CENTRALIZED AND DISTRIBUTED OPERATING SYSTEMS

Gary J. Nutt

University of Colorado

PRENTICE HALL, *Englewood Cliffs, New Jersey 07632*

Library of Congress Cataloging-in-Publication Data

Nutt, Gary J.
    Centralized and distributed operating systems / Gary J. Nutt.
        p.   cm.
    Includes bibliographical references (p.   ) and index.
    ISBN 0-13-122326-7
    1. Operating systems (Computers)   I. Title.
  QA76.76.O63N88 1992   70 284
  005.4'3--dc20   91-9197
                                                            CIP

Editorial/production supervision: Bayani Mendoza de Leon
Cover design: Wanda Lubelska
Manufacturing buyers: Linda Behrens/Dave Dickey

 © 1992 by Prentice-Hall, Inc.
A Simon & Schuster Company
Englewood Cliffs, New Jersey 07632

Printed in the United States of America
10 9 8 7 6 5 4 3 2 1

TRADEMARK INFORMATION
DOMAIN is a registered trademark of HP-Apollo.
DEC, PDP-11, VAX, and VMS are trademarks of Digital Equipment Corporation.
DYNIX is a trademark of Sequent Computers.
Ethernet is a trademark of Xerox Corporation.
IBM, IBM PC, OS/2, OS/360, PC-DOS, and System/360 are registered trademarks of IBM.
iAPX 432, Intel, and iMAX are registered trademarks of Intel Corporation.
LOCUS is a registered trademark of Locus Computing Corporation.
Microsoft and MS-DOS are trademarks of Microsoft Corporation.
NonStop is a trademark of Tandem Corporation.
Sun Workstation and SunOS are trademarks of Sun Microcomputers.
System V is a trademark of AT&T.
UNIX is a registered trademark of AT&T.

ISBN 0-13-122326-7

Prentice-Hall International (UK) Limited, *London*
Prentice-Hall of Australia Pty. Limited, *Sydney*
Prentice-Hall Canada Inc., *Toronto*
Prentice-Hall Hispanoamericana, S.A., *Mexico*
Prentice-Hall of India Private Limited, *New Delhi*
Prentice-Hall of Japan, Inc., *Tokyo*
Simon & Schuster Asia Pte. Ltd., *Singapore*
Editora Prentice-Hall do Brasil, Ltda., *Rio de Janeiro*

To Mary, Debbie, and Laura

CONTENTS

PREFACE

Computing systems have experienced radical change during the last decade. Facilities have changed from predominantly time-sharing systems to networks of workstations and servers. While most of the principles of time-sharing and multiprogramming operating systems are still applicable to these new systems, there are new principles and design issues with which the contemporary operating system designer and software professional must be familiar to be effective in this new network environment.

This book describes principles that apply to both centralized operating systems for time-sharing and batch systems and to network and distributed operating systems. It then extends the study to encompass issues that are specific to operating systems that control networks of computers.

The reader is assumed to have used computers and operating systems in the past, possibly in an undergraduate course or in a professional position; however, we do not assume any previous operating system course as a prerequisite. Without the applied experience *using* systems, many of the ideas and issues addressed in the book will have little meaning. Experience with assembly language and computer architecture is also useful for understanding many of the concepts in the book.

The level of presentation is suitable for an a one-semester, introductory operating systems class in the first year of graduate study. We have used the material in this book in a first-year graduate course in operating systems at the University of Colorado. The course is offered in both the Computer Science and Electrical and Computer Engineering Departments and is suitable for first-year graduate students in both departments. The book can also be used as an advanced undergraduate textbook by omitting some of the advanced material, particularly in Chapters 10 through 12, and by spreading the material over a full year sequence.

The aforementioned graduate course has provided the stimulation for the book. While we have used other operating systems books in the course, we found that they either lacked sufficient technical depth for graduate-level work or did not address the breadth of topics that we found useful for a course of this type. This book represents our approach to the introductory graduate study of operating systems. It contains the basic content for the course, yet it still makes wide references to the operating systems litera-ture. The first-year graduate student needs to be encouraged to use the material in the book, and to become familiar with the literature. To emphasize this view, we include the following problem with each assignment in the course:

> Read and report on an operating systems paper from *ACM Computing Surveys, Communications of the ACM, Journal of the ACM, ACM Transactions on Computer Systems, ACM Transactions on Program-ming Languages and Systems, IEEE Computer, IEEE Software, IEEE Transactions on Computers, IEEE Transactions on Software Engineer-ing, AT&T Bell Labs Technical Journal, IBM Systems Journal,* ACM SIGOPS proceedings, ACM SIGMETRICS proceedings, or any paper in the bibliography. Your report should be about one page long; three-

quarters of the report should summarize the paper, and one-quarter of the report should be a critique. The report must be typewritten or typeset using **troff, nroff,** or any other word/document processor. Introduce your report with a formal citation of the paper in the following form:

> E. W. Dijkstra, "The Structure of THE Multiprogramming System," *Communications of the ACM*, Vol. 11, No. 5 (May, 1968), pp. 341-346.

The fundamental topics covered in this book are the essential elements of a centralized or a distributed operating system. Chapters 1 through 9 and 14 address issues related to sequential processes, scheduling, synchronization, deadlock, memory management, protection, device management, file systems, and fundamental performance evaluation. In addition, Chapters 10 through 12 covers other issues related exclusively to distributed operating systems: Networks, distributed storage, and distributed synchronization. Chapter 13 provides a broad discussion of operating system architectural designs, with specific discussions of traditional and contemporary centralized, networked, and distributed operating systems.

Many people have contributed to this book, either directly or indirectly. First, I must thank the students in Computer Science 5573 at the University of Colorado; the material was used in lectures for five years and as written drafts of the manuscript for two years. Tom Baring, David Goldstein, and Alan Youngblood were especially helpful in correcting a number of typographical errors in the late drafts of the manuscript. Bruce Sanders helped with typographical errors and with clarifying obscure discussions. Next, several reviews were obtained by Prentice Hall, including reviews by Fadhi Deek and Frank Gergelyi; they provided invaluable feedback concerning typographical errors, parts of the text that were not as clear as they might be, organization, and topic coverage.

The basic material that appears in this book comes from many sources, including the literature, colleagues, and several years of experience in industry. The early formation of the material was inspired by an operating system class offered by Alan Shaw at the University of Washington, and by research with Jerre Noe at the University of Washington and later with Skip Ellis at the University of Colorado and at Xerox PARC.

Gary Nutt
Boulder, Colorado

1

INTRODUCTION

Operating systems are an important part of today's computer technology. A modern computer system typically uses a large fraction of its resources, especially primary memory, to support the operating system. The operating system is often viewed as an obstacle to the effective use of hardware, both by programming professionals and the uninitiated user. The software industry invests enormous sums of money and time into the development of operating systems. Why do we tolerate such mechanisms? What do they provide in return?

An operating system is the software that directly controls the hardware. It is intended to provide a useful and effective software environment for application programs and end users, that is, the operating system provides a usable interface between application software and the hardware. Such an interface allows a reasonable degree of independence from the hardware so that a **print** statement will write formatted information to a device without the application programmer having to know any of the details of the device's operation. In fact, the same **print** statement can be used with several different devices without changing the program in which it appears.

A computer is often shared among a set of different programs and/or a set of different users. The operating system ensures that the sharing is safe and equitable among the programs or users. It also provides boundaries between the programs or users so that errors in one program do not affect the operation of other programs.

This book is about principles of contemporary operating systems for network and distributed computer systems; much of the discussion also applies to traditional centralized operating systems. It describes the issues that arise in designing an operating system, as well as different approaches that have been used to analyze and resolve the issues.

One may choose to study operating systems for different reasons: It may be that the student wants to understand how to make better use of them. The computer science

1

scholar may want to understand how they behave. The aspiring systems designer will study them to understand how to design better computer systems in the future.

Operating systems have been designed under a variety of different constraints and circumstances. Often, design decisions are reflected in the system's user interface as discontinuities, anomalies, or other logical inconsistencies. The user can make better use of an operating system if he† can understand the rationale behind some of these inconsistencies; it may be the case that a perceived inconsistency only points out a flaw in one's own model of how the system operates. The professional software engineer will understand how to write better software for operating systems environments if he understands some of the design issues, trade-offs, and design decisions with which the operating systems designer was faced when he designed the system.

Operating systems are traditionally one of the largest "programs" that any machine supports. They are also difficult to describe functionally, that is, it is difficult to infer the reaction of the program from its inputs. Software engineering techniques and methodologies were inspired by the need to understand how operating systems behaved in order to build operating systems that displayed the kind of behavior that was expected from them.

Some of the readers of this book will eventually design and build an operating system, or perhaps they have built one in the past. This book is intended to identify and describe the important issues in the design of centralized and distributed operating systems in order to understand the issues in organizing an operating system, to consider different techniques for resolving the issues, and to serve as a reference for the knowledge gained in the past.

The topics covered in this book are the essential elements of any operating system, including sequential processes, scheduling, process synchronization, device management, file systems, memory management, and protection and security. Chapters 10 through 12 are devoted to topics that apply primarily to distributed operating systems. The last two chapters discuss some of the conventional means by which operating systems are implemented and also introduce performance prediction methodologies.

1.1 VIEWS OF OPERATING SYSTEMS

There are two popular views of an operating system. First, one can think of an operating system as being a *resource manager* for a collection of resources. Second, the operating system can be viewed as one layer in a set of *layered abstract machines*.

1.1.1 The Resource Manager View

Computer hardware is made up of CPUs, memory, and peripheral devices. During the 1950s and 1960s, computer hardware was capital intensive. For a single programmer to use the machine it was analogous to allocating a large vehicle to transport a single person. To aggravate the situation, even when the programmer was allocated the machine, he often did not make effective use of it or was only able to use small parts of the machine at a time.

---

† Throughout this book, the author uses the masculine gender when referring to an individual person; all such masculine references are to a hypothetical person that may be either male or female.

To make more effective use of the hardware, the idea of sharing the machine among two or more programmers came into being. This could be done as long as one programmer was not using the same facilities as another programmer (at least at the same time). Thus, it was only necessary to introduce some mechanism that could ensure that two or more programmers were not attempting to use the same part of the machine at one time.

Any particular part of the machine can be thought of as a *resource* of the machine. For example, a block of primary memory is a resource; a tape or disk drive is a resource; and the CPU is a resource. Thus, for two or more programmers to share a single machine, some mechanism had to be derived to exclusively allocate control of parts of the machine to each programmer. A programmer should be able to request required resources from the mechanism, and then proceed when those parts had been allocated, safe in the knowledge that another programmer would not disturb the allocated resources.

An operating system fulfills this task. All the computer hardware resources belong to the operating system. Whenever a programmer — or other user of the computer system — wishes to use some of the resources, then he must request that the operating system allocate such resources. The programmer is expected to release control over the resources when he is through with them.

Thus it is natural to think of the operating system as a mechanism that manages the system resources among a group of clients.

1.1.2 The Abstract Machine View

The abstract machine view of operating systems has grown in popularity over the last several years. It is a more comprehensive model of operating systems than the resource manager model.

An architecture for a system has been defined to be a description of the interface to the system [4]. An architecture for a building is a description of how the building will be perceived by its occupants. Similarly, an architecture for hardware is a description of the how the components of the system interact with one another as viewed by the user of the system.

Since an architectural description of computer operation may be very complex, it is common to divide the architecture into manageable parts so that one can concentrate on one part of the architecture at a time. A *vertical division* of the architecture compartmentalizes parts of the architecture on the basis of functions (as perceived by the user of the system) and how they are implemented. A *horizontal division* of the architecture compartmentalizes the architecture into complete interfaces while ignoring implementations.

For example, if an office information system were to be designed using vertical division, then one part of the system might be electronic mail and its implementation, while another part of the system would be a calendar system and its implementation. The vertical division would discourage the use of common parts between the electronic mail subsystem and the calendar subsystem. Information might be stored entirely differently in the two subsystems, even though both would require the use of some type of file system. However, it would be easy to delegate the design of such a system, since the electronic mail system would be assigned to one group while the calendar subsystem was assigned to another. Development could proceed in parallel, with little worry about cooperation among the groups.

If the same office system were to be designed using horizontal division, then one part might be the user interface, a second part the file system, and so on. In this case, the calendar subsystem and the electronic mail subsystem would employ the same user interface and the same file system. This would reduce the number of redundant parts in the system, but would tend to serialize production unless some strong agreement were made between the group implementing the user interface and the groups implementing the specifics of the calendar or the electronic mail packages.

Abstract machines embrace the horizontal division of the architecture. The architecture is described as a family of n *abstract machines*, $\{A_i \mid 0 \leq i \leq n-1\}$, where A_i is built on top of the interface to A_{i-1} (see Figure 1.1). The interface to A_i is a *description* of the behavior of a mechanism that can be used by an implementer of A_{i+1}. The user of A_i need not know the details of the implementation of A_i, only its interface.

The bottom layer machine, A_0, is usually thought of as the "hardware," but of course the same layering technique can be applied to the design of the hardware itself. In this case, A_0 might be construed as the logic level of the hardware, while A_1 is a machine implemented by microcoding a control unit. Therefore, we ignore the actual definition of the base substrate and rely only on a sound interface to the hardware, A_H.

Assume that level A_H is implemented by the hardware of the machine, that is, the mechanism that implements A_{H+1} is software. Then A_H can be described in terms of machine instructions, registers, buses, controllers, interrupts, and memory.

Assembly language-level programmers work with A_H as a regular practice. At this level, many details must be kept in mind in order to successfully control the hardware. For example, the A_{H+1} machine programmer must always distinguish between floating point and integer addition (instead of simply using "+" to denote summation of two variables of the same type). In fact, variable typing itself is no more than a convention at the A_{H+1} level.

A_{n-1}
...
A_{i+1}
A_i
A_{i-1}
...
A_1
A_0

Figure 1.1 Layered Abstract Machine Division

What should be the purpose of the mechanism that implements A_{H+1}? It could, of course, provide service directly to the end users of the computer system. That is, A_H could be used as the basis for constructing all application programs. However, we have pointed out the need for resource management in systems that support multiple users or programs. It is reasonable to think of implementing resource management at level A_{H+1} and then implementing application programs at level A_{H+2}. Recalling the office information system example, it is easy to see that there is good reason to make room for other abstract machines between the resource manager and applications programs, for example, a file system. As a result, the abstract machine model for operating systems begins to take on the appearance shown in Figure 1.2.

Although the layered abstract machine model is widely used for designing computer systems in general and operating systems in particular, there is limited agreement about the details of the operating system interface, A_S, and even less agreement about the layers between A_H and the user interface, A_U. In Chapter 13, we will return to a discussion of abstract machine layering approaches that have been used between A_H and A_S.

1.1.3 Commercial Examples

Operating systems have evolved from a laboratory curiosity into an important part of commercial products. Computer manufacturers are generally unable to market hardware without including an operating system. Because operating systems provide an abstract machine interface to the application software, the *portability* of the application software depends on the nature of A_S — the operating system interface. (In some markets, the important interface is A_H instead of A_S, that is, portability is at the *object code level* as opposed to the operating system call level.)

Some manufacturers have taken the position that this is a strategic position to maintain: Once a customer has purchased application software that is not portable to another manufacturer's operating system interface, then the customer is captured. (Of course, this may also work against the manufacturer, since it prevents him from changing his own hardware and operating system to take advantage of technology changes.)

Because of this commercial influence, a few operating systems have become very visible over the years. We mention them here because of that importance and because they have either pushed the state of the art or popularized many different notions in the

A_U The user's interface to the computer
$\cdots$ various layers of application software
A_S The operating system interface
$\cdots$ various layers of the operating system $\cdots$
A_H The software/hardware interface
$\cdots$ various hardware layers $\cdots$

Figure 1.2 The Operating System Abstract Machine

field. Because of their popularity, many readers of this book will have encountered some of these operating systems; thus we will use them to illustrate various concepts throughout the remainder of the book.

IBM OS/360

In the early 1960s, IBM introduced a revolutionary new machine called the *System/360*. The 360 was intended to accommodate customers who intended to upgrade from older IBM equipment and to address the "scientific" and "commercial" markets with a single system. The System/360 was marketed as a family of machines, each with the same functional A_H. This was accomplished through extensive use of microcode at level A_{H-1}.

System/360 was delivered with a new operating system called *OS/360*, which provided a consistent A_S across the family of computers. Thus, the family of machines provided application program portability at either the source or object code level; software compiled for a small machine could run directly on a larger machine in the line. This was the first time that such a family had been offered in a commercial marketplace.

OS/360 was also the largest piece of software that had been built until that time. It used a number of new techniques for controlling the hardware and for providing a sophisticated multiprogramming environment. Ironically, OS/360 also provided the primary motivation for the development of the software engineering discipline. Fredrick Brooks was the project leader for the development for OS/360; he wrote a series of revolutionary software engineering articles reviewing his experiences with the development of OS/360 [4].

AT&T UNIX

In 1974, Dennis Ritchie and Ken Thompson of AT&T Bell Laboratories published a paper describing a "small" time-sharing operating system for a DEC PDP 11/45 minicomputer [26]. UNIX had been influenced by Multics (an important research time-sharing operating system developed at Project MAC at M.I.T), but had taken many simplifying assumptions in its design and implementation.

UNIX became very popular among computer scientists since it was reasonably compact, it could be ported onto various A_H without great difficulty, and since it provided the most important aspects of a resource sharing operating system without an undue amount of other mechanism. UNIX was easy to extend so that one could build a customized programming environment. While UNIX was described in the technical literature in the early 1970s, AT&T was restricted from freely distributing the operating system due to certain regulatory agreements. These agreements did not apply to distributions of UNIX to universities; as a result, UNIX was widely distributed among universities and has subsequently become well-entrenched in that community.

In the late 1970s and early 1980s, variants of UNIX began to appear, largely due to the fact that the UNIX source code had been widely distributed within the academic community. Here, the most prominent version soon became the *Berkeley Software Distribution* or *BSD* from the University of California at Berkeley. In the 1990s three primary variants of the operating system exist: Research UNIX in the AT&T Bell Laboratories, AT&T UNIX now widely distributed by AT&T, and BSD UNIX.

Because of the relative ease with which UNIX can be ported among different A_H, and because of the relatively wide use of the UNIX A_S by application programs and application-support packages, various versions of UNIX are experiencing increasing commercial success. Most universities now support their educational program, at least in part, through the use of UNIX.

1.2 HISTORY OF OPERATING SYSTEMS

In the 1940s and 1950s, computers were often "personal computers" in the sense that the machine would only support a single user at a time. Operating systems were degenerate, since their primary purpose was resource management and since all resources were allocated to a single user at a time.

Once a user was allocated the machine, then he could use the peripheral devices to load a program into the memory and to execute the program. In general, a program would read data from some input device, process them, and then write a result to an output device.

I/O operations were an important part of the program functionality then, as they are today. I/O involves the management of a mechanical device under programmable control. Early systems had only a single programmable unit — the CPU, thus I/O operations required the full attention of the CPU to manage the operation of the device.

As hardware grew in sophistication, it soon became apparent that one could design hardware so that a special-purpose *channel* processor could be built to manage the mechanical input/output function, freeing up the processor to do other things. This allowed the CPU to be utilized for other processing while I/O was in progress. It also required that certain standard operations be performed on the channel in order to instruct it to perform specific I/O operations. Libraries of software to control channels soon evolved; these were the first examples of system software.

The existence of channels greatly increased the complexity of software. A program could only be made to be efficient by being constructed so that it maximized the overlap of operation between the CPU and the channel. This required that the program be written so that it started an I/O operation and then proceeded to do other processing until the channel had completed. Thus the program would have to be constructed so that it initiated the I/O operation well before the data were actually required, then it could perform independent tasks in parallel with the channel operation. Detecting the completion of the I/O operation was accomplished by periodically sampling the channel status.

1.2.1 Multiprogrammed Batch Systems

A *batch processing system* is an operating system that will service individual *jobs* from a queue. To use the batch processing system, a job is prepared (usually as a file or deck of punched cards) by specifying all the steps that are required to fulfill the processing needs and by supplying specific data that will be needed during processing. For example, a job might consist of three different parts: a control section, a program, and data (see Figure 1.3a). The control section in Figure 1.3a requests the operating system to compile the next record in the *batch stream*, the source code, then to link and load the relocatable object code with library routines, and finally to execute the resulting binary program on the data supplied in the last record of the batch stream.

In some cases, batch control directives are embedded in the batch stream rather than being in a separate control section (see Figure 1.3b); but in either case the operating

Control Section:
    Compile command
    Link & Load command
    Execute command
Program Section:

```
            <record separator>
                    MAIN()
                    READ(5,9001) A, I
                    ...
                    WRITE(6,9101) X
            9001    FORMAT(...)
            9101    FORMAT(...)
                    <record separator>
```

Data Section:

```
            <record separator>
            123.45   67
            234.56   78
            ...      ...
            567.89   12
```

         (a)

    Compile command

```
            <record separator>
                    MAIN()
                    READ(5,9001) A, I
                    ...
                    WRITE(6,9101) X
            9001    FORMAT(...)
            9101    FORMAT(...)
```

    Link & Load command
    Execute command

```
            <record separator>
            123.4567
            234.5678

            567.8 912
```

         (b)

Figure 1.3 A Batch Job

system is responsible for executing some set of commands on the supplied information.

The batch system operator provides a series of jobs to the system, usually by reading decks of cards into a system queue (on magnetic tape) as shown in Figure 1.4. This process is called *job spooling*, since the operator enqueues jobs on the system queue much as one would wind thread onto a spool. The operating system removes jobs from the system queue whenever it is capable of processing another job.

Uniprogrammed batch systems are not much different from the simpler machines discussed in the previous section (except that the device that holds the job queue must be protected from user programs). Once a job has been removed from the system queue and allocated the processor and memory, it controls the entire machine (other than the system queue).

Multiprogrammed machines provide for the management of the simultaneous execution of jobs. The various components of the system are generally *serially reusable*, meaning that a unit of the resource may be allocated to a single job at a time, but as soon as one job has completed using a resource, then the resource can be reused by another job. The CPU, memory, and devices are serially reusable resources. To support multiprogramming, the operating system must manage the sharing of serially reusable resources among several jobs. That is, if two or more jobs are to share the resources, then they must share the memory of the machine (either by partitioning the memory and giving each exclusive control of a partition or by multiplexing the jobs in and out of the same section of memory).

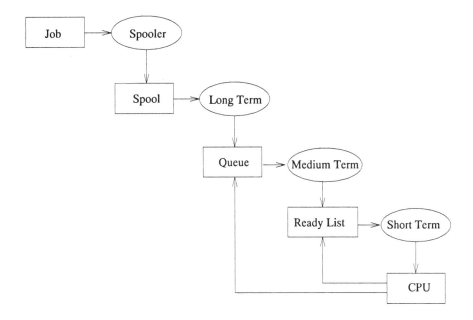

Figure 1.4 A Batch System

In a multiprogrammed operating system, there is *competition* for resources among the jobs, first for memory and later for other resources. Competition for resources is managed by *resource schedulers*, as shown in Figure 1.4. In some systems, jobs are not even allowed to enter the job queue unless they win a preliminary competition among other jobs; this competition to enter the job queue is called *long-term scheduling*. Jobs are removed from the job queue and allocated memory by a *medium-term scheduler*, and the CPU is allocated to memory-resident jobs by a *short-term scheduler*. (Short-term scheduling for uniprocessors is discussed in Chapter 6. Chapter 7 addresses medium-term scheduling in more detail.)

At the same time that multiprogrammed batch systems emerged, operating systems were typically designed to provide *device independence*. In earlier systems, programs typically referenced specific devices for I/O operations. (The FORTRAN read and write statements specifically included a device address — device number 5 for the card reader and device number 6 for the line printer.) This made programs difficult to port or to operate on different devices. Operating systems began to support the notion of a *logical device*. The characteristics of a device can be described in general terms. For example, does the device read/write characters or blocks, is it sequential or directly addressable, and so on. Furthermore, two different card readers could both have the same logical device number as long as the operating system took care to bind the logical device number to a particular physical device prior to performing an I/O operation. As simple as this abstraction may seem now, it was a revelation at the time it was introduced.

1.2.2 Time-sharing and Interactive Systems

Batch systems provided a major step forward in allowing multiple users to share a machine through multiprogramming of jobs. However, batch systems discouraged real-time interaction between the user and the computer. In the very early systems, the user was able to sit at the system console and debug a program; in batch systems, programs could only be debugged by preparing a job, submitting it to the spooler, and waiting for the job to be executed and returned. To aggravate the problem, batch users are typically not allowed to enter their own jobs into the system nor to remove the paper from the line printer; in fact, the batch system could be located at some geographically distant point. In the 1960s, it was not unusual for a professional programmer to get only two opportunities per day to enter a job into the batch stream.

Time-sharing systems are multiprogrammed systems that support multiple terminals, one for each active user of the system. Thus, to use a time-sharing machine, it is not necessary to prepare a batch job and submit it to the computer center; instead, the user is allowed to *log into* the system by typing an appropriate key sequence on a terminal.

As shown in Figure 1.5, each time-sharing user operates as if he had a system console to the machine so that he can direct the machine to perform different commands at his whim. Since a single time-sharing system provides this illusion to every user, there must be some limitations on the logical system console. A time-sharing machine provides an abstract machine to the individual user rather than the real machine. Thus, the A_S that is observed from the real system console is replaced by an A_{S+1} built on top of the real machine. The terminal is a system console to an abstract machine.

The abstract machine that implements time-sharing must support multiprogramming in order to support multiple users simultaneously. Thus, it must incorporate short-term scheduling at a minimum. Time-sharing systems also incorporate medium-term scheduling, but using significantly different strategies from those used in batch systems.

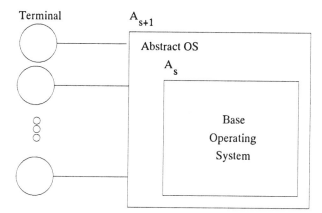

Figure 1.5 A Timesharing System

It is common for the individual time-sharing abstract machines to also provide a form of multiprogramming. The idea is that a user that has logged into a machine may wish to have a program continue to run even after the user has discontinued his session (or turned his attention to a different program that was previously *dispatched*). Thus, the single user has initiated two or more programs in execution, each competing with the others, much as any set of programs would compete for resources if it were attempting to execute simultaneously. Informally, these individual running programs are called *processes* or sometimes *tasks*; a system that supports multiple processes per user is often called a *multitasking* system. More precise descriptions of processes are given in the next chapter.

While all multiprogrammed machines support multiple users, time-sharing systems began to emphasize the importance of establishing barriers and safeguards among the users. Without such barriers, one job or user may inadvertently damage the memory being used by another job or user. The barriers also extend into the file system shared by the users. In many cases, it is desirable for a user to create files that are not to be written by other users and sometimes not even to be read by other users. *Protection and security* became major issues in the early days of time-sharing; however, these issues apply equally well to batch systems as time-shared systems. They are also crucial issues in today's systems, and so they are discussed in Chapter 8.

The roots of time-sharing technology are closely associated with three research systems: CTSS and Multics developed at M.I.T., and the Cal time-sharing system developed at the University of California at Berkeley. Time-sharing has been widely popularized by UNIX.

CTSS, the *Compatible Time Sharing System*, was developed for the IBM 7090 in the mid 1960s. CTSS was the vehicle that supported the initial research on radical scheduling algorithms and virtual memory. CTSS was replaced early in its life by Multics. Multics was intended to be viewed more like a utility than a time-sharing computer, that is, it should be extremely capable and reliable. Multics was the operating system with which fundamental knowledge about virtual memory, protection, and security was discovered.

Independently, the Cal time-sharing system was being designed and implemented at about the same time as CTSS and Multics. The research results to come from Cal are generally focused on time-sharing technology and protection and security.

1.2.3 Personal Computers and Workstations

In the mid 1970s a hardware revolution began to take place. For the first time, it was possible to construct small computers, *minicomputers*, that did not require a specialized environment in which to run. (These specialized environments included conditioned power, air conditioning, raised floors, and so on.) The first minicomputers were machines such as the DEC PDP 8 and the Data General Nova. Typically, such machines had small words (8 bits), limited instruction sets, and limited peripheral devices. However, they were relatively inexpensive and easy to install in any location.

Minicomputers quickly grew in computational power — and size. Today, a minicomputer essentially requires conditioned power, air conditioning, and a raised floor. As minicomputers grew, new small machines were built, *microcomputers*. The fundamental element of a microcomputer is a single integrated circuit implementation of a CPU. Early microcomputers were built around Intel 4004 or 8008 microcomputer chips,

Motorola 6800 family chips, AMI 6502 chips, and others, with clock rates around 1 MHz. Contemporary microcomputers employ 16- or 32-bit microprocessors with typical clock rates on the order of 10 MHz. Such microprocessors were incredibly inexpensive and enabled the creation of a *personal computer* or *PC* that even a hobbyist could afford to buy.

Early personal computers incorporated the barest essentials for an operating system — usually encoded into a read-only memory, but much more primitive than the software in an IBM PC ROM. These "operating systems" typically serve the same function as the device interface aids did on the very early systems; they provided a few routines to control the personal computer's devices. Soon, ROM-based systems were enhanced by additional (RAM-resident) software to manage files. The most popular of the early PC operating systems was CP/M, which has ultimately been replaced by MS/PC-DOS.

PCs are traditionally single-user systems. In general, they do not support multiple users and often do not support multitasking or multiprogramming. Just as microcomputers grew to large machines, microcomputer-based machines have also grown into more sophisticated systems called *workstations*. Informally, a workstation differs from a PC in that it supports multiprogramming; however, it is intended to be used by a single user.

Workstation hardware is generally more flexible and faster than PC hardware (although sometimes it is hard to draw a clean distinction along these lines). Most workstations of the 1990s employ 32-bit microprocessors with clock rates on the order of 20 MHz. In some cases, the workstations even employ RISC (reduced instruction set computer) processors.

Workstations incorporate considerably more resources than personal computers, including more memory, a faster, more powerful CPU, larger disk storage, and higher-resolution graphics monitors for the console. Thus, these workstations generally require a more complex operating system to manage the resources; because of the increased resources, sharing among processes is also natural.

The forerunner of workstations was the Xerox Alto computer. The Alto was built in the early 1970s as an experimental personal computer to support research scientists. It was a 16-bit machine built around a microprogrammed bit slice processor. The Alto incorporated a relatively high resolution graphics display, a small disk, up to 128 K bytes of memory, and a 3 megabit/second Ethernet controller. During the first 3 years of its life, the Alto was programmed almost exclusively in the BCPL programming language. Later it became the original Smalltalk machine, and in the latter part of the decade the Alto supported the Mesa programming language.

The Alto used different operating systems depending on the language system it was supporting. For example, the basic operating system supported the BCPL and Mesa environments, while Smalltalk used its own operating system. Eventually, Mesa was supported on the Alto using the Pilot operating system.

The Alto and its operating systems were a fundamental part of the early research into local area networks, clients and servers in a local area network environment, network protocols, integration of languages and systems, and object-oriented programming.

Commercial workstations have relied heavily on UNIX. While UNIX was designed as a time-sharing system, the multiprogramming support as well as the extensibility of function has fit naturally into the workstation environment, particularly when the workstation is used for software development. UNIX grew with the workstation market; as the market called for graphics support, UNIX incorporated means to support high-resolution graphics. Similarly, as network protocols became important to workstation technology, UNIX grew to accommodate network protocols.

Workstations and PCs have popularized computing. As part of that process, commercial products in these two areas have become closely associated with UNIX and DOS, respectively. With the increasing numbers of such machines, the need to have the machines communicate increases. In the simplest case, this means that individual machines need to be able to exchange files or electronic mail; in the more complex situation, the individual machines might be used as a team to work on a single problem. (Note the irony of this latter scenario compared to the requirements for batch and time-sharing systems!)

The simplest interconnection of a PC or a workstation with another computer is for the system to emulate the actions of a terminal. The PC or workstation performs only the simplest of computations, while the program executes on a remote machine.

1.3 COMPUTER ARCHITECTURES

A significant challenge of contemporary operating systems designers is to be able to build effective systems to manage a wide spectrum of computer architectures, ranging from personal computers to parallel and distributed computer systems. While there may be no requirement that a single operating system be able to span all hardware architectures, similar design issues must be addressed in all the systems. The computer environment is often a heterogeneous collection of computer systems, each individual system having a set of local resources that may be exclusive to the users of that machine or globally accessible to users of other machines in the environment. Within individual computer systems, contemporary computer architectures often employ multiple processors as a cost-effective mechanism for providing extended hardware computational cycles to the consumer. Prior to continuing our study of operating systems, it is useful to consider several of the more crucial aspects of computer architectures.

The general class of machines we consider are all *von Neumann* computers — as uniprocessors and multiprocessors. There are other multiprocessor architectures that do not employ the von Neumann architecture for the basic process implementation environment, for example, a SIMD machine or a connection machine; we do not specifically address those machines in our discussion of operating systems.

Multiprocessor operating systems implementation strategies are highly influenced by the interconnection mechanism among the multiple processors. Networks of *local memory machines* define one type of environment, while other environments include processors that are able to read and write a common memory; these machines are called *shared memory machines*.

1.3.1 The von Neumann Machine

Conventional computers conform to the von Neumann architecture (see Figure 1.6). That is, the computer is composed of a central processing unit (CPU), a control unit, a memory unit, and input/output units.

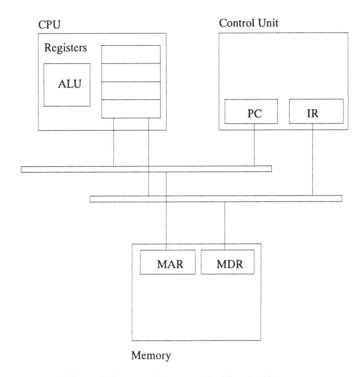

Figure 1.6 A von Neumann Machine Architecture

The Memory Unit

The memory unit stores programs and data while they are being operated on by the CPU and the control unit. A program and its data are loaded into the memory and then the program is initiated.

The memory has an interface composed of three relevant parts: the *memory address register* (MAR), the *memory data register* (MDR), and the *command register*. To write information into the memory, data are placed in the MDR, a memory address is placed in the MAR, and then a command is placed in the command register to cause the memory to store the contents of the MDR into the memory location that is loaded in the MAR. A read operation is accomplished by placing an address in the MAR and placing a read command into the command register; after a memory cycle, the memory unit places the data in the MDR.

The Central Processing Unit

The CPU operates on the data stored in memory by fetching data from the memory, performing arithmetic and logical operations on them, then storing the data back into the memory. Since the arithmetic logical unit (ALU) portion of the CPU is not designed to operate on data unless they are internal to the CPU, data fetch and store instructions are included in the instruction set to augment the arithmetic-logical instructions. Interim data are held in CPU registers. Registers are also used to represent the status of certain operations that span a machine instruction, for example, conditional branching instructions. Thus, registers are an important component of the *state of a process* at any given instant.

The Control Unit

The control unit is responsible for fetching an instruction from the memory and either executing the instruction itself or causing the CPU to execute the instruction (the control unit executes control flow instructions). The control unit contains a *program counter register* (PC) and an *instruction register* (IR). The PC contains the memory address of the next instruction to be executed when a program is executed. The IR contains a copy of the instruction that is currently being executed by the control unit and/or CPU.

The control unit operation is described by a *fetch-execute cycle* of operation (see Figure 1.7).

```
while (IR.op_code ≠ "halt")
{
        IR ← memory[PC];
        PC ← PC + 1;
        execute(IR);
};
```

Figure 1.7 The Fetch-Execute Cycle

In Chapter 2, control unit operation will be extended to handle process multiplexing. The notion of a *timer interrupt* is required to ensure fair sharing of the CPU among a set of users.

Input/Output Units

The input/output units of the von Neumann machine are used to introduce and disseminate data into and out of the memory. Input/output units also include interrupt hardware to facilitate communication between the input/output units and the program on the CPU.

1.3.2 Local Memory Architectures

A *local memory computer system* is a collection of autonomous von Neumann processors, each with its own private memory (these machines are also often called *distributed memory systems*). The machines are interconnected using some form of network (see Figure 1.8).

In some cases, the interconnection network is a full, multidrop mechanism allowing any CPU to directly communicate with all other CPUs. In other cases, there are limited interconnections, so an information item may have to be *forwarded* from the source to the destination by one or more intermediate nodes in the network. (Additional discussion of physical network topologies appears in Chapter 10.)

A collection of von Neumann machines interconnected with an IEEE 802 compliant (for example, Ethernet or Token Ring) local area network is an example of a local memory multiprocessor system.

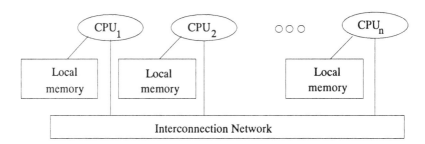

Figure 1.8 A Local Memory System

There is a subclass of local memory systems that are thought of as multiprocessors rather than as networks of machines. Ordinarily, the interconnection network in these machines is faster than a general-purpose communication network, and the interconnection mechanism may include low-level software (below the usual A_S, but above A_H) to control information routing. The hypercube and successor grid network machines are examples of this type of local memory multiprocessor.

An important issue for the operating system in a local memory system environment is related to how the application programs will be written to use the interconnection mechanism. If the local memory system and operating system provide the ability to distribute the function of a single application program across the processors in the machine such that the granularity of the sharing is "fine," then the operating system is a distributed operating system. Such support will require the operating system to allow the application to be partitioned into processes and for the processes to be able to interact by sending and receiving application-specific messages. If the grain of the application partitions tends toward "large" amounts of computation per interprocess communication, then the operating system may take on more of the characteristics of a network operating system.

1.3.3 Shared Memory Architectures

A *shared memory multiprocessor* is a collection of individual CPUs, each of which can read and write a common set of memory locations. Figure 1.9 is a conceptual block diagram of a shared memory multiprocessor. There are n CPUs attached to a common switch; there are m memory modules also attached to the switch.

As the number of processes in the system increases, the load on the memory modules increases, particularly on those modules that contain information used by programs on more than one CPU. This can be alleviated by implementing the primary memory as a collection of individual memory modules. For example, addresses 0 to F_0 - 1 may be in the first module, addresses F_0 to F_1 - 1 in the second module, and so on. Now, if most of a process's memory is not shared (the usual case) then a processor will tend to use a small number of memory modules with few other processors competing for access. Memory modules that contain shared primary memory will still be subject to contention.

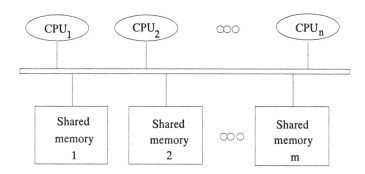

Figure 1.9 A Shared Memory Multiprocessor

An alternative is to *interleave* the memory so that if there are m memory modules, then address i is in module i mod m. This distributes a process's memory over all the modules, which may or may not relieve contention. (Memory interleaving is used in some architectures to allow a CPU to overlap several memory accesses by starting an access to module i, then immediately starting one on i + 1 before the access to i is complete, and so on. This is very effective for vector storage and retrieval.)

Even if we are able to solve the memory contention problem, the interconnecting bus then becomes a bottleneck. As each process attempts to access some part of the primary memory, it needs to gain control of the bus during the access. Since memory speeds are much slower than CPU speeds, all processors tend to wait on the bus. This problem is attacked by placing a *cache memory* between the CPU and the bus (see Figure 1.10).

Because of the load placed on the switch, contemporary shared memory multiprocessors incorporate a cache memory between each CPU and the switch. A cache memory is a buffer for retaining a copy of recent memory references by the CPU. Each time the CPU reads a primary memory location, the request is first routed to the local cache; if a copy of the memory content is loaded in the cache, then it is returned to the CPU without using the bus. If the information is not in the cache, then a normal memory access occurs, with the result being deposited in the cache when it has been retrieved from the primary memory. Subsequent reads of the location will result in a *cache hit*, eliminating the need to use the bus and the primary memory.

Caching can be enabled for the fetch cycle, the execution cycle, or both cycles. That is, whenever a CPU begins to execute a program, a copy of the portions of the program being executed may be placed in the CPU's cache memory. As the program executes, the data may also be copied into the cache memory when it is referenced. Now subsequent references to instructions and memory (by the CPU) are satisfied by the copy of the primary memory that is loaded into the cache memory.

Instruction caching has been observed to be extremely effective in shared memory multiprocessors. However, data caching can lead to subtle problems.

Suppose that CPU A caches a value from location i (on a read operation), and then CPU B creates its own copy of location i in its cache. As long as processes on both

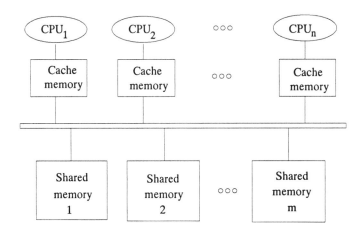

Figure 1.10 A Multiprocessor with Cache Memory

CPUs only read the value, there is no difficulty; if either writes the location, then there is a problem. The CPU that writes the value will write into its cache, which means that the copies of the location that exist in the primary memory and in other caches are invalid. Notice that the big problem in keeping the caches *coherent* stems from the fact that the location is shared. One way to avoid the problem is to forbid shared primary memory locations from being cached. There are other cache coherence strategies as well.

The *write-through* strategy specifies that the CPU immediately perform a write to the primary memory, only making effective use of the cache for read operations. Then, if there is a shared location involved, the primary memory will be made consistent. However, the other cache memories must be made aware that a write-through operation occurred in case they happen to be holding a copy of the location. If a cache does have a copy, then it must flush the copy since it is no longer valid; if the cache does not hold a copy, then the write is irrelevant. (There are several other strategies for managing the cache memory; for example, the primary memory write may not necessarily happen at the same time as the cache write, but can occur at some later time provided that it guarantees cache coherence.)

The *write-back* strategy for cache coherence also writes the cached information back into the shared memory, but as a background activity. However, even though it may delay the write into the shared memory, it must take measures to ensure that the other cached values are not used after the write has occurred. This can be accomplished by having the cache memory manager of the writing CPU coordinate its activity with all other cache memory managers.

Both strategies must include a certain amount of intelligence to handle the cache coherence problem. Essentially, each cache memory manager needs to keep a record of the status of each primary memory location corresponding to a datum loaded in the cache. All the information necessary to keep this status current will be placed on the bus when the shared memory is referenced and is therefore available for each cache memory handler to read. *Snooping caches* (sometimes called *snoopy caches*) take advantage of this information to record information about read and write operations for all primary memory locations loaded in their cache. Given this information, it is easy to implement the write-through strategy described above. As a corollary, one can expect that there is significant cost in the cache memory mechanism in a shared memory multiprocessor.

Most of the operation of the cache memory manager is implemented in hardware, although it may be necessary for the operating system to occasionally provide some low-level (software) assistance to the cache coherency hardware, depending on the design of the hardware.

A distributed operating system for a shared memory multiprocessor will take advantage of the existence of the shared memory in implementing synchronization primitives among the parts of the distributed computation. It may also rely on the architecture in implementing processes.

Not all shared memory multiprocessors incorporate a true distributed operating system. In such cases, parallel computations either communicate infrequently, that is, they resemble application programs for a network operating system, or they are inefficient.

1.4 CONTEMPORARY OPERATING SYSTEMS

Contemporary operating systems have been built around multiprogrammed uniprocessor systems. Many of the difficult issues in operating system design were first addressed in this environment for centralized operating systems, and then later extended for networked and distributed operating systems.

As a result of the physical distribution of computers systems, communication networks have become a fundamental element of the computer system and of operating systems. The contemporary operating system must provide an abstract machine hierarchy that manages network-wide as well as local resources. Two general approachs are employed in operating systems for these hardware environments: *network operating systems* and *distributed operating systems*. In the remainder of this section we identify contemporary operating system architectural strategies that can be used in centralized and distributed systems. After we have considered each of the issues in detail in Chapters 2 through 12, we provide specific examples of the approaches in Chapter 13.

1.4.1 Operating System Organization

Basic Functionality

Operating systems were the first large computer programs, their complexity becoming unavoidably apparent in OS/360 [4]. They are among the more complex software systems in existence; Lauer argues that a nontrivial operating system requires about 7 years to develop [17]!

Figure 1.11 represents a general partitioning of the functionality of a contemporary operating system: the parts that are primarily concerned with the management of the CPU or CPUs in the hardware platform, another part to manage the sharing and operation of the hardware devices, and a third part to manage the use of the memory. The devices and memory are also often used as if they were files, that is, files are part of an abstract machine built on top of some combination of devices and sometimes memory.

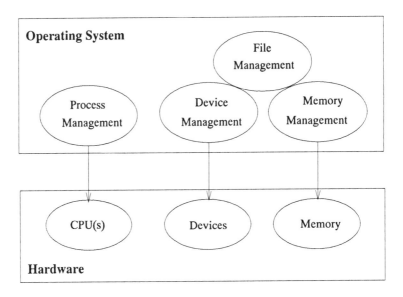

Figure 1.11 General Block Diagram for an Operating System

Processes are units of computation that coexist within the domain of control of an operating system. A process is the instantiation of an individual execution of an individual program; it is the entity that implements the intuitive notion of an algorithm. The operating system provides various mechanisms to allow algorithms to execute and to allow individual executions of algorithms to share information. This aspect of an operating system is called *process management.*

Each process relies on directly accessible memory to store the program and data on which the algorithm will be applied. The memory will usually be sharable among a set of coexisting processes in multiprogramming operating systems, which suggests the need for careful control of memory access by the supported processes. For example, if processes p_1 and p_2 are using the memory, then p_1 should not be able to write into the memory currently being used by p_2 and neither should it be able to read the other's memory (unless the memory is to be used specifically for sharing information). The memory management portion of the operating system also extends the *address space* used by the process so that the process can behave as if it had more physical memory than has actually been allocated to it. The *memory management* aspect of the operating system is a specialized resource allocation mechanism for controlling the "directly executable" memory.

Hardware devices may have a broad spectrum of uses and interfaces. Rotating media such as magnetic and optical disks exhibit a particular set of performance characteristics related to their physical characteristics, while magnetic tape shares some of that behavior and has other characteristics that differentiate it from rotating media. Networks and interactive terminals are also interfaced to the computer as hardware communications devices. Their behavior differs in detail from both rotating and sequential block storage devices, yet there are some common elements to managing such devices. *Device management* is the part of the operating system that focuses on the control of the spectrum of devices.

File management is an abstraction of the storage devices and, in some cases, to the memory management. The file management abstraction allows programs to be written without their having to know the details of device operations nor the details of memory allocation.

Providing the Functionality

In abstraction, the fundamental purpose of the operating system is to manage resource sharing among multiple users and multiple processes, providing an effective abstract machine interface to the application programmers, and subsequently to the end users of the machine. This suggests the alternative view of the operating system as shown in Figure 1.12.

Each user may have multiple processes in operation at one time, especially in a contemporary workstation with windows. In addition to the controlled resource sharing, the operating system must multiplex the CPU across different processes, upholding the virtual machine abstraction. It must also address deadlock through prevention, detection, or avoidance; operate in a deterministic manner, and be cost effective.

The facilities provided by the operating system may be used by the application process through *system call* (see Figure 1.13a) or through *interprocess communication* (see

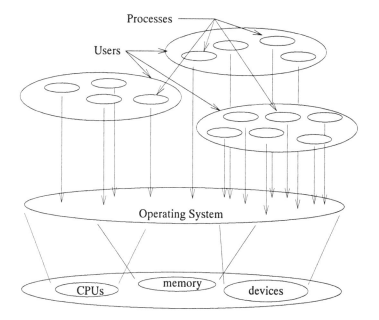

Figure 1.12 Multiple User, Multiple Process Operating Systems

Figure 1.13b). That is, an operating system may be built as a collection of system procedures that the user's process executes or as a set of processes that provides service.

The system call interface implies that each process uses operating system rights whenever it is executing system code; the state of the operating system is kept in a set of tables within the operating system's memory. A process can only access the system state tables when it is executing operating system procedures (see the discussion on rights amplification in Chapter 8).

Process-based implementations require that the operating system be layered in the sense that a lower-level machine implement processes (so that they can be used to implement the operating facilities seen by the application processes). This adds complexity to the operating system and also poses a greater challenge to constructing an efficient implementation.

1.4.2 Architectural Strategies

A number of approaches can be taken for configuring the components of an operating system, ranging from a monolithic to a functionally distributed system. To conclude our introduction, we identify several of the approaches that have been used to build operating systems.

Monolithic Organization

The monolithic organization does not attempt to implement the various functions — process, file, device, and memory management — in distinct modules. Instead, all functions are implemented within a single module that contains all system routines or processes and all operating system data structures.

The rationale for this approach is that the operating system will be written once (by experts) and then be used by many others. If it can be written carefully and correctly, the operating system may be able to avoid generalities and modularity that might affect run-time performance.

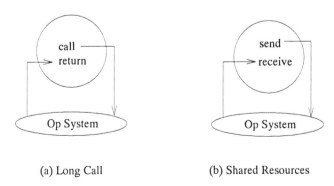

(a) Long Call   (b) Shared Resources

Figure 1.13 Operating Systems as Procedures or Processes

Modular Nucleus

A modular nucleus provides the basic functionality as a collection of distinct modules, usually conforming to the general functionality partition. Interactions among the modules may take place using procedure call or interprocess communication.

The designers that choose the modular nucleus approach are more concerned with the software engineering aspects of the operating system than with raw performance. They recognize that the operating system *will* change and will need to be maintained by different people than the original implementors. This approach is explicitly aware of the potential performance penalty of maintaining modules in exchange for maintainability and correctness.

Extensible Nucleus

The extensible nucleus approach is a mix of the monolithic and modular approaches. Here, a skeletal nucleus is constructed and then used as an underlying abstract machine for constructing the remaining functionality required of different operating systems. This approach is especially important in commercial computers, since the nucleus can hide differences among hardware family members from the bulk of the operating system implementation.

Layered Architectures

Layered architectures were inspired by the desire to divide and conquer the functionality (using horizontal partitioning). For example, process management might be implemented as a very low layer of the abstract machine, with the file management implemented using processes.

This approach was first used because it potentially allowed the operating system designer to *prove* that the operating system was correct. Commercial operating systems use the approach because of its modularity and because it encourages the construction of correct systems without actually performing the proofs.

Message-passing Operating Systems

This class of operating system is intended to support process-based implementations. The operating systems incorporates processes and interprocess communication using messages as a fundamental part of its design (as opposed to adding messages at some high level of abstraction). This approach encourages distribution and, to some extent, security.

Network Operating Systems

As users require higher functionality of interconnection among individual systems, the operating system must become more comprehensive than traditional operating systems. A file is a fundamental collection of information in a system, and it is natural to consider information sharing among systems at the file level. If an operating system can support the exchange of files between two machines, then the two systems can begin to be used to solve one problem. Such a system would allow a user at one machine to prepare a file containing a memorandum and another user on another machine to read the memorandum, that is, one could implement electronic mail.

A *network operating system* is one that provides all the function provided by a multiprogrammed operating system and that also allows information to be shared among different machines, at least at the granularity of files. Typically, a network operating system will also support remote entry, as jobs in a batch system or as remote log-in in a time-sharing system. UNIX is ordinarily thought of as a network time-sharing operating system with file transfer and remote log-in capability.

A network operating system relies on some mechanism for interconnecting with other machines, for example, an asynchronous serial line similar to that used to support interactive terminals. However, contemporary network operating systems are designed to use considerably higher speed telecommunication media, such as *local area networks* (*LANs*). A LAN is a multidrop, shared communication medium used to switch packets of information among some set of physically close host machines. Thus, besides managing the logical sharing of files among other machines, the network operating system must manage devices that interface to LANs.

More recently, network operating systems have begun to support *diskless workstation* environments. In this configuration, a collection of workstations that does not have disk drives is connected to a single *disk server* machine using a LAN. The diskless workstations share a disk drive on the server by reading and writing the shared disk via the LAN. In this case, the network operating system must make another jump in sophistication, since it must now be built so that software that attempts to read or write a disk results in information flowing out of one machine to the disk server where the access takes place, and the result of the access is routed back over the LAN to the original *client* machine.

Distributed Operating Systems

Previously, we have focused on operating systems that are concerned with managing the resources on a single A_H (hardware abstract machine). A *distributed operating system* treats an entire set of machines connected with a network or shared memory as a single "system," with physical machine boundaries transparent to the application programmer and end user. Thus, it is intended to support application programs that themselves may be distributed over distinct machines. Notice that a distributed operating system may share information among the machines at a much finer granularity than files, for example, as records in a high level programming language, strings, or other simple data structures.

The distributed operating system must control resources (such as memory) to support this fine grained interaction. For example, the distributed operating system will provide facilities to allow two parts of the distributed computation to synchronize prior to reading or writing memory cells shared between themselves.

1.5 ORGANIZATION OF TOPICS

Processes are the fundamental unit of computation managed by the operating system. Thus, we start our discussion of operating systems in Chapter 2 by describing sequential process properties and multiprogramming. Scheduling is introduced in this chapter. Basic mechanisms to support resource sharing are the subject of Chapters 3 and 4. Chapter 3 discusses an approach that relies on structure among processes, while Chapter 4 explores operating system mechanisms for synchronizing the operation among processes. Deadlock is a specialized issue in resource sharing, so it is given its own treatment in Chapter 5. Chapter 6 addresses single and multiple processor scheduling techniques. Thus, Chapters 2 through 6 are directed at process management.

Chapter 7 covers memory management, including a background discussion of memory allocation and swapping, in addition to the primary topics of segmentation and paging virtual memory approaches.

Protection will have been introduced in process and memory management discussions. In Chapter 8, the discussion focuses on protection and security as a separate topic. Most of the ideas in Chapter 8 are required to understand distributed file systems and distributed operating systems.

File systems are an abstraction of the management of most devices, providing a model of operation for input/output that transcends individual device characteristics. File systems and storage devices are discussed in Chapter 9. In Chapter 10, networks are introduced and then extended to support distributed storage in Chapter 11. Chapter 12 describes process synchronization techniques for distributed computations.

Chapter 13 reviews the approaches to designing an operating system and provides more detail about each approach. More significantly, this chapter provides several examples of each category of operating system.

Chapter 14 addresses performance modeling and prediction for operating systems. There is an introduction to queueing theory, another introduction to system simulation, and finally an extension of the distributed system techniques as they apply to simulation.

1.6 FURTHER READING

The very early history of computer systems, from 1940 to 1960, is fascinating reading. Robert Rosin and Saul Rosen have written interesting reviews of the technical challenges of the era [28, 29]. In addition, Saul Rosen edited a book containing a number of fundamental technical papers from the era [27]. Randell also edited a collection of early papers about the origins of computers and systems [24].

Layered machines were introduced in Dijkstra's THE operating system [7]. Subsequently, the idea has been extended, for example, see [20, 30] for operating systems kernel design, networks [35], and various other software systems.

A number of papers have been published about UNIX; the original paper by Ritchie and Thompson appeared in [26]. The *AT&T Bell Laboratories Technical Journal* devoted an entire issue to UNIX in 1984 [1]. Quarterman, Silberschatz, and Peterson wrote a survey paper describing the evolution of the Berkeley Software Distribution of UNIX [23]. More recently, the book by Leffler and others has provided a comprehensive discussion of BSD UNIX [18]. Multics, the forerunner of UNIX, is described in detail in Organick's book [22], and CTSS can be reviewed in the paper by Corbato, Daggett, and Daley [5].

IBM OS/360 and its variants have also been described in many different books and articles, (see [6, 15, 21]). Brooks perspective on building OS/360 does not directly address the details of the operating system, but it does provide considerable insight into the size and complexity of building large operating systems [4].

The DOS operating system is perhaps the most widely used operating system today, since it is a fundamental part of all IBM PCs and PC-compatible computers. DOS is described in detail in the IBM and Microsoft documentation, as well as in a number of books, (see [6, 15]).

The Cal TSS time-sharing system project was an important vehicle for studying capability-based protection [33]. Most of the researchers from the project contributed in one form or the other to the Alto operating system.

The Xerox Alto personal computer was a revolutionary machine because of the user interface, programming language, network, and systems research that was conducted on it. The machine itself is described in [36]. The base operating system is described in a paper by Lampson and Sproull [16], and the Pilot operating system is described in a paper by Redell and others [25]. Finally, discussion of the Smalltalk experiment on the Alto appears in papers by Kay in [14], and by Ingalls [13].

Tanenbaum and van Renesse have provided a useful elaboration on the distinction between network operating systems and distributed operating systems [34].

An understanding of computer architecture is a mandatory prerequisite for understanding operating systems. Siewiorek, Bell, and Newell have collected a number of classic architecture papers in [31]. Hennessy and Patterson have written a comprehensive book on contemporary uniprocessor computers systems, especially addressing performance issues [10]. Hwang and Briggs's book covers most of the fundamental parallel computer architectures in use today [12]. There are many other fine books on the topic, including Hayes's book [9]. The book by Levy and Eckhouse provides a lucid description of a particular machine, the DEC VAX computer [19].

While the specific issues in cache memory design for multiprocessors differ from virtual memory design, there is considerable overlap. Dubois, Schuerich, and Briggs have published a recent paper introducing cache memory approaches [8]. Archibald and Baer analyze contemporary algorithms [3], and Smith surveys the area as of the mid 1980s [32]. The interested reader should also consider papers in the performance literature, such as Hill and Smith [11], Wang and Baer [37], and Agarwal, Hennessy, and Horowitz [2].

REFERENCES

1.   *AT&T Bell Laboratories Technical Journal*, AT&T, October 1984.

2.   A. Agarwal, J. Hennessy, and M. Horowitz, "Cache Performance of Operating System and Multiprogramming Workloads," *ACM Transactions on Computer Systems 6*, 4 (November 1988), 393-431.

3.   J. Archibald and J. L. Baer, "Cache Coherence Protocols: Evaluation Using a Multiprocessor Simulation Model," *ACM Transactions on Computer Systems 4*, 4 (November 1986), 273-298.

4.   F. P. Brooks, *The Mythical Man-Month: Essays on Software Engineering*, Addison-Wesley Publishing Co., Reading, MA, 1975.

5.   F. J. Corbato, M. M. Daggett, and R. C. Daley, "An Experimental Time-Sharing System," *Proceedings of the Spring Joint Computer Conference 21* (1962), 335-344.

6.   H. M. Deitel, *Operating Systems, Second Edition*, Addison-Wesley Publishing Co., Reading, MA, 1990.

7.   E. W. Dijkstra, "The Structure of the THE Multiprogramming System," *Communications of the ACM 11*, 5 (May 1968), 341-346.

8.   M. Dubois, C. Schuerich, and F. Briggs, "Synchronization, Coherence, and Event Ordering in Multiprocessors," *IEEE Computer 21* , 2 (February 1988), 9-21.

9.   J. P. Hayes, *Computer Architecture and Organization, Second Edition*, McGraw-Hill Book Co., New York, 1988.

10. J. L. Hennessy and D. A. Patterson, *Computer Architecture: A Quantitative Approach*, Morgan Kaufmann Publishers, Inc., San Mateo, CA, 1990.

11. M. D. Hill and A. J. Smith, "Evaluating Associativity in CPU Caches," *IEEE Transactions on Computers 38*, 12 (December 1989), 1612-1630.

12. K. Hwang and F. A. Briggs, *Computer Architecture and Parallel Processing*, McGraw-Hill Book Co., New York, NY, 1984.

13. D. H. H. Ingalls, "The Smalltalk-76 Programming System Design and Implementation," *Proceedings of the Fifth Annual ACM Symposium on Principles of Programming Languages*, 1978, 9-16.

14. A. C. Kay, "Microelectronics and the Personal Computer," *Scientific American 237*, 3 (September 1977), 231-244.

15. L. S. Keller, *Operating Systems Communicating with and Controlling the Computer*, Prentice Hall, Inc., Englewood Cliffs, NJ, 1988.

16. B. W. Lampson and R. F. Sproull, "An Open Operating System for a Single-User Machine," *Proceedings of the Seventh Symposium on Operating Systems Principles*, December 1979, 98-105.

17. H. C. Lauer, "Observations on the Development of an Operating System," *Proceedings of the Eighth ACM Symposium on Operating Systems Principles*, December 1981, 30-36.

18. S. J. Leffler, M. K. McKusick, M. J. Karels, and J. S. Quarterman, *The Design and Implementation of the 4.3 BSD UNIX Operating System*, Addison-Wesley Publishing Co., Reading, MA, 1989.

19. H. M. Levy and R. H. Eckhouse Jr., *Computer Programming and Architecture: The VAX, Second Edition*, Digital Press, Bedford, MA, 1989.

20. B. H. Liskov, "The Design of the Venus Operating System," *Communications of the ACM 15*, 3 (March 1972), 144-149.

21. G. H. Mealy, B. I. Witt, and W. A. Clark, "The Functional Structure of OS/360," *IBM Systems Journal 5*, 1 (1966), 3-51.

22. E. I. Organick, *The Multics System: An Examination of Its Structure*, MIT Press, Cambridge, MA, 1972.

23. J. S. Quarterman, A. Silberschatz, and J. L. Peterson, "4.2BSD and 4.3BSD as Examples of the UNIX System," *ACM Computing Surveys 17*, 4 (December 1985), 379-418.

24. B. Randell, ed., *The Origins of Digital Computers*, Springer-Verlag, New York, NY, 1987.

25. D. D. Redell, Y. K. Dalal, T. R. Horsley, H. C. Lauer, W. C. Lynch, P. R. McJones, H. G. Murray, and S. C. Purcell, "Pilot: An Operating System for a Personal Computer," *Communications of the ACM 23*, 2 (February 1980), 81-92.

26. D. M. Ritchie and K. Thompson, "The UNIX Time-Sharing System," *Communications of the ACM 17*, 7 (July 1974), 365-375.

27. S. Rosen, *Programming Systems and Languages*, McGraw-Hill Book Co., New York, NY, 1967.

28. S. Rosen, "Electronic Computers: A Historical Survey," *ACM Computing Surveys 1*, 1 (March 1969), 7-36.

29. R. F. Rosin, "Supervisory and Monitoring Systems," *ACM Computing Surveys 1*, 1 (March 1969), 37-54.

30. A. R. Saxena and T. H. Bredt, "A Structured Specification of a Hierarchical Operating System," *Proceedings of the International Conference on Reliable Software*, April 1975, 310-318.

31. D. P. Siewiorek, C. G. Bell, and A. Newell, *Computer Structures: Principles and Examples (2nd Ed.)*, McGraw-Hill Book Co., New York, NY, 1981.

32. A. J. Smith, "Disk Cache -- Miss Ratio Analysis and Design Considerations," *ACM Transactions on Computer Systems 3*, 3 (August 1985), 161-203.

33. H. W. Sturgis, "A Postmortem for a Time Sharing System," University of California, Berkeley, Ph.D. thesis, 1973.

34.   A. S. Tanenbaum and R. van Renesse, "Distributed Operating Systems," *ACM Computing Surveys 17*, 4 (December 1985), 418-470.

35.   A. S. Tanenbaum, *Computer Networks, Second Edition*, Prentice Hall, Inc., Englewood Cliffs, NJ, 1988.

36.   C. P. Thacker, E. M. McCreight, B. W. Lampson, R. F. Sproull, and D. R. Boggs, "Alto: A Personal Computer," in *Computer Structures: Principles and Examples (2nd Ed.)*, D. P. Siewiorek, C. G. Bell, and A. Newell (ed.), McGraw-Hill Book Co., New York, NY, 1981.

37.   W. H. Wang and J. L. Baer, "Efficient Trace-Driven Simulation Methods for Cache Performance Analysis," *ACM Sigmetrics Performance Evaluation Review 18*, 1 (May 1990), 27-36.

EXERCISES

(1)   High level programming languages are abstract machines for machine language instruction sets. Given the C assignment statement

        a = b + c;

(a) Describe an implementation of the abstract machine (using pseudo assembly language) if the statement is preceded by a declaration of the form

        int a, b, c;

(b) Describe an implementation of the abstract machine (using pseudo assembly language) if the statement is preceded by a declaration of the form

        float a, b, c;

(c) Describe an implementation of the abstract machine (using pseudo assembly language) if the statement is preceded by a declaration of the form

        int a;
        float b, c;

(2)   Explain how the UNIX **stdio** library is an abstract machine for device input/output operations.

(3)   What abstraction do the IBM PC BIOS routines provide to the Intel 8088 abstract machine?

(4)   Let $T_{compute}$ be the amount of CPU time and $T_{channel}$ be the amount of channel time that a job requires in a batch processing system. Assuming that no other job interferes with the execution of this job, write an expression that shows the expected upper bound and lower bound of time required for the job to complete processing.

(5)   Most interactive time-sharing systems support some form of batch processing. In UNIX, shell scripts describe a batch operation, and in DOS a .bat file serves the same purpose. Write a shell script that will interrogate the operating system to determine the number of processes that are active at any given time, then append the result (along with a time-stamp) on a log file. (Hint: See the **ps** and **wc** commands.)

(6)   Describe how the shell script (or any other file) could "automatically" be executed once every hour in a UNIX system. (Hint: See the **cron** facility.)

(7)   The general behavior of the write-through cache coherence strategy was explained in the chapter, and the snooping cache idea was mentioned. Provide a pseudo code description of the operation of a snooping cache.

(8)   A *single-instruction-multiple-data (SIMD)* computer architecture employs one control unit to fetch and decode the instruction stream and multiple processing elements to execute an instruction concurrently on distinct data streams. How might an operating system for a SIMD computer differ from an operating system for a von Neumann machine?

(9)   Interleaving is sometimes used in multiple memory bank systems to allow the memory to respond to new read/write requests before pending ones have completed. Suppose that a processor had a special vector ALU that could operate on the scalar values in a vector in parallel. How would the interleaved memory be especially useful for such a system?

(10)   Commercial shared memory machines make extensive use of a shared bus for interconnecting processors and memories, even though the bus becomes a bottleneck for systems with a relatively small number of processors, for example, 15. How might the processor-memory interconnection be made to be more effective in shared memory multiprocessors?

(11)   Successive overrelaxation (SOR) is a method to solve linear $n \times n$ systems of equations

$$A*x = b$$

That is, given the coefficient matrix A, the right-side vector b, and an initial estimated solution vector x, then the algorithm recomputes each x_i based on the x_j $(i \neq j)$, A, and b. Notice that we can write the n equations as:

$$a_{11}x_1 + a_{12}x_2 + \cdots + a_{1n}x_n = b_1$$
$$a_{21}x_1 + a_{22}x_2 + \cdots + a_{2n}x_n = b_2$$
$$\vdots$$
$$a_{n1}x_1 + a_{n2}x_2 + \cdots + a_{nn}x_n = b_n$$

Arbitrarily use the ith equation to solve for x_i, yielding

$$x_i = (b_i - a_{i1}x_1 - a_{i2}x_2 - \cdots - a_{in}x_n)/a_{ii}$$

Now one can implement SOR on an n-processor system by having the ith processor compute x_i.

(a) Describe an implementation of SOR for an (n + 1)-processor system in pseudo code.

(b) Specify some conditions under which the program would work well on a shared memory machine?

(c) Specify some conditions under which the program would work well on a local memory machine?

2

PROCESS MANAGEMENT

Processes are the most widely used unit of computation in programming and systems, although object and threads are becoming more prominent in contemporary systems (see Section 2.4). Because of this dependency on the process model, much of the work of the operating system is to provide an abstract machine environment in which application programmers can define processes, execute them, and generally control their behavior.

In this chapter, we begin to examine the characteristics of processes. After providing a high-level description of a process, miscellaneous basic considerations are addressed: a model for describing multiple processes and their implementations, basic issues relating to providing a multiple-process environment in a single-processor context, the resulting fundamental issues that arise from maintaining multiple processes, and approaches to scheduling in the single processor environment. While the discussion in this chapter may seem diverse, it provides the foundation for more detailed discussions relating to coordinating communities of multiple processes; these more detailed discussions appear in the next three chapters.

2.1 A MODEL OF OPERATION

2.1.1 Processes

A process is a program in execution. The components of a process are the program to be executed, the data on which the program will execute, resources required by the program (for example, memory), and the status of the execution. For the process to execute, it must have a suitable abstract machine environment. The environment will provide an engine for executing the program, memory for storing the program and the data, and status information indicating the progress of the process.

Definition 2.1. A *process* is a sequential unit of computation. The action of the unit of computation is described by a set of instructions executed sequentially on a von Neumann computer, using a set of data associated with the process.

A *resource* is any abstract machine environment object required by the process for it to execute.

A process can run to completion only when all resources that it requests can be allocated to the process. ∥

The notion of process can be made more precise by expanding on this description. In particular, a process can be described by providing a formal model of the operation of the process. There are many different models, each important for studying some particular aspect of processes. The general model is intended to be intuitive and descriptive as well as precise, so it is patterned after running programs on traditional von Neumann computers. That is, the operation of the memory, CPU, and control unit describe a program in execution for a von Neumann computer. The locus of the PC contents is a sequential list — a thread — of instructions that is executed in behalf of the process. We will use more detailed and formal models for different analyses of process behavior in later chapters.

2.1.2 Multiple Processes

Suppose that we would like to execute two processes concurrently by time multiplexing the CPU or by incorporating two CPUs into the application environment. If the two processes depend on one another in any way, they will need to communicate with one another (at least to coordinate their respective operation). If the two processes are totally independent, then they will never need to synchronize nor communicate with one another, except to share resources.

In contemporary software systems, individual applications may be implemented as a set of processes, which suggests that these related processes will need to share information and/or synchronize their operation. Therefore, part of the requirement for an abstract machine to support multiple processes is that it must provide a means for the processes to share information.

There are a number of strategies that one might employ; in this section, we consider three obvious ones:

(1)   Allow the processes to have their own machines, requiring that processes communicate with one another using a message-passing paradigm (*networking*).

(2)   Allow the processes to share the memory yet have their own CPU and control unit, allowing interprocess communication to take place in the common memory (*multiprocessing*).

(3)   Allow the processors to share memory and the (single) processor (*multiprogramming*).

Networking

The networking organization of a set of processes is patterned after the hardware concept of local memory systems (see Chapter 1). Conceptually, the simplest strategy is to replicate the hardware abstract machine, A_H (see Figure 2.1). In this case, the process model is provided with its own A_H. Since the processes must be allowed to share information, the individual processors are interconnected with a message-passing mechanism. Information sharing is accomplished exclusively by *passing messages* among the processes (and in the underlying A_H). In particular, it is entirely possible to implement the message-passing mechanism on a communications network or on a shared memory architecture.

For the network approach to be effective, it must have an effective communication mechanism. That is, the interconnect will be supporting processes that execute several million instructions per second; if the network transmits information at a rate of 1,000 bytes per second (for example, 9,600 baud), then the network is likely to be a bottleneck if the processes transmit more than one byte per thousand instructions executed.

State of the art network technology supports bit-serial or byte-serial interconnection mechanisms. It is, of course, easy to imagine that the transmitter and the receiver could agree on some pattern of linear collections of bits as representing bytes; this allows higher-layered machines to treat the network as if it were a byte-serial interconnection even if it actually transmits and receives bits serially.

Processes can share information by encoding the information into a sequential stream of bytes that can be transmitted from one processor to another, for example, a file or message. A process that intends to use the network to communicate with another process must find some way for converting its information into a serial byte stream prior to transmitting the information to the receiving process. If the sender wishes to send an electronic mail message to a receiver, then the sender needs to encode the header for the message and the message body into a byte stream prior to transmission. The receiver must then decode the serial stream into information that conveys the meaning that the sender intended. For example, the receiver must be expecting a mail message in order to decode the byte stream as a mail header and body. The sending and receiving processes must have agreed on the particular method of encoding and decoding when the programs that implement the processes were designed; such an agreement between two processes is

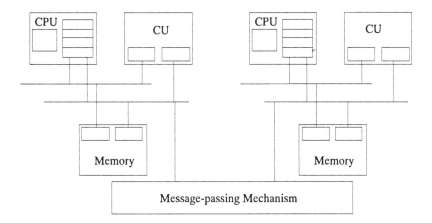

Figure 2.1 Network Support of Processes

called a *communication protocol*. Networks of processors that support processes are only effective when there is a functional and efficient protocol among the communicating processes.

The network solution is adequate for many collections of processes, for example, for processes that do not require high-bandwidth information sharing. Low-bandwidth requirements may be the only requirement if the processes are independent or if they do not communicate with one another very often with very much information (compared to the amount of time they spend performing isolated computations). Processes that have low traffic between them are called *loosely connected* processes. If the processes are actually some decomposition of a larger computation into a set of loosely connected processes, the computation is called a *large-grained* parallel computation. (Notice that, for any pair of processes to need to communicate, logically they are part of some larger computation.)

Network organizations of processors are economically attractive, since they take advantage of existing, isolated computers — from personal computers to large machines — as components to be used in executing large-grained parallel computations. Large problems can be solved with systems that might ordinarily be dedicated to nonshared use, by constructing a large-grained parallel program that solves the large problem. In a typical corporate business environment, this is often the situation; an organization within the corporation uses its "own" computers to perform computations unique to its charter. However, when the corporation needs to solve a larger problem, for example, communication among workers in the corporation, it may need to interconnect the individual systems so that they share information and so that the larger problem may be solved on the collection of corporate machines.

The granularity of a parallel program is related to the number of computations within a single processor with respect to the amount of information transmitted among the processors. Thus network-based communities of processes can be implemented so that the number of computations between communications can decrease with the speed of the interconnect (size of the communication) relative to the speed of the processor. As these trade-offs begin to balance, the granularity of the process becomes finer. Slow processors interconnected with high-speed networks can support *medium-grained* or possibly even *fine-grained* parallel computations.

Multiprocessing

If two processes need to communicate relatively frequently, that is, they are medium- or fine-grained computations, then the network will likely be a bottleneck. A faster physical interconnection is needed between the processors that support the two processes. In Figure 2.2, the two processors that implement the processes share the internal bus of a machine; such an architecture is called a *shared memory multiprocessor* architecture, since a single machine supports two or more processors with common access to a shared memory module. Each process will have some partition of the memory containing its program and private data. Communication is implemented by allowing each process to access a shared partition of the memory.

Multiprocessor support of multiple processes simplifies the protocol problem, since structured information never needs to be encoded and decoded for sharing (assuming that the programs that implement the two processes share common data type definitions). The programs that implement the processes are constructed so that they agree on the nature of

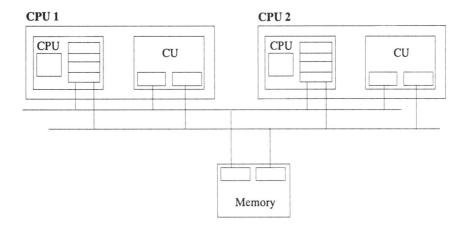

Figure 2.2 Multiprocessing Support of Processes

the information structure, then they are allowed to proceed in parallel.

Consider a variable in the shared memory that two processes, p_1 and p_2, wish to use. If process p_1 is writing a multiword record into the shared memory while p_2 is reading it, then there must be some mechanism to allow p_1 to write the entire record to all memory words before p_2 reads any of them. Otherwise, p_2 may read a record from the memory in which some of the fields are information that was in the record prior to p_1's updating, while other fields reflect the update. The overall record will be incorrect, neither representing the information in the record prior to nor after the update. If the multiprocessor operating system were to ensure that arbitrary (program-defined) records could be written and read strictly serially, then the operating system would be said to support *atomic transactions* on the memory.

Multiprogramming

A process often has time in which it is unable to proceed until some external event has occurred, for example, an input/output operation has completed. During these time intervals, the process "idles" on the CPU, performing no useful work. (Typically, the process executes a loop, checking a flag to be set by a device, in the case of input/output; when the flag is set, the process can proceed with useful work.)

Since these situations occur frequently, the process may "waste" large amounts of CPU time. If another program were ready to execute, then the first process could temporarily be made dormant while the second program were put into execution. That is, two or more processes could share a single machine by time multiplexing the CPU and control unit and space multiplexing the memory (see Figure 2.3). This approach to concurrency is referred to as *multiprogramming* a single processor. A multiprogramming system, A_S, simulates an A_H for each program that will implement the processes. It can result in more efficient use of the A_H (hardware), which, in turn, will allow two independent programs to be completed in a shorter amount of time than if they were executed serially.

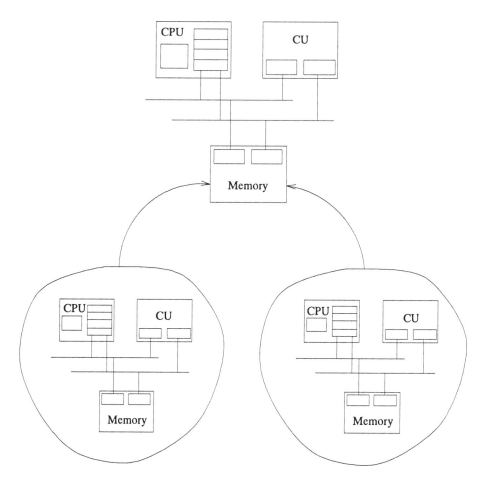

Figure 2.3 Multiprogramming Support of Processes

The information sharing problem for multiprogramming machines is similar to that for multiprocessors. Two problems make it very difficult for a multiprogramming abstract machine to present the perfect A_H model to the program: First, the operating system will have to allow every process to perform atomic transactions on arbitrary shared records. Second, since the single hardware processor is shared among some set of *virtual machines*, each virtual machine must be guaranteed of receiving its "fair share" of the physical processors cycles. Programs, particularly those under development or those that have unexpected input data, may contain infinite execution loops; in many cases, the loop contains no input/output instructions. This can result in a process that will never yield the CPU, thus destroying the multiprogramming approach. For multiprogramming to be successful, it must solve both of these problems. We will address this problem in more detail in Section 2.2.

Sharing Information

Supporting concurrent processes is difficult due to the need to share information among the processes. If they were always independent, that is, they never shared information, then any of the solutions would be adequate (provided that the multiprogramming solution were able to solve the infinite loop problem).

Most of the study of operating systems is concerned with choosing an architecture for the abstract machine to support multiple processes and then implementing mechanisms for controlled information sharing.

2.2 BASIC TASKS

The general purpose of the process management portion of the operating system is to provide the abstract machine environment in which processes can be created, controlled, operated, and removed. The first issue is related to sharing a processor among a set of competing processes. Next, the process and resource management issues can be described; then one can identify three fundamental problems that must ultimately be addressed by the application programmer using the process management facilities.

2.2.1 Multiplexing a Processor

Multiprogramming is employed in almost all forms of multiple processing, including networks and multiprocessor approaches. Part of the reason for this is that operating systems themselves may be implemented as one or more processes on a processor (sometimes the operating system is implemented as a set of procedures that can be called by the user process, for example, as is done in DOS). The other major factor in favor of multiprogramming is the need for processes to perform input/output operations in the normal course of computation. Since input/output operations ordinarily require orders of magnitude more time to complete than CPU instructions, multiprogramming systems often allocate the CPU to another process whenever a process invokes an input/output operation. (That is, whenever a process invokes an input/output operation, the process is voluntarily releasing its control of the CPU to some other process.)

The Yield Instruction

The simplest means by which time multiplexing can be accomplished is by requiring that no program contain a potentially infinite loop without executing a **yield** instruction within the loop. (The **yield** instruction may be buried in a procedure call.) When **yield** is executed by process p_1, then the control unit executes the algorithm shown in Figure 2.4.

The parameter p is related to p_1 by virtue of the operating system's internal *process identifier* for the process. It is often convenient to abbreviate the setting of this parameter by writing "**yield**(*, q)" to mean that the first parameter is associated with the process identifier of the process that executes the instruction.

Prior to the execution of **yield**, memory[p] contains the value of the PC the last time the process executed **yield**; after **yield** has completed execution, memory[p] contains the address of the instruction following the **yield**, and the PC has been reset to resume execution on the process that was suspended at the PC value stored in memory[q]. That is, the CPU is switched from running the program that executes the

```
yield(p, q):
{
        memory[p] ← PC;
        PC ← memory[q];
}
```

Figure 2.4 The Yield Instruction

yield to another program at the location stored in memory[q]. For example, suppose that memory[q] contains the last PC value for p_2; then when process p_1 executes the **yield** instruction, it yields control of the CPU to process p_2 [which could then cooperate by executing **yield**(*, p) to restart p_1].

If more than two processes were being shared, then p_2 could act as a process *scheduler* by choosing some memory location, q´, that contained the PC value for process p_3, and then executing **yield**(*, q´). Now, all user processes execute **yield**(*, q), while the scheduler executes **yield**(*, q´) for some q´ depending upon the identity of the process that the scheduler desires to execute next.

In this example, every compute-intensive process is always in one of two states: *running* or *ready* (see Figure 2.5). Process p_i moves from the running state to the ready state by executing **yield**(*, q), and process p_j moves from the ready state to the running state when the scheduler executes **yield**(*, q´) where memory[q´] contains the last PC value for the process p_j. While there can be only one process in the running state (per processor), there may be many processes in the ready state, each being ready to use a processor should one be available and each having the address of the instruction to be executed upon restart in a table maintained by the scheduler.

The *blocked* state is included in Figure 2.5 to represent that a process has requested a resource from the abstract machine environment (for example, the process has initiated an input/output operation and cannot proceed with computation until the operation is complete). In the figure, we have marked the transition from the running-to-blocked state

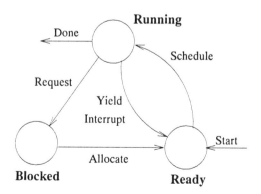

Figure 2.5 Process States

by *request* to represent an input/output operation request. (In Chapter 5, we will see that a process's request for any resource that may not be immediately available is effectively the same as an input/output operation invocation, hence the term "request" for the transition.)

Building a system that relies on the **yield** instruction is not without its difficulties. A process may behave properly, behave like a "cad," or behave like a "knave." Proper behavior has been described. A "cad" program ignores the **yield** instruction; once a cad process gets control of the CPU, no other process will ever get control of the CPU unless an operator intervenes. A "knave" program also ignores the **yield** instruction, albeit inadvertently. The effect is the same, so in the context of this discussion, there is no difference between a cad and a knave.

The **yield** instruction can be effective on a *personal* system, meaning one that supports only a single user at a time. The rationale is that, if the single user chooses to run an ill-behaved process, then that is the business of the user. If the user does this inadvertently, then he can override the machine by restarting it. The Xerox Alto used a variant of the **yield** instruction to accomplish multiprogramming.

Interval Timers and Interrupts

Hardware can be designed to enforce periodic interruption of any program, that is, to force it to effectively execute a **yield** instruction. The basic extension is to incorporate an *interval timer* device and extend the control unit so that it can handle *interrupts* from the interval timer.

An interval timer behaves like an egg timer; to use the timer, one sets an interval of time in the device and then proceeds with other processing. When the time interval has passed, the timer raises an alarm in the form of an interrupt.

The basic operation of the interval timer is summarized by the Interval_Timer procedure in Figure 2.6. The interval timer is implemented in hardware, and is invoked once each time a real-time clock ticks. The interval (K = number of ticks) can be specified by the Set_Interval call shown in the figure.

The control unit fetch-execute cycle (implemented in hardware) is now altered so that the algorithm shown in Figure 1.7 behaves as shown in Figure 2.7. After the current instruction is executed, the control unit checks to see if the interval timer has expired. If it has not, the control unit continues normal operation; if it has, the controller executes a form of the **yield** instruction in behalf of the process that is in execution.

The control unit, in general, cannot detect the identity of the process that is in execution. Instead, it saves the old PC in a standard place (memory[0]) and loads the new PC from a standard place (memory[1]). Thus, the address of the *clock interrupt routine* is loaded in memory[1]; the clock interrupt routine will determine the identity of the interrupted process from a CPU status table and then save memory[0] in an internal data structure for the interrupted process. In the hardware algorithm it is assumed that the clock interrupt software will immediately reset the Int_Req flag back to false after it has detected the interrupt.

In principle, the clock interrupt routine could also be the scheduler, but in practice the clock interrupt routine generally runs the scheduler as a separate process. This can be accomplished using the **yield** instruction. (Briefly, this is done just in case another interrupt should arrive when the scheduler is being executed, a more complex situation than we have described in this example.)

```
Interval_Timer:
{
        Int_count ← Int_count - 1;
        if (Int_count ≤ 0)
        {
                Int_Req ← TRUE;
                Int_count ← K;
        }
}


Set_Interval(programmable_value):
{
        K ← programmable value;
        Int_count ← K;
}
```

Figure 2.6 The Interval Timer

```
while (IR.op_code ≠ "halt")
{
        IR ← memory[PC];
        PC ← PC + 1;
        execute(IR);
        if (Int_Req)
        { /* Interrupt current process */
                memory[0] ← PC;
                PC ← memory[1];
        }
};
```

Figure 2.7 The Fetch-Execute Cycle with an Interrupt

Interval timers, interrupts, and schedulers can ensure that the CPU will be shared among a set of user processes. However, they introduce a new problem much like the atomic update of records (above).

2.2.2 Process Operation

The process management aspect of the operating system provides facilities that will enable one process to create another one, to allocate resources to it, to block its progress, and to destroy the process. Thus, the system is put into operation by initiating one process that is the "parent" process of all other processes; this process is essentially the agent of the computer's operator and is started when the system is initialized.

The most widely used process model employs a controlling hierarchy established by the process creation activity. The initialization process is the root of the hierarchy; each process that it creates is the root's child. The children, of course, may subsequently create their own children, which will propagate the hierarchy.

Resource management may be delegated to each child process when it is created, implying that the child must be prepared to manage the resources of child processes that it creates. In other cases, resource management is implemented as a part of the process manager (independent of the creation hierarchy).

Figure 2.5 provided a simplified state diagram for a process that was useful for introducing processor multiplexing; however, the diagram does not address the set of states relating to resource allocation and control. Figure 2.8 (inspired by Shaw [3]) reflects these other issues.

A process is created in the *ready-suspended* state. It can be moved to the *ready-active* state once its controlling process, for example, its parent, decides to activate it. When the process becomes *ready-active*, it is placed in the CPU ready list, that is, it is blocked waiting for the CPU to be allocated to it by the scheduler. The controlling process may choose to deactivate a process in the *ready-active* state, or the scheduler may allocate the CPU to the process; in the former case, the process returns to the *ready-suspended* state and in the latter it becomes a *running* process on the CPU.

A process in the *running* state may be removed from the CPU if the operating system chooses to do so, or it may move to the *blocked-active* state if it makes a request for an unavailable resource. That is, a process is "ready" if it needs the CPU to proceed and "blocked" if it needs a different resource to proceed. The state diagram essentially reflects the medium-term scheduling strategy, but is also applicable for any resource management.

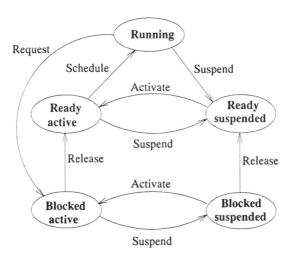

Figure 2.8 A Process State Diagram

A *blocked-active* process can become *ready-active* if the requested resource is allocated to it, or it can become *blocked-suspended* if a controlling process chooses to suspend it while it is blocked. A release operation by some other process is required for the process to moved from either of the blocked states to the corresponding ready states, and an activate operation is required to move the process from a suspended state to the corresponding active state.

A large part of process management is to implement the state diagram for each process it supports. (Providing facilities to coordinate the execution of the processes is the other large part.) It should be apparent that there are many different engineering approaches to designing a process manager for an operating system. Each must provide these facilities and address three major pitfalls: determinacy, critical sections, and deadlock.

2.2.3 Fundamental Process Management Issues

Determinacy and Critical Sections

Suppose that processes p_1 and p_2 share an integer variable, I, and that process p_1 will execute a high level language statement

$$I \leftarrow I + J;$$

while process p_2 will execute the statement

$$I \leftarrow I - K;$$

Then Figure 2.9(a) illustrates machine language that might be generated for p_1's statement, and Figure 2.9(b) represents machine language for p_2's statement.

If the interval timer happens to expire when process p_1 is executing the instruction marked by †, and process p_2 begins to execute before p_1 resumes its execution, then a *race condition* will exist to see if p_1 will manage to complete the high-level language statement before p_2 begins to execute it. If p_1 wins the race, then the values that it had previously read into its version of R1 and R2 (in its simulated hardware) can be added together and written back to the shared memory with no harm. If p_2 wins the race, then it will read the old value of I from the shared memory, subtract K from it, and write it back to the memory location that contains I; later, p_1 will resume on the old value of I that is loaded in R1. Process p_1 will compute old I plus J and overwrite the value of I that p_2 had written when p_1 was blocked. The update of I by p_2 will be lost.

```
Load  R1, I              Load  R1, I
Load† R2, J              Load  R2, K
Add   R1, R2             Sub   R1, R2
Store R1, I              Store R1, I
```

         (a)   (b)

Figure 2.9 Machine Code for Processes p_i

The programs that define processes p_1 and p_2 each have a *critical section* with respect to their use of the shared variable. The concurrent execution of the two processes is not guaranteed to be *determinate*, since different instances of execution of the same programs on the same data may not produce the same result.

Either process can enter its corresponding section any time it needs except when the other process is currently in the critical section. There are two general approaches to handling this problem: precedence relations can be established between the two processes to ensure that they execute in the proper order (Chapter 3), or the two processes will behave correctly only if they *synchronize* their entry into their critical section (Chapter 4).

How can the two processes cooperate on the use of the critical sections? In a multiprogrammed system, the problem is caused by the interrupt. If a pending interrupt could be delayed while the process in the running state were in its critical section and then allowed to occur when it departed its critical section, it would not cause the problem described above.

Suppose that the operating system provided two special system procedures, **disable()** and **enable()**, to temporarily disable the interval timer interrupt (but buffering the interrupt if it should happen to occur while disabled) and enable the interval timer interrupt. Then the processes would behave properly if the program for processes p_1 and p_2 were written as shown in Figure 2.10.

The **disable** and **enable** routines are very powerful, since they override the interval timer, a device intended to force sharing among processes. The routines must be used judiciously; otherwise, the system is equivalent to one that provides only a **yield** instruction. There are a number of other primitives for synchronizing processes, and these are elaborated on in the remainder of the book.

Deadlock

Suppose that processes p_1 and p_2 read and write two variables, I and J, such that when I is updated then J must also be updated, and vice versa (for example, I and J are related and must be consistent). Then, to avoid the critical section problem, p_1 might encapsulate operations on I and J as shown in Figure 2.11.

If processes p_1 and p_2 are executed concurrently on a multiprogramming system, then a clock interrupt may occur after p_1 updates I, but before it updates J. If p_2 updates J and I before p_1 resumes, then the values of I and J will not necessarily be consistent with one another.

Program for p_1	Program for p_2
```disable();```	```disable();```
```I ← I+J;```	```I ← I-K;```
```enable();```	```enable();```

Figure 2.10 Disabling Interrupts to Implement the Critical Section

Program for p_1 Program for p_2

```
...                                  ...
disable();                           disable();
<access variable I>                  <access variable J>
enable();                            enable();
<intermediate computation>;          <intermediate computation>
disable();                           disable();
<access variable J>                  <access variable I>
enable();                            enable();
...                                  ...
```

Figure 2.11 Long Computations with Disabled Interrupts

Reexamination of the code suggests that p_1 could be rewritten as shown in Figure 2.12.

This solution is sufficient unless the <intermediate computing> within each critical section causes it to be so long as to cause other interrupts to be missed. In this case, one could use a flag so that p_1 and p_2 could coordinate their respective accesses to I and J, so that p_1 and p_2 appear as shown in Figure 2.13. In this solution, if p_1 is currently in a critical section relative to I, then p_2 will be prevented from entering its critical section with respect to I by its test of "lock_I", and vice versa. The same case also holds for accessing J. (While this is conceptually a good solution, since it prevents <intermediate computing> from disabling interrupts for long periods of time, it has a subtle form of critical section problem related to testing and setting the lock. If a process is interrupted after testing the lock but before it sets it, then the solution fails. This can be corrected by using **enable** and **disable**; see the exercises.)

Suppose that p_1 is interrupted during the <intermediate computation> (after having set lock_I to TRUE) and p_2 begins to execute. It will lock J and then wait for access to I

Program for p_1 Program for p_2

```
...                                  ...
disable();                           disable();
<access variable I>                  <access variable J>
<intermediate computation>;          <intermediate computation>
<access variable J>                  <access variable I>
enable();                            enable();
...                                  ...
```

Figure 2.12 Modified Long Computations with Disabled Interrupts

```
boolean lock_I = FALSE; /* shared variable */
boolean lock_J = FALSE; /* shared variable */
```

Program for p_1 Program for p_2

```
...
while (lock_I){null};          while (lock_J){null};
lock_I ← TRUE;                 lock_J ← TRUE;
<access variable I>            <access variable J>
<intermediate computation>    <intermediate computation>
while (lock_J){null};          while (lock_I){null};
lock_J ← TRUE;                 lock_I ← TRUE;
<access variable J>            <access variable I>
lock_I ← FALSE;               lock_J ← FALSE;
lock_J ← FALSE;               lock_I ← FALSE;
...                           ...
```

Figure 2.13 Critical Sections Using Locks

at the **while** statement; eventually, the clock interrupt will resume at p_1, which will be blocked at the **while** statement prior to updating J.

Neither process can ever proceed, since each holds the exclusive right to update a variable that the other needs. This situation is called a *deadlock* between p_1 and p_2. It is a recurring problem in systems that support multiple communicating processes. Chapter 5 is devoted to the study of deadlock.

2.3 OTHER UNITS OF COMPUTATION

Processes are the classic unit of computation, derived from the operation of the software on a von Neumann architecture. There are other models of units of computation stemming from other principles. The most prominent of these models are *lightweight processes* (also called *threads*) and *objects*.

2.3.1 Lightweight Processes

Processes of the form described above are sometimes called "heavyweight processes" in contrast to processes that are designed to have a minimum of internal state and resources. Since these lightweight processes have less state, a scheduler has less work to do when multiplexing among a set of such processes. Hence, a major motivation for lightweight processes is to minimize context switching time, allowing the CPU to switch from one unit of computation (a process) to another unit of computation with minimal overhead.

The context of a lightweight process can be reduced over that for a heavyweight process by reducing the amount of resources associated with the process. For example, a set of lightweight processes might all execute the same program, simplifying the amount of information stored in the physical memory for any given lightweight process (and reducing the amount of memory management performed by the operating system in behalf of the particular lightweight process). The implication is that the operating system may support some parent heavyweight process for a group of similar lightweight processes, and each lightweight process is merely a thread of execution through the corresponding program. Since all lightweight processes are sharing a procedural description, their behavior toward one another is symmetric. This allows the programmer to (relatively) easily construct a program in which a community of lightweight processes interacts with one another, managing shared resources that have been allocated to the parent heavyweight process.

As lightweight processes have become more widely used, it has become apparent that there is an important issue related to how they should be scheduled. If lightweight processes were to be scheduled by an application heavyweight process, then the application programmer could use the heuristics of the problem to decide the most effective manner for scheduling. Application programmers make this type of decision in traditional heavyweight processes (programs) whenever the process has many different tasks to perform at any given time, but they must be accomplished sequentially.

If lightweight process scheduling is implemented within the application program, then the operating system must ensure that the resulting scheduling decisions are fair to the other heavyweight and lightweight processes competing for the CPU. This might suggest a two-level scheduler: the first level might allocate quanta to heavyweight processes, and the second level might divide the resulting quanta among each heavyweight process's lightweight children.

If the lightweight process scheduler operates in the application program (that is, in the heavyweight process), then the operating system scheduler must also ensure that the application-provided lightweight process scheduler is secure and safe. This will ordinarily require that the operating system invoke the application's lightweight process scheduler based on interrupts, which suggests the need for efficient context switching between the operating system and the scheduler.

Lightweight processes are especially useful in scenarios in which several different processes need to utilize shared, logically remote facilities. The shared facility is managed by a community of lightweight processes, defined by a common program; each lightweight process acts in behalf of an external heavyweight process.

Contemporary window systems may use the lightweight process paradigm for managing virtual terminal sessions in the context of a physical terminal. Suppose that a window system were built with a heavyweight physical screen manager, with several related virtual screen lightweight processes (see Figure 2.14). Each lightweight process is running the same code, and all are sharing the physical screen. Since response time is very important is this type of system, context switching among individual virtual screen managers is important. Lightweight processes are an ideal mechanism for implementing such a system (and are used in commercial windowing systems).

2.3.2 Objects

Object-oriented systems have been in existence since the late 1960s, first being widely known in the Simula 67 system [5]. Simula 67's original purpose in using objects was similar to the motivation for lightweight processes, that is, a simulation program can be construed as the management of a large number of individual units of computation, each of which performs little computation and each of which is closely correlated with sibling units of computation.

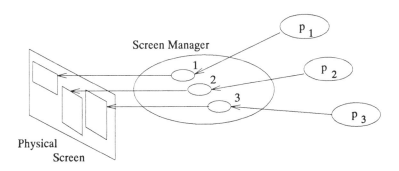

Figure 2.14 Network Support of Processes

Simula 67 used the idea of *classes* to define a unit of computation. The simulation application programmer defined a number of classes, then at run time, different *instances* of each class were created to model behavior in some target system. The simulation run-time system does instance (process) management by scheduling the individual instances in such a manner that their execution conforms to the advancement of the simulated time.

Contemporary object-oriented systems use the same general model for defining the behavior of a unit of computation, an *object*. An object is an independent unit of computation that reacts to messages. Once an object is created, other objects send it messages and it responds by performing computation on its local data and by sending other messages (either back to the original sender or possibly on to other objects).

The behavior of an object is defined by its class definition, just as a Simula class defines the behavior of an instance. The object-oriented programmer designs a system by defining a set of classes and then instantiating objects from the class definitions.

While there are many more aspects to object-oriented programming, for example, the idea of data abstraction (which we will revisit in Chapter 4) and the inheritance of the behavior of one class from some other class definition(s), the significant part of objects is the notion that they are another mechanism for specifying the behavior of a distributed system by specifying the behavior of individual units of serial computation.

2.4 FURTHER READING

Multiprogramming was the mainstay of operating systems in the 1970s, thus there are several detailed presentations of multiprogramming strategies, for example, see Brinch Hansen [4] and Habermann [7]

Additional discussion on clocks and interrupts can be found in several systems programming books, for example, Tanenbaum's introductory operating systems book [13].

Processes have various descriptions in the literature. Horning and Randell provide a relatively complete discussion of processes independent of the context of any particular operating system [8]. In contemporary operating systems, other forms of processes have begun to appear, including objects [6], mobile objects [2, 10], and lightweight processes and threads [1, 11, 12].

Processes are the fundamental unit of computation for parallel and distributed programming. Jamieson, Gannon, and Douglass edited a book on parallel programming; several papers in the collection address computations, granularity, coupling, and the like. [9].

REFERENCES

1. M. Acetta, R. Baron, W. Bolosky, D. Golub, R. Rashid, A. Tevanian, and M. Young, "Mach: A New Kernel Foundation for UNIX Development," *Proceedings of the 1986 USENIX*, Atlanta, GA, 1986, 93-112.

2. J. L. Bennett, "Distributed Smalltalk," *Proceedings of the 2nd ACM Conference on Object-Oriented Systems, Languages, and Applications*, Orlando, FL, October 1987, 318-330.

3. L. Bic and A. Shaw, *The Logical Design of Operating Systems, Second Edition*, Prentice Hall, Inc., Englewood Cliffs, NJ, 1988.

4. P. Brinch Hansen, *Operating System Principles*, Prentice Hall, Inc., Englewood Cliffs, NJ, 1973.

5. O. J. Dahl, B. Myhrhaug, and K. Nygaard, "The SIMULA 67 Common Base Language," Norwegian Computer Center technical report, Oslo, Norway, 1968.

6. A. Goldberg and D. Robson, *Smalltalk-80: The Language and its Implementation*, Addison-Wesley Publishing Co., Reading, MA, 1985.

7. A. N. Habermann, *Introduction to Operating System Design*, Science Research Associates, Inc., Chicago, IL, 1976.

8. J. Horning and B. Randell, "Process Structuring," *ACM Computing Surveys 5*, 1 (March 1973), 5-30.

9. L. H. Jamieson, D. B. Gannon, and R. J. Douglass, *The Characteristics of Parallel Algorithms*, MIT Press, Cambridge, MA, 1987.

10. E. Jul, H. Levy, N. Hutchinson, and A. Black, "Fine-Grained Mobility in the Emerald System," *ACM Transactions on Computer Systems 6*, 1 (February 1988), 109-133.

11. B. Liskov, D. Curtis, P. Johnson, and R. Scheifler, "Implementation of Argus," *Proceedings of the Eleventh ACM Symposium on Operating Systems Principles*, Austin, TX, December 1987, 111-122.

12. G. Popek, B. Walker, J. Chow, D. Edwards, C. Kline, G. Rudison, and G. Thiel, "LOCUS: A Network Transparent, High Reliability Distributed System," *Proceedings of the Eighth ACM Symposium on Operating Systems Principles*, December 1981, 169-177.

13. A. S. Tanenbaum, *Operating Systems: Design and Implementation*, Prentice Hall, Inc., Englewood Cliffs, NJ, 1987.

EXERCISES

(1)   A SIMD computer architecture employs one control unit to fetch and decode the instruction stream and multiple processing elements to execute an instruction concurrently on distinct data streams. Provide a definition of a process in such a system.

(2)   Why are parallel programs implemented on a SIMD processor ordinarily considered to be fine-grained programs?

(3)   Explain how the "networking" model for processes (described in Section 2.1.6.) might be implemented on a shared memory multiprocessor.

(4)   Explain how the "multiprocessing" model for processes (described in Section 2.1.6.) might be implemented on a local memory multiprocessor.

(5)   The *degree of multiprogramming* is the maximum number of processes that may be supported by a uniprocessor at any given time. (Traditionally, jobs and processes had a

one-to-one correspondence.) Discuss the factors that must be considered in determining the degree of multiprogramming for a particular system. You may assume a batch system with the same number of processes as jobs.

(6)   The control unit algorithm described in the text requires that the interrupt handler determine which device caused the interrupt it can branch to a "sub" interrupt handler for the particular device. Some computers include hardware *interrupt vectors* so that when a device raises an interrupt, then the specific handler for that device is invoked directly. Modify the control unit algorithm so that the interrupt request flag is a vector with individual coordinates representing different devices.

(7)   Suppose that a hardware system does not incorporate a timer interrupt. Illustrate how **yield** can be used to implement a critical section in this environment.

(8)   Suppose that a hardware system includes a timer interrupt and **disable** and **enable** system calls. Illustrate how **yield** can be used with interrupts to increase the average effective utilization of the processor for implementing critical sections.

(9)   Suppose that processes p_0 and p_1 share variable V_2, processes p_1 and p_2 share variable V_0, and processes p_2 and p_3 share variable V_1. Show how the processes can use **enable** and **disable** to coordinate access to I, J, and K so that the critical section problem does not occur.

(10)   The solution to the critical section problem shown in Figure 2.12 is flawed by the possibility of an interrupt occurring in p_1 immediately after it executes

                                    while(lock_I){null};

but before it executes

                                    lock_I ← TRUE;

This might allow p_2 to run and to enter the critical section in which it references I. Modify the **while**-loop and assignment statement so that *they* are in a critical section protected by **enable** and **disable**.

(11)   Consult the documentation of your local operating system, then draw a state diagram to represent the states and transitions for a user process.

(12)   Numerical quadrature is a technique for approximating the value of the integral of a function. Intuitively, quadrature can be thought of as "finding the area under a curve." If $f(x)$ is some arbitrary function, then the integral of $f(x)$ is defined on the interval [a, b], and represents the area bounded by $f(x)$, x = a, x = b, and the x axis. For any particular continuous function, the trick is to approximate the shape of $f(x)$. The simplest approximation, called the *trapezoidal rule*, is to use a straight line between $f(a)$ and $f(b)$ to represent the various values of $f(x)$ on [a,b].

        A better approximation can be made by computing $f((b - a)/2)$, the value of $f(x)$ at the midpoint of [a, b]. This new value could be used to fit a quadratic equation to the three points (*Simpson's rule*) or it could be used to approximate the integral as the sum of the areas of two adjacent trapezoids, one bounded by x = a, $f(x)$, x = (b - a) / 2, and the x axis; and the other being bounded x = (b - a) / 2, $f(x)$, x = b, and the x axis. This subdividing of the x axis can be carried on indefinitely, with the approximation to the integral being computed as the sum of the areas of the trapezoids. Ignoring round-off error, the increasing number of intervals increases the accuracy of the approximation of the integral.

        Write a C program that will use the trapezoidal rule to compute the integral of

$$f(x) = x^2 + 2x + 4$$

between LEFT and RIGHT as N intervals. You should be able to run your program with a command of the form

                                    trapezoid LEFT RIGHT N

UNIX shell commands that are terminated with a "&" rather than a carriage return cause the shell to run the command and to immediately prompt the user for another command. Write a UNIX shell script to use your trapezoid program to compute the integral of f(x) from 0 to 6 as six partial sums computed by six instances of your program running in parallel.

3

PRECEDENCE
AMONG PROCESSES

A scheduling mechanism allows a group of processes to share a CPU resource, providing the illusion that each process is proceeding concurrently. In our earlier remarks about scheduling, we assumed that a process either required the CPU or had requested some unavailable resource. If the processes are to share information, then a process may need to avoid the ready state, because it is waiting for some other process to perform certain computations. For example, suppose that process p_1 is intended to write information into a shared memory cell and then process p_2 should read the memory cell; that is, the execution of p_1 must precede the execution of p_2 for the computation to be correct. Thus, the scheduler or some other part of the operating system must provide a means by which p_2 can avoid becoming ready (even though it is not waiting for an explicit resource) until p_1 has completed the required write operation.

In this chapter, we introduce a formal graph model of processes that can be used to precisely describe the desired behavior of parallel operation among the processes. We first use the underlying visual aspects of graph models to develop an intuition about relationships that can exist among processes. Next, programming language constructs that represent relationships among processes are described. Then the model is used to revisit scheduling (in a multiprocessor context) among a community of processes whose computational outcome depends on the order in which the processes execute. A variant precedence model is then used to derive necessary and sufficient conditions related to the *determinate* operation of a computation that is implemented as a community of parallel processes. Finally, we consider a means by which one can transform determinate models of computation into computationally equivalent models that exhibit maximal parallelism.

Critical sections are an instance of the more general problem of coordinating processes. Chapter 4 builds on the basic computational models introduced in this chapter to address process synchronization and interprocess communication.

In Chapter 5, the basic model is again extended to study necessary and sufficient conditions for deadlock to exist in a community of related processes with varying types of resources.

3.1 THE PROBLEM: COORDINATING PROCESSES

Suppose that two procedures have been encoded as shown in Figure 3.1. The variables, x and y, are assumed to be shared between the two procedures, so that proc_A computes for some indeterminate amount of time and then writes a value into the shared variable x; it enters another computation phase and then reads the value of y before looping. Proc_B begins its loop by reading x. (Since x and y are shared variables, we may assume that the procedures *read* and *write* have been constructed using *enable* and *disable* in order to prevent a critical section with respect to accessing the variable.) Proc_B then computes, writes y, computes, and starts its loop over again.

If these two procedures are called by a single process, then the order in which values are read and written in x and y is well determined, since the process will provide a serial ordering on the calls. However, we may not be able to achieve the desired effect since, if proc_A (proc_B) is called first, it may not read the correct value for variable y (variable x). Also, if the compute sections are relatively time consuming, then one may choose to define two processes, p_1 and p_2, to execute proc_A and proc_B, respectively, obtaining parallel execution of the program; that is, the process that executes proc_A can be in *<compute A2>* while the process that executes proc_B is concurrently executing *<compute B1>*.

But if the two procedures are used to define two processes, again there is a problem: How can one ensure that p_2 is reading the correct value of x and that p_1 is reading the correct value of y when the corresponding read statements are executed? If p_1 starts and runs once through the loop (using values initially written into y) and then proceeds through the loop a second time, then p_2 will never see the first value written to x by p_1. Similarly, p_2 may write to y twice before the value is ever read by p_1.

```
proc_A()                    proc_B()
{                           {
   while (TRUE)                while(TRUE)
   {                          {
      <compute Al>;              read(x);
      write(x);                  <compute Bl>;
      <compute A2>;              write(y);
      read(y);                   <compute B2>;
   }                          }
}                           }

        (a)                         (b)
```

Figure 3.1 Procedures A and B

The order in which the code is to be executed by the two processes is important. For example, it may have been intended that proc_B's *read(x)* be executed once after each time proc_A's *write(x)* statement was executed. If this were the intent, then some mechanism must be included to enforce the execution of parts of p_1 and p_2 in concert.

There are two basic approachs to handling this problem: interprocess synchronization and partitioning with precedence among the parts. The synchronization approach introduces new operating system constructs that can be used by each process to coordinate the progress of each process. The partitioning approach requires that the two processes be partitioned into smaller subprocesses, and the subprocesses have a set of precedence constraints to dictate the order in which they are executed.

In this chapter, we focus on the precedence approach, and in Chapter 4 we examine the synchronization approach.

3.2 GRAPH MODELS

Many formal models of computation have been derived since 1960 (for example, see [2]). The family of precedence models has been widely used to represent computations in operating systems, compilers, parallel programming, and computer architecture.

Petri nets are an independent model used to study precedence in operating systems, parallel programming, and computer architecture (but not so much in compiler technology, for example see [14, 15]).

While the mainstream of our studies is based on the precedence graph models, Petri nets provide a useful, alternative view of a system or computation.

3.2.1 Precedence Models

Suppose that proc_A and proc_B are implemented by many subprocesses (the subprocesses are not necessarily small amounts of computation). For example, the computation shown in Figure 3.1 can be partitioned into eight subprocesses. Let

> $p_{1,1}$ be a subprocess that executes *<compute A1>;*
> $p_{1,2}$ executes *write(x);*
> $p_{1,3}$ executes *<compute A2>;*
> $p_{1,4}$ executes *read(y);*
> $p_{2,1}$ executes *read(2);*
> $p_{2,2}$ executes *<compute B1>;,*
> $p_{2,3}$ executes *write(y);*
> $p_{2,4}$ executes *<compute B2>;*

Now, for any particular pass through the respective loops, $p_{2,1}$ can be executed only after $p_{1,2}$ has terminated. And $p_{1,4}$ can only be executed after $p_{1,3}$ and $p_{2,3}$ have both terminated. Notice that $p_{1,3}$ and $p_{2,2}$ can be executed in parallel. Figure 3.2 represents the situation as a *precedence graph* for the computation, where an edge from p_i to p_j represents the fact that p_i must terminate before p_j can be initiated.

Precedence graphs are an intuitive mechanism for representing this cooperation among a set of (sub)processes; they are also a formal mechanism for studying properties of groups or processes.

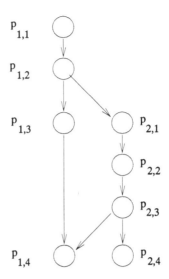

Figure 3.2 Precedence Graph

The Formal Precedence Model

Definition 3.1. Let

$$P = \{p_i \mid 1 \le i \le n\}$$

be a set of processes, and "$<\cdot$" be a partial order on P

$$<\cdot = \{(p_i, p_j) \mid 1 \le i, j \le n\}$$

The partial order includes (p_i, p_j) if and only if process p_i must terminate before process p_j can be initiated.

A *computation* π is an ordered pair

$$\pi = (P,\,\bar{}\, <\cdot)$$

where P is a finite, nonempty set of processes and $<\cdot$ is a partial order on P. ∥

Thus, the intuitive precedence graph can be represented as a directed, acyclic graph in which the nodes are subprocesses and the edges represent precedence among the subprocesses.

The precedence graph shown in Figure 3.2 is represented by the formal model

$$\pi = \begin{aligned} &(\{p_{1,1}, p_{1,2}, p_{1,3}, p_{1,4}, p_{2,1}, p_{2,2}, p_{2,3}, p_{2,4}\}, \\ &\{(p_{1,1}, p_{1,2}), (p_{1,2}, p_{1,3}), (p_{1,2}, p_{2,1}), (p_{1,3}, p_{1,4}), \\ &(p_{2,1}, p_{2,2}), (p_{2,2}, p_{2,3}), (p_{2,3}, p_{2,4}), (p_{2,3}, p_{1,4})\}) \end{aligned}$$

The example illustrates how precedence graphs can be used to represent medium- or large-grained organizations of processes. The same model can also be applied to fine-grained parallelism. Consider a procedural specification of a computation such as that shown in Figure 3.3.

There is statement-level parallelism in this code segment; for example, $a \leftarrow x + y$ can be executed in parallel with $b \leftarrow y + 2$. If one wished to exploit this parallelism, it could be done by mapping each statement to a process and deriving a precedence graph of the resulting processes to represent data dependencies among the statements (processes).

Denote each statement as a "small" process, p_i, to execute the statement on line i. Initially assume that it is possible to execute all six p_i in parallel and then look for data dependencies among the processes. Notice that p_2 cannot be initiated until p_1 has terminated, since it depends on x being defined in order for y to be computed. By analyzing the program text for "definition-before-use," one can derive a full set of constraints on the amount of parallelism for the program segment. For this particular program segment, the resulting precedence graph is shown in Figure 3.4.

3.2.2 Petri Nets

Precedence graphs are acyclic since a cycle describes untenable precedence semantics. That is, if we have

$$<\cdot = \{(p_i, p_j), ..., (p_j, p_k), ..., (p_j, p_i)\}$$

then p_j cannot initiate until p_i has terminated, p_i cannot initiate until p_k has terminated, and p_k cannot initiate until p_j has terminated. No process can ever be initiated.

So precedence graphs cannot be used to directly represent the while loop composed of the four processes in Figure 3.2, since a loop from $p_{1,4}$ back to $p_{1,1}$ would indicate that $p_{1,1}$ cannot initiate until $p_{1,4}$ has terminated. Of course, the intent is that the loop can be executed a second time once it has completed the first iteration.

Petri nets can represent the loop condition while accommodating the precedence semantics in the static graph. This is accomplished by using the Petri net to describe a schema of operation and a *marking* of the Petri net to describe execution sequences of the processes.

```
Line
1        x ← 5;
2        y ← x+input();
3        a ← x + y;
4        b ← y + 2;
5        c ← a - b;
6        w ← c+1;
```

Figure 3.3 A Fine-Grained Computation

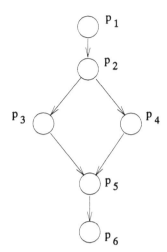

Figure 3.4 Precedence Graph for the Program Segment

A Petri net is composed of a set of *places* and a set of *transitions*, interconnected with arcs, such that each place is connected only to transitions, and vice versa. (More formally, a Petri net is a bipartite graph with the node set being the union of the places and transitions.) Figure 3.5 is a Petri net corresponding to the precedence graph shown in Figure 3.4.

In Figure 3.5, transitions are represented by rectangular boxes and places are represented by circles. A transition can be *fired* if and only if there is a *token* on each input place of the transition. Thus, transition t_3 can fire if and only if there is a token on location p_3 and another on p_4. Whenever a transition terminates, it places a token on each of its output places; thus, when t_2 terminates, it places a token on p_3 and on p_4. The distribution of tokens on the Petri net — the marking of the net — represents the state of the individual processes that make up the computation. A token or set of tokens flowing through the Petri net represents an execution of the corresponding code.

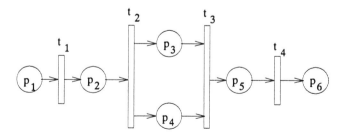

Figure 3.5 A Petri Net

Now consider a Petri net for the multiprocess implementation of the example shown in Figure 3.1, where we wish to represent iterations through the loop. Figure 3.6 is a Petri net to represent the computation including the cycles. Since the precedence is represented by the token marking on the graph, then whenever a token is placed on the two **start loop** places (as indicated in the figure), the execution of the two corresponding *while* loops is modeled by the continuous activity of the loops through the $p_{1,i}$ places and the $p_{2,j}$ places, with appropriate coordination at t_3 and t_6.

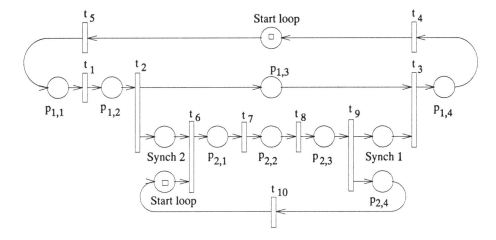

Figure 3.6 A Petri Net with Loops

3.3 LINEAR REPRESENTATIONS OF PARALLELISM

To partition a serial computation into components that may be executed in parallel, or to combine independent units so that they cooperate, the coordination of the units must be determined either implicitly by the compiler or system, or explicitly through the definition of the program(s). The precedence constraints on the resulting partition of the serial computation are important, since they affect the functionality of the parallel computation. The resulting parallel program must reflect the precedence suggested by the graph.

The automatic detection of parallelism is an important topic that is usually included in the compiler literature. Automatic detection algorithms take a linear, sequential program specification as input and produce a precedence graph as the output.

In this text, we limit our study to the specification of parallelism (and of the implied precedence graph) through explicit statements in the language. In either case, the operating system will be required to provide mechanisms to support the policy, whether the specification is generated from a compiler or by the programmer.

There are several linear specification mechanisms for the programmer to define the precedence among a set of processes. The most general set uses the three statements: *FORK*, *JOIN*, and *QUIT*. *PARBEGIN* and *PAREND* represent a smaller class of computations (but most agree that the subset is large enough to characterize all "interesting" computations). The *AND* primitive is computationally equivalent to *PARBEGIN* and *PAREND*.

Contemporary procedural programming languages have been extended or created to use these parallel programming constructs. See Further Reading for some examples.

3.3.1 FORK, JOIN, and QUIT

There are several variants of *FORK*, *JOIN*, and *QUIT*, the original work being done by Conway in 1963 [6] and Dennis and Van Horne in 1966 [7].

The statement set enables the programmer to specify that certain parts of a program may be executed (as processes) in parallel. *FORK(label)* results in the creation of a second process (defined by the procedure currently being executed), which begins execution at the statement with the specified *label*. The process that executed the FORK continues execution at the next instruction. Once the new process has been created, then the original process and the new process coexist and proceed concurrently.

A process terminates by executing *QUIT()*. This results in the process being destroyed.

JOIN(count) is used to merge two or more processes back into a single process. When a process executes the statement, it executes code equivalent to that shown in Figure 3.7 on a shared variable named *count*. *QUIT* is assumed to execute an *enable()* instruction as its last action.

FORK, JOIN, and QUIT can be used to describe computations that have been represented as precedence graphs or Petri nets. Consider the precedence graph shown in Figure 3.2 (which represents one pass through the loops in the procedures shown in Figure 3.1). To show the ordering among the subcomputations, one could rewrite the procedures as shown in Figure 3.8. (The encoding of the two procedures into a single body of code is the result of the JOIN instruction's name space being within a single procedure. Also, since the FORK construct uses a label to specify the point at which the newly spawned process will begin execution, these language constructs propagate labels. It is possible to formulate equivalent constructs that eliminate the need for labels, but at the cost of a slightly more complex paradigm.)

Fine-grained code segments can also be encoded using these primitives. Suppose that we have the code segment shown in Figure 3.9. Since the code segment contains a loop, we will use a Petri net to represent the precedence constraints among the statement executions.

Figure 3.10 is a Petri net representation of the fine-grained computation with a loop. From the figure, one can infer that there can be tokens on the processes (places) labeled a ← y ˆ 2, r ← y + 20, and s ← y - 1 simultaneously, so these three processes can

```
disable();
count ← count - 1;
if (count ≠ 0) QUIT();
enable();
```

Figure 3.7 Manipulating the 'count' Shared Variable

```
          count ← 2;
          <compute A1>;
          write(x);
          FORK(L2);
          <compute A2>;
     L1:  JOIN(count);
          read(y);
          QUIT();
     L2:  read(x);
          <compute B1>;
          write(y);
          FORK(L3);
          goto L1;
     L3:  <compute B2>;
          QUIT();
```

Figure 3.8 FORK, JOIN, QUIT Example

```
w ← 10;
while (w < 0)
{
          y ← input();
          a ← y ^ 2;
          r ← y + 20;
          s ← y - 1;
          b ← r * s;
          c ← a - b;
          w ← c+1;
}
```

Figure 3.9 Fine-Grained Computation with a Loop

be scheduled to execute concurrently. Also, the Petri net indicates that b ← r * s can have its execution overlap that of a ← y ^ 2, even though b ← r * s must be preceded by the assignment statements for variables r and s. Similarly, c ← a - b cannot be initiated until both a and b have had values assigned to them.

The Petri net representation can be used to generate the FORK, JOIN, QUIT linear representation of a set of processes. There must be a process in existence for each place. Thus, once the y ← input() process terminates, two processes must be created through the FORK call. Whenever two or more edges enter a transition, a JOIN operation is required, since that represents the case that the corresponding processes all must terminate prior to the process(es) on the output be initiated. Figure 3.11 is a linear representation of the process coordination indicated in the Petri net.

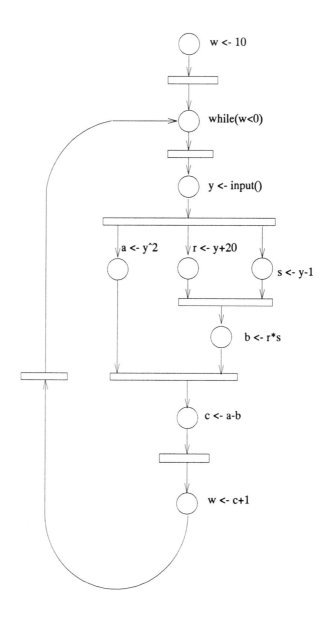

Figure 3.10 Petri Net Representation of the Fine-Grained Computation with a Loop

```
w ← 10;
while (w < 0)
{
        y ← input();
        count1 ← count2 ← 2;
        FORK(L1);
        FORK(L2);
        a ← y ^ 2;
        goto L4;
L1:     r ← y + 20;
        goto L3;
L2:     s ← y - 1;
L3:     JOIN(count1);
        b ← r * s;
L4:     JOIN(count2);
        c ← a - b;
        w ← c+1;
}
```

Figure 3.11 Fine-Grained Computation with FORK, JOIN, and QUIT

3.3.2 PARBEGIN and PAREND

The PARBEGIN and PAREND statements were proposed as extensions to Algol 60 in [8] as an alternative mechanism to FORK, JOIN, and QUIT. Any collection of statements can be bracketed by PARBEGIN and PAREND; the result is that the statements may be executed concurrently.

In some cases, one needs to represent a case where $p_i <\cdot p_j$, but p_k can be executed concurrently with the block of p_i and p_j. This is accomplished through the use of sequential block brackets such as BEGIN-END or { - } pairs (see Figure 3.12. For example the code segment in Figure 3.9 can be rewritten as shown in Figure 3.13.

3.3.3 The AND Statement

Wirth's AND statement is equivalent to PARBEGIN and PAREND. Whereas the latter are used to bracket a collection of statements that may be executed concurrently, AND is

```
PARBEGIN
        {
                p_i;
                p_j;
        };
        p_k;
PAREND
```

Figure 3.12 Bracketing Parallel Statements

```
w ← 10;
while (w < 0)
{
        y ← input( );
        PARBEGIN
                a ← y ^ 2;
                {
                PARBEGIN
                        r ← y + 20;
                        s ← y - 1;
                PAREND
                b ← r * s;
                };
        PAREND
        c ← a - b;
        w ← c+1;
}
```

Figure 3.13 A Fine-Grained Computation with a Loop

placed between any pair of statements (in lieu of a ";") to indicate that the pair can be executed in parallel. Sequential blocks are delimited by curly braces or BEGIN-END pairs, as with PARBEGIN-PAREND.

The previous example can now be encoded as shown in Figure 3.14.

```
w ← 10;
while (w < 0)
{
        y ← input( );
        a ← y ^ 2
        AND
        {
                r ← y + 20
                AND
                s ← y - 1;
                b ← r * s;
        };
        c ← a - b;
        w ← c+1;
}
```

Figure 3.14 FORK, JOIN, QUIT Example

3.3.4 Classes of Precedence Graphs

Ignoring looping constructs, consider the class of precedence graphs that can be generated from the various language constructs. The FORK command maps directly into a process that enable two successors [see Figure 3.15(a)], and JOIN corresponds to a process that has two or more predecessors [see Figure 3.15(b)]. QUIT is executed by a sink process, that is, one that has no successors.

Using FORK, JOIN, and QUIT, it is possible to build precedence graphs that are binary trees, that is, FORK can be used to generate a node in a binary tree, and QUIT determines a leaf node. If paths from a root node are to merge, then JOIN is used to combine any number of such paths. There are no other constraints on the form of the resulting precedence graphs. As a result, precedence graphs and Petri nets with complex patterns can be encoded using these primitives. Consider the graph shown in Figure 3.16; it can be constructed using the primitives.

Because FORK is a binary fork, it is not possible to exactly produce all precedence graphs without the introduction of "dummy" nodes.

Suppose that you were given a series of programs that employed PARBEGIN and PAREND and were asked to construct precedence graphs for each of them. Then, for each occurrence of PARBEGIN and PAREND, you would construct a portion of the graph similar to that shown in Figure 3.17(a). It is possible to nest PARBEGIN-PAREND expressions, so the precedence graphs themselves would be nested to reflect this possibility; see Figure 3.17(b). Notice that the AND construct generates exactly the same class of precedence graphs.

Now reconsider the precedence graph shown in Figure 3.14. While it is possible to construct a FORK-JOIN-QUIT schema that corresponds to the precedence graph, it is not possible to do so for the PARBEGIN-PAREND or AND constructs, since they only generate precedence graphs (and subgraphs) with a single entry point and a single exit point, that is, a unique source process and a unique sink process.

The latter class of precedence graphs has considerably more structure imposed on it. Thus, it may be argued that such graphs result in more structured concurrent programs, that is, ones with simpler control flow.

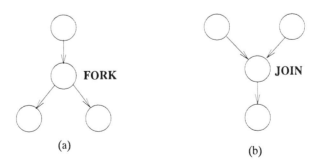

(a)   (b)

Figure 3.15 Precedence Graph Atoms for FORK and JOIN

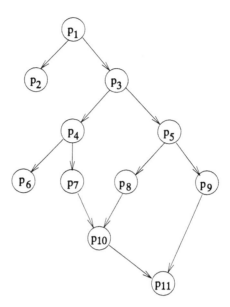

Figure 3.16 A Precedence Graph Constructed from FORK, JOIN, and QUIT

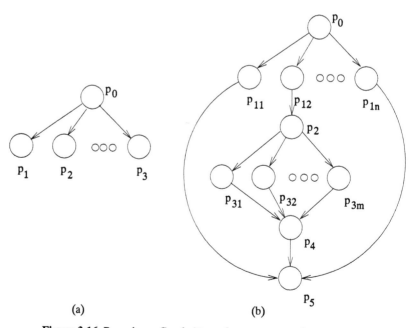

(a)   (b)

Figure 3.16 Precedence Graph Atoms for PARBEGIN and PAREND

3.4 DETERMINATE COMPUTATIONS

A sequential computation may be decomposed into processes to allow the underlying abstract machine to execute the parts in parallel, and hence to achieve a decrease in the amount of time required to execute the entire program. There are pitfalls to decomposing the computation, such as deadlock and violation of a critical section. Critical section violations often manifest themselves as a faulty supporting abstract machine. For example, a program is decomposed into procedures that can be executed by distinct processes; but the program does not produce the same result with the same input data when it is executed repeatedly.

Many mechanisms provided by operating systems provide tools for protecting critical sections, but the tools do not guarantee that the program that uses the tools will be *functional* or *determinate*. A program is said to be determinate if it will always produce the same result with the same input data each time it is executed.

Determinacy can be guaranteed if (and only if) a computation is decomposed into processes that satisfy certain conditions. First, the resulting processes must not violate *Bernstein's conditions* [4]:

(1) If process p_i writes a memory cell, then no process p_j can read the cell.
(2) If process p_i reads a memory cell, then no process p_j can write the cell.
(3) If process p_i writes a memory cell, then no process p_j can write the cell.

Clearly, such constraints are too strong for our purposes, since they define away the possibility of processes p_i and p_j sharing information. The constraints can be relaxed by allowing p_i and p_j to share access to a memory cell, provided that there is precedence between them, that is, if one process is going to write a shared memory cell, then the other process must execute before or after the first, but not concurrently.

In the remainder of this section, we formally argue why this observation must be true.

Refined Precedence Graph Model

Let $\pi = (P, <\cdot)$ be a computation. For every $p \in P$, there are two significant events known as the *initiation* of p, denoted $\bar{p}$, and the *termination* of p, denoted p. The initiation of p represents the event that p is created and allowed to begin execution; p is assumed to read a value from each memory cell in its set of input cells, D_p, when it is initiated. When p terminates, it writes new information to each memory cell in the set of output cells for the process, R_p, and then terminates. Thus, each process, p, can be thought of as a function that maps a set of points from the domain D_p into a set of points in the range R_p,

$$f_p(D_p) = (R_p)$$

If there are no cycles in the precedence graph, then the computation can be represented as the occurrence of $2 * |P|$ events, that is, the initiation and termination of each $p \in P$.

Definition 3.2. Given $\pi = (P, <\cdot)$ with $|P| = n$. An *execution sequence* for the computation is a string

$$\xi = x_1, x_2, \cdots, x_{2n}$$

where every x_i is an initiation or a termination for some $p \in P$, and

(1)   if $x_i = \bar{p}$, then $x_j \neq \bar{p}$ for all $i \neq j$,
(2)   if $x_i = p$, then $x_j \neq p$ for all $i \neq j$,
(3)   if $x_i = \bar{p}$ and $x_j = p$, then $i < j$,
(4)   if $x_i = p_r$, $x_j = \bar{p}_s$, and $p_r <\cdot p_s$, then $i < j$. ∥

Reconsider the precedence graph shown in Figure 3.2 [and described as a formal precedence graph $(P, <\cdot)$ in Section 3.1]. There are several execution sequences for the precedence graph, but all of them must begin with $\bar{p}_{1,1}$, followed by $p_{1,1}$ since $p_{1,1}$ is the predecessor of all other processes in the precedence graph. Two full execution sequences are

$$\xi_1 = \bar{p}_{1,1}, p_{1,1}, \bar{p}_{1,2}, p_{1,2}, \bar{p}_{1,3}, \bar{p}_{2,1}, p_{2,1}, \bar{p}_{2,2}, p_{2,2}, \bar{p}_{2,3}, p_{1,3}, p_{2,3}, \bar{p}_{1,4}, \bar{p}_{2,4}, p_{1,4}, p_{2,4}$$

$$\xi_2 = \bar{p}_{1,1}, p_{1,1}, \bar{p}_{1,2}, p_{1,2}, \bar{p}_{1,3}, \bar{p}_{2,1}, p_{2,1}, \bar{p}_{2,2}, p_{1,3}, p_{2,2}, \bar{p}_{2,3}, p_{2,3}, \bar{p}_{1,4}, \bar{p}_{2,4}, p_{1,4}, p_{2,4}$$

Thus, execution sequences are strings that represent the possible orderings of process initiation and termination in the precedence graph. Notice that this process model provides for the simultaneous execution of processes, but not the simultaneous execution of events associated with the initiation and termination of processes.

A computation will pass through a sequence of *states*, beginning at an initial state and terminating in a final state. The execution sequence determines the particular sequence of states for the computation.

Let

$$S = \{s_i \mid i < \infty\}$$

be the set of states for a computation (where s_i are defined in more detail below). Then the *state sequence* corresponding to ξ is

$$\sigma(\xi) = s_0, s_1, \cdots, s_{2n}$$

where the computation begins in s_0 and moves to state s_1 due to event x_1 in ξ. In general, each state transition in σ is determined from the execution sequence ξ by defining that the computation move from state s_{i-1} to state s_i due to the occurrence of x_i in ξ.

Let $\mu = \{M_i \mid 1 \leq i \leq m\}$ be the set of memory cells shared among the $p \in P$.

Let $M_i(k)$ represent the value stored in M_i after x_k has occurred in ξ. See Figure 3.18. Then

$$s_k = \text{the sequence of } M_i(k) \text{ for } 1 \leq i \leq m$$

that is, a column in memory representation shown in Figure 3.18, and in particular,

$$s_0 = \{M_i(0) \mid 1 \leq i \leq m\}$$

Suppose that we had the following execution sequence for the precedence graph shown in Figure 3.2:

$$\xi = \bar{p}_{1,1}, p_{1,1}, \bar{p}_{1,2}, p_{1,2}, \bar{p}_{1,3}, \bar{p}_{2,1}, p_{2,1}, \bar{p}_{2,2}, p_{1,3}, p_{2,2}, \bar{p}_{2,3}, p_{2,3}, \bar{p}_{1,4}, \bar{p}_{2,4}, p_{1,4}, p_{2,4}$$

in which $p_{1,2}$ writes into memory cell M_1, $p_{1,4}$ reads from memory cell M_2, $p_{2,1}$ reads

	0	1		k		2n
M_1	$M_1(0)$	$M_1(1)$	...	$M_1(k)$	...	$M_1(2n)$
M_2	$M_2(0)$	$M_2(1)$	...	$M_2(k)$	...	$M_2(2n)$
...	...		...		...	
M_m	$M_m(0)$	$M_m(1)$	...	$M_m(k)$	...	$M_m(2n)$

Figure 3.18 Memory States

from memory cell M_1, and $p_{2,3}$ writes into memory cell M_2, (compare with Figure 3.1). Then $m = 2$, and

$$s_0 = (M_1(0), M_2(0)) = (?,?)$$

$$x_4 \text{ is } p_{1,2},$$

so

$$s_4 = (M_1(4), M_2(4)) = (\text{output of } p_{1,2}, ?)$$

The domain and range of a process can now be defined more precisely:

$$D_p = \{M_i \mid p \text{ reads from } M_i \text{ at } \bar{p}\}$$

$$R_p = \{M_i \mid p \text{ writes to } M_i \text{ at } p\}$$

The transition from state s_k to s_{k+1} is defined by

(1)   if $x_{k+1} = \bar{p}$, then $M_i(k+1) = M_i(k)$, $1 \le i \le m$.

(2)   if $x_{k+1} = p$, then $M_i(k+1) = f_p(M_{j_1}(h), M_{j_2}(h), ..., M_{j_a}(h))$

for all $M_j \in D_p$,
where x_h is $\bar{p}$,
for all $M_i \in R_p$.

and

$M_i(k+1) = M_i(k)$ otherwise.

Consider the sequence of values that any memory cell will exhibit during any execution sequence. Notice that the sequence of values simply represents the changes in the value of M_i, so it does not correspond directly to a row in Figure 3.18, but to the elements in the figure when a process terminates and writes into the corresponding cell. Let $V(M_i, \xi)$ represent the sequence of values written into memory cell M_i by execution sequence ξ. Then, if λ represents the empty string,

$$V(M_i, \lambda) = M_i(0)$$

and $V(M_i, x_1x_2 \cdots x_k)$ is defined by
(1)   If x_k is p and $M_i \in R_p$, then the value is

$$V(M_i, (x_1x_2 \cdots x_{k-1})),M_i(k)$$

(that is, the value sequence before the termination concatenated with the value written into M_i by the process).
(2)   Otherwise, the value is

$$V(M_i, (x_1x_2 \cdots x_{k-1}))$$

(that is, the same value sequence as before the event occurred).
Denote the last value written into M_i under the execution sequence ξ by $F(M_i, \xi)$,

Mutually Noninterfering Process Systems

The formal definition for a determinate computation may now be stated:

Definition 3.3. A computation is *determinate* if

$$V(M_i, \xi) = V(M_i, \xi')$$

for $1 \le i \le m$, for any given initial state, S_0, and for all execution sequences ξ, ξ'. ‖

We are now ready to formally define the necessary and sufficient condition for a computation to be determinate:

Definition 3.4. A computation $\pi = (P, <\cdot)$ contains *mutually noninterfering processes* if, for every pair of processes p, q $\in$ P,
(1) p is a successor or predecessor of q, or
(2) Bernstein's conditions are true for p and q.
    That is,
    i) $R_p \cap R_q = \emptyset$, and
    ii) $R_p \cap D_q = \emptyset$, and
    iii) $D_p \cap R_q = \emptyset$. ‖

The example from Figure 3.1, refined in Figure 3.2 and again earlier in this subsection, is determinate. For each pair of processes that read and write a common memory location (x and y in the example), there is precedence between them.
    Before reviewing the determinacy theorem, we need to consider the following lemma, which, is used in the arguments for the necessary and sufficient theorem:

Lemma 3.1. Let $\pi = (P, <\cdot)$ be a computation with $|P| = n$, such that π contains mutually noninterfering processes, and t is a terminal process of π. If

$$\xi = \gamma_1 \top \gamma_2 \underline{t} \gamma_3$$

is an execution sequence of π, then

$$\xi' = \gamma_1 \gamma_2 \gamma_3 \top \underline{t}$$

is an execution sequence of π such that

$$V(M_i, \xi) = V(M_i, \xi')$$

for all $1 \leq i \leq m$. ‖

That is, if π contains mutually noninterfering processes, then any process that has no successors can appear in an execution sequence as the last two events. Terminal processes may be the last processes to write to any memory cell in their range.

Argument
If t is a terminal process, then there is no t' such that $t <\cdot t'$. Therefore, ξ' is a legal execution sequence.

Suppose that $M_i \notin R_t$. Then $R_t \cap D_{t'} = \varnothing$ for any $t' \in \gamma_3$, since π contains mutually noninterfering processes. Thus, each $D_{t'}$ is the same in ξ and ξ' since t could not have affected any memory cell that t' used in computing values for the memory cells in its range. Therefore, $V(M_i, \xi) = V(M_i, \xi')$ for every $M_i \notin R_t$.

Suppose that $M_i \in R_t$. For any $M_j \in D_t$, $V(M_i, \gamma_1) = V(M_i, \gamma_1\gamma_2\gamma_3)$ since $D_t \cap R_{t'}$ is empty for all t' such that $\underline{t}$ could appear in $\gamma_2 \gamma_3$. That is, t' cannot write into any of the memory cells that t reads. Therefore , $F(M_i), \gamma_1 = F(M_i, \gamma_1 \gamma_2 \gamma_3)$ and t must write value, v, into each M_i in ξ and ξ'.

$$
\begin{aligned}
V(M_i,\xi) &= V(M_i,\gamma_1 \top \gamma_2 \underline{t} \gamma_3) \\
&= V(M_i,\gamma_1 \top \gamma_2 \underline{t}) \\
&= (V(M_i,\gamma_1 \top \gamma_2 \; v) \\
&= (V(M_i,\gamma_1 \top) \; v) \\
&= (V(M_i,\gamma_1 \; v) \\
&= (V(M_i,\gamma_1 \; \gamma_2 \; \gamma_3) \; v) \\
&= V(M_i,\gamma_1 \; \gamma_2 \; \gamma_3 \top \underline{t}) \\
&= V(M_i,\xi')‖
\end{aligned}
$$

The necessary and sufficient theorem can now be stated, and the lemma will be used in the argument:

Theorem 3.1. Let π be a computation. Then π is determinate if and only if it contains mutually noninterfering processes. ‖

Argument

Show that if π contains mutually noninterfering processes it is determinate.

Let $|P| = 1$. Then π is determinate because $P = \{p\}$ $\xi = \bar{p}\,p$ is the only execution sequence.

Assume that π is determinate for $|P| = n - 1$. Let $|P| = n$. If there is only one execution sequence, then π is determinate; so assume that there are at least two execution sequences, ξ_1 and ξ_2. Let $t \in P$ be a terminal process in π. Then consider

$$\xi_1' = \xi_1'' \top t, \text{ where } V(M_i, \xi_1) = V(M_i, \xi_1'), \text{ for } 1 \leq i \leq m$$

and

$$\xi_2' = \xi_2'' \top t, \text{ where } V(M_i, \xi_2) = V(M_i, \xi_2'), \text{ for } 1 \leq i \leq m$$

We are sure that ξ_1' and ξ_2' both exist by the previous lemma. Now, show that for $M_i \in R_t$, ξ_1' and ξ_2' write the same values into each M_i, respectively. Consider $\pi' = (P - \{t\}, <\cdot')$, where $<\cdot'$ is obtained from $<\cdot$ by removing all $p <\cdot t$ from $<\cdot$. Now ξ_1'' and ξ_2'' are execution sequences of π', since they are the same as ξ_1' and ξ_2', respectively, with the terminal process t omitted. Notice that $|P - \{t\}| = n - 1$; so

$$V(M_i, \xi_1'') = V(M_i, \xi_2''), \text{ for } 1 \leq i \leq m$$

by the induction hypothesis. Therefore, $F(M_j, \xi_1'') = F(M_j, \xi_2'')$ for all $M_j \in D_t$. Thus, t writes the same value, v, into $M_i \in R_t$ in ξ_1' and ξ_2'.

Now suppose that $M_i \notin R_t$. $M_i \notin R_t$

$$
\begin{aligned}
V(M_i, \xi_1) &= V(M_i, \xi_1') && \text{by the lemma} \\
&= V(M_i, \xi_1'') && \text{since } M_i \notin R_t \\
&= V(M_i, \xi_2'') && \text{induction hypothesis} \\
&= V(M_i, \xi_2') && \text{since } M_i \notin R_t \\
&= V(M_i, \xi_2) && \text{by the lemma}
\end{aligned}
$$

and π is determinate. Now suppose that $M_i \in R_t$. $M_i \in R_t$ implies that

$$
\begin{aligned}
V(M_i, \xi_1) &= V(M_i, \xi_1') && \text{by the lemma} \\
&= (V(M_i, \xi_1''), v) && t \text{ writes } v \\
&= (V(M_i, \xi_2''), v) && \text{induction hypothesis} \\
&= V(M_i, \xi_2') && t \text{ writes } v \\
&= V(M_i, \xi_2) && \text{by the lemma}
\end{aligned}
$$

and π is determinate. This completes the sufficient part of the theorem.

Show that, if π is determinate, it contains mutually noninterfering processes. Suppose that $t, t' \in P$ and t, t' interfere with one another. Then t and t' are independent by definition of interference, and there is some $\xi = \gamma_1 \top t \top t' \, t' \, \gamma_2$ and $\xi' = \gamma_1 \, t' \, t' \top t \, \gamma_2$. Since t and t' interfere with one another and are executed in parallel, there is some $M_i \in (R_t \cap R_{t'})$, $M_j \in (R_t \cap D_{t'})$, or $M_k \in (D_t \cap R_{t'})$.

Suppose that $M_i \in (R_t \cap R_{t'})$. Choose interpretations of f_t and $f_{t'}$ such that t writes u into M_i and t' writes v into M_i, where $u \neq v$. Then

$$V(M_i, \gamma_1 \top \underline{t}\, \overline{t'}\, t') \; = (V(M_i, \gamma_1), u, v)$$

$$V(M_i, \gamma_1 \, \overline{t'}\, \underline{t'}\, \top t) \; = (V(M_i, \gamma_1), v, u)$$

But then π is not determinate. Therefore, $R_t \cap R_{t'} = \varnothing$.

Suppose that $M_j \in (D_t \cap R_{t'})$, and let $M_i \in R_t$ (we assume that R_t is nonempty). Choose interpretations of f_t and $f_{t'}$ such that $F(M_j, \gamma_1) \neq F(M_j, \gamma_1 \overline{t'} t')$. Now t reads different values from M_j in ξ and ξ'. Choose interpretations of f_t and $f_{t'}$ such that t writes u when it appears in ξ and t writes v when it appears in ξ', where $u \neq v$. Then

$$V(M_i, \gamma_1 \top \underline{t}\, \overline{t'}\, t') \; = V(M_i, \gamma_1 \top t) = (V(M_i, \gamma_1), u)$$

$$V(M_i, \gamma_1 \, \overline{t'}\, \underline{t'}\, \top t) \; = V(M_i, \gamma_1 \, \overline{t'}\, t') = (V(M_i, \gamma_1), v)$$

But then π is not determinate. Therefore, $D_t \cap R_{t'} = \varnothing$.

Finally, exchange the roles of t and t´ and use the same argument as above to show that $R_t \cap D_{t'} = \varnothing$.

Therefore, π is determinate => mutual noninterference. $\|$

3.5 MAXIMALLY PARALLEL COMPUTATIONS

The determinacy proofs magnify the importance of precedence and shared memory references related to parallelism and functional operation. If too many processes are allowed to execute in parallel, then the computation is not determinate. If too few are enabled to run in parallel, that is, there are too many precedence constraints, then the implementation will not run the maximum number of parts in parallel. While precedence may have been introduced into a parallel computation for external reasons (for example, synchronization with external entities such as users), it should be possible to compute a precedence graph based only on the shared memory references.

For example, suppose that all processes were assumed to run in parallel ($<\cdot = \varnothing$). If any pair of processes shares memory in which one of the processes writes memory and the other reads or writes the same memory, then the resulting computation will not be determinate. Therefore, modify the computation such that a precedence relation exists between the two processes, specifying that the two should not be executed in parallel. By repeating this step until all such pairs of processes have been identified, it is possible to construct a new precedence graph that has a minimal number of precedence relations and that represents the maximum amount of parallelism that can exist in the computation based on the shared memory references.

A slightly simpler problem is to create a maximally parallel graph from an existing determinate graph.

Generating a Maximally Parallel Graph

Suppose that a computation is known to be determinate, since it contains mutually noninterfering processes. How can one relax the precedence constraints such that the computation maintains its determinacy?

   If one were to construct another precedence graph from the same components, yet the processes were still mutually noninterfering, then the two computations would be equivalent. Suppose that the constructed precedence graph included a precedence arc between *every* pair of processes that violated Bernstein's conditions.

   For example, suppose that we had a precedence graph, corresponding to the one in Figure 3.19, in which the following memory references occur:

P_1 writes to M_1 and M_2
P_2 reads from M_1 and writes to M_4
P_3 reads from M_2 and writes to M_5
P_4 reads from M_2 and M_3 and writes to M_6
P_5 reads from M_3
P_6 reads from M_1 and M_4
P_7 reads from M_5

We can systematically determine all cases where Bernstein's conditions would be violated in a graph with no precedence by constructing a table such as the one shown in Figure 3.20.

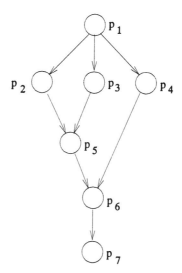

Figure 3.19 A Determinate Computation

	M_1	M_2	M_3	M_4	M_5	M_6
P_1	write	write				
P_2	read			write		
P_3		read			write	
P_4		read	read			write
P_5			read			
P_6	read			read		
P_7					read	

Figure 3.20 Read/Write References in the Computation

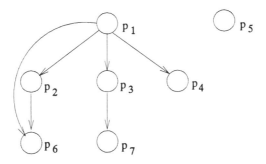

Figure 3.21 Maximally Parallel Graph with Redundant Precedence

Using the table, one can determine the processes that violate Bernstein's conditions by identifying rows (processes) that contain conflicting read/write operations on a common memory cell (columns). For example, P_1 writes M_1 and P_2 reads it; therefore, precedence is required between the two processes. Continuing, we can construct the precedence graph shown in Figure 3.21 by comparing every pair of processes to see if they share a memory cell (where at least one of the processes is writing the memory cell), adding precedence wherever necessary.

Notice that the arc from P_1 to P_6 is redundant, since if $P_1 <\cdot P_2$ and $P_2 <\cdot P_6$, then $P_1 <\cdot P_6$. Therefore, we can construct a new precedence graph in which all such redundant precedence edges are removed, such as shown in Figure 3.22.

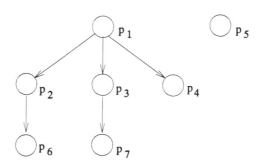

Figure 3.22 Maximally Parallel Graph

3.6 FUNCTIONAL PROGRAMMING LANGUAGES

Functional programming languages are another approach to explicitly specifying the parallelism in a program. A functional programming language disallows constructs that introduce ambiguity into potential parallelism, that is, functional programs are specified using language constructs that infer explicit concurrency.

Functional and applicative programming languages have a strong mathematical underpinning. (Functional languages differ from applicative languages in that they support the idea of manipulating functions as objects within the language.) These languages depend on the formal properties of the model to specify computation in such a manner that it is relatively easy to recognize parallelism in the program. As a result, functional language specifications are especially well suited for programming concurrent computations.

Each statement in a functional language is treated as a mathematical function definition. Thus, if one writes

$$y = (a + b) * x;$$

then the value of y is defined for the program. In particular, there can be no other statement in the program that assigns a different value to y, that is, the "=" operator is mathematical equality rather than assignment.

Given this constraint on the language, the precedence graph representing the statement-level parallelism is trivial to construct. Each statement is cast as a process; since a variable may appear only once on the left side of any statement (or otherwise have a result assigned to it), the statement that defines the variable determines the root of a subtree in the precedence graph. Descendants of the root are all statements that reference the variable defined in the given statement. (Combinations of such subtrees will result in a general graph structure rather than a tree, since a statement will generally reference more than one variable.)

The given precedence graph is determinate. The techniques used in the previous section can be incorporated into the compiler so that the precedence graph is maximal. Thus, functional programming languages allow a programmer to write high-level programs that never explicitly identify parallelism, yet that are easily analyzed to generate maximally parallel precedence graphs for statement-level parallelism.

This single-assignment constraint radically alters the way one thinks about certain programming constructs, for example, arrays and loops. Just as loops are not allowed in a precedence graph, they cannot appear in the functional language program. Multielement structures and loops are generally handled by maintaining versions of the structures and by using recursion. This, of course, adds substantially to the "intellectual baggage" required to use a functional programming language.

Petri nets are variants of precedence graphs that allow loops to be introduced through the introduction of tokens to identify instances of control flow. The generalization of functional programming into data flow languages uses a similar extension, that is, a data flow language is closely related to functional languages, yet it explicitly allows loops by encoding all memory for a computation into the token itself. As the token moves from process to process, it brings its own data environment for the computation, again allowing very high degrees of parallelism.

3.7 FURTHER READING

Precedence graphs were used to represent parallelism in automatic parallelism detection compilers [2]. These techniques are still widely used in compilers for contemporary multiprocessors.

SCHEDULE [9], The Force [12], and PPL [16] are examples of procedural languages that have been extended to allow programmers to explicitly specify concurrent operation. Phred is an experimental parallel programming language that explicitly addresses determinacy [3].

Much of the material in this chapter is discussed in more detail, with complete formalisms and proofs in Coffman and Denning's advanced operating systems book [5].

Additional details concerning maximal parallelism in determinate systems can be found in Keller's paper [13].

General aspects of functional and applicative languages are discussed in many books and articles, for example, see [1, 10, 11].

REFERENCES

1.   J. Backus, "Can Programming Be Liberated from the von Neumann Style? A Functional Style and Its Algebra of Programs," *Communications of the ACM 21*, 8 (August 1978), 613-641.

2.   J. L. Baer, "A Survey of Some Theoretical Aspects of Multiprocessing," *ACM Computing Surveys 5*, 1 (March 1973), 31-79.

3.   A. L. Beguelin, "Deterministic Parallel Programming in Phred," University of Colorado, Department of Computer Science, Ph. D. dissertation, May 1990.

4.   A. J. Bernstein, "Program Analysis for Parallel Processing," *IEEE Transactions on Electronic Computers EC-15*, 5 (October 1966), 757-762.

5.   E. G. Coffman and P. J. Denning, *Operating Systems Theory*, Prentice Hall, Inc., Englewood Cliffs, NJ, 1973.

6. M. Conway, "A Multiprocessor System Design," *Proceedings of the AFIPS Fall Joint Computer Conference,*, 1963, 139-146.

7. J. B. Dennis and E. C. Van Horne, "Programming Semantics for Multiprogrammed Computations," *Communications of the ACM 9*, 3 (March 1966), 143-155.

8. E. W. Dijkstra, "Co-operating Sequential Processes," in *Programming Languages*, F. Genuys (ed.), Academic Press, New York, NY, 1968, 43-112.

9. J. J. Dongarra and D. C. Sorenson, "SCHEDULE: Tools for Developing and Analyzing Parallel Fortran Programs," in *The Characteristics of Parallel Algorithms*, L. H. Jamieson, D. B. Gannon, and R. J. Douglass (ed.), MIT Press, Cambridge, MA, 1987, 363-394.

10. H. Glaser, C. Hankin, and D. Till, *Principles of Functional Programming*, Prentice Hall, Inc., Englewood Cliffs, NJ, 1984.

11. P. Henderson, *Functional Programming*, Prentice Hall, Inc., Englewood Cliffs, NJ, 1980.

12. H. F. Jordan, "The Force," in *The Characteristics of Parallel Algorithms*, L. H. Jamieson, D. B. Gannon, and R. J. Douglass (ed.), MIT Press, Cambridge, MA, 1987, 395-436.

13. R. M. Keller, "On Maximally Parallel Program Schemata," *Proceedings of the 11th Symposium on Switching and Automata Theory*, October 1972, 33-50.

14. T. Murata, "Petri Nets: Properties, Analysis and Applications," *Proceedings of the IEEE 77*, 4 (April 1989), 541-580.

15. J. L. Peterson, *Petri Net Theory and the Modeling of Systems*, Prentice Hall, Inc., Englewood Cliffs, NJ, 1981.

16. H. Schwetman, *PPL Reference Manual (Version 1.1)*, MCC Technical Report, January 1987.

EXERCISES

(1) Modify the code below using *FORK*, *JOIN*, and *QUIT* so that the two procedures will be synchronized properly if they are executed as parallel loops (see Figure 3.6 for a Petri net of the desired computation).

```
proc_A() proc_B()
{                              {
    while (TRUE)                   while(TRUE)
    {                              {
        <compute A1>;                  read(x);
        write(x);                      <compute B1>;
        <compute A2>;                  write(y);
        read(y);                       <compute B2>;
    }                              }
}                              }
```

(2) Encode the precedence graph shown in Figure 3.14 using the *FORK, JOIN*, and *QUIT* primitives.

(3) How can "dummy" nodes be used to extend the binary FORK into an n-way FORK?

(4) Write a PARBEGIN-PAREND program schema for the precedence graph shown in Figure 3.15(b).

(5) Write an AND program schema for the precedence graph shown in Figure 3.15(b).

(6) Draw a precedence graph (one node per line of code) to illustrate the maximum parallelism for the following code segment:

```
a = b + c;
d = a * 10 - e;
a = d / e;
i = 1;
f = a + b;
g = e - d;
h = f * g;
```

(7)   Determine if the following system is determinate. Support your answer with a logical argument.

Computation = ($\{p_0, p_1, p_2, p_3, p_4, p_5\}$,
             $\{(p_0, p_1), (p_0, p_2), (p_0, p_5), (p_1, p_3), (p_2, p_3), (p_3, p_4), (p_5, p_4)\}$)
with memory $\{M_0, M_1, M_2\}$
Domain $p_0 = \emptyset$ Range of $p_0 = \{M_1\}$
Domain $p_1 = \emptyset$ Range of $p_1 = \{M_0\}$
Domain $p_2 = \{M_1\}$ Range of $p_2 = \{M_2\}$
Domain $p_3 = \{M_1\}$ Range of $p_3 = \emptyset$
Domain $p_4 = \{M_0\}$ Range of $p_4 = \{M_2\}$
Domain $p_5 = \{M_1\}$ Range of $p_5 = \{M_0\}$

(8)   Given the following process system, draw the equivalent maximally parallel process system.

Computation = *use the graph from the previous problem*
with memory $\{M_0, M_1, M_2, M_3\}$
Domain $p_0 = \emptyset$ Range of $p_0 = \{M_1\}$
Domain $p_1 = \emptyset$ Range of $p_1 = \{M_0\}$
Domain $p_2 = \{M_1\}$ Range of $p_2 = \{M_2\}$
Domain $p_3 = \{M_1\}$ Range of $p_3 = \{M_3\}$
Domain $p_4 = \{M_0\}$ Range of $p_4 = \{M_2\}$
Domain $p_5 = \{M_1\}$ Range of $p_5 = \emptyset$

(9)   Write a formal description of the algorithm to construct the maximally parallel graph from a determinate precedence graph.

(10)   Why is it easier to construct a maximally parallel graph from an existing determinate computation that to simply start with a graph with no precedence, as suggested in the overview discussion of maximally parallel graphs?

4

SYNCHRONIZATION USING SHARED MEMORY

In the previous chapter, the parts of a computation were coordinated by partitioning the computation into processes and then arranging for the operating system to manage processes as indivisible units of computation.

The alternative is to allow processes to be more complex so that one process can coordinate its operation with another process by synchronizing its state with a particular state in another process. For example, it is possible to cast the two procedures in Figure 3.1 as two processes such that the process that executes proc_B synchronizes with the process that executes proc_A prior to executing the **read(x)** statement [and, in turn, the process that executes proc_A cooperates by providing sufficient information to the other process to accomplish the synchronization following its execution of the **write(x)** statement].

In this chapter we examine mechanisms to accomplish coordinated operation through synchronization in multiprogrammed and shared memory architecture environments. In Chapter 12, we reconsider synchronization for message-passing environments, after we have considered additional detail about the mechanisms for sharing information in local memory environments.

4.1 BASIC SYNCHRONIZATION PRIMITIVES

4.1.1 Cooperating Sequential Processes

In the previous chapters we have used the example from Section 2.2 (two processes referencing a shared variable, I) to illustrate a number of points: The first example was the situation in which two processes wish to share a variable, I, such that one of the processes adds a value to I and another subtracts a value from I. Because of a race condition that exists between the two processes, we saw that the results were not determinate if the two processes attempted to perform their respective operations on I at the same time. In Chapter 3, it became apparent why the results were unpredictable, although the solution for preventing the condition required the used of precedence. It is also possible to solve the problem by finding a mechanism to *synchronize* the two processes so that they cannot simultaneously enter their respective critical sections.

This can be accomplished if each process would synchronize with the other in those cases where simultaneous execution could happen. If a process is about to enter its critical section, then it first determines if the other process is in its critical section. If it is, then the second process synchronizes its continued operation with the event corresponding to the first process exiting the critical section.

Processes that intend to cooperatively share information will need to synchronize the means in which they share that information. In some cases, a simple synchronization operation will suffice, while in others it is necessary to provide synchronizing primitives to enforce exclusive entry into a critical section.

If we intend to solve the critical section problem, then there are some constraints on acceptable solutions:
(1)   Only one process at a time should be allowed to enter its critical section (*mutual exclusion*).
(2)   Suppose that a critical section is free; if a set of processes indicates a need to enter into the critical section, then only those processes competing for the critical section participate in the selection of the process that will enter the critical section. A process cannot be postponed indefinitely.
(3)   After a process requests entry into its critical section, a bounded number of other processes may be allowed to enter their related critical sections before the original process enters its critical section.

4.1.2 Software Solutions

The critical section problem is construed as a software problem in our formulation of it; thus, it makes sense to solve it with ordinary software control constructs such as conditionals, loops, and the like.

The general critical section problem should be thought of in terms of many processes, each of which has a critical section. For purposes of discussion, one can begin to see the issues and solutions using only two processes. For the discussion, assume that there are two processes of the form shown in Figure 4.1.

For the solutions shown in this subsection, the following assumptions are used:
(1)   Writing and reading a memory cell that is common to the two processes is an indivisible operation. Any attempt at simultaneous read or write operations by the two processes will result in some unknown serial ordering of the two operations.
(2)   The processes are not assumed to have any priority, where one or the other would take precedence in the case of simultaneous attempts to enter the critical section.
(3)   The relative speeds of the processes are unknown, so one cannot rely on speed differentials (or equivalence) in arriving at a solution.
(4)   As indicated in Figure 4.1, the processes are assumed to be sequential and cyclic.

```
global declarations;

proc_0()                        proc_1()
{                               {
   while (TRUE)                     while (TRUE)
   {                               {
      compute;                        compute;
      critical_section;               critical_section;
   };                              };
};                              }:

initial processing;
proc_0() AND proc_1();
```

Figure 4.1 Process Schema

Figure 4.2 is a pure software solution to the critical section problem, credited to Dekker in Dijkstra's paper [7]. Let us consider an argument for the correctness of the solution, that is, it satisfies the assumptions mentioned above and solves the critical section problem:

Argument
First, suppose that **turn** is set to 1, and process 0 attempts to enter the critical section while process 1 is in its compute section. Then **flag**[0] = TRUE and **flag**[1] = FALSE; therefore, process 0 is allowed to enter its critical section since the **while** test fails immediately.

Suppose that **turn** is set to 1, and process 0 is in the critical section when process 1 attempts to enter the critical section. Then process 1 sets **flag**[1] to TRUE and executes the **while** test; it finds **flag**[0] is TRUE, so it checks **turn**. Since **turn** is equal to 1, process 1 ignores the remaining statements in the range of the **while** loop and proceeds directly to retest **flag**[0]. Eventually, process 0 will exit the critical section and set **turn** to 0 and **flag**[0] to FALSE. Process 1 will detect the changing value of **flag**[0] and proceed to the critical section without rechecking the value of **turn**.

Suppose that **turn** is set to 1 and processes 0 and 1 simultaneously attempt enter the critical section. Then each will set **flag**[i] to TRUE and each will evaluate the condition in the **while** statement to be TRUE. Process 0 will then fail the nested **if** test and will set its **flag** to FALSE; it will then wait for **turn** to be set to its own value. When this eventually happens (by virtue of process 1 exiting its critical section), process 0 will exit the loop and retry the entire process. Meanwhile, process 1 will behave as in the previous paragraph, waiting for **flag**[0] to go FALSE (in this case, that happens by the tie-breaking code rather than by process 0 finishing its critical section). ‖

```
int turn;
boolean flag[2];

proc(i)
int i;
{
        while (TRUE)
        {
                compute;
        try:    flag[i] ← TRUE;
                while (flag[i+1 mod 2])
                {
                        if (turn = i) continue;
                        flag[i] ← FALSE;
                        while (turn ≠ i);
                        goto try;
                };
                critical_section;
                turn ← turn+1 mod 2;
                flag[i] ← FALSE;
        };
};

turn ← 0;
flag[0] ← FALSE;
flag[1] ← FALSE;

proc(0) AND proc(1);
```

Figure 4.2 Dekker's Software Solution

There are a few other scenarios that must be considered in order to completely argue the correctness of this solution (see [7]).

Dekker's solution was published in 1968 and seemed to be the only one until Peterson published the solution shown in Figure 4.3 in 1981 [18]. To convince oneself that this solution is correct, it is necessary to argue that the three conditions described at the beginning of the chapter hold for the solution.

Argument

First, only one process at a time should be allowed to enter its critical section (*mutual exclusion*).

For both processes to be in their critical sections, then they would have had to simultaneously set their own **flag** to TRUE, that is, **flag[0]=flag[1]** = TRUE. Thus, the two processes are simultaneously attempting to enter their critical section. Also, process 0 (process 1) only enters its critical section after it has set the **turn** variable to 1 (0) and if **flag[1]** (**flag[0]**) is FALSE or **turn** is 0 (1 in the case of process 1). But only one of the processes could have last set the value of **turn**, so it is

```
int turn;
boolean flag[2];

proc(i)
int i;
{
      while (TRUE)
      {
            compute;
            flag[i] ← TRUE;
            turn ← i+1 mod 2;
            while ((flag[i+1 mod 2]) & (turn = i+1 mod 2));
            critical_section;
            flag[i] ← FALSE;
      };
};

turn ← 0;
flag[0] ← FALSE;
flag[1] ← FALSE;

proc(0) AND proc(1);
```

Figure 4.3 Peterson's Software Solution

either 0 or 1 at any instant. Suppose **turn** is 0; then process 1 will pass the **while** test and continue to evaluate the expression; process 0 will set **turn** to 1 (if it had not yet executed the statement, which means that process 1 will evaluate the expression FALSE on its next attempt), or it will evaluate the expression FALSE and will enter the critical section. Only one of the processes will be allowed to enter its critical section.

Second, once a process indicates a need to enter into its critical section, it cannot be postponed indefinitely.

A process can only be blocked from entering its critical section at the **while** loop. Thus, if process 0 is blocked, then it finds **flag[1]** TRUE and **turn** set to 1. Process 1 must be in its critical section, otherwise **flag[1]** would be FALSE. If process 1 is attempting to enter its critical section, then either **turn** is 0 or 1, thus one or the other is allowed to proceed. If it is 1, then process 1 will enter the critical section (or it is already in its critical section). In either case, process 1 will eventually exit its critical section and set **flag[1]** to FALSE. Process 0 will then fail the **while** test and enter the critical section. Notice that if process 1 exits the critical section and then attempts to reenter it it will block itself from competing with process 0 by setting **turn** to 0.

Third, after a process requests entry into its critical section, a bounded number of other processes may be allowed to enter before the original process

enters the critical section. This follows by the same argument used for condition
(2). ‖

4.1.3 Semaphores

The software solutions are most useful to illustrate the difficulty in arriving at correct
solutions using accepted software constructs in a multiprogramming environment.
Dijkstra's solution to the problem was to introduce semaphores.

> **Definition 4.1.** A *semaphore*, s, is a nonnegative integer variable that can only be
> changed or tested by one of two indivisible access routines:
>
> $$V(s): [s \leftarrow s + 1]$$
> $$P(s): [\text{while } (s = 0) \ wait; \ s \leftarrow s - 1]‖$$

The brackets around the definitions are intended to indicate that P and V are atomic
operations. However, the **wait** statement in the P definition requires additional explanation. Just as Dekker's solution required that the waiting process temporarily give up its
claim to the critical section, it was allowed to essentially queue itself on the critical section by performing the nested **while** test. The **wait** in the P definition is a similar operation; if a process is blocked on the zero value of the semaphore, then it must wait for
some other process to perform the V operation. Thus, we allow the indivisible operation
of P to be broken by other processes wishing to queue upon the semaphore and by the V
operation.

Given Dijkstra's semaphores, it is easy to write a solution to the two problems we
described at the beginning of this chapter. Figure 4.4 is a solution to the problem introduced in Section 2.2. The P and V operations are used to bracket the critical section,
with the semaphore identifying related critical sections of code in different procedures.
In a multiprogramming system, we could achieve a similar effect by replacing the "P(s)"
operations with a *disable()* and the "V(s)" with *enable()* in the figure.

Figure 4.5 is a solution to the problem introduced in Figure 3.1. Notice that we
cannot simply substitute enable/disable calls for P and V in this example, since more than
one semaphore is used to accomplish synchronization.

The P and V operations on semaphores have extremely general use; we consider
two more complex examples to illustrate their utility.

Example 4.1: The Bounded Buffer (Producer-Consumer) Problem

Suppose that a system incorporates two processes, one of which produces information (the
producer process) and another (the *consumer* process) that uses the information produced by
the first. The two processes can communicate the desired information by having the producer obtain an empty buffer from an empty buffer pool, fill it with information and then
place it in a pool of full buffers. The consumer should obtain information by picking up
buffers from the full buffer pool, copying the information out of the buffer, and then placing
it in the empty buffer pool for recycling. It is likely that we would not like to give the producer and consumer an unbounded number of buffers; instead, N buffers are allocated to the

```
semaphore s = 1;
proc_0()                          proc_1()
{                                 {
    ...                                   ...
    P(s);                             P(s)
    I ← I + J;                        I ← I - K;
    V(s);                             V(s);
    ...                                   ...
};                                };

proc_0() AND proc_1();
```

Figure 4.4 Using Semaphores to Protect Critical Sections

```
semaphore s1 = 0;
semaphore s2 = 0;
proc_A()                          proc_B()
{                                 {
    while(TRUE)                       while(TRUE)
    {                                 {
        <compute A1>;                     P(s1);
        write(x);                         read(x);
        V(s1);                            <compute B1>;
        <compute A2>;                     write(y);
        p(s2);                            V(s2);
        read(y);                          <compute B2>;
    };                                };
};                                };

proc_A() AND proc_B();
```

Figure 4.5 Using Semaphores to Synchronize Two Processes

pair for information exchange. Figure 4.6 illustrates program schemata for the producer and consumer processes.

Notice that the s semaphore has been included to protect the access to the two buffer pools. Realistically, the buffers are some contiguous block of memory that has been logically split into N parts. Each buffer must contain space for links to associate the buffer with other empty or full buffers and space for the data itself. Since the producer and consumer each manipulate links, it is necessary to treat buffer pool manipulation as a critical section.

Consider the ordering of the first two P operations in the producer and the consumer. Suppose that the P(full) and the P(s) instructions were reversed in the consumer (the same argument holds for the producer). Then, if all the buffers ever became empty at one time, the consumer would obtain the s semaphore and then block on the full semaphore (while

```
semaphore s = 1;
semaphore full = 0;
semaphore empty = N;
buf_type buffer[N];
```

```
producer()                          consumer()
{                                   {
    buf_type *next, *here;              buf_type *next, *here;

    while (TRUE)                        while (TRUE)
    {                                   {
        produce_item(next);
        P(empty);                           P(full);
        P(s);                               P(s);
        here ← obtain(empty);               here ← obtain(full);
        V(s);                               V(s);
        copy_buffer(next, here);            copy_buffer(here, next);
        P(s);                               P(s);
        release(here, full);                release(here, empty);
        V(s);                               V(s);
        V(full);                            V(empty);
                                            consume_item(next);
    };                                  };
};                                  };
```

```
proc_0() AND proc_1();
```

Figure 4.6 Bounded Buffer Problem

holding the s semaphore). This is a deadlock situation (why?). The order of appearance of the P operations is significant. Does the same argument hold for the V operations at the end of the loop?

Example 4.2: The Readers-Writers Problem

Courtois, Heymans, and Parnas posed another interesting synchronization problem in 1971 [6]. Suppose that a resource is to be shared among a community of processes of two distinct types, called *readers* and *writers*. A reader process can share the resource with any other reader process, but not with any writer process. A writer process requires exclusive access to the resource whenever it acquires any access to it.

Thus, this scenario is similar to one in which a file was to be shared among a set of processes. If a process only wants to read the file, then it may share the file with any other process that also only wishes to read the file. But if a writer wants to modify the file, then no other process should have access to the file when a writer has access to it (compare with Bernstein's conditions in Chapter 3).

Several different policies could be implemented for managing the shared resource. For example, it may be that whenever any reader has access to the resource then any writer that requests the resource must wait for it to become available. This policy is implemented by the algorithm shown in Figure 4.7.

```
resource_type *resource;
int read_count = 0;
semaphore s = 1;
semaphore write_block = 1;

reader()
{
    while (TRUE)
    {
        other_computing;
        P(s);
        read_count ← read_count+1;
        if (read_count = 1) P(write_block);
        V(s);
            access(resource);
            P(s);
        read_count ← read_count-1;
        if (read_count = 0) V(write_block);
        V(s);
    };
};

writer()
{
    while (TRUE)
    {
        other_computing;
        P(write_block);
            access(resource);
        V(write_block);
    };
};
```

```
/* There could be many readers and many writers */
    reader() AND writer();
```

Figure 4.7 First Policy for Coordinating Readers and Writers

In this policy, it is necessary for the first reader to access the shared resource to compete with any writers, but any succeeding readers may pass directly into the critical section provided that a reader is still in the critical section. Thus, the readers keep account of the number in the critical section with the **read_count** variable (updated and tested inside its own critical section). Only the first reader executes the P(**write_block**) operation, while every writer does so, since every writer must compete with the first reader. Similarly, the last reader to yield the critical section must perform the V operation for all readers that were accessing the shared resource.

While this solution implements the desired policy, it is easy to see that the policy may be faulty. Readers can dominate the resource so that no writer ever gets a chance to access it. In real systems, this is analogous to the case in which a pending update of a file must wait until all reads have completed. In most cases, one would like the updates to take place as soon as possible; this leads to an alternative policy in which a writer process requests access to the shared resource, and then any subsequent reader process must wait for the writer to gain access to the shared resource and then release it.

An algorithm to implement the second policy is shown in Figure 4.8. This implementation still allows a stream of readers to enter the critical section until a writer arrives; the writer should take priority over subsequent readers, but not those already accessing the shared resource. When the first writer arrives, it will block on the **read_block** semaphore; readers that arrive after the first writer blocks will block on **write_pending** instead of on **read_block**. (If the readers also blocked on **read_block**, then a reader may take priority over a blocked writer; thus, the solution would not implement the desired policy.)

4.1.4 Implementing Semaphores

In Chapter 2, we described how interrupts could be disabled during critical sections in order to eliminate race conditions. Such a solution is radical, since it disables all input/output activity for the entire machine while any process is in a critical section (the relationship between interrupts and input/output will be discussed in Chapter 7). Semaphores are much more useful for managing critical sections, since they only "disable" processes that are attempting to enter an individual critical section rather than debilitate input/output operations or other processes that are independent of the critical section.

Implementing semaphores can be significantly easier if the hardware makes a few special provisions than if it does not. While one may wish for hardware P and V instructions, this is reasonably difficult to implement directly because of the need to accommodate the *wait* command in the P operation. That is, uniprocessor implementation will generally want to interact with the operating system for the implementation of P, so part of the instruction will be implemented in hardware and part in software.

The *test-and-set* instruction can be shown to be sufficient for implementing semaphores.

Definition 4.2. *Test-and-set* or *TS* of a memory location causes the contents of the specified memory location to be loaded into a CPU register and the memory to be written with a value of TRUE. ‖

Assume that we have TS in the instruction repertoire of a machine. Then the critical section problem can be solved using TS as shown in Figure 4.9(a). [Figure 4.9(b) is the corresponding code using P and V, for comparison].

TS is not difficult to implement on a conventional von Neumann machine. While memory is built to act as though read operations were nondestructive, they generally are not. That is, when the contents of a memory are read into the MDR, then the memory location's state is obliterated; so a second phase is added to the memory design such that the contents of the MDR can be multiplexed to the data bus and then written back into the original memory location. TS is simply a memory fetch in which the MDR is set to TRUE before the write-back phase is performed.

It follows that the test-and-set instruction is also easy to implement on shared memory multiprocessors, since the memory on such a machine is conventional (it is the sharing among the processors that is unconventional). Local memory multiprocessors,

```
reader()
{
   while (TRUE)
   {
      other_computing;
      P(write_pending);
         P(read_block);
            P(s1);
               read_count ← read_count+1;
               if (read_count = 1) P(write_block);
            V(s1);
         V(read_block);
      V(write_pending);
      access(resource);
      P(s1);
         read_count ← read_count-1;
         if (read_count = 0) V(write_block);
      V(s1);
   };
};

writer()
{
   while (TRUE)
   {
      other_computing;
      P(s2);
         write_count ← write_count+1;
         if (write_count = 1) P(read_block);
      V(s2);
      P(write_block);
         access(resource);
      V(write_block);
      P(s2);
         write_count ← write_count-1;
         if (write_count = 0) V(read_block);
      (s2);
   };
};
```

Figure 4.8 (a) Reader and Writer for the Second Policy for Coordinating Readers and Writers

```
resource_type *resource;
int read_count = 0, write_count = 0;
semaphore s1 = 1, s2 = 1;
semaphore read_block = 1;
semaphore write_pending = 1;
semaphore write_block = 1;

reader()
{
    see Figure 4.8(a)
};
writer()
{
    see Figure 4.8(a)
};

/* There could be many readers and many writers */
reader() AND writer();
```

Figure 4.8 (b) Second Policy for Coordinating Readers and Writers

```
boolean s = FALSE;              semaphore s = 1;
...                             ...
while (TS(s));                  P(s);
critical_section;              critical_section;
s = FALSE;                      V(s);
...                             ...
        (a)                             (b)
```

Figure 4.9 Process Schema

including networks of computers, pose a considerably more difficult problem: How can one make a memory access appear as a single instruction when part of the operation involves network message passing? TS is usually replaced by some other P/V implementation in the network environment.

One shortcoming of TS is that it only replaces the P operation for *binary semaphores*, that is, ones that take on only the values of zero and one. Dijkstra's definition allowed a semaphore to take on any nonnegative value (or at least more than two values). Figure 4.10 illustrates how TS can be used to implement these *general semaphores*.

Notice that the **sem** boolean array is used for mutual exclusion while a process manipulates **value** (which corresponds to the implied value of the general semaphore). The **hold** boolean is used to stage a process that is blocked by the semaphore. So any process that is waiting for the semaphore will be waiting at the statement

while (TS(hold[s]));

```
#define N  number of semaphores
{
    int value[N];
    boolean sem[N];
    boolean hold[N];

    P(s)                              V(s)
    int s;                            int s;
    {                                 {
        while (TS(sem[s]));               while (TS(sem[s]));
        value[s] ← value[s]-1;            value[s] ← value[s]+1;
        if (value[s] < 0) then            if (value[s] ≤ 0) then
        {                                 {
            sem[s] ← FALSE;                   while (¬hold[s]);
            while (TS(hold[s]));              hold[s] ← FALSE;
        }                                 };
        else                              sem[s] ← FALSE;
            sem[s] ← FALSE;           };
    };

    for i = 0 to N
    {
        value[i] ← initial_value;
        sem[i] ← FALSE;
                                      hold[i] ← TRUE;
    };
    ...
}
```

Figure 4.10 Implementing the General Semaphore with TS

in the P procedure. When the process finds that **hold[s]** returns a value of FALSE (since the V operation will have set the value FALSE in those cases when it detected that there were processes queued on semaphore s), it will return to the original TS in the outer **while** loop. Also note that a process that executes the P operation will release the critical section related to manipulating the "value" entry before it begins waiting on the **hold[s]**.

One other statement in the solution requires careful consideration; in the V operation, the

while (¬hold[s]);

is required. This follows since a race condition can occur in which a process believes that it is blocked in the P procedure, yet the V procedure encounters **hold[s]** being TRUE. You should study the two procedures until you see the conditions under which this situation can arise.

Other Implications of the Implementation

The solution to the general semaphore problem using the test-and-set instruction has one unpleasant property in certain circumstances. Suppose that this implementation were used in a multiprogrammed system with a single processor. Then, whenever a process is scheduled to run and it blocks on a semaphore, it will repeatedly execute the

$$\textbf{while (TS(hold[s]));}$$

instruction until the timer interrupt invokes a scheduler to multiplex the process off and another process onto the processor. And when the blocked process obtains its next time slice, it will resume this *busy waiting* if **hold[s]** is still TRUE. The result is that the blocked process is effectively slowing down some other process that would eventually execute a V operation and allow the first to proceed.

The problem is that the blocked process needs to indicate to the operating system that it cannot do anything useful at the moment, that is, it needs to execute the equivalent of the **yield** instruction discussed in Chapter 2. Each time the process detects that it is blocked, it might simply **yield**. This would suggest that the busy waiting statement be changed to

$$\textbf{while (TS(hold[s])) yield(q);}$$

in order to eliminate wasting the unused portion of the time slice.

Suppose that the software is being supported by a shared memory multiprocessor. Now the shared memory will support TS (as discussed above), and the effect of letting the blocked process continue its busy wait is that *only* the processor on which the blocked process executes is idling; another process that can execute the V operation can be running on another process. Therefore, the busy wait is a mechanism for very fast recognition of the instant at which a process becomes unblocked. That is, in some cases it may be worth using one of N processors to *poll* the **hold[s]** variable in order to detect the earliest possible moment that the blocked process becomes unblocked.

Operating systems for shared memory multiprocessor systems typically support this scenario by including *spin locks* in the operating system call interface. A spin lock is merely a system call to a procedure that repeatedly performs the test-and-set instruction on a specified variable, the lock. To complete the abstract machine interface to the lock, there will be a call to create the lock, calls to lock and unlock it, a call to block on the spin lock, and often a nonblocking call on the spin lock. This latter call is used so that if a process detects that it is locked out of a critical section, it can do other operations.

Alternatively, we can think of semaphores as being consumable resources. Thus, a process blocks if it requests a semaphore value and none is available; that is, the process should become blocked. Thus, at any instant a process is either in the *running* state or a *blocked* state. A process moves from the running state to a blocked state by executing some request operation where the resource is unavailable. A process moves from blocked to running when it acquires the desired resource (semaphore).

This is consistent with the state diagram shown in Figure 2.8. A process moves from running to blocked whenever it requests an unavailable resource — a unit of memory, a semaphore, and so on. When some other process releases a resource, for example, performs a V operation, then the resource allocator can move the first process from blocked to ready. Being in the ready state does not mean that the process is physically executing on the CPU, but it is "runnable" if the CPU were available. Thus, any process that is runnable (ready) is enqueued in the ready list.

Let us consider one more subtlety of the implementation of semaphores. Notice that many of these solutions require that when one process executes a V operation, a process that is blocked on the corresponding semaphore should "notice" that change in some reasonably short time. Figure 4.11 illustrates a pair of processes that synchronize on a semaphore. Suppose process 0 obtained the semaphore and entered the critical section; process 1 subsequently blocked on the P(s) operation. If process 0 exits the critical section, executes V(s), executes the **small_compute_section**, and then executes its own P(s) prior to the time that process 1 was able to detect that the semaphore took on a positive value, then the process could be permanently prevented from entering its critical section even though the semaphore took on positive values.

This scenario is likely to happen on a multiprogrammed uniprocessor if the process that executes the V(s) does not give up the CPU immediately after incrementing the semaphore, that is, in implementing the V operation, it would be judicious to add a **yield** to the procedure definition immediately after incrementing the semaphore. This form of implementation is called the *active V operation* as opposed to the implementation that increments the semaphore with no opportunity for a context switch (the *passive V operation*).

```
semaphore s;

proc_0()                          proc_1()
{                                 {
   while (TRUE)                       while (TRUE)
   {                                  {
      P(s);                              P(s);
      critical_section;                  critical_section;
      V(s);                              V(s);
      small_compute_section;             compute_section;
   };                                 };
};                                }:

s ← 1;
proc_0() AND proc_1();
```

Figure 4.11 The Passive V Operation Problem

4.2 OTHER SYNCHRONIZATION MECHANISMS

Semaphores are useful for defining concepts, but are sometimes less useful for defining applications. The active versus passive V operation is one example of such a property. Another case is the arbitrary ordering of processes blocked on a semaphore; this was a problem that had to be handled quite specifically in the second readers-writers problem by adding a semaphore (**write-pending**).

A number of alternatives to semaphores have been described in the literature. In this section, we consider a few alternative approaches to attaining synchronization with semaphore alternatives.

4.2.1 AND Synchronization

In many parallel programs, processes must synchronize on some set of conditions rather than just on a single condition. The dining philosophers problem is a good example of such problems.

Example 4.3: The Dining Philosophers Problem

The dining philosophers problem represents a situation that can occur in large communities of processes. Dijkstra introduced the problem as an analogy in which five philosophers spend their lives alternately thinking and eating. Suppose that the five philosophers are seated around a table on which are placed five plates of pasta and five forks. While a philosopher thinks, he ignores the pasta and does not require a fork; when a philosopher decides to eat, then he must obtain two forks, one from the left of his plate and one from the right of his plate. To make the analogy fit the behavior of sequential processes, it is assumed that a philosopher can only pick up a single fork at one time. After consuming food, the

```
semaphore fork[5];

philosopher(i)
int i;
{
      While (TRUE)
      {
      /* Think */
      /* Eat */
            P(fork(i));
            P(fork(i+1));
            eat();
            V(fork(i+1));
            V(fork(i));
      };
}

fork[0] ← fork[1] ← fork[2] ← fork[3] ← fork [4] ← 1;
philosopher(0) AND
philosopher(1) AND
philosopher(2) AND
philosopher(3) AND
philosopher(4);
```

Figure 4.12 The Dining Philosophers with Semaphores

philosopher replaces the forks and resumes thinking. A philosopher to the left or right of a dining philosopher cannot eat while the philosopher is eating since forks are a shared resource.

Simple solutions to the problem are fraught with difficulties relating to deadlock or unsafe conditions. Figure 4.12 is a typical semaphore solution to the problem. Unfortunately, the solution is not safe, since if all philosophers decide to eat simultaneously, deadlock occurs.

The difficulty with this class of problems is that the P operation obtains the first semaphore and then blocks on another; this establishes a classic environment in which deadlock can occur (see Chapter 5).

The Petri net shown in Figure 4.13 illustrates the desired solution. The places labeled **fork$_i$** represent the case that the ith fork is available when a token resides on it. When a token is on the **think$_i$** (**eating$_i$**) place, the ith philosopher is thinking (eating). In this model of activity, the transitions marked with P_i are essentially P operations on two

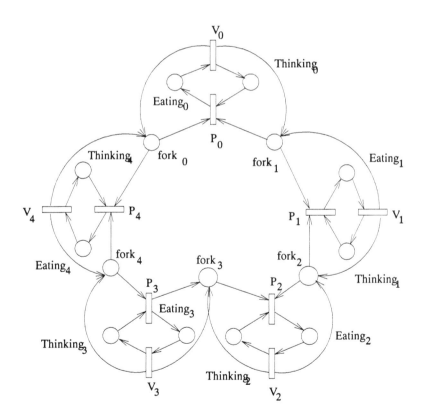

Figure 4.13 Petri Net of the Dining Philosophers

semaphores, modeled by the "fork" places. The marking shown in the figure represents the state in which all forks are available and all philosophers are thinking.

Suppose a P operation could be guaranteed to obtain all semaphores in a set or none of them (it would block the calling process in the case that not all semaphores could be obtained). This *simultaneous P* would have the form

$$P_{simultaneous}(S_1,...,S_{2n})$$

Figure 4.14 illustrates one possible implementation of $P_{simultaneous}$ for two semaphores.

```
/* Shared variables */
int S1, R1;
semaphore mutex;
semaphore block;

P(S,R)
{
        P(mutex);
        S1 ← S1 - 1;
        R1 ← R1 - 1;
        if((S1 < 0) or (R1 < 0))
        {
                V(mutex);
                P(block);
        }
        else  V(mutex);
}

V(S,R)
{
        P(mutex);
        S1 ← S1 + 1;
        R1 ← R1 + 1;
        if((S1 ≤ 0) OR (R1 ≤ 0)) V(block);
        V(mutex);
}

    ...

/* Initialize semaphores */
        mutex ← 1;
        block ← 0;
```

Figure 4.14 An Implementation of $P_{simultaneous}$ for n = 2

```
struct condition *create_event(details)
struct *details;
{
        struct condition *event_name;
```

        Set up queue[condition_name] for this event

```
        return(condition_name);
}

post(condition_name)
struct condition *condition_name;
{
        if  (queue[condition_name] has no waiting processes )
        {
```

                enqueue a signal on queue[condition_name]

```
        }
        else
        {
```

                dequeue a process, change its state to ready

```
        }
}

wait(condition_name)
struct condition *condition_name;
{
        if  (queue[condition_name] has no pending signals )
        {
```

                enqueue the process, change its state to blocked

```
        }
        else
        {
```

                dequeue a signal from queue[condition_name]

```
        }
}
```

Figure 4.15 Condition Variable System Calls

4.2.2 Events and Conditions

Synchronization can be viewed as the problem of placing precedence on the occurrence of the set of all "important" events that occur in the collective processes. For example, if event x in p_i cannot be allowed to occur until event y has occurred in p_j, then one could require that

$$(\text{occurrence of } y \text{ in } p_j) <^\cdot (\text{occurrence of } x \text{ in } p_i)$$

be a constraint on the operation of p_i and p_j. Notice that many processes, p_k, are unconcerned about the occurrence of x and y. Thus, proper operation of $\{P_i\}$ could then be defined by specifying a partial order on all events in all the processes (compare with the partial order used in Chapter 3 for coordination among processes rather than events) that reflects the important causal relations.

Signals are used to indicate that an *event occurrence* has taken place; *condition variables* can be used to record signals. An operating system will typically support many different condition variables, each associated with the occurrence of some type of event (much as it would support many different semaphores). Thus, the operating system would likely have **post** and **wait** system calls such as those shown in Figure 4.15.

A set of processes that intended to use signals for synchronization would create a condition as a shared variable; the pointer to the condition is disseminated among the processes that intend to synchronize on the signal. Now, whenever a process wishes to signal another process, it executes a **post**-operation on the specified condition; to determine that an event has occurred at some time in the past, a process executes a **wait**-operation.

Figure 4.16 is an example of the use of signals for solving the bounded buffer problem.

OS/360 used a form of conditions (called **events** in OS/360), signal (called **post** in OS/360), and **wait** for process synchronization.

Example 4.4: Synchronizing by Event Occurrences in UNIX

UNIX signals are used by one process to inform another that some event has occurred. Traditionally, signals are used by the UNIX kernel to synchronize with user processes. For example, when a child process terminates, then the **exit** system call by the child process results in a signal being sent by the kernel to the parent of the child. When the parent executes a **wait** system call, then it will proceed only if a child has terminated.

While signals are used in other places besides for synchronization between a parent and child process at the child's death, it is illustrative to see how UNIX employs events with variants of the FORK and JOIN primitives to allow the programmer to explicitly identify processes that should run in parallel. (In addition, UNIX uses other mechanisms for finer-grained synchronization.)

The **fork**() system call creates a copy of the program for the process that executes the call, including the PC and all currently defined data (for example, file descriptors). The call returns a pointer to a *process identifier* in memory. Both the old (*parent*) and the new (*child*) process execute the next instruction following the **fork**, since they have the same PC value. In the parent process's version of the program, the pointer returned by *fork* addresses the system process description of the child process; the pointer is null for the child process. That is the only mechanism by which the two processes can infer which is the child and which is the parent.

The **exec**(file_name) system call is often used in conjunction with **fork**. It causes the executing process to replace its current program with one stored in the given *file_name*. Notice, then, that a call to exec never results in a return (unless there is an error in the **exec** call).

```
{
/* Shared variables */
    struct condition *s;
    struct condition *full, *empty;
    buf_type buffer[N];

    producer()
    {
        while (TRUE)
        {
            produce_item(next);
            wait(empty);
            wait(s);
            here ← obtain(empty);
            signal(s);
            copy_buffer(next, here);
            wait(s);
            release(here, full);
            signal(s);
            signal(full);
        }
    };

    consumer()
    {
        while (TRUE)
        {
            wait(full);
            wait(s);
            here ← obtain(full);
            signal(s);
            copy_buffer(here, next);
            wait(s);
            release(here, empty);
            signal(s);
            consume_item(next);
        };
    };

    s ← create_condition(1);
    full ← create_condition(0);
    empty ← create_condition(N);
    proc_0() AND proc_1();
}
```

Figure 4.16 Bounded Buffer Problem with Condition Variables

```
    . . .
pid = fork();
if (pid == 0)
{ /* This is the child process */
        exec(child_program.out);
        printf("Error in the exec");
        exit(0);            /* terminate the child */
};
/* Parent code resumes here */
    . . .
wait(status);
    . . .
```

Figure 4.17 UNIX Process Creation

Now, suppose that a program has been compiled and linked into a module stored in a file named "child_program.out" and a parent process wishes to create a child to execute it. Then the parent would execute code similar to that shown in Figure 4.17.

At some point, the child process will terminate, making an **exit** call on the UNIX kernel. When this event occurs, then a signal is sent to the parent of the child. If the parent has executed the **wait** system call, it will be blocked at the call waiting for the signal; otherwise, the signal is queued until the parent executes the call. Once the **wait** call has succeeded, an effect similar to the JOIN statement will have taken place, that is, the child will have terminated and the single surviving parent process will not continue until it has synchronized with the death event.

The example from Figure 3.1 might be encoded in UNIX as shown in Figure 4.18. (This solution is not really suitable for a UNIX system, since it makes simplifying assumptions about the use of shared variables between processes.) To implement a solution equivalent to the previous solutions, it would be necessary to reduce the grain of the processes to be equivalent to the processes in the precedence graphs and then use **fork** and **wait** among the resulting processes.

Sequencers and Eventcounts [20]

Effective coordination of processes can be accomplished by maintaining a partial order among all event occurrences, that is, by maintaining a total order among the occurrence of *related* events. This can be accomplished using eventcounts:

Definition 4.3. An *eventcount* is an integer variable, initially with a value of 1, that takes on a strictly increasing set of nonnegative values. An eventcount can only be manipulated by:

advance. The **advance**(E) procedure is used to announce the occurrence of an event related to E, causing the eventcount E to be incremented by 1.

read. A process determines the value of the eventcount by **read**(E), which returns the current value of E.

await. The **await**(E, v) causes the calling process to block as long as $E \leq v$. ∥

```
proc_A()
{
        while (TRUE)
        {
                <compute A1>;
                write(x);
                flag1 = FALSE;   /* Mark x full */
                <compute A2>;
                while (flag2) { null };      /* Wait for y to be full */
                read(y);
                flag2 = TRUE;   /* Mark y empty */
        }
}

proc_B()
{
        while (TRUE)
        {
                while (flag1) { null };      /* Wait for x to be full */
                read(x);
                flag1 = TRUE;   /* Mark x empty */
                <compute B1>;
                write(y);
                flag2 = FALSE;  /* Mark y full */
                <compute B2>;
        }
}

main()
{
flag1 = flag2 = TRUE;  /* x and y are empty */
if ((pid = fork() == 0)
{ /* This is the child process */
        exec(prog_A.out);
        exit(0);      /* Should never get here, terminate */
};
if ((pid = fork() == 0)
{ /* This is the child process */
        exec(prog_B.out);
        exit(0);      /* Should never get here, terminate */
};
wait();
wait();
}
```

Figure 4.18 UNIX Processes

An eventcount is analogous to a global clock that ticks at the occurrence of each significant event by the explicit execution of an **advance** call; the **advance** call is the signaling mechanism. A process synchronizes with the global clock using the **await** call by blocking until the global clock reaches a predefined time, that is, there have been "v" **advance** calls. **Read** returns the count of the number of **advance** calls that has occurred in the case that the synchronization operation is more complex than the simple case.

These primitives will allow many synchronization problems to be solved. Their use in solving the producer-consumer problem (ignoring simultaneous buffer manipulation) provides a good illustration of how eventcounts can be used (see Figure 4.19).

The producer and consumer each maintain a private integer counter, **i**, used to select an eventcount value for synchronization. When the processes are initiated, the producer has N empty buffers and the consumer has no full buffers. The value i - N (in the producer) initially takes on the value -(N - 1), causing the **await** call in the producer to initially block until **out** (initially 1) is greater than -(N - 1) (a nonpositive number

```
eventcount in, out;
struct buffer[N];

producer()
{
        int i ← 1;

        while (TRUE)
        {
                await(out, i-N);
                produce(buffer[i-1 mod N]);
                advance(in);
                i ← i+1;
        }
}

consumer()
{
        int i ← 1;

        while (TRUE)
        {
                await(in, i);
                consume(buffer[i-1 mod N]);
                advance(out);
                i ← i+1;
        }
}
```

Figure 4.19 Using Eventcounts for the Producer-Consumer Problem

initially). Thus, for N ≥ 1 the producer passes through the **await** call, produces a buffer, and then **advance**s the **inf** eventcount. Meanwhile, the consumer will have encountered **await** with **in** initially set to 1 and **i** initially set to 1, that is, it will have blocked until **in** is **advance**d.

Just as the processes use **in** to establishes a total order on the events related to the manipulation of the full buffers, **out** establish a total order on the events related to the manipulation of the empty buffers. However, there is no specific ordering on the individual events within the two sets; the producer may periodically have many full buffers waiting for the consumer and at other times be blocking the consumer.

Eventcounts establish a partial order (on the events related by the reference to the common eventcount), but they cannot help with the synchronization of "unrelated" events. However, it is sometimes useful to be able to make a decision about orderings based on arbitrary conditions that might exist in the computation. A *sequencer* can be used to detect race conditions among events that are unrelated by eventcount references and establish a larger order between the two partial orders.

> **Definition 4.4.** A sequencer is an integer variable, with an initial value of 1, that takes on strictly increasing values. Only **ticket**(T) can be applied to a sequencer, T, resulting in T being incremented with the previous value being returned. A call to **ticket** is atomic. That is, T is used to place a total order on some set of partially ordered events. ‖

Sequencers are used to establish order among event occurrences within distinct eventcount orders. The sequencer is not intended to place a total order on all events, but just to establish order on some subset of otherwise unrelated events.

Eventcounts and sequencers are sufficient to implement semaphores (see Figure 4.20). The solution uses an eventcount to coordinate between P and V and a sequencer to coordinate among processes competing for the semaphore with P operations.

```
struct semaphore
{
    int initial_value;   /* Initial value of the semaphore */
    eventcount e;
    sequencer t;
} s;

P(s)                             V(s)
semaphore s;                     semaphore s;
{                                {
    int i;                           advance(s.e);
    i ← ticket(s.t);             }
    await(s.e, i-s.initial_value);
}
```

Figure 4.20 Implementing P and V

```
eventcount E;
sequencer T;

Pboth(R,S)
semaphore R, S;
{
        int g, r, s;

        g ← ticket(T);
        await(E, g);
                r ← ticket(R.t);
                s ← ticket(S.t);
        advance(E);
        await(R.e, r-R.initial_value);
        await(S.e, s-S.initial_value);
```

Figure 4.21 Implementing Simultaneous P

The **semaphore** structure contains fields to represent the initial value of the semaphore, an eventcount, and a sequencer. Assuming that the **initial_value** field has been set in a **semaphore**, the P operation first obtains a value from the sequencer, **s.t.** If several processes simultaneously attempt to execute the P operation, then **ticket** will establish a strict order on the processes. The strict order is used by the **await** call in a manner analogous to the way **out** was used by the producer in the previous figure; this will result in sequential occurrence of the P operation in the order established by **ticket**, since the V operation uses **advance** to signal waiting processes.

Sequencers and eventcounts can also be used to implement the simultaneous P operation discussed earlier in the chapter (see Figure 4.21). The eventcount, **E**, is used to enforce mutual exclusion on the manipulation of **r** and **s**. The two **await** calls accomplish the actual synchronization due to the values or the semaphores **R** and **S**.

4.3 CONCURRENT LANGUAGES

Some high-level languages attempt to address synchronization issues related to supporting multiple processes. These languages must provide for process instantiation and control, determinacy, synchronization, and interprocess communication (IPC). Not all languages address every issue, but several attempt to address some subset, particularly synchronization and IPC.

There are essentially two approaches, roughly characterized as shared memory languages and local memory languages. The shared memory languages concentrate on mechanisms for synchronization and information sharing by assuming that processes can access common memory directly, such as through the use of shared data structures and abstract data types. The local memory languages focus on IPC mechanisms whose implementations do not depend on the existence of shared memory. Concurrent Pascal,

Modula, and Mesa are examples of shared memory languages. Argus, CSP, Gypsy, PLITS, and SR are examples of languages that incorporate message passing into their semantics. Some of the issues of the message-passing languages have been described above; in the remainder of the section, we focus on shared memory aspects of information sharing.

4.3.1 Abstract Data-type Extensions

An *abstract data type* is a module that encapsulates storage, private procedures for manipulating the storage, and a public interface (including procedures and type declarations) that can be used to manipulate the information in the storage.

Abstract data types hide the implementation of the information manipulation. A process can use an abstract data type by understanding the interface definition and by calling the public procedures at the interface. The abstract data type will not allow one to write one's own procedures to manipulate information stored inside the abstract data type.

Abstract data types can be used to manipulate an arbitrary resource, instead of being limited to storage. In this case, users of the abstract data type utilize the resource via the interface without direct manipulation of it.

In a multiple-process environment, it is natural to share abstract data types, that is, two processes may each wish to call interface procedures to manipulate the abstract data type. Since the internal implementation of the abstract data type is unknown to its users, it is possible that any particular operation at the interface may cause inconsistent computations to occur within the abstract data type if two processes simultaneously invoke distinct public interface procedures.

For example, suppose that an abstract data type has been defined to manage a variable, I, and that there are interface routines to "credit" values to I and to "debit" values from I (see the example illustrated in Figure 2.8). That is, **credit(I, J)** will result in J being added to the current value of I, and **debit(I, K)** will result in K being subtracted from I. Then no two processes should execute **credit** and **debit** simultaneously, since that may result in the effect of one of the operations being lost.

4.3.2 Monitors

Monitors are a special form of abstract data type designed to eliminate the concurrent access problem. Monitors are generally credited to Hoare [12] and Brinch Hansen [3]. We generally follow Hoare's definition of monitors.

> **Definition 4.5.** A *monitor* is an abstract data type for which only one process may be executing procedures in the abstract data type at any given time. ‖

A monitor inherently incorporates a critical section into a standard abstract data-type template. Figure 4.22 illustrates how a monitor might be implemented as a standard abstract data type with the hidden **mutex** semaphore to ensure that only one process is in the monitor at a time.

Consider the management of a shared variable, **I**, as described in Figure 2.10, that is, some processes wish to increment the shared variable and others wish to decrement it. A monitor could be constructed as shown in Figure 4.23 to protect the access of the shared variable. The public interface includes procedures **increment** and **decrement** to

```
"module"
{
      semaphore mutex = 1;
      <ADT data structures>
      ...
      public proc_i(...)
      {
            P(mutex);
            <processing for proc_1>
            V(mutex);
      }
      ...
}
```

Figure 4.22 Critical Section within a Monitor

allow processes to manipulate I. Even though the assignment statements may generate a sequence of machine code as in the example in Chapter 2, a process is guaranteed to be able to complete the assignment statement as a critical section since the statements appear inside the **shared_I** monitor.

     In many cases, a process will be in a monitor and discover that it cannot proceed until some other process takes some particular action on the information protected by the monitor (compare with the *wait* action required in the P operation in Definition 4.1).

```
monitor shared_I
{
      int I;

      public increment(amount)
      int amount;
      {
            I ← I + amount;
      }

      public decrement(amount)
      int amount;
      {
            I ← I - amount;
      }
}
```

Figure 4.23 A Shared Variable Monitor

For example, suppose that one were to attempt to solve the second readers-writers problem using monitors as they have been defined. In Figure 4.24 we show a monitor public procedures, **start_read**, **start_write**, **finish_read**, and **finish_write** to be executed when a reader or a writer enters and leaves the critical section.

The solution fails for one reason: in the **start** procedures, a process will obtain exclusive access to the monitor and then not relinquish it again if the critical section is currently in use, since the process will perform a busy wait at the while loop in either procedure. As long as the process busy waits, it maintains exclusive control of the monitor, even to the exclusion of a process that attempts to perform a **finish** operation. It is necessary to allow the process to temporarily relinquish the monitor, while maintaining its intent to detect a state change in the monitor at a later time.

```
monitor reader_writer_1
{
        int number_of_readers = 0;
        int number_of_writers = 0;
        boolean busy = FALSE;

        public start_read
        {
                while (number_of_writers = 0);
                number_of_readers ← number_of_readers+1;
        }

        public finish_read
        {
                number_of_readers ← number_of_readers-1;
        }

        public start_write
        {
                number_of_writers ← number_of_readers+1;
                while (¬busy && (number_of_readers = 0));
                busy ← TRUE;
        }

        public finish_write
        {
                number_of_writers ← number_of_readers-1;
                busy ← FALSE;
        }
}
```

Figure 4.24 Attempted Solution for Readers-Writers Using a Monitor

To accommodate this situation, monitors may have special condition variables (embellished over the condition variables introduced earlier in the chapter).

Definition 4.6. A *condition variable* is a structure that may appear within a monitor, global to all procedures within the monitor, that can have its value manipulated by three operations:

wait: The invoking process is suspended until another process performs a **signal** on the condition variable.

signal: Resumes exactly one process if any is currently suspended due to a **wait** operation on the condition variable.

queue: Returns a value of TRUE if there is at least one process suspended on the condition variable, and FALSE otherwise. ‖

Condition variables are used to allow a process to temporarily relinquish its exclusive control of the monitor until some relevant condition changes. Suppose that we write *condition.op* to indicate that *op* be applied to the condition variable, *condition*. Now the readers-writers solution shown in Figure 4.24 can be modified to so that it performs correctly, as shown in Figure 4.25.

A reader process is expected to invoke **start_read** whenever it attempts to use the shared resource and **finish_read** when it has finished. Similarly, writers use **start_write** and **finish_write** to bracket their access of the shared resource.

The **start_read** monitor routine waits if either the critical section contains a writer (**busy** is TRUE) or there is a writer queued on the monitor. If the reader proceeds, then it increments the number of readers in the shared resource and signals other readers to proceed. When a reader finishes, it signals the writers if there are no other readers waiting.

When a writer attempts to enter the critical section, it waits if there are any readers or another writer in the critical section. When a writer finishes, it signals readers if any are waiting or else it signals a writer. (This is a solution to a slightly different problem than either of the Courtois-Heymans-Parnas reader-writer problems. A more complete discussion of the solution may be found in Hoare's monitor paper [12].)

Example 4.5: Monitor Solution to the Dining Philosophers Problem

Earlier in the chapter we introduced the dining philosophers problem and provided an attempted solution using semaphores; the solution shown in Figure 4.26 employs monitors.

All philosophers are initially thinking, represented by the **state[j]** being set to **thinking**. When philosopher i wishes to eat, he calls **pick_up_fork(i)**; this monitor procedure allows the process to proceed only if both adjacent forks are available; see the private procedure **test**. The philosopher moves to state **eating** only if his two neighbors are not **eating**, otherwise, he waits for a signal.

Suppose that the philosopher had been blocked. Then he needs to be signaled when either of his neighbors calls **put_fork_down**. However, the signal should not be issued until both neighbors have left the eating state; thus whenever any philosopher finishes eating, he **tests** the forks of both of his neighbors. If both of the neighbors were eating and the philosopher attempted to eat, then both will have to call **put_fork_down** before the philosopher can move from state **hungry** to state **eating**. This solution allows a situation in which the philosopher never obtains both forks at once, since either his left or right neighbor always has a fork.

Monitors can still be misused. Suppose that one encapsulated a monitor call (to a distinct monitor) within a monitor, that is, we have *nested monitor calls*. Then there is a danger that one process could hold the outer monitor while it waited for the inner monitor to become available, while another process holds an outer monitor that is the same as the inner monitor requested by the first process, while it requests an inner monitor that is the same as the outer monitor held by the first process. The result is a deadlock.

4.4 INTERPROCESS COMMUNICATION

Semaphores, events, and signals are intended to synchronize the operation of two processes, but not to convey other information between them.

Processes need to communicate with one another in order to share information. In early systems, processes were allowed to share one another's entire memory space; the results were often chaotic since synchronization needs to coordinate the access to the shared information in order for the processes to be determinate.

The simple alternative is to disallow sharing. But then two or more processes cannot cooperate on a single problem. Modern systems disallow all sharing of variables with specific exceptions, that is, the operating system must include some mechanism by which the processes can copy information from one process's space into another process's space.

In this section, we address message-based *interprocess communication* (IPC) mechanisms. In many cases, these mechanisms have been employed in multiprogrammed uniprocessors and shared memory multiprocessors, even though the solutions do not generally assume the existence of a shared memory.

4.4.1 Primitives

There are many different forms of the IPC primitives, defined to suit the requirements of a particular operating system and application environment. In this subsection, the issues that arise in defining the IPC primitives are described.

Messages can be used to synchronize processes and to transmit information among a set of processes. For our purposes, a message is a block of unspecified information formatted by a sending process in such a manner that it is meaningful to the receiving process.

Messages can be transmitted from one process to another by copying the body of the message from the memory of the sending process into the memory of the receiving process.

In some cases, the receiving process may not be ready to receive a message transmitted to it, but it would like to have the operating system enqueue the message for later reception. In these cases, the operating system will rely on the receiver having a *mailbox* in which messages can be stored prior to the receiving process executing specific code to process the message.

Thus, the logical path of information flow for passing a message from one process to another is illustrated in Figure 4.27. The message is copied from the sending process's

```
monitor reader_writer_2
{
        int number_of_readers = 0;
        boolean busy = FALSE;
        condition OK_to_read, OK_to_write;

        public start_read
        {
                if (busy | (OK_to_write.queue))
                        OK_to_read.wait;
                number_of_readers ← number_of_readers+1;
                OK_to_read.signal;
        }

        public finish_read
        {
                number_of_readers ← number_of_readers-1;
                if (number_of_readers = 0)
                        OK_to_write.signal;
        }

        public start_write
        {
                if ((number_of_readers ≠ 0) | busy)
                        OK_to_write.wait;
                busy ← TRUE;
        }

        public finish_write
        {
                busy ← FALSE;
                if (OK_to_read.queue)
                        OK_to_read.signal
                else
                        OK_to_write.signal;
        }
}
```

Figure 4.25 Monitor for Readers-Writers

```
#define N    5

status∈{eating, hungry, thinking};

monitor dining_philosophers
{
      status state[N];
      condition self[N];
      int j;

/* This procedure can only be called from within the monitor */
      private test(i)
      int i;
      {
            if ((state[i-1 mod N] ≠ eating) &&
                  (state[i] = hungry) &&
                  (state[i+1 mod N] ≠ eating))
            {
                  state[i] ← eating;
                  self[i].signal;
            }
      }


/* The following 2 procedures can be called externally*/
      public pick_up_fork(i)
      int i;
      {
            state[i] ← hungry;
            test(i);
            if (state[i] ≠ eating) self[i].wait;
      }

      public put_fork_down(i)
      int i;
      {
            state[i] ← thinking;
            test(i-1 mod N);
            test(i+1 mod N);
      }

      for j = 0 to N
            state[j] ← thinking;
}
```

Figure 4.26 Monitor for The Dining Philosophers

memory into the receiving process's mailbox, and then copied from the mailbox to the receiver's memory when the receiver calls for the message. In general, two copy operations will need to be performed.

The receiver's mailbox may be located in the operating system's memory or in the receiver's memory. If it is located in the operating system memory, then mailboxes are a system resource that must be allocated to processes as required. This will tend to limit the number of messages that an individual process may keep in its mailbox.

If the mailbox is located in the receiving user's memory, then the operating system will have to rely on the process allocating an appropriate amount of memory, protecting the mailbox from mishaps, and so on.

In shared memory multiprocessor architectures, the copy operations are straight forward. However, message copying in a local memory architecture will require network communication, since information must be transmitted from the memory of the sender's processor, to the receiver's processor, to the mailbox in the memory of the receiver's machine.

The scenario in Figure 4.27 suggests the need for two more system calls to transmit and receive messages. The *send* call will accomplish the placement of the message into the mailbox of the receiver. The *receive* call will move the message from the mailbox into the memory of the calling process.

The send call may be *synchronous* or *asynchronous*. The synchronous send blocks the transmitting process until the message has been successfully received by the destination process. Notice that if a message is enqueued in a mailbox the process that transmits the message using the synchronous send technique will be blocked until the receiving process retrieves the message from the mailbox. That is, the sender is assured that the message is received before it continues. The synchronous send acts as if the transmission were immediately followed by a P operation; the corresponding V operation occurs when the receiver accepts the message.

A degenerate case of the synchronous send occurs if the mailbox is null, that is, the synchronous send does not succeed until the receiving process executes a receive command. In this case, the message need not be copied from the sender's memory until the receiver performs a receive operation, and then it can be placed directly in the target memory location of the receiver. Only a single copy is required.

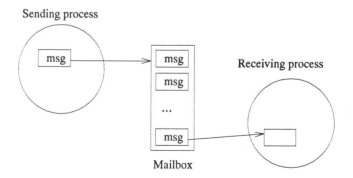

Figure 4.27 Message Path for Interprocess Communication

The asynchronous send ignores synchronization, but is unreliable. The sending process passes the message to the operating system via a system call and then proceeds. A successful send operation does not imply that any process will ever receive the message.

In either the synchronous or asynchronous send, the destination process may be nonexistent, that is, it has not yet been created or it has already been destroyed. Generally, either form of send operation will return an error to the caller in this case (although it is conceivable that asynchronous send may succeed, with the hope that the process may soon exist).

A send operation will fail if there is inadequate mailbox space at the receiving process (of course, the operation will always fail if the receiver has no mailbox and is not currently requesting a message). In this case, most forms of the synchronous send return an error code to the transmitter indicating that the operating system was unable to deliver the message. Asynchronous send operations may simply fail without notification to the sending process.

A receive operation can be *blocking* or *nonblocking*. A blocking receive will cause the receiving process to halt until a message is available in the mailbox — or has been transmitted from some sender. Thus, the blocking receive synchronizes its operation with that of some sending process. If there is a mailbox, the synchronization only ensures that the receiving process has reached a given point in the computation after the sending process has reached some corresponding point in its computation. That is, a blocking receive corresponds to a P operation by the receiver, while a send operation corresponds to a V operation.

If there is no mailbox, then the blocking receive must be used in conjunction with synchronous send operation if messages are not to be lost (why?). The blocking receive and synchronous send guarantee that the two processes are synchronized at the time IPC takes place.

The nonblocking receive call will return to the calling process immediately, either with a message or with an indicator that no message is available.

Example 4.6: UNIX Pipes

UNIX provides an IPC mechanism that employs asynchronous send, blocking receive, and communication links [5]. (UNIX also supports nonblocking receive operations, although the "normal" mode for using pipes is with the blocking receive.)

The mailbox and the link are combined into a first-in-first-out queue of bytes called a *pipe*, that is, a message is a stream of bytes of arbitrary length.

If two UNIX processes intend to communicate with one another, then they must have some common ancestor establish a pipe prior to their creation. When each process is born (through the **fork** command discussed Example 4.4), it uses the same program as the parent, but it inherits its own copy of the data space; that copy contains a pipe descriptor (the "names" of the read end and the write end of the pipe). If two children have been **fork**ed, then they will each have both ends of the pipe. One end is a read end, and the other end is a write end, that is, if the two processes wish to exchange information then it will be necessary to have two pipes between them — one in each direction.

A process can send information to another process through the UNIX **write** system call. This call accepts parameters that identify the write end of a pipe, a buffer address, and the number of bytes to be written into the pipe. This is an asynchronous send, since the writer simply places the information in the pipe and continues. If the pipe is "full" when the write operation is attempted, it will block or fail and return an error.

The UNIX **read** operation checks the read end of the pipe to see if there are any bytes in it; if the read calls for N bytes, and there are only K bytes in the pipe, then the calling process is blocked until there are N bytes or until another process writes an end-of-file mark to the pipe. Thus the read is a blocking receive operation.

BSD UNIX employs sockets to implement pipes that span address spaces. The interface is the socket interface described in Chapter 10, but the logical model is quite similar to the UNIX pipe.

Figure 4.28 revisits the example in Figure 3.1 (also see Figure 3.2).

4.4.2 Communication Links

Experience with IPC mechanisms uncovered a practical problem: When a process receives a message, how does it know who the message is from (how can it prevent unwanted messages from "clogging" the transmission of other messages)? How can the receiver classify various types of messages?

CSP is a hypothetical language for writing cooperating sequential programs [11], that addresses both of these problems. In CSP, the send operation is written as

$$p_1 \,!\, m_1$$

to mean that the transmitting process should send a message, m_1, of a specific *type*, to some process p_1. That is, the send operation is a synchronous operation that transmits a typed message to a specified receiver.

If the corresponding receiver executes

$$p_2 \,?\, m_2$$

then this will result in a blocking receive for a message of a specified type (the type of the variable, m_2) from the specified sender process, p_2. The effect is as if there were a *typed communication link* between the two processes, that is, any message that is received over the link will have a specified type and will come from a specified sender. The IPC mechanism is used to transmit previously agreed on information between previously agreed on parties; the mechanism provides synchronization.

CSP's strong semantics are used on the IPC mechanism to force it to achieve type-checked transmission of information; if p_2 executes the send statement at the same time that p_1 executes the receive statement, then the effect will be as if

$$m_2 \leftarrow m_1;$$

had been executed across the two processes.

The CSP mechanism suggests the existence of typed communication links between the processes and that the links are unidirectional. If two processes wish to communicate both ways, then two unidirectional links are required.

CSP communication has led to implementations of practical communication links, for example, in the DEMOS operating system [2]. A *link* is a unidirectional communication path between two specific processes, which supports information of a particular

```
int A_to_B[2];   /* Read by proc_A, written by proc_B */
int B_to_A[2];   /* Read by proc_B, written by proc_A */

main()
{
      pipe(A_to_B);
      pipe(B_to_A);
      if ((pid = fork() == 0)
      { /* This is the first child process */
            exec(prog_A.out);
            exit(0);   /* Error - terminate the child */
      };
      if ((pid = fork() == 0)
      { /* This is the second child process */
            exec(prog_B.out);
            exit(0);   /* Error - terminate the child */
      };
      wait();
      wait();
}

proc_A()
{
        while (TRUE)
        {
                <compute A1>;
                write(A_to_B[1], x, sizeof(int));
                <compute A2>;
                read(B_to_A[0], y, sizeof(int));
        }
}

proc_B()
{
        while (TRUE)
        {
                read(A_to_B[0], x, sizeof(int));
                <compute B1>;
                write(B_to_A[1], y, sizeof(int));
                <compute B2>;
        }
}
```

Figure 4.28 UNIX Processes

format. A link is created by a process that wishes to receive messages from another task; the link is passed to the sending task by the receiver.

There are two problems with this scenario: naming across the process name spaces, and providing initial links to allow processes to generate other links. The naming problem can be handled by the process manager in the operating system (or by a more general naming facility described in Chapter 10); a global authority must exist that can span all processes' name spaces. References among the name spaces must be mapped by the global authority.

The DEMOS solution to managing the external name, once it has been assigned by the global authority, is to have each process maintain a link table that is easily accessible to the kernel as well as to the process. A link ID is used to index the link table; when the process obtains a link to another process, it enters the information into the link table, essentially as capability information. Upon message transmission, the sender passes the link ID to the kernel along with the message. The kernel reads the link information from the link table and delivers the message to the appropriate link.

A process must be created with a basic set of links to the fundamental services in its environment, for example, to the link server and file system. The process requests service by creating a link to itself and then passing the link over one of its base links to the service. The service then uses the passed link to send messages to the original process. (In the case of DEMOS links, the communication mechanism can be expanded to allow the client and service to exchange bulk data as a result of a specific protocol established by the link mechanism.)

4.5 FURTHER READING

Most of the fundamental work described in the chapter stems from early work done by Dijkstra, reported in his classic paper on cooperating sequential processes [7]. Peterson and Silberschatz also provide an excellent discussion of process synchronization in either of their books [19, 22].

As mentioned in the body of the chapter, the paper by Courtois, Heymans, and Parnas introduces the readers-writers problem and the two solutions presented early in the chapter [6]. Another interesting example in resource synchronization (the cigarette smokers' problem) was posed and solved by Patil in [17]. The book by Holt, and others describes a number of classes of problems with solutions to each [13]. Lamport and his coworkers have also reported a number of interesting results on synchronization, particularly in distributed systems; for example, see [14, 15].

Additional information about spin locks and the test-and-set instruction in contemporary shared memory multiprocessors may be found in the paper by Dubois, Schuerich, and Briggs [8].

There have also been several interesting alternative mechanisms for accomplishing synchronization, including Reed and Kanodia's sequencers and eventcounts [20]; Campbell and Kolstad's path expressions [4], and Hewitt's serializers [10].

Monitors are described in detail in papers by Hoare [12] and Brinch Hansen [3]. Lampson and Redell discuss some practical problems with implementing software using monitor in the Pilot-Mesa environment [16]. A more recent high-level primitive is Raddle's n-party transaction [9].

Finally, Andrews and Schneider provide an excellent survey of concurrent programming languages in [1], updated by Schlichting and others [21].

REFERENCES

1.   G. R. Andrews and F. B. Schneider, "Concepts and Notations for Concurrent Programming," *ACM Computing Surveys 15*, 1 (March 1983), 3-43.
2.   F. Baskett, J. H. Howard, and J. T. Montague,Task Communication in DEMOS, November 1977.
3.   P. Brinch Hansen, *The Architecture of Concurrent Programs*, Prentice Hall, Inc., Englewood Cliffs, NJ, 1977.
4.   R. H. Campbell and R. B. Kolstad, "An Overview of Path Pascal's Design," *ACM SIGPLAN Notices Notices 15*, 9 (September 1980), 13-24.
5.   *Unix User's Manual Reference Guide, 4.3 BSD*, Computer Systems Research Group, Computer Science Division, Department of Electrical Engineering and Computer Science, University of California, Berkeley, April 1986.
6.   P. J. Courtois, F. Heymans, and D. L. Parnas, "Concurrent Control with 'Readers' and 'Writers'," *Communications of the ACM 14*, 10 (October 1971), 667-668.
7.   E. W. Dijkstra, "Co-operating Sequential Processes," in *Programming Languages*, F. Genuys (ed.), Academic Press, New York, NY, 1968, 43-112.
8.   M. Dubois, C. Schuerich, and F. Briggs, "Synchronization, Coherence, and Event Ordering in Multiprocessors," *IEEE Computer 21* , 2 (February 1988), 9-21.
9.   I. R. Forman, "On the Design of Large Distributed Systems," MCC Technical Report No. STP-098-86, Rev. 1.0, January 1987.
10.   C. E. Hewitt and R. R. Atkinson, "Specification and Proof Techniques for Serializers," *IEEE Transactions on Software Engineering SE-5*, 1 (1979), 10-23.
11.   C. A. R. Hoare, "Cooperating Sequential Processes," *Communications of the ACM 21*, 8 (August 1978), 666-677.
12.   C. A. R. Hoare, "Monitors: An Operating System Structuring Concept," *Communications of the ACM 17*, 10 (October 1974), 549-557.
13.   R. C. Holt, G. S. Graham, E. D. Lazowska, and M. A. Scott, *Structured Concurrent Programming with Operating Systems Applications*, Addison-Wesley Publishing Co., Reading, MA, 1978.
14.   L. Lamport, "Proving the Correctness of Multiprocess Programs," *IEEE Transactions on Software Engineering SE-3* , 2 (March 1977), 125-133.
15.   L. Lamport, "Time, Clocks and the Ordering of Events in a Distributed System ," *Communications of the ACM 21* , 7 (July 1978), 558-565.
16.   B. W. Lampson and D. D. Redell, "Experience with Processes and Monitors in Mesa," *Communications of the ACM 19*, 5 (February 1980), 105-117.
17.   S. S. Patil, "Limitations and Capabilities of Dijkstra's Semaphore Primitives for Coordination among Processes," MIT Project MAC Computation Structures Group Memorandum No. 57, MIT, February 1971.
18.   G. L. Peterson, "Myths About the Mutual Exclusion Problem," *Information Processing Letters 12*, 3 (June 1981), 115-116.
19.   J. L. Peterson and A. Silberschatz, *Operating Systems Concepts, Second Edition*, Addison-Wesley Publishing Co., Reading, MA, 1985.
20.   D. P. Reed and R. K. Kanodia, "Synchronization with Eventcounts and Sequencers," *Communications of the ACM 22*, 2 (February 1979), 115-123.
21.   R. D. Schlichting, G. R. Andrews, N. R. Hutchinson, R. A. Olsson, and L. L. Peterson, "Observations on Building Distributed Languages and Systems," Department of Computer Science, University of Arizona, Tech. Rep. 87-25, Tucson, AZ, October 1987.

22.   A. Silberschatz and J. L. Peterson, *Operating System Concepts, Alternate Edition*, Addison-Wesley Publishing Co., Reading, MA, 1988.

EXERCISES

(1)   Criticize the following software solution intended to solve the critical section problem

```
{
        int turn;
        proc(i)
        int i;
        {
                while (TRUE)
                {
                        compute;
                        while (turn ≠ i);
                        critical_section;
                        turn ← i+1 mod 2;
                };
        };
        turn ← 1;
        proc(0) AND proc(1);
}
```

(2)   Criticize the following software solution intended to solve the critical section problem

```
{
        boolean flag[2];
        proc(i)
        int i;
        {
                while (TRUE)
                {
                        compute;
                        while (flag[i+1 mod 2]);
                        flag[i] ← TRUE;
                        critical_section;
                        flag[i] ← FALSE;
                };
        };
        flag[0] ← FALSE;
        flag[1] ← FALSE;
        proc(0) AND proc(1);
}
```

(3)   Criticize the following software solution intended to solve the critical section problem:

```
{
                boolean flag[2];
                proc(i)
                int i;
                {
                        while (TRUE)
                        {
                                compute;
                                flag[i] ← TRUE;
                                while (flag[i+1 mod 2]);
                                critical_section;
                                flag[i] ← FALSE;
                        };
                };
                flag[0] ← FALSE;
                flag[1] ← FALSE;
                proc(0) AND proc(1);
}
```

(4)   Assume that the **write_pending** semaphore was omitted from Figure 4.8. Describe a simple sequence of reader and writer activity that would cause the solution to fail (for the policy specified in the example).

(5)   Provide a scenario in which a process that executes the V procedure in Figure 4.10 will detect **value[s]** being less than or equal to zero and then **hold[s]** being TRUE.

(6)   The discussion of implementation identified the wasted CPU cycles that are spent when busy waiting is used for locks. However, commercial shared memory multiprocessors all include spin locks for synchronization. Provide some possible rationale that the manufacturers might use to justify their choice for implementing locks.

(7)   Spin locks in shared memory multiprocessors can introduce a subtle problem with cache coherence. Suppose that five processes on five different processors are "spinning" on a single lock while a sixth process on a sixth processor holds it. Explain what will happen to the cache contents when the sixth process releases the lock.

(8)   Suppose that a machine's instruction set included an instruction named **swap** that operates as follows (as an indivisible instruction):

```
                swap(a, b)
                boolean a, b;
                {
                        boolean t;
                        t ← a;
                        a ← b;
                        b ← t;
                }
```

Show how **swap** can be used to implement the P and V operations.

(9)   Figure 4.14 provides a solution for implementing the P and V operations for the simultaneous use of two semaphores. Notice that the V operation executes **V(block)** if *either* S1 or R1 is less than or equal to zero. Explain why the test is an *OR* rather than an *AND* of the two conditions.

(10) The following solution has been posed for the dining philosophers problem, but has been shown to be faulty. Criticize the solution.

```
{
        semaphore fork[n] = (1, ...,1);
        while (TRUE)
        {
                P(fork[i]);
                P(fork[i+1 mod 5]);
                eat;
                V(fork[i]);
                V(fork[i+1 mod 5]);
                think;
        };
}
```

(11) The following solution has been posed for the dining philosophers problem, but has been shown to be faulty. Criticize the solution.

```
{
        semaphore fork[n] = (1, ...,1);
        while (TRUE)
        {
                P(s);
                P(fork[i]);
                P(fork[i+1 mod 5]);
                V(s);
                eat;
                V(fork[i]);
                V(fork[i+1 mod 5]);
                think;
        };
}
```

(12) *The Sleepy Barber Problem.* A barbershop is designed so that there is a private room containing the barber chair and an adjoining waiting room with a sliding door that contains N chairs. If the barber is busy, then the door to the private room is closed and arriving customers sit in one of the available chairs (If a customer enters the barbershop and all chairs are occupied, then the customer leaves the shop without a haircut.) If there are no customers to be served, the barber goes to sleep in the barber chair with the door to the waiting room open. If the barber is asleep, the customer wakes the barber and obtains a haircut. Write a monitor to coordinate the barber and the customers.

(13) Write a solution to the sleepy barber problem using sequencers and eventcounts to coordinate the barber and the customers.

(14) Suppose that a two-way (two-lane) north-south road contains a one-lane tunnel. A southbound (or northbound) car can only use the tunnel if, when the car arrives at the entrance to the tunnel, there are no oncoming cars in the tunnel. Because of accidents, a signaling system has been installed at the entrances to the tunnel; when a car approaches and when it exits the tunnel, traffic sensors notify the tunnel controller computer. The traffic controller sets signal lights — green means proceed and red means stop. Write a program skeleton to achieve synchronization using monitors.

(15) Construct a C program for a UNIX environment to use the trapezoidal rule (described in Exercise 2.12) to approximate the integral of

$$f(x) = 1/(x+1)$$

for the interval [0,2]. Construct your solution so that you compute the areas of n small trapezoids by N individual slave processes.

The master process should spawn N slave processes using the *fork* and *exec* UNIX system calls. There should be one pipe with which all N slave processes send results to the master, and N pipes that the master uses to assign a trapezoid to a slave process. Thus, whenever a slave process is ready to compute the area for another trapezoid, it sends the master a result on the shared "input" pipe. When the master process receives all the sums from the slave processes, it should sum them and print the answer, along with the amount of time required to obtain the solution (ignoring the time to set up the processes and the pipes).

Experiment with various values of N between 1 and 8 for n = 64 trapezoids. Plot the respective times versus N.

The code shown below can be used to read the time-of-day clock (accurate in the microsecond range).

```
/* This is a timer routine */

#include     <sys/time.h>

float getTime()
{
     struct timeval now;

     if(gettimeofday(&now, 0)) printf("Time call error");
     return((float) (now.tv_sec % 1000) + ((float) now.tv_usec)/1000000.0);
}
```

Use **getTime()** to instrument your program so that you can measure the amount of time spent processing your code. (Include a suitably large *for* loop in your procedure to evaluate the area of a trapezoid so that you can measure the time to accomplish the computation.) Plot the amount of time versus the number of trapezoids used in the approximation.

5

DEADLOCK

5.1 INTRODUCTION

Deadlock occurs in many guises in the real world, from processing documents in an office to automobile traffic patterns in large cities. In some cases, deadlock may be purposely defined into a system so that a human operator of the system can intervene to resolve a conflict that is too difficult for the system to solve; this is common in office procedures.

In other cases, the deadlock is inadvertent and catastrophic. There is a time-worn story of an early operating system that included a program that could be run to free memory space whenever necessary. Unfortunately, the program required memory space in order to be executed, and it was only needed when there was no memory available.

In Chapter 2, deadlock was introduced as a side effect of allowing interrupts and shared information. Because two processes wished to update a pair of shared variables in a consistent manner, they used the idea of a lock flag to ensure that when one variable's value was changed, the other would also be updated. We also saw several instances of deadlock when studying synchronization.

The example recurs frequently in communities of processes that share resources. Suppose that a process is allowed to request exclusive use of an arbitrary resource from some authority, for example, the operating system. As long as the process has exclusive control of the resource, no other process is allowed to use it. In the previous example, the authority was the interrupt hardware, and the resource was exclusive access to a shared variable.

A resource, then, can be very general; in fact, it is convenient to characterize *anything that a process needs to proceed* as being a resource. Memory is a resource, a tape drive is a resource, and access to a shared variable is a resource.

Suppose that we make the following assumptions about the way that a process uses resources:

(1)   The process has exclusive use of the resource once the resource has been allocated to the process (this is called *mutual exclusion*).
(2)   A process may hold one resource while it requests another one.
(3)   A situation can arise in which process p_1 requests resource R_1 and then it requests resource R_2, while process p_2 and requests resource R_2 then resource R_1 (*circular waits* are possible).
(4)   Resources can only be released by the explicit action of the process, that is, resources cannot be *preempted*. This includes the case in which a process places a request for a resource, and the resource is not available, then the process cannot withdraw its request.

These assumptions are not unusual and occur in almost all communities of processes that share resources.

Consider a pair of processes on a multiprogrammed system, where the two processes share a pair of resources. We can plot the progress of processes p_1 and p_2 on a Cartesian coordinate system in which the X axis represents the progress made by process p_1, and the Y axis represents the progress made by process p_2. Assume that process p_i requires n_i time units to complete. Now, any "step function" from the origin to (n_1, n_2) represents the progress made by the individual processes. That is, the plot is horizontal when it represents the fact that p_1 is using the CPU, and the plot is vertical when it represents the fact that p_2 is using the CPU.

Suppose that p_1 uses R_1 from time $t_{1,1}$ to time $t_{1,3}$ and R_2 from time $t_{1,2}$ to $t_{1,4}$. Similarly, p_2 uses R_2 from time $t_{2,1}$ to time $t_{2,3}$ and R_1 from time $t_{2,2}$ to $t_{2,4}$. By the assumptions above, the plot is always up and to the right (no preemption). Also, when one process has been allocated the resource, the other process is not allowed to proceed through the portion of its computation when it too requires the resource; the second process must wait for the first to release the resource (mutual exclusion). The processes use the resources in opposite order (circular wait). And a process may hold one resource while requesting another.

Figure 5.1 is a Cartesian coordinate space for representing the progress of the two processes. There are certain regions in the plane that do not represent feasible operation, for example, after p_1 has reached $t_{1,1}$ (assuming that p_2 has not reached $t_{2,2}$), p_1 has control of R_1, so p_2 cannot proceed past $t_{2,2}$ until p_1 has reached $t_{1,3}$. These *infeasible regions* are crosshatched in the figure; there is one region for R_1 and another for R_2. Portions of the plane can never be reached since the step function would have to go down or to the left to get there after avoiding the infeasible portion of the plot.

Consider the situation in which the plot enters the portion of the plane above and to the right of $(t_{1,1}, t_{2,1})$. Since preemption is disallowed, the plot cannot go down or to the left; therefore, the plot will end up at $(t_{1,2}, t_{2,2})$. And from that point, neither process can ever proceed; the two processes are deadlocked.

5.2 DEADLOCK STRATEGIES

How can operating systems (or communities of processes) be constructed to ensure that deadlock is handled properly? There are three basic approaches: prevention, avoidance, and detection and recovery.

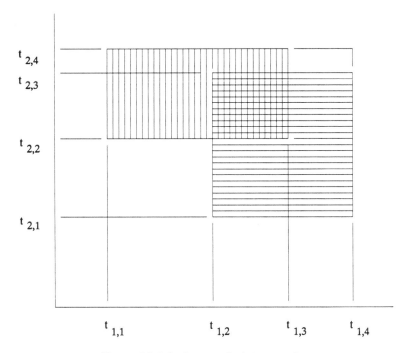

Figure 5.1 Joint Progress Path for p_1 and p_2

5.2.1 Prevention

Deadlock is only possible if all four conditions exist in the community of processes, that is, these conditions are *necessary* for deadlock to exist, but not *sufficient*. Deadlock *prevention* strategies ensure that at least one of the conditions is false at all times.

One way of preventing deadlock is to violate the preemption requirement. Suppose the operating system allowed processes to "back out of" a request for a resource if it is not available. For example, the system could be implemented such that, whenever a process requests a resource, the system responds immediately by allocating the resource or indicating that there are not sufficient resources to satisfy the request. In cases where resources are unavailable, this will force the requesting process to poll the resource manager until they become available; it also implicitly assumes that the process has other useful work to do that does not require the specified resource. And, of course, there is likely to be competition for these resources; without priorities on the requests (how can the operating system tell who has been waiting the longest?) some processes may "starve" while waiting for resources to become available. This approach removes the condition that resources cannot be preempted.

It is also possible to attack the circular wait condition. Suppose that a process could only request resources at initiation time. Then it would never be in a position of holding some resources while requesting others, and deadlock could be prevented in the system.

It would also be possible to prevent circular waits from occurring if processes always requested resources in exactly the same order. For example, suppose that the system had resources R_1, R_2, ..., R_m; then, if each process only requested R_j after it had obtained R_i, for $i < j$, circular waits could never occur.

While prevention is a legitimate theoretical attack on deadlock, it is not often used in general-purpose systems, since the constraints are too strong for the general multiprogramming environment.

5.2.2 Avoidance

The avoidance strategy relies on being able to construct a resource allocation mechanism that can predict the effect of honoring individual allocation requests. If a request can lead to a situation in which deadlock may occur, then avoidance strategies will refuse the request.

Since avoidance is a predictive approach, it relies on some information about the resource activity for the process that will occur in the future. For example, if a process always announced the maximum number of resources that it would ever request when it began, then it would be possible to avoid deadlock when individual resource requests are made. We discuss this *maximum claim* strategy in a subsection below.

Avoidance is a conservative strategy. It tends to underutilize resources by refusing to allocate them if there is a danger of deadlock. As a consequence, it is rarely used in commercial operating systems.

5.2.3 Detection and Recovery

Some systems are designed to allow resource allocation to proceed with no particular intervention. Instead, the system is checked to see if deadlock exists, either periodically or whenever certain events occur (or do not occur!).

There are two phases to this strategy: First, the system is checked to see if deadlock currently exists (detection). If a deadlock is detected, then the system is recovered, either manually or automatically, by preempting resources from processes. This ordinarily means that processes are destroyed.

Detection and recovery is the most widely used strategy in commercial systems. The conditions under which it is invoked are often manual; that is, the "operator" of the system manually executes the detection algorithm when he detects potential inactivity or when users begin to complain about a lack of progress.

5.2.4 Commercial Overtones

Many commercial systems simply ignore the possibility of deadlock. Historically, deadlock has not been a major problem for commercial machines, partly because processes did not often share resources, and partly because the systems were relatively simple compared to those that will be commonplace in the next five years. It has not been cost effective to include deadlock strategies in these systems; when it does become costly (customers send their machines back to the manufacturer), deadlock strategies will be considerably more important in the commercial world.

In those cases that deadlock does occur, it is up to the users of the system to detect the deadlock by comparing perceived response time with expected response time. If all the users' perceived response time far exceeds their expected response time, then all processes are destroyed and the system is restarted.

There are several flaws in this approach. First, it assumes that all users *can predict the run time* of their processes; if any user is debugging a program, there is the ever-present possibility of an infinite loop. We also often employ processes that have widely varying response times; if we stop the process "too soon," then we will have lost considerable processing time. (The problem is actually much worse; suppose that the process has partially updated some set of disk files, but not completed its task when it is destroyed. Then the secondary storage may be in an unrecoverable state.)

There is also evidence that, as systems incorporate more allocatable resources and support more processes, the probability of deadlock increases. It will become increasingly dangerous to ignore the possibility of deadlock as one builds increasingly complex systems. We return to this discussion in the next subsection.

The evolution of network systems emphasizes the growth of resources and processes. It also aggravates the deadlock problem due to unreliable, noninstantaneous communication. Not only will deadlock occur more frequently, but it will be harder to avoid or detect.

5.3 A PROCESS-RESOURCE STATE MODEL

In Chapter 3, a state model was introduced to study formal properties associated with determinate computation. In this section, a similar model is used to study deadlock.

To analyze a system composed of processes and shared resources, it is necessary to construct a formal model of the components. The model uses states and execution sequences, although the state definitions will differ considerably from those used to study determinacy.

Definition 5.1. Let

$$P = \{p_i \mid 1 \leq i \leq n\}$$

be a set of processes,

$$R = \{R_j \mid 1 \leq j \leq m\}$$

be a set of resources, and

$$T = \{t_j \geq 0 \mid \text{for each } R_j \in R\}$$

indicating the total number of units of resource type R_j that exist in the system. $\parallel$

The resource utilization pattern can be described by considering allocation status at any given moment, that is, the system is in some state determined by the process-resource allocation pattern. State transitions occur whenever some process requests, acquires, or releases resources.

Definition 5.2. Let

$$S = \{s_i \mid i \text{ unbounded}\}$$

be the set of states for a computation. Designate state s_0 to be the initial state for the system, in which all resources are unallocated. ‖

The pattern in which units of different resource types are requested, acquired, and released will determine if the system is deadlocked or not. All other activities that the process performs are not relevant to this particular aspect of the process's behavior. While we were interested in the sequence of occurrences of process initiations and terminations in studying determinacy, the sequence is not as important here as the set of possible state transitions that could occur. So, instead of redefining the execution sequence, we concentrate on individual state transitions.

Definition 5.3. Given a set of processes, P, each process, $p_i \in P$, is a mapping

$$p_i : S \times E \rightarrow 2^S$$

where

$$E = \{r_i, a_i, d_i\} \,\|$$

Each state transition is determined from the current state and the action of some process by defining that the computation move from state s_j to state s_k due to the occurrence of x_i in E. Such a state transition is denoted by

$$s_j - d_i \rightarrow s_k$$

The three process events that will cause state transition are:
(1)   If $x_i = r_i$, then there is a request event by p_k.
(2)   If $x_i = a_i$, then there is an acquisition event by p_k.
(3)   If $x_i = d_i$, then there is a release event by p_k.

Definition 5.4. If $s_j - {}^* \rightarrow s_k$ then

(1) $s_j = s_k$, or
(2) $s_j - x_i \rightarrow s_k$, for all $0 \le i \le n$ or
(3) $s_j - x_i \rightarrow s_h$, for all $0 \le i \le n$ and
       $s_h - {}^* \rightarrow s_k \,\|$

Definition 5.5. Process p_i is *blocked* in s_j if there is no s_k such that

$$s_j - x_i \rightarrow s_k \,\|$$

A blocked process is incapable of changing the state of the system. Some other process may change the state of the system so that the process may proceed.

Definition 5.6. Process p_i is *deadlocked* in s_j if for all s_k such that

$$s_j -^* \to s_k$$

then p_i is blocked in s_k. ‖

Thus, if a process is permanently blocked, independent of all future transitions in the state diagram, the process is deadlocked. If there is a process deadlocked in a state, then the state is called a *deadlock state*.

Example 5.1: Single Resource Type

Consider a very simple system that is composed of two processes and a single resource type with two units of the resource. For example, the system supports two processes in a system with two floppy disk drives. Assume that a process is only allowed to request a single unit of the resource at a time (and cannot ask for a cumulative total of more that two units, since there are only two units in the system).

Figure 5.2 is a state diagram for one of the processes. State s_0 represents the case when the process neither holds nor requests any units of the resource. The only possible state transition from s_0 is by a request, r, on the resource. This will cause the system to move to state s_1, representing the case that the process still holds no resources, but now needs one unit. The system can transition to s_2 if the process acquires a unit of the resource. From s_2, two transitions are possible: First, the process may release the resource, changing the state to s_0 (the initial state). Second, the process may request the second unit of the resource, causing the new state to be s_3, that is, the process holds one unit of the resource and needs another.

In our example, there are two processes competing for the two units of the resource, that is, the state diagram in Figure 5.2 needs to be replicated and the two copies combined in order to describe the total system state as a combination of the states for the individual processes. Figure 5.3 represents that combination.

The states and transition events have been relabeled to distinguish between the two processes. That is, $s_{i,j}$ refers to the fact that p_1 is in s_i in Figure 5.2, and p_2 is in s_j. Of course several states from the "cross product" are not feasible, for example, $s_{4,4}$ would represent the case where both processes had acquired both units of the resource. Therefore, several states have been eliminated to represent the possible actions in the system.

State $s_{3,3}$ is a deadlock state. In this case, each process is holding one unit of the resource and requesting the other. If the systems reaches this state, then there are *no* transitions out of the state, thus both processes are blocked for all states that can be reached from $s_{3,3}$, that is, no other states.

Suppose that $|S| < \infty$, as it is in many state models. Then the model is a finite-state

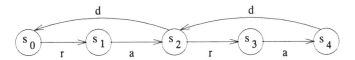

Figure 5.2 State Diagram for One Process

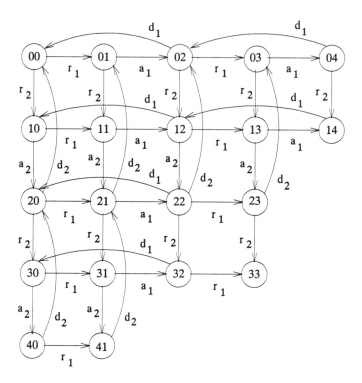

Figure 5.3 State Diagram for Two Processes

automaton. Attach probabilities to each transition in the model to reflect the probability that the corresponding transition will be taken from the given state. Ellis uses a generalization of this example to show that as the number of processes and the number of resources increase (where $|P| = |R|$), the probability of deadlock increases [4]. This is a concrete statement of the danger of ignoring deadlock as systems grow more complex.

5.4 AVOIDANCE

Avoidance strategies are designed to allocate resources only when it is certain that deadlock cannot occur as a result of the allocation. The basic observation behind avoidance strategies is that the set of all states can be partitioned into *safe* states and states that are not safe (*unsafe* states). A safe state is one in which it can be determined that the system can allocate resources in some order (for all pending requests) and still avoid deadlock.

If a state is unsafe, it does not mean that the system is in a deadlock state, nor even that a deadlock state is imminent. It simply means that the matter is "out of the hands" of the resource allocator and will be determined solely by future actions of the processes. For example, processes that are holding resources in an unsafe state may subsequently release them rather than ask for more; the system would transition from an unsafe state back into a safe state.

Definition 5.7. A state is *safe* if there is at least one s_k such that

$$s_j -x_i \rightarrow s_k \text{ (for all i)}$$

where no process is deadlocked in s_k. The state is *unsafe* otherwise. ‖

5.4.1 The Banker's Algorithm

Dijkstra's banker's algorithm is the best known of the avoidance strategies [3]. The strategy is modeled after the lending policies often employed in banks.

A bank has a limited amount of funds (resources) that can be lent to different borrowers (processes). To accommodate borrowers, the bank will often extend a line of credit to a customer; the line of credit is an indication by the bank that it is prepared to loan funds to the customer up to some agreed on limit. The customer is agreeing that he will not ask for more than the line of credit without entering into a totally new agreement; it is a *maximum claim* for resources by the customer. There is an important tacit assumption in the model: if a customer borrows some portion of the line of credit, and then requests additional funds, the amount borrowed can only be returned by satisfying the additional loan request. That is, there is no preemption in the model.

The bank's strategy for distributing resources can now be guided by the total lines of credit that it has extended to its customers and the total amount of loan funds owned by the bank. At any moment, the loan department looks at the funds that have been allocated to all customers and the maximum amount that could be requested by each customer. If there is some sequence of activity in which at least one customer's full line of credit could be met, then assume that the customer could borrow to his line of credit then repay his entire loan. After this customer has repaid his loan, then iterate on the other accounts; if all customers could exercise their lines of credit and repay, then the current state is safe.

Now reconsider the example as a set of processes, P, using a set of resources, R. The current state, s_k is determined by the pattern of resources allocated to processes. The state is defined by **alloc**(i, j), the number of units of resource $R_j \in R$ held by process $p_i \in$ P. Let **maxc**(i, j) be the maximum claim on resource $R_j \in R$ by process $p_i \in$ P; then one can compute the number of available units of R_j as

$$\textbf{avail}(j) = t_j - \sum_{i=1}^{n} \textbf{alloc}(i, j)$$

It is possible to inspect T, **maxc**(i, j), and **alloc**(i, j) and determine if the current allocation state is safe or not. Essentially, the avoidance algorithm determines if there is some sequence of allocations and deallocations such that all processes' unmet needs are smaller than the unallocated units of resource. If there is such a sequence, then the state is safe; otherwise, it is unsafe (and possibly deadlocked) (see Figure 5.4).

Example 5.2: Using the Banker's Algorithm

Suppose that a system were in a state as inferred from Figure 5.5. Let the total number of resources, T, be (8, 5, 9, 7); thus, **alloc** = (7, 3, 7, 5) and **avail** = (1, 2, 2, 2). The state is

(1)   Using **maxc, avail**, and **alloc**, determine if any process's maximum claim can be met. If all the processes have been marked **safe**, then the state is **safe**; if not all processes are marked **safe** and no unmarked process can have its maximum claim met, then the state is unsafe.

(2)   If any can be met, then mark them as **safe** processes and release their resources. Go to step 1.

Figure 5.4 The Banker's Algorithm

safe: process p_2 can exercise its maximum claim and then release all its resources, causing **avail** to be (5, 2, 2, 5). Next, p_4 could exercise its maximum claim and then release its resources, resulting in **avail** being (6,2,5,5). At this point any of the other three processes could exercise its maximum claim.

Notice that the state illustrated in Figure 5.6 is unsafe, since there is no process that can exercise its maximum claim to the resources. Also notice that this is not a deadlock state, because no process may need to use its maximum claim prior to more resources becoming available.

One view of a safe state, then, is that it is some state such that there exists some sequence of state transitions $s_j -^* \rightarrow s_k$ where some process makes a maximum request and then a full release of all its resources. If this can be accomplished for all processes, then the system can be returned to s_0, and s_j is safe.

Maximum Claims					Resource Assignments				
Process	R_0	R_1	R_2	R_3	Process	R_0	R_1	R_2	R_3
P_0	3	2	1	4	P_0	2	0	1	1
P_1	0	2	5	2	P_1	0	1	2	1
P_2	5	1	0	5	P_2	4	0	0	3
P_3	1	3	5	0	P_3	0	2	1	0
P_4	3	0	3	3	P_4	1	0	3	0

Figure 5.5 A Safe Process-Resource State

Maximum Claims					Resource Assignments				
Process	R_0	R_1	R_2	R_3	Process	R_0	R_1	R_2	R_3
P_0	3	2	1	4	P_0	2	0	1	1
P_1	0	2	5	2	P_1	0	1	2	1
P_2	5	1	0	5	P_2	4	0	0	3
P_3	1	3	5	0	P_3	1	2	1	0
P_4	3	0	3	3	P_4	1	0	3	0

Figure 5.6 An Unsafe Process-Resource State

5.5 DETECTION AND RECOVERY

Detection algorithms are less conservative than avoidance algorithms; such an algorithm is used to inspect the current state of the system and determine if the system has any deadlocked processes or not. It makes no prediction about states that can be reached from the current state, although it will determine if there is any sequence of transitions in which every process is unblocked in some state in the sequence.

We have defined resources loosely as "anything that a process needs to proceed ..." This could mean a block of primary memory, a file, or exclusive access to a device. Such resources are called *serially reusable resources*, since a process requests that the operating system allocate the resource exclusively to the process, and since the process will later release that resource for another process to reuse.

Processes also use *consumable resources*. When a process blocks on a read operation, for example, attempting to read the next character from a keyboard, then the character is something that the process needs to proceed. However, the process will never "release" the character; instead it will consume it.

So, there are two classes of resources that a process may need, and instances of the two classes are treated differently. We will begin our study by considering only serially reusable resources, then consider consumable resources, and finally consider systems that contain both classes of resources.

5.5.1 Serially Reusable Resource Systems

Definition 5.8. A *serially reusable resource* R_j has a finite number of identical units such that:

(1)   The number of units of the resource, t_j, is constant.
(2)   Each unit of R_j is either available or allocated to one and only one p_i at any instant.
(3)   A unit of R_j can be released only if it was previously acquired. ‖

Now we will define a new family of graph models to describe system states for systems containing only serially reusable resources.

Definition 5.9. A *reusable resource graph* is a directed graph, (N, E), such that:

(1) $N = P \bigcup R$, where $P \bigcap R = \phi$.
 $P = \{p_0, p_1, ..., p_n\}$ is a set of processes.
 $R = \{R_0, R_1, ..., R_m\}$ is a set of resources.
(2) (N, E) is a bipartite graph. For every $(a, b) \in E$,
 (i) If $a \in P$ and $b \in R$, then the edge is called a *request edge*.
 (ii) If $a \in R$ and $b \in P$, then the edge is called an *assignment edge*.
(3) For each $R_j \in R$, there is $t_j \geq 0$, called the *number of units of* R_j .
(4) Let $|(a, b)|$ be the number of edges from a to b.
 (i) For every j, $\Sigma |(R_j, p_i)| \leq t_j$.
 (ii) For every i and j, $|(R_j, p_i)| + |(p_i, R_j)| f \leq t_j$. ‖

Notice that parts of this definition are consistent with the definition used for a state diagram. Each reusable resource graph is a refinement of a state, and so the definitions are refinements of the state diagram definition.

One can define the actions of request, acquisition, and release of serially reusable resources more precisely than has been done up to this point

Request: Assume that the system is in s_j; then p_i is allowed to request any number of units of any number of resource types R_h ($\leq t_h$), provided that p_i has no outstanding requests for resources. A request causes a state transition, $s_j -r_i \to s_k$, where the serially reusable resource graph for s_k is derived from the serially reusable resource graph for s_j by adding an edge (p_i, R_h) for each unit requested.

Acquisition: Assume that the system is in s_j; then p_i is allowed to acquire units of R_h if and only if there is a request edge, (p_i, R_h) in the serially reusable resource graph representing s_j, and all such requests can be satisfied at one time. An acquisition causes a state transition, $s_j -a_i \to s_k$, where the serially reusable resource graph for s_k is derived from the serially reusable resource graph for s_j by changing each edge (p_i, R_h) to (R_h, p_i).

Release: Assume that the system is in s_j; then p_i can release units of R_h if and only if there is an allocation edge, (R_h, p_i), and there is no request edge, (p_i, R_g), in the serially reusable resource graph representing s_j. A release causes a state transition, $s_j -d_i \to s_k$, where the serially reusable resource graph for s_k is derived from the serially reusable resource graph for s_j by deleting all edges (R_h, p_i).

Example 5.3: The Single Resource System Revisited

A simple system was introduced in Example 5.1 in which two processes shared two units of a single resource type. The example implicitly assumed that the resources were serially reusable. The state diagram for the system was provided in Figure 5.3; we can now refine the view of each state.

In a serially reusable resource graph, denote processes by circles and resources by squares. Also, use small circles inside a square to represent the number of units of that resource type. Then Figure 5.7a represents $s_{0,0}$; neither process holds nor needs a unit of the resource. If p_2 requests a unit of the resource, r (only single-unit requests were permitted in

Example 5.1), then the system moves to $s_{0,1}$, corresponding to the serially reusable resource graph shown in Figure 5.7b. If p_1 were to request a unit of the resource, that is, the system were to move from state $s_{0,1}$ to $s_{1,1}$, then the new state would be represented as shown in Figure 5.7c. An acquisition is represented in the diagram by reversing a request edge; see Figure 5.7d representing $s_{2,1}$. In the state diagram, it is possible for $s_{2,1} -d_1 \rightarrow s_{0,1}$ (Figure 5.7b) by removing the allocation edge from the graph. Figure 5.7e illustrates the serially reusable resource graph for $s_{3,3}$, which is a deadlock state. Notice the cycle in the serially reusable resource graph.

5.5.2 Analyzing a Serially Reusable Resource Graph for Deadlock

Serially reusable resource graphs can be analyzed to determine if they represent deadlock states or not. A process is deadlocked in a state if it is blocked in the current state and in any state that is reachable from the current state (see Definition 5.6). Thus, to detect deadlock, it must be possible to analyze a serially reusable resource graph to determine if there is a process that is blocked and that will remain block under all possible transitions.

By the semantics associated with request, acquisition, and release events, it follows that the conditions for a process to be blocked can be restated as follows:

Theorem 5.1. If there is R_j such that

$$|(p_i, R_j)| + \sum_{k=1}^{n} |(R_j, p_k)| > t_j$$

process p_i is *blocked* in s_j. ‖

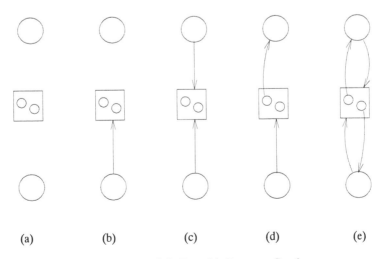

(a)   (b)   (c)   (d)   (e)

Figure 5.7 Serially Reusable Resource Graph

Argument

Suppose that $|(p_i, R_j)| + \sum_{k=1}^{n} |(R_j, p_k)| > t_j$ for some R_j. Then $\sum_{k=1}^{n} |(R_j, p_k)|$ of the t_j units are currently allocated to processes. Now there are $t_j - \sum_{k=1}^{n} |(R_j, p_k)|$ units of R_j available. But p_i requires $t_j - \sum_{k=1}^{n} |(R_j, p_k)| + x$ units of R_j; thus p_i cannot cause a transition out of the current state, and it is blocked in the current state. ‖

To detect deadlock, one must be assured that there is no sequence of state transitions that unblocks a blocked process. Graph reductions can be used to investigate possible state sequences. A graph reduction represents optimal action by a process; that is, an unblocked process acquires available resources and then releases all its resources.

Notice that graph reductions are similar to individual steps in testing to see if a state is unsafe in the banker's algorithm. In the banker's algorithm, the intent was to avoid unsafe states, and in the detection algorithm it is to decide if the current state is a deadlock state or not.

Definition 5.10. A serially reusable resource graph can be *reduced* by p_i if the process is not blocked and if there are edges incident to p_i. The reduction results in removing all edges incident to p_i.

A serially reusable resource graph is *irreducible* if it cannot be reduced by any $p \in P$.

A serially reusable resource graph is *completely reducible* if there is a sequence of reductions leading to a graph where $E = \emptyset$. ‖

Theorem 5.2. Given a serially reusable resource graph representing state s_j. State s_j is a deadlock state if and only if the serially reusable resource graph is not completely reducible. ‖

Argument

Assume that s_j is a deadlock state. Let p_i be deadlocked in s_j. Then, for every s_k such that $s_j -^* \!\!\rightarrow s_k$, p_i is blocked in s_k. Suppose that the graph is reduced by p_h. Then p_h is not blocked; that is, $t_g \geq |(p_h, R_g)| + \sum_{k=1}^{n} |(R_j, p_k)|$ for each request edge associated with p_h. The reduction results in the removal of all (request and acquisition) edges incident to p_h, leaving p_h isolated. This corresponds to state transitions a_h and d_h, leading to s_k. p_i is still deadlocked in s_k for all such reductions leading to all such s_k. Therefore, the serially reusable resource graph corresponding to s_j is not completely reducible.

[The remainder of the argument is an outline, with the details left as an exercise to the reader. Assume that s_j is not completely reducible. Show that all reduction sequences of a given serially reusable resource graph lead to the same irreducible graph (see Exercise 5.7). Notice that this implies that there is a p_i that remains blocked in all such sequences. Now show that p_i is deadlocked.]‖

If a serially reusable resource graph represents a deadlock state, then the graph must contain a cycle. For the graph to represent a deadlock state, there is a circular wait in the system. A circular wait suggests that p_1 holds R_1 and requests R_2 while p_2 holds R_2 and requests R_1. Thus, the following edges belong to E: (R_1, p_1), (p_1, R_2), (R_2, p_2), and (p_2, R_1). And this is a cycle in the serially reusable resource graph.

But a cycle is not sufficient for the state to be deadlocked, since that depends on the number of resources that are available for each resource type.

Example 5.4: Serially Reusable Resource Graph

Suppose that a system is in the state represented by the serially reusable graph shown in Figure 5.8a. Notice that p_2 and p_3 are both blocked (p_2 on R_1 and p_3 on both R_2 and R_3). But p_1 is not blocked; if we reduce by p_1, we obtain the reduced graph shown in Figure 5.8b. At that point, the graph can be reduced by p_2, yielding the graph shown in Figure 5.8c. Reducing by p_3 gives us the completely reduced graph shown in Figure 5.8d.

Figure 5.9 illustrates a similar state that is not reducible, since no process is unblocked.

5.5.3 Consumable Resource Systems

Consumable resources are differentiated from serially reusable resources in that a process may request such resources, but never releases them. Typically, a consumable resource is a signal, message, or input data.

Because consumable resources may have an unbounded number of units and because allocated units are not released, the model for analyzing serially reusable resources does not apply to consumable resources. By redefining the model for consumable resources, it is possible to find conditions for testing a system for deadlock.

Definition 5.11. A *consumable resource*, R_j has an unbounded number of identical units such that:

(1)   The number of units of the resource, t_j, varies.
(2)   There is one or more *producer processes*, p_i that increase t_j for R_j.
(3)   *Consumer processes*, p_i, decrease t_j for R_j. ‖

Definition 5.12. A *consumable resource graph* is a directed graph, (N, E) such that:

(1) $N = P \bigcup R$, where $P \bigcap R = \emptyset$. $P = \{p_0, p_1, ..., p_n\}$ is a set of processes. $R = \{R_0, R_1, ..., R_m\}$ is a set of resources.
(2)   (N,E) is a bipartite graph. For every $(a,b) \in E$,
       (i) If $a \in P$ and $b \in R$, then the edge is called a *request edge*.
       (ii) For each $r \in R$ there is a set of processes, $P_r \subset P$ ($P_r \neq \emptyset$) such that $a \in R$ and $b \in P$; these edges are called *producer edges*.
(3)   For each $R_j \in R$, there is $w_j \geq 0$, called the *available units of R_j* . ‖

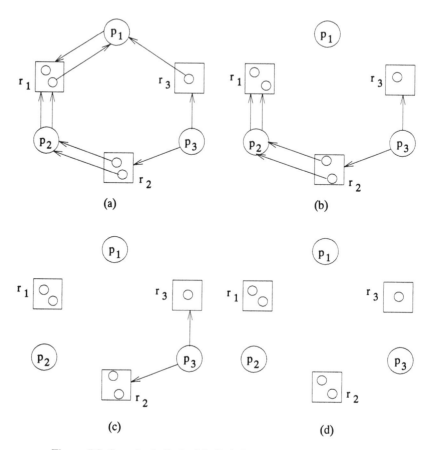

Figure 5.8 Completely Reducible Serially Reusable Resource Graph

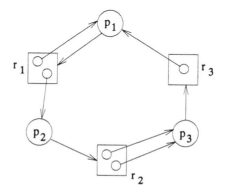

Figure 5.9 Deadlocked Serially Reusable Resource Graph

Request: Assume that the system is in s_j; then p_i is allowed to request any number of units of any number of resource types R_h, provided that p_i has no outstanding requests for resources. A request causes a state transition, $s_j -r_i\rightarrow s_k$ where the consumable resource graph for s_k is derived from the consumable resource graph for s_j by adding an edge (p_i, R_h) for each unit requested.

Acquisition: Assume that the system is in s_j; then p_i is allowed to acquire units of R_h if and only if there is a request edge (p_i, R_h) in the consumable resource graph representing s_j, and all such requests can be satisfied at one time. An acquisition causes a state transition, $s_j -a_i\rightarrow s_k$ where the consumable resource graph for s_k is derived from the graph for s_j by deleting each edge (p_i, R_h) and by decrementing w_h once for each edge deleted.

Release: Assume that the system is in s_j; then p_i can release units of R_h if and only if there is a producer edge (R_h, p_i) and there is no request edge (p_i, R_g) in the consumable resource graph representing s_j. A release causes a state transition $s_j -d_i\rightarrow s_k$ where the graph for s_k is derived from the consumable resource graph for s_j by incrementing w_h once for each unit of the resource produced.

Example 5.5: Consumable Resource Graph

Figure 5.10 represents a series of state transitions for a simple consumable resource system. Processes p_1 and p_2 share a single consumable resource. The first state represented in the system shows that p_2 is a producer of the resource, that there are currently no units of the resource available, and that there are no pending requests for the resource.

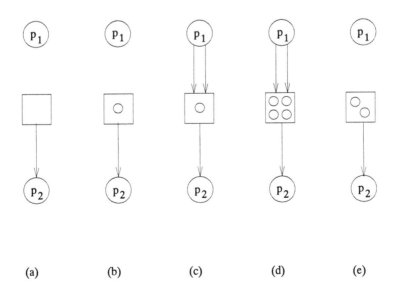

| (a) | (b) | (c) | (d) | (e) |

Figure 5.10 State Transitions in Consumable Resource Graph

The system state changes when p_2 releases one unit of the resource and again when p_1 requests two units of the resource. At this point, p_1 is blocked, but p_2 continues to run. The next transition shows that p_2 releases an additional three units of the resource. And in the final state illustrated in Figure 5.10, p_1 has obtained two units of the resource, leaving two units available. No process is blocked.

5.5.4 Analyzing a Consumable Resource Graph for Deadlock

Consumable resource systems behave differently than serially reusable resource systems, since there are potentially an unbounded number of units of the resource available. That is, if a process is blocked in some state, it is difficult to know if it will always be blocked (unless, of course, *all* processes are blocked in the state, in which case all processes are deadlocked).

Second, every state in the system is unsafe, since there is no maximum claim on consumable resources.

However, consumable resource graphs can also be analyzed to determine if they represent deadlock states or not. A process is deadlocked in a state if it is blocked in the current state and in any state that is reachable from the current state (see Definition 5.6). Thus, to detect deadlock, it must be possible to analyze the graph to determine if every process is permanently blocked in all states reachable from the current state.

> **Definition 5.13.** A consumable resource graph can be *reduced* by p_i if the process is not blocked and if there are edges incident to p_i. The reduction results in
> (1)   Decrementing w_j for all outstanding requests on R_j by p_i and deleting the edges from the graph.
> (2)   For each R_j such that (R_j,p_i), release an unbounded number of units of R_j and delete the edge from the graph. ‖

Figure 5.11 shows a consumable resource graph representing a particular system state. In this example, p_i is the producer for R_i. There are three requests for R_1 by p_2, and $w_1 = 2$. Since p_1 is not blocked, it may release (produce) units of R_1 to satisfy the request by p_2. Thus, the state is not a deadlock state.

The analysis of a consumable resource graph is different from serially reusable graphs, we cannot use complete reducibility as a necessary and sufficient condition for deadlock. Consider the consumable resource graph shown in Figure 5.12. We can reduce by either p_1 or p_2, but once we reduce by one, we cannot reduce by the other; yet this state is not a deadlock state. (After any state transition this particular example will result in a deadlock state.)

> **Theorem 5.3.** Given a consumable resource graph representing state s_j. Process p_i is not deadlocked in s_j if and only if there is a sequence of reductions leaving a state in which p_i is not blocked. ‖

Argument

Suppose that there is a sequence of reductions leaving a state in which p_i is not blocked. Each reduction corresponds to a legal transition in the corresponding

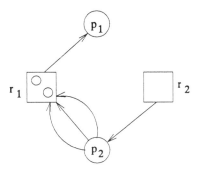

Figure 5.11 Consumable Resource Graph

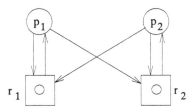

Figure 5.12 A More Complex Situation in a Consumable Resource Graph

consumable resource graph. Therefore, the series of reductions corresponds to a legal sequence of states; since p_i is not blocked, it is not deadlocked.

Suppose that p_i is not deadlocked in s_j. Then there exists some sequence of requests, acquisitions, and releases, ξ, by processes

$$p_{i_1}, p_{i_2}, \cdots, p_{i_k},$$

leading to a state s_t in which p_i is not blocked. Now consider a sequence of reductions,

$$\rho = p_{j_1}, p_{j_2}, \cdots, p_{j_g}.$$

Now we have

$$\xi = \alpha_{i_1}, \alpha_{i_2}, \cdots, \alpha_{i_k}$$

and

$$\rho = p_{j_1}, p_{j_2}, \cdots, p_{j_g}$$

Now, α_{i_h} is the first event in ξ such that i_h is not an an index in

$$p_{j_1}, p_{j_2}, \cdots, p_{j_h}$$

and such that p_h is not an isolated node in s_j. By the definition of reduction, no additional request edges will be placed in the graph during reduction. So we can use ρ to reduce s_j since, before a reduction by any p_{j_k}, the available units of each resource must be at least as large as that preceding the first operation by α_{j_k} in ξ. Thus p_i is not blocked following the reduction sequence ρ, because it is not blocked in ξ. ∥

5.5.5 General Resource Systems

Real systems will incorporate some combination of serially reusable and consumable resources; thus deadlock detection will need to combine the analysis techniques in the previous discussion.

While the formal definitions for handling general resource systems are not provided here, it should be clear that such a system has a set of resources $R = R_S \cup R_C$ where the first subset is the collection of serially reusable resources, and the second subset is the collection of consumable resources. Analysis of a state — a general resource graph — amounts to the application of the appropriate technique for the corresponding resource type.

For example, suppose we had a general resource graph as shown in Figure 5.13a. Let R_1 and R_3 be serially reusable resources and R_2 be a consumable resource. Then p_1 and p_3 are both producers for R_2. Figure 5.13b shows the graph after a reduction by p_4, Figure 5.13c indicates the graph after reduction by p_1, and so on.

5.6 FURTHER READING

Deadlock was very widely discussed in the early 1970s. One of the better discussions of prevention, avoidance, and detection and recovery can be found in the survey paper by Coffman, Elphick, and Shoshani [2]. Holt's Ph.D. thesis presents a very general model for describing deadlock and for necessary and sufficient conditions for deadlock to exist in various types of systems; his work is surveyed in Bic and Shaw's book [1] and in his survey paper [5]. The exposition in this chapter follows Holt's work.

We have not covered the difficulties associated with detecting deadlock in local memory multiprocessor systems, for example, a network of computers. The major new difficulty is unreliable communication, slow communication among the parts of the detection algorithm. As the detection algorithm navigates the network to obtain the local state, the state in previously read machines changes [6]. We return to this problem in Chapter 12.

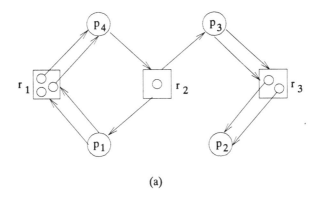

(a)

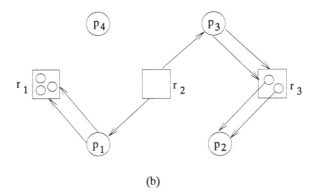

(b)

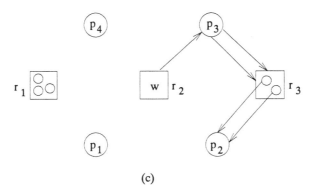

(c)

Figure 5.13 General Resource Graph

REFERENCES

1.   L. Bic and A. Shaw, *The Logical Design of Operating Systems, Second Edition*, Prentice Hall, Inc., Englewood Cliffs, NJ, 1988.
2.   E. G. Coffman, M. T. Elphick, and A. Shoshani, "System Deadlocks," *ACM Computing Surveys 3*, 2 (June 1971), 67-78.
3.   E. W. Dijkstra, "Co-operating Sequential Processes," in *Programming Languages*, F. Genuys (ed.), Academic Press, New York, NY, 1968, 43-112.
4.   C. A. Ellis, "On the Probability of Deadlock in Computer Systems," *Proceedings of the Fourth ACM Symposium on Operating Systems Principles* , 1973, 88-95 .
5.   R. C. Holt, "Some Deadlock Properties of Computer Systems," *Computing Surveys 4*, 3 (September 1972), 179-196.
6.   E. Knapp, "Deadlock Detection in Distributed Databases," *ACM Computing Surveys 19*, 4 (December 1987), 303-328.

EXERCISES

(1)   Suppose that a system is composed of three processes, p_1, p_2, and p_3, sharing three resources, R_1, R_2, and R_3. p_1 acquires R_1 at process time $t_{1,1}$ and R_2 at process time $t_{1,2}$ and then releases R_1 at time $t_{1,3}$ and R_2 at $t_{1,4}$. p_2 acquires R_2 at process time $t_{1,1}$ and R_3 at process time $t_{2,2}$ and then releases R_2 at time $t_{2,3}$ and R_3 at $t_{2,4}$. p_3 acquires R_3 at process time $t_{3,1}$ and R_1 at process time $t_{3,2}$ and then releases R_3 at time $t_{3,3}$ and R_1 at $t_{3,4}$. Draw a joint progress path for the three processes.

(2)   Given a system that uses the banker's algorithm for avoiding deadlock and the resource state shown below (total number of units = <6 4 4 2>):

Maximum Claims					Max Add. Resources Needed				
Process	R_0	R_1	R_2	R_3	Process	R_0	R_1	R_2	R_3
P_0	2	0	1	1	P_0	1	2	0	0
P_1	1	1	0	0	P_1	0	1	0	2
P_2	1	1	0	0	P_2	0	0	2	0
P_3	1	0	1	0	P_3	2	2	0	0
P_4	0	1	0	1	P_4	2	0	0	0

Is this state safe? Why or why not?

(3)   Reconsider the simple process-resource model in Example 5.1. Describe a state diagram for a system with three process and a single resource type with two units of the resource. How many deadlock states are there in the graph?

(4)   A system is composed of four processes, {p1, p2, p3, p4} and three types of serially reusable resources, {s1, s2, s3}. The number of units of the resources are t1 = 3, t2 = 2, and t3 = 2. Process p1 holds one unit of s1 and requests one unit of s2. p2 holds two units of s2 and requests one unit each of s1 and s3. p3 holds one unit of s1 and requests one unit of s2. P4 holds two units of s3 and requests one unit of s1. Show the serially reusable resource graph to represent this system state. Show the reduced form of the graph. Which, if any, of the processes are deadlocked in this state?

(5)   The system is composed of four process, {p1, p2, p3, p4} and three types of consumable resources, {c1, c2, c3}. There is one unit each of c1 and c3 available. p1 requests a unit of

c1 and a unit of c3. p2 produces c1 and c3 and requests a unit of c2. p3 requests one unit each of c1 and c3. p4 produces c2 and requests a unit of c3. Show the consumable resource graph to represent this system state. Which, if any, of the processes are deadlocked in this state?

(6)   The system is composed of four processes, {p1, p2, p3, p4}, two types of serially reusable resources, {S1, S2}, and two types of consumable resources, {C1, C2}. S1 has two units and S2 has three units. C1 and C2 each have one available unit. p1 produces C1 and is requesting two units of S2. p2 holds two units of S1 and one unit of S2 while it requests two units of C2. p3 holds one unit of S2 and requests one unit of C1. p4 produces C2 and requests one unit each of C1 and S1. Show the general resource graph to represent this system state. Which, if any, of the processes are deadlocked in this state?

(7)   Given a serially reusable resource graph representing state s_j. Suppose that the resource graph is not completely reducible. Prove that all reduction sequences of a given serially reusable resource graph lead to the same irreducible graph.

(8)   Prove that a cycle in a serially reusable resource graph is not a sufficient condition for deadlock to exist.

(9)   Investigate the documentation of your local computing facility to determine how the operating system handles deadlock.

6

SCHEDULING

In Section 2.2, processor multiplexing was introduced as a fundamental aspect of process management. The discussion in Chapter 2 focused on mechanisms for ensuring that a scheduler would be invoked, but did not describe scheduling strategies. This chapter discusses those strategies, first as they apply to uniprocessor (multiprogramming) systems and then to multiprocessors.

The scheduler is the fundamental mechanism to support CPU sharing (multiprogramming) in centralized, networked, and distributed operating systems. Recall from the earlier discussion that the scheduler can be invoked voluntarily by a processor — explicitly with a **yield** system call or implicitly with a clock interrupt or by a resource request.

The task of the scheduler is to evaluate the set of processes in the ready list, to select one of them, and then to dispatch it to the idle processor. The part of this process that is a design issue is selecting the process from the ready list. Thus, the scheduler will change the state of the running process to ready or blocked, save the state of the process, select a new process that is ready, load the process's state into the CPU registers, and then change the process's state to running (that is, activate the process).

Whenever a processor becomes idle, there is competition among the ready processes for the processor. The *scheduling strategy* (or *scheduling policy*) for the operating system is used to specify how the competition is to be resolved.

In the first section of the chapter we examine uniprocessor schedulers, then we discuss multiprocessor schedulers.

6.1 UNIPROCESSOR SCHEDULING

In the uniprocessor schedule, only one process will ever be running at any given time; the other processes will either be ready to run (and competing for the processor) or be blocked on a resource request.

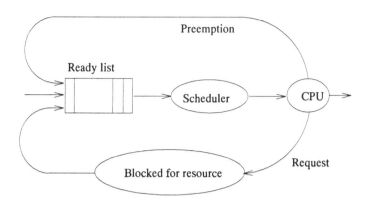

Figure 6.1 Process Scheduling

Figure 6.1 is a schematic diagram of a uniprocessor system in which the process that is in the running state resides in the CPU circle, each process that is currently in the ready state is enqueued in a *ready list*, and blocked processes are in the resource allocation portion of the system. The *scheduler* is an algorithm (or mechanism) for implementing a particular scheduling strategy; it chooses one process from the ready list and then allocates the CPU to that process. Thus processes may be *preempted* through a **yield** instruction or clock interrupt, leaving the CPU and entering the ready list; processes may block themselves, yielding the CPU, and making requests on the resource allocation portion of the system; and departing processes may exit the system.

What is the policy for selecting a process from the ready list? The details of the policy depend on the overall policy for the operating system, for example, if the system is a real time system, then processes must be scheduled so that they meet very specific deadlines. If the operating system is for a time-sharing system, then the criteria may focus on providing an equitable share of the processor per unit time to each user or process. The criteria for selecting a scheduling strategy will depend on the goals of the operating system, as well as priority among processes (and the corresponding users), fairness, overall resource utilization, maximized throughput, average or maximum turnaround time, average or maximum response time, maximized system availability, and deadlines.

Before describing some of the more popular scheduling algorithms, we will establish a formal definition of the objects that the scheduler will manipulate.

Definition 6.1. Let $P = \{p_i \mid 1 \leq i \leq n\}$ be a set of *processes*. $S(p_i)$ is the *state of* process p_i, where $S(p_i) \in \{\text{blocked, running, ready}\}$. The *service time request*, $\tau(p_i)$, is the amount of time that a process requires in the running state before it is completed. The *priority* of the process at time t, $\mathbf{pri}_t(p_i)$ is a mapping:

$$\mathbf{pri}_t: P \to \text{nonnegative integers} \cup \{\Omega\}$$

The priority may be invariant with respect to time, in which case we will omit the subscript t. ‖

The scheduling policy of a particular scheduling algorithm can be defined by specifying the priority mapping. If a process is ready or running, then its priority is defined, that is, processes that are mapped to Ω are in the blocked state and cannot be scheduled. By specifying the priority for all processes and by assigning the processor to the process with the top priority (lowest number), we have specified the scheduling policy.

The performance of an algorithm can be estimated by the expected amount of time that will be required to obtain service when a process enters the ready state. There are two often-used measures of such time.

Definition 6.2. The *waiting time* for a process p_i, $T_{WAIT}(p_i)$, is the amount of time that the process spends waiting to use the processor.

The *expected waiting time* for all processes in a system is the average of the waiting times of all processes in the system at any given moment. ‖

For example, suppose that no two processes have the same priority and that no other processes will enter the ready list after p_i. Then

$$T_{WAIT}(p_i) = \sum_{k=1}^{n} \tau(p_k)$$

where $pri_t(p_k) < pri_t(p_i)$, and $pri_t(p_j) = \Omega$ if p_j is blocked.

The expected waiting time of a process is an indicator of the amount of time that an "average" process will spend in the ready list waiting for service. The expected waiting time is not necessarily the best measure of performance of a scheduling algorithm, since, for example, it may favor these "average" processes over long-running processes (which may not be consistent with the overall operating system policy).

Definition 6.3. The *turnaround time* for a process p_i, $T_{TURNAROUND}(p_i)$, is the amount of elapsed time between the moment that a process enters the ready state and the moment that the process exits the running state.

The *expected turnaround time* for all processes in a system is the average of the turnaround times of all processes in the system at any given moment. ‖

For example, suppose that no two processes have the same priority and that no other processes will enter the ready list after p_i. Then

$$T_{TURNAROUND}(p_i) = T_{WAIT}(p_i) + \tau(p_i)$$

The measured waiting and turnaround time in a system will depend on several factors and assumptions, some of which we ignore for now (such as arrivals of new processes in the ready list once the process begins to wait, the scheduler's treatment of processes with the same priority as process p_i, and that the CPU is busy if there are any processes in the ready state). We return to analyze systems performance in general, including schedulers, in Chapter 14; the definitions are provided now so that we can describe different scheduling strategies.

Consider the model of systems operation shown in Figure 6.13, representing scheduling algorithms. The system load can be characterized by the arrival rate of new processes into the ready list and the nature of the service times, $\tau(p_i)$.

Let α represent the mean arrival rate of new processes (that is, the rate in processes/time at which processes enter the ready list) and β represent the mean service rate; $1/\beta$ is the mean service time of the processes. Ignoring context switching time and assuming that the CPU has sufficient capacity to service the load, the fraction of time that the CPU is busy is expressed by

$$\rho = \alpha \cdot \frac{1}{\beta} = \frac{\alpha}{\beta}$$

If the arrival rate, α, exceeds the service rate, β, then the CPU will be saturated independently of the scheduling algorithm employed in the system, that is, in time, any finite-length ready list will overflow since processes arrive at a higher rate than they can be serviced. Systems will reach a *steady state* if $\alpha < \beta$, that is, $\rho < 1$.

Notice that the system will not be viable in the long run if $\alpha \geq \beta$, since processes will arrive at least as fast as the CPU can process them. Systems that operate under conditions where $\rho \to 1$ may require arbitrarily large ready lists, so such conditions are also going to be problematic for continued operation of the system.

6.1.1 Nonpreemptive Algorithms

Nonpreemptive scheduling algorithms do not forcefully interrupt a process to move it to the ready state once the process has been allocated the CPU. That is, there is no path from the CPU directly back to the ready list (in Figure 6.1) in systems that use a nonpreemptive scheduling algorithm.

Because of this lack of practical control for CPU allocation, nonpreemptive algorithms may be altered so that they allow for preemption from a clock interrupt. For our introduction to this class of algorithms, we assume that the processor using the CPU will never be preempted, but that a process will always move from the running to the blocked state.

There are many nonpreemptive scheduling algorithms. In the remainder of this section we review a few of the most well known.

First-Come-First-Served (FCFS)

This scheduling strategy assigns priority to processes in the order in which they request the processor. Thus,

$$\mathbf{pri}(p_i) = t_{i,0}$$

where $t_{i,0}$ is the time at which the process last requested service and

$$\mathbf{pri}(p_i) < \mathbf{pri}(p_j)$$

if p_i became ready (entered the ready list) at time $t_{i,0} < t_{j,0} = \mathbf{pri}(p_j)$ prior to the time that p_j did so. The priority of the process does not change over time.

FCFS is easily implemented, since the ready list need only be a standard FIFO queue of processes. A process is added to the end of the queue whenever it requests a processor, and the process at the head of the queue is allocated the processor at scheduling time.

When a process p_i requests service, then the turnaround time is the sum of the times of all the processes that are already in the ready list and the process's own service time *independent of subsequent arrivals*:

$$T_{TURNAROUND}(p_i) = \tau(p_i) + T_{TURNAROUND}(p_j) = \sum_k \tau(p_k)$$

where p_j is the process at the end of the queue when the new process arrives (that is, for all processes, p_k, currently in the queue). And the expected waiting time is the turnaround time for the last process in the ready list divided by the number of processes in the ready list:

$$T_{WAIT}(p_i) = \frac{T_{TURNAROUND}(p_j)}{|\text{ready list}|}$$

Suppose that there are four processes in the ready list, as illustrated in Figure 6.2. FCFS will schedule the processes as shown in Figure 6.3. The expected turnaround time is

$$\frac{40 + 60 + 110 + 140}{4} = \frac{350}{4} = 87.5$$

The turnaround time for a new process, p_n is $\tau(p_n) + 140$. The expected waiting time is

$$\frac{0 + 40 + 60 + 110}{4} = \frac{210}{4} = 52.5$$

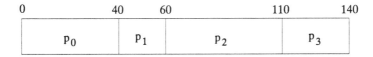

Figure 6.3 FCFS Schedule

We can use the service rate, β, to estimate the wait time in a FCFS system. Suppose that a process arrives at the ready list in a nonpreemptive FCFS system. Then, the time that the new process, called the *tagged process*, will have to wait before it begins to receive service can be estimated by

Process	Service Time	Priority
0	40	4
1	20	2
2	50	1
3	30	3

Figure 6.2 An Example Load

$$T_{WAIT}(p) = \frac{L}{\beta} + \frac{1}{2\beta}$$

where L is the length of the queue at the time the tagged process arrives. The FCFS assumption ensures that only the load that is present when the tagged process arrives is relevant, since any subsequent processes will be served after the tagged process. The tagged process must wait for all processes currently in the ready list to complete in addition to (on the average) half of an average service time for the process currently on the CPU to complete. The relationship between wait time and queue length can be generalized for many scheduling algorithms (see the discussion of Little's law in Chapter 14).

While the FCFS algorithm is easy to implement, it ignores the service time request and all other criteria that may influence the performance with respect to turnaround or expected waiting time. FCFS generally does not perform well under any specific set of system requirements and is not often used.

Shortest Job Next (SJN)

Suppose that the service time is known *a priori*. The SJN (also known as "shortest job first" or "SJF") scheduling algorithm will choose the next job to receive service to be the one with minimum service time. That is,

$$\mathbf{pri}(p_i) = \tau(p_i)$$

The turnaround time for p_i is determined by the processes in the ready list with lower service time than this process. That is,

$$T_{TURNAROUND}(p_i) = \sum_j (\tau(p_j) \leq \tau(p_i))$$

Given the processes in the ready list shown in Figure 6.14, SJN will produce the schedule shown in Figure 6.4.

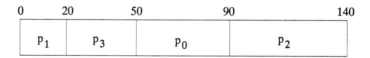

Figure 6.4 SJN Schedule

The expected turnaround time is

$$\frac{20 + 50 + 90 + 140}{4} = \frac{300}{4} = 75$$

and the expected waiting time is

$$\frac{0 + 20 + 50 + 90}{4} = \frac{160}{4} = 40$$

SJN minimizes the average wait time, since it services small processes before large ones. To see why this is true, consider the simple case in which no new processes arrive: SJN will repeatedly schedule the process with minimum τ. Suppose that τ orders the n processes in the ready list as $p_0, p_1, ..., p_{n-1}$, that is, $\tau(p_0) \leq \tau(p_1) \leq \cdots \leq \tau(p_{n-1})$. Then we have

$$T_{WAIT}(p_0) = 0$$

$$T_{WAIT}(p_1) = T_{WAIT}(p_0) + \tau(p_0)$$

$$\cdots$$

$$T_{WAIT}(p_i) = T_{WAIT}(p_{i-1}) + \tau(p_{i-1})$$

$$\cdots$$

$$T_{WAIT}(p_{n-1}) = T_{WAIT}(p_{n-2}) + \tau(p_{n-2})$$

and the expected wait time is the average of the n individual wait times,

$$\sum_{i=0}^{n-1} \frac{\tau(p_i)}{n} = \frac{(n-1)\tau(p_0) + (n-2)\tau(p_1) + \cdots + \tau(p_{n-2})}{n}$$

For any other scheduling algorithm, there will be a numerator of the form

$$(n-1)x_0 + (n-2)x_1 + \cdots + x_{n-2}$$

where $x_i = \tau(p_i)$ for SJN. Thus, small service times have larger multipliers in SJN, and the resulting sum is at least as small for SJN as it is for any other algorithm. Therefore, SJN will have an expected waiting time that is less than or equal to the expected waiting time for any other algorithm.

While SJN minimizes average wait time, it may penalize processes with high service time requests. If the ready list is saturated, then processes with large service times tend to be left in the ready list while small processes receive service. In the extreme case, where the system has little idle time, processes with large service times will never be served. This *starvation* may be a serious liability of the scheduling algorithm.

Suppose that a SJN scheduling policy controls CPU allocation where $\rho = 1 - \varepsilon$. As new processes arrive with service times distributed around the mean service time, $1/\beta$, those few processes with very large service times (much larger than the mean) will tend to have a lower priority than the average incoming process. And since the CPU utilization is very high, there will tend to be two or more processes in the ready list. As a result, the processes with very large service time requests will starve even though $\rho < 1$.

Priority Scheduling

In priority scheduling, the processes are allocated the CPU on the basis of their assigned priorities (in our explanation, lower numbers have higher priority; some schedulers use the opposite ordering).

The turnaround time will be determined by the number of jobs with higher priority that exist in the ready list.

$$T_{TURNAROUND}(p_i) = \sum_j (\tau(p_j))$$

such that

$$pri_t(p_j) < pri_t(p_i)$$

Again consider the example shown in Figure 6.14. Priority scheduling will produce the schedule shown in Figure 6.5.

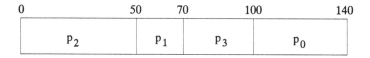

Figure 6.5 Priority Schedule

The expected turnaround time is

$$\frac{50 + 70 + 100 + 140}{4} = \frac{360}{4} = 90$$

and the expected wait time is

$$\frac{0 + 50 + 70 + 100}{4} = \frac{220}{4} = 55$$

Obviously, the key to the performance of priority scheduling is in choosing priorities for the processes. They may be some function of the user (process owner) identification or computed internally as some function of resource requests.

Again, priority scheduling may cause low-priority processes to starve. This can be compensated for if the priorities are internally computed. Suppose that one parameter in the priority assignment function is the amount of time that the process has been waiting, that is, the longer a job waits, the higher its priority (lower its priority number) becomes. This will tend to eliminate the starvation problem.

6.1.2 Preemptive Algorithms

Preemptive algorithms differ from nonpreemptive algorithms in that a process that is in the running state can be changed to the ready state at any time, rather than only when a job voluntarily releases the processor. There are different reasons for using preemptive algorithms, including quick response to high priority jobs or fairness to all jobs. It is important to note that CPU multiplexing is under the explicit control of the scheduler, not of the user processes.

We have already described nonpreemptive SJN and priority scheduling. There are also preemptive versions of these algorithms. The preemptive versions differ from the nonpreemptive versions in that they keep the highest-priority job in the running state at all times. Whenever the scheduler is invoked, it chooses the highest-priority ready process, just as in the nonpreemptive strategies. However, the scheduler is called each time a process enters the ready state, for example, because it was just started. In particular, the process that was running at the time this event occurred will have its state changed to ready. Thus, all lower-priority processes are made to yield to the highest-priority process whenever it requests the CPU.

The preemptive SJN algorithm will automatically increase the priority of the process that was preempted, since it was the high-priority job prior to the scheduling activity and it can only have increased its priority by decreasing its CPU need since it obtained the processor. The preemptive priority algorithm may alter the running process's priority when it returns it to the ready list or leave the priority as it was before the process was scheduled.

In the discussion of nonpreemptive algorithms, we ignored the cost of *context switching* among processes. In preemptive algorithms, the scheduler must run each time it is possible that a process has entered the ready queue; this results in halting the process on the CPU, saving its CPU register contents, loading the scheduler's CPU register contents, allowing it to select a new user process, and then loading the newly chosen process's register contents (including the PC register) into the CPU registers. While several hardware architectures include features to minimize the cost of context switching, it may still be a significant factor in preemptive scheduling, depending on how frequently it is necessary to run the scheduling algorithm due to preemption conditions. In preemptive scheduling systems, the cost of context switching can become a significant cost to computing optimal schedules.

Round Robin

The basic premise behind *round robin* (*RR*) scheduling is to distribute the processing time equally among all processes that request it. That is, suppose the CPU is idle, that processes $\{p_i \mid 0 \leq i < K\}$ are all ready to run, and that the processes appear in the ready list in the same order as their index, that is, p_i appears before p_j if $i < j$. At time t,

$$\mathbf{pri}_t(p_k) = 0$$

and

$$\mathbf{pri}_t(p_j) > 0$$

for some single k and for all $j \neq k$. Now, p_k has highest priority (lowest number) and will be allocated the CPU.

After some *time quantum*, q, the priorities will be adjusted such that

$$\mathbf{pri}_{t+q}(p_k) \leftarrow K$$

and

$$\mathbf{pri}_{t+q}(p_{k+1 \bmod K}) \leftarrow \mathbf{pri}_{t+q}(p_{k+1 \bmod K}) - 1$$

Let C be the time to perform a context switch between user processes (often one assumes that C is sufficiently small that it can be ignored); each of the K processes will receive q units of time on the CPU for every $K(q + C)$ units of real time.

In some cases, a process will finish with the CPU before its time quantum has expired. It will voluntarily release the CPU and call the scheduler, for example, by using the **yield** abstract machine instruction or by requesting an input/output operation. The scheduler removes the running process from the CPU, adjusts the priorities, resets the time quantum, and then reschedules the CPU.

It is easy to see that a system with a timer interrupt naturally fits with RR scheduling, since the interrupt interval can be set to the time quantum. The timer interrupt handler calls the scheduler whenever it is invoked.

Whenever a process completes, it is deleted from the ready list, and whenever a new process starts, it is entered into the ready list at an arbitrary point, for example, at the end of a linked list of processes. The scheduler removes the running process from the CPU, adjusts the priorities, resets the timer, and reschedules the CPU.

The turnaround time for RR schedules is determined by the size of the processor request, τ_i; the time quantum, q; the number of other processes sharing the CPU, K; and the amount of time required for a context switch, C. If we assume that no new jobs enter the queue while p_i is being processed and that all jobs have

$$\tau_j \geq \tau_i$$

then we can estimate the turnaround time. In this simplified case, the job requires $\lfloor \tau_i/q \rfloor$ time slices. The remainder of τ_i / q represents the part of a final quantum used by the process (the "last" quantum is not used if the remainder is zero). Thus, the turnaround time estimate (with the assumptions) is

$$T_{\text{TURNAROUND}}(p_i) = (\lfloor \tau_i/q \rfloor * (q+C)) + (q * \text{remainder}(\tau_i / q) + C)$$

Notice that this estimate is very rough, depending on strong assumptions. A more realistic estimate will require more sophisticated analysis of the type discussed in Section 14.1.

Suppose that the ready list contained the four processes shown in Figure 6.14, and the time quantum was 20 with a negligible time for context switching. Then, the *Gantt chart* describing the resulting schedule is shown in Figure 6.6. The expected turnaround time for a process is

$$\frac{40 + 100 + 130 + 140}{4} = \frac{410}{4} = 102.5$$

and the expected wait time is

$$\frac{60 + 20 + 90 + 100}{4} = \frac{270}{4} = 67.5$$

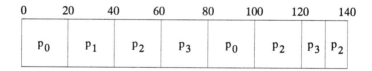

Figure 6.6 Round Robin Schedule for q = 20

Let us reconsider the example by supposing that a context switch requires 5 units of time (see Figure 6.7). The expected turnaround time has increased to reflect the context switching time to

$$\frac{45 + 120 + 160 + 175}{4} = \frac{500}{4} = 125$$

and the expected wait time is now

$$\frac{80 + 25 + 125 + 130}{4} = \frac{360}{4} = 90$$

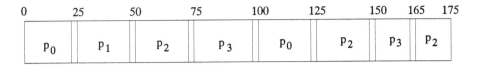

Figure 6.7 Round Robin Schedule with Context Switching

Multiple-level Queues

Multiple-level queues are a combination of priority scheduling with other strategies used within a given priority. In the simplest case, one can imagine that the ready list is partitioned into J smaller ready sublists, where all processes have some priority between one and J. Process p_i is in ready sublist k if $pri(p_i) = k$. If we assume preemptive priority scheduling, then all processes in ready sublist 1 will be completed before any process is run from ready sublists 2 through J, and so on. Since the scheduling algorithm is preemptive, if the scheduler is currently running processes from ready sublist k and a higher-priority process arrives, it preempts the currently running job.

A variant of the pure priority levels is to define the scheduler so that it favors higher-priority sublists over time, for example, it may give 2^{-j} fraction of the time to processes in the sublist j (saving the remaining 2^{-J} for various overhead functions).

Within a given ready sublist, any scheduling strategy may be used — preemptive or nonpreemptive (of course, nonpreemptive local strategies may be overridden by the global preemptive strategy). Thus, processes within a sublist could be processed using FCFS, SJN, or RR.

Time-sharing systems often support the idea of *foreground* and *background* processes. Those running in the foreground are servicing an interactive user, while background processes are intended to run whenever no foreground process requires the CPU. Thus, there is a high-priority foreground ready sublist and a low-priority background ready sublist. Any foreground job takes precedence over any background job.

It is easy to imagine a number of different strategies that follow the foreground/background rationale: For example, interrupt handler processes might run at priority 1, device drivers at priority 2, interactive processing jobs at priority 3, interactive editing jobs at priority 4, normal batch jobs at priority 5 and "long" batch jobs at priority 6. Of course, such a choice suggests that processes might change priority levels during execution, for example, if an interactive editing process became a compute-intensive process. Systems that allow processes to change ready sublists are called *multiple-level feedback queues*.

6.1.3 A Final Word about Uniprocessor Scheduling

Scheduling algorithms are an area of operating systems that have been implemented in many different ways. The more sophisticated algorithms are multiple-level feedback queue variants. However, each of the more sophisticated scheduling algorithms begins to increase the context switching time, so the most often used scheduling algorithms for time-sharing systems are preemptive round robin schedulers, with parameterized time quanta.

Any production operating system is likely to use some combination of the scheduling algorithms surveyed in this chapter, usually resulting in some form of preemptive algorithm. These combined strategies may be very effective, but are difficult to analyze. It is difficult to formulate simple mathematical models to predict how these algorithms will behave under realistic system loads.

6.2 MULTIPROCESSOR SCHEDULING

Precedence graphs provide constraints on the set of processes that are in the ready list, that is, if a process's predecessors have not terminated, then the process cannot use the CPU.

Precedence graphs represent the content of the ready list in terms of subprocesses for a particular computation; however, they are more useful for considering schedules in multiprocessor systems. Suppose we are attempting to compute an optimal nonpreemptive schedule for $m \geq 2$ processors, for a set of processes constrained by a precedence graph, where the execution time, $\tau(p_i)$, is known for each process, p_i. [Earlier, we used $\tau(p_i)$ to compute the schedule for a single processor in order to minimize average wait time, see SJN scheduling].

Given a computation, $\pi = (P, <\cdot)$, $\{\tau(p_i) \mid p_i \in P\}$, and $m \geq 2$ processors, the goal is to compute a nonpreemptive schedule for the set of processes. For example, suppose that

$$P = \{p_i \mid 1 \leq i \leq 7\}$$
$$<\cdot = \{(p_1, p_3), (p_2, p_3), (p_3, p_4), (p_5, p_6), (p_5, p_7)\}$$
$$\tau = \{(p_1, 2), (p_2, 1), (p_3, 3), (p_4, 1), (p_5, 2), (p_6, 4), (p_7, 1)\}$$

(see Figure 6.8).

Figure 6.9 illustrates two different schedules for two processors that satisfy the given precedence constraints. The schedule shown in Figure 6.9a chooses processes, left to right, across the top of the graph. A process can only be scheduled if all its predecessors have already terminated; thus, when p_2 finishes on processor CPU$_2$, then p_5 or p_3 could have been scheduled.

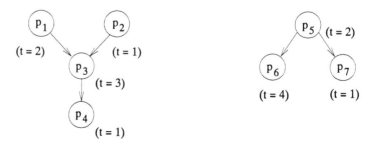

Figure 6.8 Example Precedence Graph

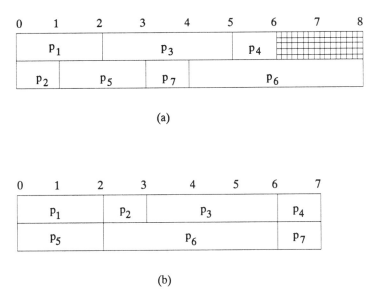

Figure 6.9 Schedules for the Precedence Graph

The order in which the processes are assigned to the two processors is called a *schedule*, resulting in a *finish time* of 8 time units in this example. It includes two units of *idle time* on processor 1 from time 6 to time 8. It is natural to consider the possibility that the two processors could be scheduled (with the given precedence constraints) so that the two units of idle time on processor 1 were eliminated and both processors were constantly busy. Perhaps, more importantly, is it possible to reduce the finish time?

In Figure 6.9b, we treat the two subgraphs as separate entities and schedule each subgraph to one processor. In this case, the latter strategy produced a schedule that has an earlier finish time than the former schedule.

It should be clear that for these systems one could compute the *optimal schedule* by simply enumerating all possible schedules (there are a finite number of them, since $|P|$ and m are both finite). However, this requires exponential time in general (that is, it is an NP complete problem); the challenge is to find the optimal schedule using an algorithm that has order polynomial time.

For the general case, there is no known optimal algorithm that does not require exponential time. However, there are interesting subcases that require polynomial time; for example, it can be shown that a polynomial time scheduling algorithm exists for each of the following cases:
(1)   The precedence graph is a tree, $m \geq 2$ and $\tau(p_i) = \tau(p_j)$ for all i and j.
(2)   The precedence graph is arbitrary, but $m = 2$ and $\tau(p_i) = \tau(p_j)$ for all i and j.
    To illustrate how the precedence model is used for these algorithms, we describe the ideas behind each.

6.2.1 Scheduling a Tree Precedence Graph

Precedence graphs that are constrained to be trees will have a single sink node and multiple source nodes. It will always be possible to consider a *path* from the unique sink node — root of the tree — to any source. Furthermore, the union of such paths will touch every node in the graph.

For this class of schedules, we assume that every process requires the same amount of execution time. Notice that one can use this equal execution time assumption as the basis for preemptive scheduling of processes with arbitrary execution times by breaking down a process into a list of smaller (sub)processes that are to be executed one after the other. The execution time for each subprocess is a time quantum. Thus, while the result may not seem to be very useful, it is the basis of an important observation about time-sliced scheduling algorithms for dual-processor systems: an optimal schedule is based on the path length if the paths all lead to a single sink node. (Graphs that have multiple sink nodes use a generalization of this observation.)

For the following algorithm, let $r \in P$ be the unique sink node (root of the tree), and let **length**(p) be the length of the path from node p to r.

Tree Scheduling Algorithm:
(1)   Wait for a processor to become idle.
(2)   Define the set, R, of all processes for which every predecessor has already completed execution, yet for which the process has not yet executed.
(3)   Define a subset R′ of R such that $p \in R'$ if **length**(p) is maximal.
(4)   Choose an arbitrary $p \in R'$ and assign it to the idle processor.
(5)   If there are no more processes to schedule, then halt; otherwise go to step 1.

Of course, since we have assumed that $\tau(p_i) = \tau(p_j)$ for all $p_i, p_j \in P$, then both processors will come idle at the same time. Arbitrarily assign processor 1 before processor 2 at each such assignment time.

Example 6.1: Scheduling a Tree Graph

Suppose we are given a computation with

$$P = \{p_i \mid 1 \le i \le 12\}$$
$$<\cdot = \{(p_1, p_7), (p_2, p_7), (p_3, p_8), (p_4, p_8), (p_5, p_{10}), (p_6, p_{10}), (p_7, p_{10}), (p_8, p_{11}),$$
$$(p_9, p_{11}), (p_{10}, p_{12}), (p_{11}, p_{12})\}$$
$$\tau = \{(p_i, 1) \mid 1 \le i \le 12\}$$

(see Figure 6.10). Our goal is to construct an optimal schedule for m = 3 processors.
Schedule first time slice:
    Processes p_1, p_2, p_3, and p_4 all have no predecessors and have **length** of 3. Processes p_5, p_6, and p_9 all have no predecessors and have **length** of 2. Assign p_3 to processor 1, p_4 to processor 2, and p_1 to processor 3.
Schedule second time slice:
    Process p_2 has no predecessors and **length**(p_2) = 3. Processes p_5, p_6, and p_9 all have no predecessors and have **length** of 2. All predecessors of p_8 have executed, and **length**(p_8) = 2. Assign p_2 to processor 1, p_5 to processor 2, and p_9 to processor 3.

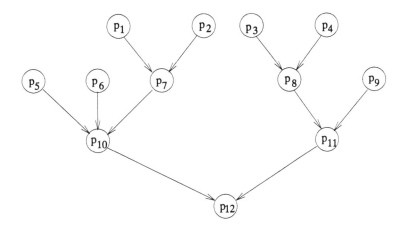

Figure 6.10 Example of Tree-Shaped Precedence Graph

Schedule third time slice:

Process p_6 has no predecessors and **length**$(p_6) = 2$. All predecessors of p_7 and p_8 have executed, and **length**$(p_7) = $ **length**$(p_8) = 2$. Assign p_8 to processor 1, p_6 to processor 2, and p_7 to processor 3.

Schedule fourth time slice:

All predecessors of p_{10} and p_{11} have executed, and **length**$(p_{10}) = $ **length**$(p_{11}) = 1$. Assign p_{10} to processor 1, p_{11} to processor 2, and leave processor 3 idle.

Schedule fifth time slice:

All predecessors of p_{12} have executed, and **length**$(p_{12}) = 0$. Assign p_{12} to processor 1, leave processors 2 and 3 idle.

Figure 6.11 is the Gantt chart for the resulting schedule.

0	1	2	3	4	5
p_3	p_2	p_8	p_{10}	p_{12}	
p_4	p_5	p_6	p_{11}		
p_1	p_9	p_7			

Figure 6.11 3-Processor Schedule for Tree-shaped Precedence Graph

6.2.2 Scheduling a Two-processor System

For this special case, assume that the system is constrained to m = 2 processors, and all execution times are equal.

This scheduling algorithm consists of two phases: In the first phase, the precedence graph is labeled with priorities as a function of the precedence. In the second phase, the processes are scheduled according to existing conditions in the schedule and to the labels on the processes.

Phase 1: Labeling the Graph

The labeling algorithm will assign a priority label, **label**$(p_i) \in \{1, 2, ..., n\}$ (n is the cardinality of P) to each process in P. The highest-numbered labels will be scheduled earlier than the lower-numbered labels (opposite from the priorities discussed earlier). The general idea is to start with the *last* process that is to be executed and give it the lowest-numbered label, then continue to its predecessors, and so on.

Definition 6.4. Denote decreasing sequences of integers by

$$N = (n_1, n_2, ..., n_t)$$

such that $n_i > n_{i+1}$. Given N and

$$N' = (n_1', n_2', ..., n_{t'}')$$

then $N < N'$ if either of the following are true:
i) For some i $(1 \le i \le t)$, $n_j = n_j'$ for all $1 \le j \le i - 1$, and $n_i < n_i'$, or
ii) $t < t'$ and $n_j = n_j'$ for $1 \le j \le t$. ‖

For example, if N = (10, 6, 2, 1) and N' = (10, 6, 3), then the first condition is true for i = 3, that is, N < N'. Similarly, N < N' for N = (4, 3, 1) and N' = (6, 2) for i = 1. If N = (8, 4) and N' = (8, 4, 2), then N < N' by the second condition in the definition.

Labeling Algorithm
(1)   Set **next_unassigned_label** = 1.
(2)   Choose an arbitrary process, p_i, such that the process has no successors; that is, (p_i, p_j) does not belong to $<\cdot$ for any p_j. Assign **label**(p_i) = **next_unassigned_label**.
(3)   Increment **next_unassigned_label**.
(4)   (Labels 1 through **next_unassigned_label**-1 have been previously assigned.) Let E be the set of all unlabeled processes for which a label has been assigned to every successor process. For every p $\in$ E, derive N(p) as the decreasing sequence of integers formed by ordering the set of labels of successors of p. At least one of these processes, p*, must satisfy N(p*) $\le$ N(p) for all p $\in$ E. Choose one such p* arbitrarily and assign **label**(p*) = **next_unassigned_label**.
(5)   If **next_unassigned_label** is equal to the cardinality of P, then halt, otherwise, go to step 3 of the algorithm.

The labeling algorithm does not produce unique labels since it is possible to choose an arbitrary process from some subset of processes as the next process to receive a label.

For example, if the precedence graph has more than one sink node, then the process that receives the first label is arbitrary among the set of sink nodes. In the fourth step of the algorithm, the sink nodes will have the "smallest" decreasing sequence of integer labels for their successor, that is, the empty list; thus, they will all have labels assigned before any process that has any successors is labeled.

Phase 2: Computing the Schedule

The second phase of the scheduling algorithm is trivial, since the analysis of the constraints is handled in the first phase.

Labeled Graph Scheduling Algorithm
(1)   Wait for a processor to become idle.
(2)   Define the set, R, of all processes for which every predecessor has already completed execution.
(3)   Choose p such that **label**(p) > **label**(p′) for all p, p′ ∈ R.
(4)   Assign p to the idle processor and go to step 1.
Again, we arbitrarily assign processor 1 before processor 2 at each such assignment time if they are both idle.

Coffman and Denning [1] provide a proof that the algorithm is optimal for m = 2 processors, following the original publication of the work in Coffman and Graham's paper [2]. We conclude our discussion of deterministic optimal schedules with an example of the application of the algorithm.

Example 6.2: Optimal Schedule for m = 2

Suppose we are given a computation with

$$P = \{p_i \mid 1 \le i \le 12\}$$
$$<\cdot = \{(p_1, p_3), (p_2, p_3), (p_3, p_6), (p_3, p_9), (p_3, p_{11}), (p_4, p_5), (p_4, p_7), (p_6, p_7),$$
$$(p_7, p_8), (p_9, p_7), (p_9, p_{10}), (p_{10}, p_8), (p_{11}, p_{10})\}$$
$$\tau = \{(p_i, 1) \mid 1 \le i \le 12\}$$

(see Figure 6.12). To compute the optimal schedule for m = 2 processors, we will first apply the labeling algorithm to the graph:

next_unassigned_label = 1
  Nodes p_5, p_8, and p_{12} are all sink nodes. Arbitrarily assign **label**(p_8) = 1.

next_unassigned_label = 2
  Now p_5 and p_{12} have no successors, and p_7 and p_{10} both have all of their successors (process p_8) labeled. So,

$$N(p_5) = N(p_{12}) = ()$$
$$N(p_7) = N(p_{10}) = (1)$$

  Assign **label**(p_5) = 2.

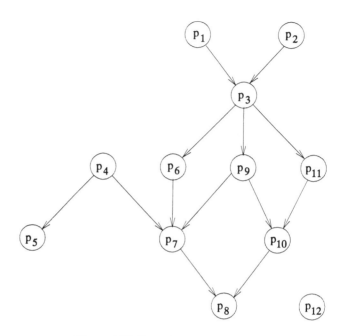

Figure 6.12 Example Precedence Graph

next_unassigned_label = 3

Now p_{12} has no successors, and p_7 and p_{10} both have $\{p_8\}$ labeled. So

$$N(p_{12}) = ()$$
$$N(p_7) = N(p_{10}) = (1)$$

Assign **label**(p_{12}) = 3.

next_unassigned_label = 4

p_7 and p_{10} both have $\{p_8\}$ labeled. So

$$N(p_7) = N(p_{10}) = (1)$$

Assign **label**(p_7) = 4.

next_unassigned_label = 5

Process p_{10} has $\{p_8\}$ labeled. Also, the successors of p_4 ($\{p_5, p_7\}$) and p_6 ($\{p_7\}$) are now labeled. So

$$N(p_4) = (4, 2)$$
$$N(p_6) = (4)$$

$$N(p_{10}) = (1)$$

Since $N(p_{10})$ is the smallest, assign **label**$(p_{10}) = 5$.

next_unassigned_label = 6

The successors of p_4 ($\{p_5, p_7\}$), p_6 ($\{p_7\}$), p_9 ($\{p_7, p_{10}\}$), and p_{11} ($\{p_{10}\}$) are now labeled. So

$$N(p_4) = (4, 2)$$
$$N(p_6) = (4)$$
$$N(p_9) = (5, 4)$$
$$N(p_{11}) = (5)$$

Since $N(p_6)$ is the smallest, assign **label**$(p_6) = 6$.

next_unassigned_label = 7

The successors of p_4 ($\{p_5, p_7\}$), p_9 ($\{p_7, p_{10}\}$), and p_{11} ($\{p_{10}\}$) are now labeled. So

$$N(p_4) = (4, 2)$$
$$N(p_9) = (5, 4)$$
$$N(p_{11}) = (5)$$

Since $N(p_4)$ is the smallest, assign **label**$(p_4) = 7$.

next_unassigned_label = 8

The successors of p_9 ($\{p_7, p_{10}\}$), and p_{11} ($\{p_{10}\}$) are now labeled. So

$$N(p_9) = (5, 4)$$
$$N(p_{11}) = (5)$$

Since $N(p_{11})$ is the smallest, assign **label**$(p_{11}) = 8$.

next_unassigned_label = 9

The successors of p_9 ($\{p_7, p_{10}\}$) are now labeled. So

$$N(p_9) = (5, 4)$$

Assign **label**$(p_9) = 9$.

next_unassigned_label = 10

The successors of p_3 ($\{p_6, p_9, p_{11}\}$) are now labeled. So

$$N(p_3) = (9, 8, 6)$$

Assign **label**$(p_3) = 10$.

next_unassigned_label = 11

The successor of p_1 and p_2 ($\{p_3\}$) is now labeled. So

$$N(p_1) = N(p_2) = (10)$$

Assign **label**(p_1) = 11.

next_unassigned_label = 12

The successor of p_2 ($\{p_3\}$) is now labeled. So

$$N(p_2) = (10)$$

Assign **label**(p_2) = 12.

Every node in the graph is now labeled (see Figure 6.13).

The scheduling algorithm will now produce the Gantt chart shown in Figure 6.14.

6.3 FURTHER READING

Scheduling has been studied heavily for several decades. The most inclusive treatment of determinate scheduling for multiple processors appears in the book by Conway, Maxwell, and Miller [3].

Coffman and Graham originally describe the optimal schedule for two-processor systems in [2] using precedence graphs (see Chapter 6).

REFERENCES

1.   E. G. Coffman and P. J. Denning, *Operating Systems Theory*, Prentice Hall, Inc., Englewood Cliffs, NJ, 1973.

2.   E. G. Coffman and R. L. Graham, "Optimal Scheduling for Two-Processor Systems," *Acta Informatica 1*, 3 (1972), 200-213.

3.   R. W. Conway, W. L. Maxwell, and L. W. Miller, *Theory of Scheduling*, Addison-Wesley Publishing Co., Reading, MA, 1967.

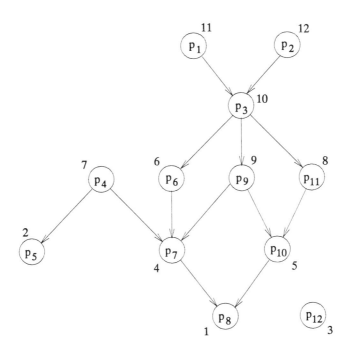

Figure 6.14 Labeled Precedence Graph

0	1	2	3	4	5	6
P_2	P_3	P_9	P_6	P_7	P_5	
P_1	P_4	P_{11}	P_{10}	P_{12}	P_8	

Figure 6.14 The Optimal Schedule

EXERCISES

For the first four questions,
assume that you have the following jobs to execute with one processor:

Job	Burst Time	Priority
1	8	2
2	2	4
3	1	3
4	2	4
5	5	1

The jobs are assumed to arrive in the order 1, 2, 3, 4, 5.

(1)   Suppose that a system uses first-come-first-served scheduling.
(a) Give a Gantt chart illustrating the execution of these jobs.
(b) What is the turnaround time for job 3?
(c) What is the average wait time for the jobs?

(2)   Suppose that a system uses shortest job next scheduling.
(a) Give a Gantt chart illustrating the execution of these jobs.
(b) What is the turnaround time for job 4?
(c) What is the average wait time for the jobs?

(3)   Suppose that a system uses round robin scheduling with a quantum of 2.
(a) Give a Gantt chart illustrating the execution of these jobs. (b) What is the turnaround time for job 3 under round robin scheduling with time quantum of 2?
(c) What is the average wait time for the jobs?

(4)   Suppose that a system uses priority scheduling, where a small integer means a high priority.

(a) Give a Gantt chart illustrating the execution of these jobs.

(b) What is the turnaround time for job 2 under priority scheduling?

(c) What is the average wait time for the jobs?

(5)   What is the effect of increasing the time quantum to an arbitrarily large number for round robin scheduling?

(6)   Given the computation shown in Figure 6.15, construct two schedules for m = 3 processors that illustrate that it is sometimes beneficial *to introduce idle time* into a nonpreemptive schedule.

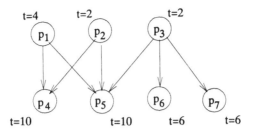

Figure 6.15 Precedence Graph

(7) Let **level**(p) be the distance of node p from the closest sink node in a precedence graph [compare with **length**(p) for tree-shaped precedence graphs]. Using the labeling algorithm described in this chapter, prove that **level**(p_i) > **level**(p_j) implies that **label**(p_i) > **label**(p_j).

7

MEMORY MANAGEMENT

7.1 PRIMARY MEMORY MANAGEMENT

General-purpose memory is used to store programs and data, the former notion being one of the elements that distinguishes computers from calculators. The *primary memory* is accessed directly by the CPU — the CU during the fetch cycle and the ALU during the execute cycle. The amount of primary memory that is configured into the machine has an enormous effect on the size of the programs that can be executed and on the amount of data that can be operated on at any given time.

The basic unit of memory in contemporary machines is the *byte*, or 8 contiguous bits of information. The primary memory is organized as some contiguous collection of bytes. The data transfer path between the memory and the CPU is usually some integral number of bytes, instructions are an integral number of bytes, and the data operands in the ALU are an integral number of bytes. For these reasons, primary memories are usually constructed so that groups of bytes can be retrieved or stored in the primary memory with a single operation; such a group is called a *word* of the memory. For binary machines, the integral number of bytes in a word is a power of 2, for example, 2, 4, or perhaps 8 (there are many counterexamples in computers of the 1960s and 1970s).

Notice that a binary byte address in a machine with $2^2 = 4$ bytes per word can be shifted right 2 bits to obtain the word address, provided that words are made up from contiguous groups of bytes (starting at address 0).

Until the mid 1980s, microprocessor CPUs were typically designed to support processes with 16-bit addresses. Thus, a process in such a hardware environment has a 16-bit *address space*. Prior to 1975, memory was relatively expensive; even very expensive computers might have only 128 K bytes of memory to be shared among all the processes sharing the CPU. Innovation was required to support more than two processes in such an environment. Part of the problem is to manage the memory sharing, and the other part is to provide some mechanism by which the address space allocated to a process can be made to appear to be larger than the primary memory space.

However, memory costs were in steep decline. By 1985, even inexpensive personal computers could be configured with more than 128 K bytes (in single-process operating system machines!). However, a process could only generate a 16-bit address; thus, it could only address 64 K words in the primary memory. Thus the relationship between the address space and the primary memory size is inverted from the situation in 1975.

The memory management problem for the 1970s was to make the primary memory appear to be larger than it really was, while the memory management problem for the 1980s, at least for inexpensive machines, was to find ways for a process to be able to access primary memories that were larger than the address space. Strangely, the same general techniques can be used to solve both problems.

In this chapter, we discuss the various aspects of memory management, ranging from mechanisms used in memory management to policies for managing contemporary virtual memories.

7.1.1 The Programmer's View of the Memory

A programmer views a system in terms of the programming language interface (with its attendant run-time system). In compiled-program environments, the source program is translated (at *compile time*), producing a relocatable object module. A collection of such modules can be combined with a linkage editor (at *link time*) to produce a load module; the load module is not typically ready to run, since it is constructed as if it were to be loaded and executed at memory location zero. The loader modifies addresses in the load module (at *load time*) to produce an executable image.

Consider a static variable in a source program: The compiler will generate code to allocate storage for the variable and then use the address of the allocated storage wherever the code references the variable. We say that the symbolic variable name is *bound* to a memory location at compile time.

Now consider a procedure entry point. The compiler may not be able to determine the address for the entry point since the procedure may be separately compiled (for example, it is a library routine or it is located in a distinct file). That is, the target address is unknown at compile time, so it cannot be bound at compile time. The compiler will annotate each reference to the external address so that the linkage editor can place the correct address in the code, that is, bind the name to an address, when it combines the relocatable object modules at link time.

The loader operates on load modules in which all symbolic addresses have been bound to memory addresses that lie within the load module or at some *absolute address* in the primary memory. Before the program can be executed, it must be loaded into the primary memory. At load time, the absolute addresses that appear in the load module remain unchanged, while all other addresses are *relocated* to reflect the location at which the load module is placed in the primary memory.

For example, suppose that we have a code segment such as that shown in Figure 7.1. The variable named **global** will have space allocated in the relocatable object module for the procedure, but the procedure named **put_record** is located in another relocatable object module.

```
static int global;
 ...
procedure a(arg)
int arg;
{
        ...
        global = 7;
        ...
        put_record(..., global, ...);
        ...
}
```

Figure 7.1 A Source Program

The compiler will generate a relocatable object module similar to that shown in Figure 7.2. The compiler reserves space for **global** at memory location 0036, recording the value in its symbol table. The assignment statement results in a reference to **global**, which is bound to 0036 by the compiler. However, the compiler does not have enough information to bind **put_record**, so it annotates the address field for the linkage editor to complete.

The linkage editor will combine the relocatable object module shown in Figure 7.2 with others, including one that contains the **put_record** procedure, producing a load

0000	...	
...		
0036	[space for "global"]	
...		
0220	load	=7, R1
0224	store	R1, 0036
...		
0366	push	0036
...		
0370	call	'put_record'
...		

Figure 7.2 The Relocatable Object Module

module of the form shown in Figure 7.3. Notice that all addresses have been altered to reflect a new base address for the load module (as if it were loaded at memory location 0000).

If the load module were to be placed in primary memory starting at location 4000, then the addresses for **global** and **put_record** references would be adjusted by the loader to reflect the relocation, for example, **global** would be loaded at primary memory location 1036 + 4000 = 5036.

7.1.2 Dynamic Binding

The programmer's view represents one in which variables are *statically bound* to primary memory locations at compile, link, and load time, but never at run time. If it were possible to defer the binding until run time, then the process could economize its use of primary memory. That is, the program would not cause primary memory to be allocated unless the particular execution of the program required it.

Dynamic Memory Allocation

An extension to this view is *dynamic memory allocation*, supported by many operating systems. In this case, a program is provided with facilities (for example, a system call) to request and free variable memory at run time. The programming language must include some mechanism for supporting the dynamic memory allocation mechanism, such as

0000	[Other modules]	
...		
1036	[space for "global"]	
...		
1220	load	=7, R1
1224	store	R1, 1036
...		
1366	push	1036
...		
1370	call	2334
...		
2334	[put_record entry point]	
...		

Figure 7.3 The Load Module

pointers to coerce a type onto blocks of memory allocated at run time. That is, the programmer declares a variable of type "pointer to a specific data structure" in the program. At run time, the process requests a specified amount of memory — enough to hold an instance of the specific data structure. The memory allocator assigns the memory and returns a pointer to it; the pointer is assigned to the pointer variable. The effect is that the programmer has extended his conceptual model of the primary memory such that he is able to dynamically bind variables to primary memory locations (at run time).

Overlay Loaders

Overlays can also be used to accomplish a form of dynamic binding. An overlay is a segment of object code that can be dynamically loaded upon an explicit command from the process. Most programs are written with large portions of the code that are used in different phases of execution. For example, certain code may only be used when an error is detected, but is not ordinarily used. Similarly, a two-pass compiler will not use any of the pass 2 code while it is executing pass 1.

Such observations, with the shortage of primary memory in the 1960s and 1970s, encouraged programmers to partition their load module such that parts of the code that made up different phases of the computation would be grouped in different submodules. Thus, a compiler might be written with one submodule to oversee the general compilation process, another submodule to implement pass 1, one for pass 2, and one for error recovery. In any short interval of time, the general submodule and one of the other three need to be loaded in the primary memory, while the other two are stored in *secondary memory* until they are needed. The general submodule is responsible for detecting phase changes in the execution and for causing the primary memory that contains a submodule that is no longer needed to be overwritten ("overlayed") by a submodule that is currently required.

The effect, once again, is that a load submodule is dynamically bound to primary memory locations at run time.

7.1.3 Automatic Dynamic Binding

It is possible for some of the dynamic binding strategies be detected by the run-time system and to be invoked without any explicit action on the part of the programmer. Such techniques typically require action on the part of the operating system and even the hardware.

Dynamic Relocation

The loader relocates a load module whenever it produces an executable image. This is accomplished by altering all relative addresses in the load module, thus, it is typically a time-intensive task for large programs.

Once the executable image has been produced, it can be stored on secondary memory (the file system) if it is not to be executed imminently. However, when the executable image is actually placed in the primary memory, it must be loaded in a precise location since all the addresses have been adjusted under that assumption.

There are two alternatives to this problem: The program can be kept in load module form on the secondary memory, or the hardware can be modified to greatly simplify relocation. The first solution is not scalable, since the time to relocate a program grows faster than linearly with the size of the program.

Suppose that the CPU-memory interface included a *relocation register*, located as shown in Figure 7.4. The relocation register is part of the process's state, although it cannot be set by an ordinary machine instruction. Each address emitted from the CPU during the fetch or execute cycle has the current content of the relocation register added to it before it is loaded into the primary memory's address register. The effect is that executable images can be produced as if they were loaded at memory location zero, but may be loaded at any location and executed properly by setting the relocation register to the address of the first location loaded in the primary memory.

This *hardware dynamic relocation* is very commonly used in contemporary processors, independently of any additional memory management strategies. It enables the operating system to have tremendous freedom concerning the location at which executable images are loaded in a primary memory, particularly when the primary memory is shared among several different processes.

Suppose that the operating system were to support four-way multiprogramming. The scheduler assumes that each process is loaded whenever it allocates the CPU to a process; with dynamic relocation facilities, it is easy to allocate the primary memory in variable-sized blocks, depending on the needs of the processes competing for the CPU. In Figure 7.5 we illustrate a primary memory snapshot in which the four processes have been allocated various parts of the primary memory. When process i is allocated the CPU, the relocation register is loaded with the pointer into process i's memory partition. Notice that this scheme allows the operating system to have its own memory partition.

Contemporary language systems are designed to separate temporary data, static data, and code into distinct submodules (within a relocatable object module). For example, C programs are compiled into a text segment (containing the code), a stack segment (containing temporary variables), and a data segment (containing static variables). To support such language models, the CPU is designed with at least three relocation registers to manage the code, stack, and data segments as separate relocatable modules. That is,

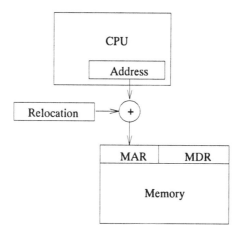

Figure 7.4 Hardware Address Relocation

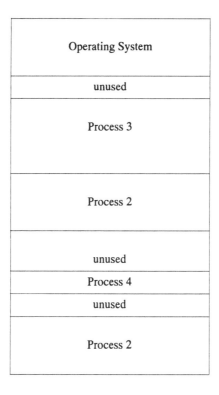

Figure 7.5 Multiprogramming Memory Support

the CPU contains a code segment relocation register, a stack segment relocation register, a data segment relocation register (and frequently an "extra" segment register); see Figure 7.6. The code segment register relocates all addresses during the fetch cycle, the stack segment register relocates addresses for stack instruction execution, and the data segment register relocates all other addresses during the execute cycle. The extra segment register is used explicitly in instruction execution, that is, the addressing mode in an instruction provides for the use of the extra segment register as a base register.

This simple mechanism is widely used in contemporary microprocessors as a first attack on the problem of enlarging a process's address space with a 16-bit address limitation, for example, see the Intel 80x86 microprocessor family which has an address formation architecture quite similar to that shown in Figure 7.6. With the four segments, each can have a 16-bit address space, so the process can now address $4 \times 64 \text{ K} = 256 \text{ K}$ locations in the primary memory. The solution requires that the compiler and the hardware be designed to work with one another in order to be successful.

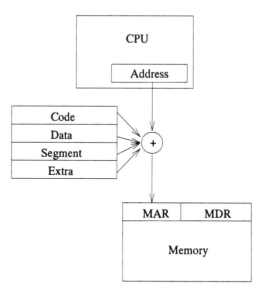

Figure 7.6 Multiple Segment Relocation Registers

Protection

The relocation register has proven to be a fundamental contribution to computer systems since it enables dynamic memory sharing. Once such a mechanism has been incorporated into the hardware, it is easy to make small additions that will substantially increase the ability of the system to support memory protection.

Suppose that each relocation register had a companion *limit register*. The limit register is loaded with the length of the memory segment addressed by the relocation register (the length is an unsigned integer). Whenever the CPU sends an address to the primary memory, the relocation register is added to the address at the same time as it is compared with the contents of the limit register; see Figure 7.7.

If the address is less than the value in the limit register, then the address refers to a location that is within the memory segment; if it is larger than the limit register value, then it is a reference to a part of the primary memory that is not allocated to the process currently using the CPU. An out-of-bounds reference will generate a program error, allowing the operating system to take diagnostic action, while an in-bounds reference behaves as before.

7.1.4 Medium-term Scheduling

Dynamic relocation mechanisms can be used by the operating system to implement memory usage policies, that is, a *medium-term scheduling* policy (see Chapter 1): processes are being scheduled into the primary memory; once a process has been allocated primary memory space, it can compete for the CPU under the short-term scheduling policy.

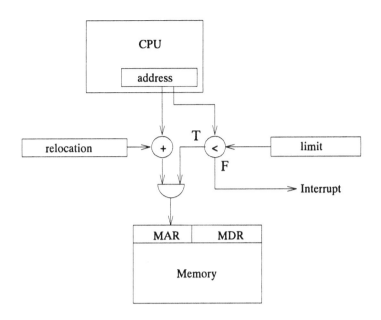

Figure 7.7 Bound Checking with a Limit Register

Multiprogramming operating systems require that some form of medium-term scheduling exist. Traditionally, this follows from the scarcity of primary memory in a machine; in contemporary machines that support multiprogramming, it is still necessary to multiplex the memory across processes.

Swapping

A *swapping* operating system multiplexes process images back and forth between the primary and secondary memories.† The loader produces an execution image and places it in the secondary memory. When the corresponding process is to be executed, the loaded process's image is written to the secondary memory, and the new process's execution image is loaded into the primary memory; this is called *context switching*. (The old image must be written back to the secondary memory since it contains data that represent the current state of the old process when it is swapped out of the primary memory.)

Swapping has considerable overhead associated with it. Before a swapped-out process can run, two process's images must be transferred (to and from) the secondary storage. The secondary storage is implemented on a rotating device such as a disk (called "the swapping device" or the "backing store"). Because of the massive device

---

† Swapping can be implemented on systems that do not incorporate hardware relocation, although typically only one process can be loaded in the primary memory at a time (but also see the discussion of fixed-sized partitions).

I/O, the speed of the device is crucial to the overall performance of the system. In a swapping system, the context switching time tends to dominate decisions related to short-term scheduling, such as the time quantum.

Fixed Partition Memory

Suppose that the primary memory were divided into N fixed size partitions (or region), where partition i, R_i, has N_i units of memory. Typically $N_i \neq N_j$; this allows small programs to be loaded into small partitions and large programs in large partitions.

Medium-term scheduling in a fixed partition system requires that a process's memory needs to correlate with a memory partition size. For example, if a process requires n_k units of memory, then it can be loaded into any R_i such that $N_i > n_k$; upon allocation of R_i to the process, $N_i - n_k$ units of the primary memory are unusable during the time that the process is loaded. This is one form of *internal fragmentation*.

Suppose that each memory partition had its own queue of processes competing for the partition, where every member of the queue meets the size criteria. Then, a process is placed in the queue for partition i, where $\min_i N_i > n_k$. The medium-term scheduler chooses processes from the corresponding queue whenever the partition is free. This policy is called the *best-fit-only* policy.

Alternatively, the operating system may keep a single queue of all processes. If the high priority process is given the first partition that is large enough to meet the process's memory requirements, then the policy is called the *best-available-fit* policy.

Fixed partition primary memory can eliminate the need for dynamic relocation hardware. If a process is intended to run in a particular partition (even if it is swapped out and then reloaded into the same partition), then it can be statically relocated by the loader. Notice that swapping can be used in conjunction with fixed partition mechanisms.

Example 7.1: OS/360 MFT

The IBM System/360 OS/360 MFT incorporates the multiple fixed partition strategy. The memory is divided into N fixed-size regions, R_1, R_2, ..., R_N determined at the time that the operating system is configured. The regions will likely, though not necessarily, differ in size. Jobs are scheduled into the smallest R_i that will satisfy the needs of the job.

Variable Partition Memory

Fixed-size partitions introduce internal fragmentation due to the mismatches between process memory needs and partition sizes. The operating system can be designed to manage memory partitions with variable size so that when a process is allocated a block of memory there will be no internal fragmentation. (As a technical detail, the partition allocator will probably allocate only on multiword boundaries, for example, 100 words; if a process requests an amount of memory that is not a multiple of that minimum size, then there will be small amounts of internal fragmentation.)

Free memory space management now becomes considerably more complex than is the case with fixed partition memory allocation. The memory manager must keep a record of the usage of each allocatable block of memory, just as a file manager maintains for free disk blocks (see Chapter 9). For primary memory allocation, it is possible to keep the list in the free memory itself! This is done by using the first few words of each unallocated block as a set of pointers to the next free block and to describe the size of the block. Again, best-fit, first-fit, and other free list policies can be implemented as required (see [8]).

The variable-sized partition environment creates the possibility for a process to dynamically request additional memory during execution; while the process would have to be fortunate for there to be a hole immediately following its allocated space, a new hole can be found that is large enough to satisfy the existing and new memory needs. However, the process's memory image will have to be moved to the new hole.

Whether or not dynamic memory allocation is supported in the policy, it will lead to *external fragmentation*, since over time, memory requests will tend to be satisfied in holes that are slightly larger than the memory request, leaving small fragments that are unusable by another process. If the system gets to a state in which only the smallest memory requests can be satisfied even when there is sufficient memory available (but in fragments), then the operating system may have to *compact* the memory by moving all loaded processes so that they are contiguous in the memory, creating one large free block. Clearly, compaction and dynamic memory allocation are most easily implemented in systems with dynamic relocation hardware.

Example 7.2: OS/360 MVT

OS/360 MVT dynamically determines the sizes of the regions, depending on the needs of the jobs in the job queue. In this case, a job is selected from the job queue and allocated region R_j; the size of the region is determined by the needs of the job. Thus, a region memory allocator dynamically determines the size of the region at schedule time.

7.1.5 Shared Memory Multiprocessors

Today a number of shared memory multiprocessors are available, most using some relatively standard operating system, for example, some extension of UNIX. The hardware architecture of such machines was discussed in Chapter 1; the machine's bus supports a shared memory module and multiple CPUs. Each CPU can read or write any memory location.

The programmer's view of such systems typically treats shared regions of the memory in a special manner. The typical compile/link/load model requires that shared memory addresses be statically bound, which suggests difficulty in compiling two programs separately when they intend to use the same shared memory locations. As a result, shared memory is generally allocated to a process at run-time.

Example 7.3: Sequent DYNIX Shared Memory

DYNIX attempts to minimize the impact on the C/UNIX programmer when he uses shared memory. Uniprocessor UNIX uses the **malloc** system call to dynamically allocate memory. DYNIX provides a **shmalloc** system call to allocate memory blocks to a process from a shared pool.

When a process calls **shmalloc**, it is returned an ordinary memory address ("pointer to a block of bytes") to a previously unallocated block of memory. This block can be shared among processes that have the pointer; this is typically accomplished by having a parent process obtain the shared memory, and then by spawning children that will use the previously allocated shared memory.

Figure 7.8 illustrates a typical code schema for using shared memory in DYNIX. Notice that the two child processes can read and write the shared memory allocated to the parent, since they each inherited their own copy of a pointer ("shared_block") to the shared memory block. But notice that the character pointer is *not* shared, each process having a private copy pointing to the shared memory.

```
char *shared_block;
 ...
main(...)
{
        char *shmalloc();
        int block_length;

        shared_block = shmalloc(block_length);
        ...
        if(fork() == 0)
        { /* first child process */
        /* Sharing with the second child process */
                ... = f(shared_block);
        };
        ...
        if(fork() == 0)
        { /* second child process */
        /* Sharing with the first child process */
                ... = f(shared_block);
        };
        wait(...);
        wait(...);
        ...
}
```

Figure 7.8 Using Sequent Shared Memory

7.2 VIRTUAL MEMORY

Virtual memory is a form of automatic overlaying. Recall that an overlay is part of a program's address space, and that an overlay system allows the programmer to manually load selected parts of the program, depending on the phase that the process is in when it executes the program. In particular, an overlay system provides for a process's full memory image to exist in secondary storage, with only part of the image being loaded in the primary memory at any given time.

Virtual memory systems automated the overlay idea by determining the part of the primary memory that is to be loaded at any given time and by handling the transfers back and forth between primary and secondary memory without manual intervention. The abstraction presented to the programmer is that he has a very large address space in which to write his programs, even though only part of the address space will be loaded in the primary memory at any given time.

Name-Location Space Mapping

In early memory management systems, there was no substantive distinction between the address space that the programmer used for building the execution image and the address space in which the program was executed. In virtual memory systems, these two address spaces are distinguished by the logical address space used to create the program and the physical address space used for execution. A virtual memory system maps elements of the logical address space into elements of the physical space at run time.

> **Definition 7.1.** A process's *name space* is an ordered set of memory locations addressable by the corresponding program execution image. An address in the name space is called a *virtual address*.
>
>   A process's *location space* is a set of physical memory locations in the primary memory. An address in the location space is called a *physical address*. ‖

For a program to be executable in primary memory — the location space — the operating system must be able to map each virtual address in the program image into a corresponding physical address, depending on which part of the name space is loaded into the location space at any given time.

> **Definition 7.2.** The *name-location map* (or *address translation*), ψ_t, is a partial map of a programs name space to a location space at time t.
>
> $$\psi_t: \text{name space} \rightarrow \text{location space} \bigcup \{\Omega\}$$
>
> where t is a nonnegative integer *virtual time* for the process [$t \in T_v(p)$ for process p], and Ω is a distinguished symbol referring to a null location. ‖

The virtual memory implements a time-varying map from the name space to the location space. When an element, i, of the name space is loaded, $\psi_t(i)$ is defined to be the location space element containing the value associated with address i. If i is not loaded in the primary memory, then $\psi_t(i) = \Omega$. If $\psi_t(i) = \Omega$ at virtual time t, and the process references location i, then the virtual memory system will interrupt the execution of the process, load the corresponding information from secondary memory into some physical location, j, redefine $\psi_t(i) = j$, and then let the program continue execution. Notice that the element from the name space that was determined to be missing from the location space at time t required that the element be loaded, the map be redefined, *and the instruction be reexecuted at virtual time t.* That is, virtual memory ordinarily requires that the CPU be able to back out of an instruction execution and execute the instruction again later after the name-location map has been defined.

Ordinarily, |name space| > |location space|, that is, there are more virtual than physical addresses. However, recall that some systems present a relatively small set of primary memory addresses to the program compared to the amount of physical memory configured into the machine; these systems provide a very simple form of mapping — the segment registers. Therefore, in these cases, we actually have |location space| > |name space|. The address translation map varies with time, depending on the setting of the segment relocation registers.

Segmentation and Paging

There are two general approaches to implementing virtual memory: segmentation and paging. Each approach is briefly described here and then in considerably more detail in the remainder of the chapter.

Segmentation employs a strategy in which the program parts that will be loaded or unloaded are defined by the programmer as *segments*, exactly like those discussed in Section 6.1.3. That is, the programmer defines a number of segments, either implicitly or explicitly, and then references information within a segment with a two-component address (segment #, offset); see Figure 7.9. The segment # identifies the segment, and the offset is a linear offset from the beginning of the segment. The virtual memory system will transfer whole segments back and forth between the primary and secondary memories, that is, a segment is the unit of loading in this technique.

The C compiler implicitly generates the three segments mentioned earlier and then generates code to reference those segments as appropriate. The particular mechanism used to enforce the C segment policy depends on the nature of the target machine. If the target machine incorporates the segment relocation registers, then the C compiler algorithms are trivial.

Paging uses single-component addresses, like those used to address cells within any particular segment. Since the name space is flat, that is, a contiguous set of nonnegative integers, the programmer has no specific mechanism for telling the virtual memory system about logical units of the name space (as is the case in segmentation). Therefore, the virtual memory system is responsible for defining the units of name space (*pages*) that will be moved back and forth between the primary and secondary memories. The programmer need not be aware of the units of virtual address space that are loaded into or unloaded from the physical memory; in fact, the size of the units is transparent to the process.

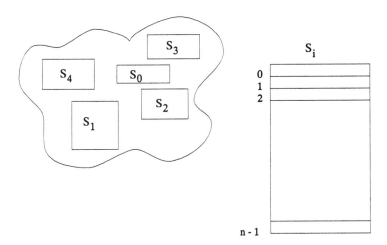

Figure 7.9 Segment Name Space Organization

Segmentation provides more programmer control of the units of transfer in the memory system than does paging. This implies that a segmentation system requires more effort to use than does a paging system (unless there are a small number of segments generated by the compiler, for instance). Segments can be more efficient than paging, since the programmer can specify the set of name space locations that will be used at about the same time in the execution, for example, "pass 2 of the compiler." However, the virtual memory system will have more difficulty placing segments in the primary memory, since they are of variable size; segmented virtual memory systems have all the same external fragmentation problems that variable-sized memory partition systems have.

7.3 SEGMENTATION

7.3.1 Address Translation

Since address translation is the fundamental concept in virtual memory, we begin looking at segmentation by considering the nature of the mapping mechanism. The name space is a two-component space, so the name-location map has the form

$$\psi_t: \text{segment space} \times \text{offset space} \rightarrow \text{primary memory space} \bigcup \{\Omega\}$$

and any individual name space reference has the form

$$\psi_t(i, j) = k$$

where i is a segment name, j is an offset within the segment, and k is the primary memory location where the information is loaded (or is Ω if the information is not loaded).

Segment names may be symbolic names to be bound at run time; or they may be simple names such as nonnegative integers. In our previous discussion, we have assumed the simple case; however, segmentation systems often allow for run-time binding of the segment name. This introduces another level of translation,

$$\sigma: \text{segment names} \rightarrow \text{segment numbers}$$

Thus, the name-location map has the refined form

$$\psi_t(\sigma(\text{name}_i), j) = k$$

where name_i is a symbolic name in the program. The name will be bound to a segment number at run time (as opposed to compile, link, or load time).

7.3.2 Implementing the Address Translation Mechanism

Figure 7.10 represents a generic implementation of the address translation facility. The operating system maintains a *segment table* for each process (the segment table is ordinarily a segment itself). The segment table can be implemented in the primary memory (as a segment that will not be removed from the primary memory). The table is a set of entries, each called a *segment descriptor*, with fields representing the *base*, *limit*, and *security* for the segment. The base field is analogous to the contents of a segment relocation register, the limit field is the length of the segment, and the security field is used to describe allowable forms of access to the segment (such as "read access" and "execute access"; see Chapter 8).

When the process accesses memory, the name-location map translates the segment name into a segment number, that is, the operating system implements some specific form of σ. The result, $\sigma(\text{seg\_name})$ is an offset into the segment table, addressing a segment descriptor in the segment table. The base field points to a primary memory location where the segment is loaded, and the offset is added to the base to obtain the address of the specific primary memory location. Just as in Figure 7.7, the segment base and limit values are used to relocate and bound check the reference at run time.

The address translation mechanism is straight forward, except for the constraint that it must be used for *each* reference to memory. A simple-minded implementation could result in drastic overhead costs. Contemporary segmentation systems must be designed so that the operating system, compilers, and hardware work together to implement a segmentation policy.

Suppose that the hardware incorporates additional registers, loaded when a process is loaded onto the CPU (see Figure 7.11). The *segment table register* (STR) points to the location of the segment table, while a *code base register* (CBR) contains an offset into the STR to index a segment descriptor for the procedure currently being executed. Similarly, a *data base register* (DBR) and a *stack base register* (SBR) address segment descriptors for static data and a stack, respectively. The σ map is evaluated and the result is stored in the appropriate base register. As long as the process references the same code, data, and stack segments for some period of (virtual) time, then the CBR, DBR, and SBR will not change. If the hardware also incorporates dynamic relocation hardware for the code, data, and stack registers, that is, base and limit registers, then those registers can be loaded by the hardware each time the corresponding base register is changed.

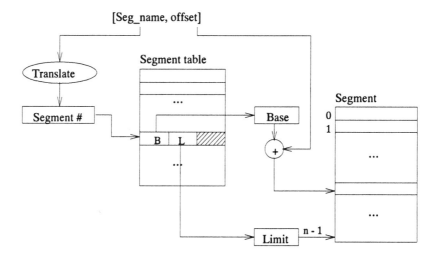

Figure 7.10 Segment Mapping Mechanism

Now, the three segment base-limit pair registers can be used by the instruction set as described in Section 6.1.3. Notice that the extreme memory access time overhead is now limited to cases where the process changes the context — code, data, or stack segment — in which it is executing.

Early segmentation hardware used this approach, although it did not typically include the data and stack registers. For example, the GE 645 system used a single *procedure base register* to relocate instruction fetch references and explicit base registers for all execute references.

The programming language and compiler must be designed to make effective use of the segmentation hardware. The language must provide some mechanism by which the programmer can specify symbolic segment names. In assembly language programs this is typically accomplished by a pseudo operation, for example, *using*. In Figure 7.12, the assembler will initially generate code for **segment_A** into its own segment; the reference to **lab_1** will be a simple call instruction within the current segment, that is, the CBR will not change when the instruction is executed. However, the call to **[segment_C, lab_20]** will assemble to instructions that load the CBR with a value determined by the segment name, in addition to the call instruction. The CBR load operand will be an external, symbolic reference for **segment_C**, which will be bound by σ at run time. The call instruction will follow the CBR load instruction and will be of the same form as the previous call, with an operand of **lab_20**. (For our discussion, we assume that the value of **lab_20** is resolved before run time; this label can also be bound at run time if necessary.)

The **using** pseudo operation will cause the assembler, link editor, and loader to generate separate execution images for **segment_B** and **segment_C**. It will be the task of the operating system to dynamically link the segments at run time.

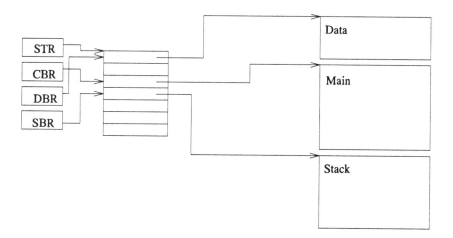

Figure 7.11 Segmentation Address Translation Implementation

```
                    using    segment_A
                    ...
                    call     lab_1
                    ...
                    call     [segment_C, lab_20]
                    ...
          lab_1:    ...
                    ...
                    using    segment_B
                    ...
                    using    segment_C
                    ...
          lab_20:   ...
                    ...
```

Figure 7.12 Intersegment References

When **segment_A** is to be executed, it is loaded through a standard operating system command. When the process encounters the symbolic segment reference to
segment_C, it will be necessary to bind the symbolic address to one in the location space
(primary memory). The CBR load instruction must cause a trap to the operating system,
that is, the normal instruction sequence will be interrupted and control will be given to
the operating system just as if an interrupt had occurred. The operating system will
obtain the symbolic reference and use it to search the file system for the executable
image of **segment_C**. Once found, it is loaded into the primary memory, and an entry is
made in the segment table to record the fact that **segment_C** is now present. Now the
CBR load instruction is modified (possibly using indirect links to avoid actual
modifications to code) to point to the newly created segment descriptor. Finally, the
CBR is loaded with the segment descriptor offset and the instruction is restarted. On the
second execution, the CBR load will encounter a segment descriptor offset, which will be
loaded into the CBR, enabling the remainder of the address translation to occur as if
segment_C had been present on the first execution of the instruction.

7.3.3 Segment Sharing

Since segments are defined by the logical requirements of the programmer, it is natural
for segments to be shared among processes. For example, suppose that a programmer
designed a multiple-process implementation where each process incorporated a standard
set of error recovery actions. The error recovery code could be placed in a single segment, and then either process could use the segment as required.

The mechanism described above will have to be enhanced to support general segment sharing. For example, when the operating system loads a new segment, it may have
to unload another segment; if the operating system chose to unload a shared segment in
behalf of process A while process B was actively using it, then the segment would be
reloaded into the primary memory as soon as process B resumed execution.

Our original implementation has other problems associated with sharing. We used the CBR as an offset into the process's segment table in order to address the appropriate code segment. Furthermore, the system bound the segment name to that entry at run time, modifying the code when it loaded the segment. This will cause a conflict among the two processes if we allow for run time segment binding. One alternative is to bind segment names to segment numbers prior to run time and then ensure that the loader binds the references prior to execution. This will result in a situation similar to the one shown in Figure 7.13.

Code in the shared segment references other segments by segment number, referring to a specific offset in the segment table. For example, the **load** [1,i] instruction will cause either process to load data from the ith location in the segment loaded at segment table entry 1. To ensure correct operation, it is necessary that the data segments be loaded in the proper place in the segment table.

This solution, called the *uniform address approach*, is difficult to manage, since it causes the system to require inordinate amounts of information about a program at link time. This can be accomplished through a registry of shared segments, but is error prone and tedious.

Unless the registry is carefully managed, the uniform address solution may lead to conflicts in which process A uses shared segments X and Y, and process B uses shared segments Y and Z. Each of X, Y, and Z has requirements about positions in the segment table. It is necessary for process A to "reserve" all segment indexes used in X, Y, and Z

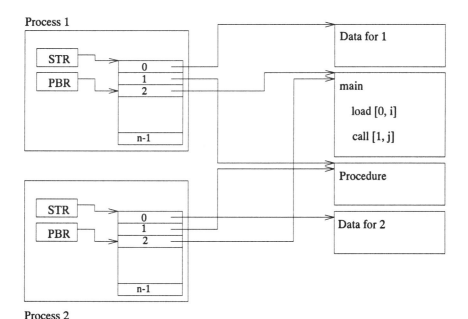

Figure 7.13 Shared Segments with Uniform Addresses

even though it never uses segment Z. By transitivity, each segment table will have to be very large to accommodate a system with more than a few sharable segments.

The Multics Segmentation System

The Multics operating system was designed to support a very general form of shared segments. The basic approach used in the design relies on adding a level of indirection between the shared segment's references and the segment table, as explained in more detail below.

In hardware that supports Multics, for example, the Honeywell/GE 645 computer, there are three segment table registers: the usual STR to point at the segment table, a *procedure base register* (PBR), which serves the same purpose as the CBR in our discussion above, and a *linkage base register* (LBR) used to manage the level of indirection. Figure 7.14 describes the segment table mechanism used in Multics.

The PBR points to the segment descriptor for the code that is currently being executed (there are no pointers for data or stack segments). In the example used above, the current procedure segment contains a data access on segment 1 and a call to segment 2 (see Figure 7.14). When the shared segment is compiled, the compiler produces a template for an indirection table called a *linkage segment*. Whenever the shared segment is "made known" using the binding process described above, a unique linkage segment is

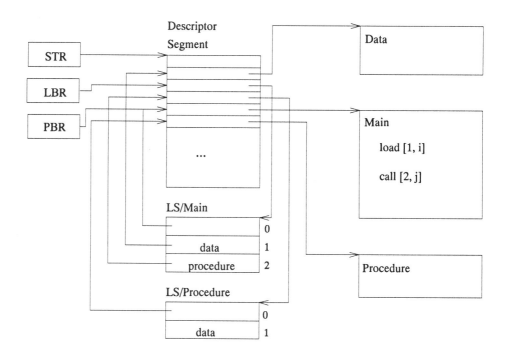

Figure 7.14 Multics Shared Segments Mechanism

constructed from the template for the process that is invoking the shared segment. In the figure, the shared segment is called "MAIN" and the linkage segment is called "LS/MAIN." The linkage segment is pointed to by the segment table (since it is just another segment), and the LBR is set to point at the segment descriptor for the current linkage segment. Since the linkage segment is created from a compile-time template, it is correlated with the segment indexes compiled into the shared segment, that is, the references to segments 1 and 2 refer to offsets in the linkage segment, not in the segment table.

Assume that the linkage segment pointers have been set (see below); then, when the **access segment 1** instruction is executed, the hardware will use LBR to find the linkage segment and the "1" to identify an entry in the linkage segment. Entry "1" in the linkage segment, in turn, will point to a segment descriptor in the segment table for the data reference. The linkage segment has simply provided a one-level indirect addressing mechanism for the data reference.

The procedure call instruction causes the PBR and the LBR to change, since the process is moving to a different segment for continued execution. The **call 2** instruction causes the hardware to use the LBR to find the linkage segment entry and the pointer to a new segment descriptor. When the link is traversed, the system will change the LBR to point to the segment pointed to by **LS/MAIN**. By convention, the first entry in the linkage segment points to the procedure segment to which it belongs. Thus, the system will follow the first pointer in the linkage segment to the segment descriptor for the called procedure segment and the PBR will be set to address the new procedure segment descriptor, which points to the new procedure segment.

Linkage segments and procedure segments are constructed to allow run time binding of symbolic references to other segments (see Figure 7.15). That is, when the compiler encounters a inter segment call of the form

call   [segment_name, offset]

it first creates an entry in an *outsymbol table* that will contain the symbolic reference, **segment_name**. Next, the compiler adds an entry to the linkage segment at entry k that contains a pointer to the outsymbol table entry; the entry also contains a *fault flag* that is initialized to cause a fault the first time the outsymbol is referenced. Finally, the compiler generates code of the form

call   [<*linkage_segment, k>, offset]

Now, when the call instruction is executed, it will branch indirectly to the kth entry in the linkage segment. On the first execution of the instruction, the fault flag will be set to cause a trap to the operating system. The trap handler will follow the pointer in the linkage segment to the entry in the calling procedure's outsymbol table. The system can then retrieve the symbolic segment name, retrieve it from secondary storage, enter it into the segment table, and then modify the linkage segment so that it points to the appropriate segment descriptor. The fault flag is also cleared to prevent subsequent missing segment faults.

The Multics segmentation system is very general and complex. While it appears that the complexity of the solution might drastically impact the performance, the

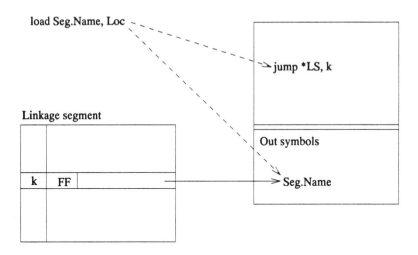

Figure 7.15 Multics Run-time Binding Mechanism

hardware has been designed to specifically support the segment mechanism. Also, most of the mechanism is only used when there is an intersegment reference. Few contemporary systems — hardware and operating system — match the generality of the 645/Multics approach.

7.4 PAGING

Paging systems present a flat name space to the programmer. He can construct his program and data images in a set of G memory locations, with virtual addresses ranging between 0 and G - 1. The paging system treats the name space as a set of $n = 2^k$ *pages*, each of size $c = 2^h$ (see Figure 7.16). The name space is the set of all pages accessible to the programmer, that is,

$$N = \{ p_0, p_1, ..., p_{n-1}\}$$

Page boundaries are transparent to programmers; the system will use pages as the atom of transfer between the primary and secondary memory.

Primary memory is divided into a set of $m = 2^j$ *page frames*, each the same size as a page ($c = 2^h$). The location space is the set of all page frames in the primary memory allocated to a process,

$$L = \{ b_0, b_1, ..., b_{m-1}\}$$

Since $|N| > |L|$, that is, $n > m$, the name space cannot all be loaded into the location space at any given time. The paging system will load selective pages into page frames as required when the program is executed, saving page images on secondary storage when

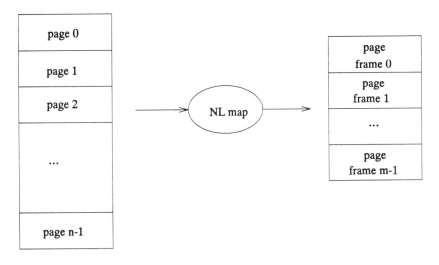

Figure 7.16 Pages and Page Frames

they are removed from the location space. Thus, the paging system implements the name-location map and the page transfer system.

7.4.1 Address Translation

A virtual address is a nonnegative integer, i, where

$$0 \le i \le G - 1 = 2^{k+h} - 1$$

(since there are $n = 2^k$ pages each of size 2^h words). If

$$H = 2^j \cdot 2^h = 2^{j+h}$$

that is, the number of page frames times the page size, then the name-location map has the form

$$\psi_t: [0:G - 1] \rightarrow [0:H - 1] \bigcup \{\Omega\}$$

In binary machines, virtual and physical addresses can be easily translated into two-component addresses with hardware. Let i be a virtual address written in binary notation; then a $(k + h)$-bit register will contain the address, where the k most significant bits represent the page and the h least significant bits represent an offset within a page. Thus, the first $c = 2^h$ addresses $(0, \ldots, c - 1)$ are in page 0 since these binary representations all have the k most significant bits set to zero. The k most significant bits are called the *page number* and the h least-significant bits are called the *line number* within the page. Similarly, the primary memory address can be partitioned into a *page frame number* and a line number using a $(j + h)$-bit MAR. Thus, we can focus on the mapping of pages to page frames, ignoring the line numbers. So

$$\psi_t(p_i) = \begin{cases} b_j & \text{if } p_i \text{ is loaded in } b_j \text{ at time } t \\ \Omega & \text{otherwise} \end{cases}$$

Figure 7.17 represents a typical address translation mechanism for a paging system. The k most significant bits of the virtual address are passed to the name-location map (to translate a page number to a page frame number). The result of the mapping operation can be a *missing page fault* or a resulting page frame number. The page fault will cause an operating systems trap, allowing it to locate the missing page on the secondary storage, to place the page in the primary memory, to adjust the page table (name-location map), and to restart the instruction. If the translation resulted in a page frame number, then it is concatenated with (shifted left and added to) the line number and passed to the primary memory.

Address translation must take place on each memory reference in a paging system; thus, paging requires hardware support to be cost effective. The name-location map is conceptually a table of the form shown in Figure 7.18. Page 0 maps to page frame 3, page 1 is not loaded, page 2 maps to page frame 7, and so on.

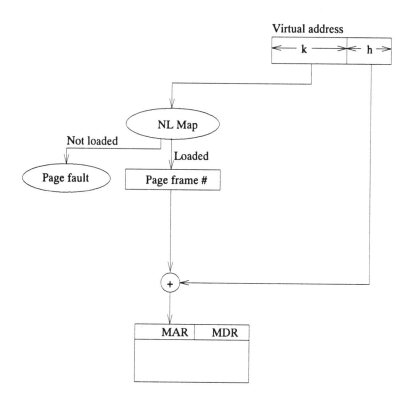

Figure 7.17 Page Translation

Page #	Page frame #
0	3
1	Ω
2	7
...	...
2^k-1	9

Figure 7.18 The Conceptual Page Table

A software implementation would result in tremendous overhead per memory reference and so is obviously not a reasonable alternative. An *associative memory* is an effective hardware mechanism in which to implement the page map. An associative (content-addressable) memory is designed with each cell containing a key and data. The data are addressed by the key content rather than by cell address; as a bonus, the key search is implemented as a parallel pattern match, meaning that the associative memory access is very fast. Small associative memories (less than 1 K cells) have been feasible since the early 1980s.

The page table of Figure 7.18 could be implemented with an associative memory as shown in Figure 7.19. The associative memory need only have as many entries as there are page frames, since unmapped pages do not appear in the memory. If a page does not appear in the memory, then the access will fail and cause a missing page fault.

7.4.2 The Page Replacement Model

There are three basic issues in defining a paging policy: deciding when to fetch pages into the primary memory (*fetch policy*), deciding what page should be removed from primary memory if all page frames are full (*replacement policy*), and deciding where the fetched page should be loaded in the primary memory (*placement policy*). Most paging

Key (Page #)	Data (Page frame #)
0	3
2	7
...	...
2^k-1	9

Figure 7.19 The Associative Memory Page Table

policies use a degenerate placement policy, that is, once a page has been picked for replacement, the page frame that it vacates will be the page frame that will hold the new page. The fetch and replacement policies differentiate among well-known paging algorithms.

We can build a formal model to consider various policies.

Definition 7.3. Let the *initial state* of the location space, $S_0(m) = \emptyset$, represent the state in which no pages are loaded in the $m = |L|$ primary memory page frames. In general, $S_t(m)$ is the set of pages from M loaded in L at time t:

$$S_t(m) = S_{t-1}(m) \bigcup X_t - Y_t$$

where t is the process's virtual time, X_t is the set of pages fetched at time t ($X_t \subseteq N - S_{t-1}(m)$), and Y_t is the set of pages replaced at time t ($Y_t \subseteq S_{t-1}(m)$). ‖

Thus, $S_t(m) \subseteq N$ (the page frame contents are images of the pages in the name space), $|S_t(m)| \leq m = |L|$ (the number of pages loaded is less than or equal to the number of page frames allocated to the process), and $r_t \in S_t(m)$ (the page referenced at time t is loaded into the primary memory).

The virtual time represents the progress that the process makes as it executes. With respect to the paging model, one can define the sequence of pages referenced by the process and then use the index on the sequence as the time.

Definition 7.4. The *page reference stream*, ω, is an unbounded sequence of page numbers,

$$\omega = r_1, r_2, r_3, ..., r_i, ...$$

representing the page numbers referenced by the process during its execution. The *virtual time* of a process is the index of the page reference stream. ‖

Thus, if ω is a page reference stream for some process, then at time i the process will reference page r_i. The page reference stream and the paging algorithm determine the sequence of memory states for the process. Thus, $S_t(m) \subseteq N$, $|S_t(m)| \leq m = |L|$ and $r_t \in S_t(m)$.

7.4.3 Demand Paging

The fetch policy determines when a page should be brought into the primary memory. The paging mechanism will not ordinarily have *a priori* knowledge about the programs that will be executed on the machine and, in particular, has no knowledge of the page reference stream for a process. Therefore, it is difficult to construct paging mechanisms that use a *prefetch* policy in which pages are fetched into the memory prior to the time they are referenced. Instead, the majority of general-purpose paging mechanisms use a fetch policy by which a page is loaded in the primary memory only when the page reference stream calls for the page. These paging algorithms are called demand paging algorithms.

Definition 7.5. If a paging algorithm satisfies

$$
S_t(m) = \begin{cases} S_{t-1}(m) & \text{if } r_t \epsilon S_{t-1}(m) \\ S_{t-1}(m) \cup r_t & \text{if } r_t \not\in S_{t-1}(m) \,\&\, |S_{t-1}(m)| < m \\ S_{t-1}(m) \cup \{r_t\} - \{y\} & \text{if } r_t \not\in S_{t-1}(m) \,\&\, |S_{t-1}(m)| = m, y \epsilon S_{t-1}(m) \end{cases}
$$

then it is a *demand paging algorithm.* ‖

Static Demand Paging Algorithms

We start our discussion of specific paging algorithms by considering only those that use static page frame allocation, that is, when the process begins to run, it requests a fixed number of page frames and then does not change that allocation during its lifetime. Later we will consider some dynamic page frame allocation strategies.

Once the fetch and placement policies have been established, then a paging policy can be described by defining the replacement policy. The performance of any particular paging algorithm depends on the the page reference stream, that is, there is no realizable paging algorithm that is an optimal demand paging algorithm, since that would require that the replacement policy have perfect knowledge of the page reference stream before the process executed it.

> **Definition 7.6.** Given some primary memory state sequence, $\{S_i(m)\}$, and a page reference stream, $\omega = r_1, r_2, \dots$ Let $R(S_t(m), r_t)$ designate the page that is replaced under a given demand paging algorithm when the location space is in state $S_t(m)$ when the process references page r_t.
> The *forward distance* of page r_t at time t is
>
> $$\text{dist}_f(r_t, t) = \begin{cases} k & \text{if } r_{t+k} \text{ is the first occurrence of } r_t \text{ in } r_{t+1}, r_{t+2}, \dots \\ \infty & \text{if } r_t \text{ does not appear in the remainder of } \omega \end{cases}$$
>
> Similarly, the *backward distance* of page r_t at time t is
>
> $$\text{dist}_b(r_t, t) = \begin{cases} k & \text{if } r_{t-k} \text{ is the most recent occurrence of } r_t \text{ in } r_1, r_2, \dots r_{t-1} \\ \infty & \text{if } r_t \text{ does not appear in } r_1, \dots, r_t \end{cases}$$
>
‖

Less formally, the forward (backward) distance is the measure of the next (last) occurrence of the given page in the reference stream. The distance is always greater than 0; the forward distance is infinite if the page is not referenced again, and the backward distance is infinite if the page has not been referenced previously.

We can now define demand paging algorithms by defining the replacement policy. Assume that the primary memory is full; that is, $|S_t(m)| = m$ and $r_{t+1} \notin S_t(m)$. Then

$$
S_{t+1}(m) = S_t(m) \cup \{r_t\} - R(S_t(m), r_{t+1})
$$

for some $R(S_t(m), r_{t+1})$ determined by the particular replacement strategy.

Random Replacement. The replaced page is chosen at random, that is,

$$R(S_t(m), r_{t+1}) = y \text{ with probability } \frac{1}{m}$$

Random replacement does not perform well, since it uses no knowledge of the reference stream in selecting a page to replace. Early paging systems used random replacement page only to discover that the paging system performed more poorly than no paging, since it incurred large amounts of paging activity.

Belady's Optimal Algorithm. At the other end of the extreme is the replacement policy that has perfect knowledge of the page reference stream. The replaced page is the one with maximal forward distance; that is,

$$R(S_t(m), r_{t+1}) = y, \text{ where } dist_f(y) = \max_{x \epsilon S_t}(dist_f(x))$$

Of course, some pages that are loaded at time t may never appear again in the reference stream, so there may be more than one loaded page with maximal forward distance. In this case, the optimal algorithm will choose an arbitrary loaded page with maximal forward distance.

For example, suppose that $\omega = 0\ 1\ 2\ 3\ 0\ 1\ 2\ 3\ 0\ 1\ 2\ 3\ 4\ 5\ 6\ 7$ with m = 3. Then this algorithm will produce the following behavior (incurring 10 page faults, each marked with *):

Page Frame	ω															
	0	1	2	3	0	1	2	3	0	1	2	3	4	5	6	7
0	0*	0	0	0	0	0	0	0	0	1*	1	1	4*	4	4	7*
1		1*	1	1	1	1	2*	2	2	2	2	2	2	5*	5	5
2			2*	3*	3	3	3	3	3	3	3	3	3	3	6*	6

Notice that the optimal algorithm can only be implemented if the full page reference stream is known *a priori*. Since it is rare that this occurs, the optimal algorithm is not generally realizable; instead it can be used to compare the performance of realizable algorithms with the optimal performance.

Least Recently Used (LRU). The LRU algorithm relies on the existence of *locality* in the page reference stream. Since programs are usually written as loops, then it is likely that the loop body will fit within some small number of pages. That is, if a page has been referenced recently, it is likely to be referenced again soon. LRU relies on locality by using the backward distance to approximate optimal performance, that is,

$$R(S_t(m), r_{t+1}) = y, \text{ where } dist_b(y) = \max_{x \epsilon S_t}(dist_b(x))$$

For example, suppose that $\omega = 0\ 1\ 2\ 3\ 0\ 1\ 2\ 3\ 0\ 1\ 2\ 3\ 4\ 5\ 6\ 7$ with m = 3. Then this algorithm will produce the following behavior (with 16 page faults):

Page Frame	ω															
		0	1	2	3	0	1	2	3	0	1	2	3	4	5	6	7
0	0*	0	0	3*	3	3	2*	2	2	1*	1	1	4*	4	4	7*
1		1*	1	1	0*	0	0	3*	3	3	2*	2	2	5*	5	5
2			2*	2	2	1*	1	1	0*	0	0	3*	3	3	6*	6

Least Frequently Used (LFU). The LFU replacement algorithm selects a page for replacement if it has not been used much since the process started. Let $freq(r_t, t)$ be the number of references to r_t in r_1 through r_{t-1}, then

$$R(S_t(m), r_{t+1}) = y, \text{ where } freq(y, t) = \min_{x \in S_t}(freq(x, t))$$

There may be more than one page that satisfies the criteria for replacement, so any of the qualifying pages can be selected for replacement. Suppose that we use a random rule for selecting among pages that have the same frequency of use (resulting in 12 page faults):

Page Frame	ω															
		0	1	2	3	0	1	2	3	0	1	2	3	4	5	6	7
0	0*	0	0	0	0	0	0	0	0	0	0	3*	3	3	3	3
1		1*	1	1	1	1	1	3*	3	1*	1	1	1	1	1	1
2			2*	3*	3	3	2*	2	2	2	2	2	4*	5*	6*	7*
			•				•		•		•	•				

The example incurs 12 page faults under LFU, with random pages loaded at time 3, 7, 9, 11, and 12 (marked with a •) due to ties in selecting pages based on frequency at those times.

Suppose that LFU used LRU as a mechanism to select a page for replacement in the case when the frequency counts are the same. This would result in 16 page faults:

Page Frame	ω															
		0	1	2	3	0	1	2	3	0	1	2	3	4	5	6	7
0	0*	0	0	3*	3	3	2*	2	2	1*	1	1	4*	5*	6*	7*
1		1*	1	1	0*	0	0	3*	3	3	2*	2	2	2	2	2
2			2*	2	2	1*	1	1	0*	0	0	3*	3	3	3	3

First in, First out (FIFO). The FIFO replacement algorithm replaces the page that has been in memory the longest. Let $age(r_i)$ be the time at which each page in $S_i(m)$ was last loaded. Then the replaced page is selected by

$$R(S_t(m), r_{t+1}) = y, \text{ where } age(y) = \min_{x \in S_i(m)}(age(x))$$

FIFO focuses on how long a page has been in memory rather than how much the page is being used. The example incurs 16 page faults under FIFO:

Page Frame	ω	0	1	2	3	0	1	2	3	0	1	2	3	4	5	6	7
0		0*	0	0	3*	3	3	2*	2	2	1*	1	1	4*	4	4	7*
1			1*	1	1	0*	0	0	3*	3	3	2*	2	2	5*	5	5
2				2*	2	2	1*	1	1	0*	0	0	3*	3	3	6*	6

Stack Algorithms

Certain demand algorithms are more well behaved than others. For example, consider the page reference stream

$$\omega = 0\ 1\ 2\ 3\ 0\ 1\ 4\ 0\ 1\ 2\ 3\ 4$$

as it is processed by FIFO with m = 3:

Page Frame	ω	0	1	2	3	0	1	4	0	1	2	3	4
0		0*	0	0	3*	3	3	4*	4	4	4	4	4
1		-	1*	1	1	0*	0	0	0	0	2*	2	2
2		-	-	2*	2	2	1*	1	1	1	1	3*	3

There are 9 page faults, each marked with a *. Now suppose that we increase the location space to m = 4 page frames and run the same page reference stream with the same algorithm:

Page Frame	ω	0	1	2	3	0	1	4	0	1	2	3	4
0		0*	0	0	0	0	0	4*	4	4	4	3*	3
1		-	1*	1	1	1	1	1	0*	0	0	0	4*
2		-	-	2*	2	2	2	2	2	1*	1	1	1
3		-	-	-	3*	3	3	3	3	3	2*	2	2

There are 10 page faults, even though the process has one more page frame that it did in the previous example. This is an example of *Belady's anomaly*, that is, the paging algorithm exhibits properties that cause it to have worse performance when the amount of primary memory allocated to the process is increased. It is natural to be concerned about the class of replacement algorithms that are susceptible to Belady's anomaly.

Suppose that $|\omega| = t < \infty$. Then $S_t(m)$ represents the pages that are loaded in the location space when the process terminates.

Definition 7.7. (The Inclusion Property) Let $|\omega| = t < \infty$. If $S_i(m) \subseteq S_i(m + 1)$ for $1 \leq i \leq t$ in ω, then the paging algorithm is called a *stack algorithm*. ‖

It is apparent from the example above that FIFO is not a stack algorithm. Are there any algorithms that satisfy the stack property for all page reference streams?

For every ω, there is a permutation of the n pages in the name space,

$$\text{Stack}_t(\omega) = [u_1, u_2, ..., u_n]$$

where the order of the pages in the stack depends on the replacement algorithm. For a stack paging algorithm that has processed reference i, there is a permutation in which the first m elements correspond to the memory state at time i for a location space of size m: That is,

$$\text{Stack}_1(\omega) = [u_1]$$

$$\text{Stack}_2(\omega) = [u_1, u_2]$$

$$...$$

$$\text{Stack}_i(\omega) = [u_1, u_2, ..., u_i]$$

$$...$$

$$\text{Stack}_j(\omega) = [u_1, u_2, ..., u_m](m \le j \le t)$$

Now, u_1 is the page at the top of the stack, u_2 is the page next to the top, and so on to u_m. $\text{Stack}_t(\omega)$ is the final memory state.

For the LRU replacement policy, the m most recently referenced pages occupy the first m slots in the permutation (stack), and the m + 1 most recently referenced pages occupy the first m + 1 slots in the permutation for $|L| = m + 1$. That is, LRU is a stack algorithm.

The stack for a reference stream is built using a specific replacement algorithm as follows: let the *stack distance* of a page p at time i, designated $dist_s(p,i)$, be its position in $\text{Stack}_i(\omega)$. Then $\text{dist}_s(p, i) = k$ if $u_k = p$ [$\text{dist}_s(p, i) = \infty$ if p has not yet been referenced]. Now, if the system with m page frames has a stack state

$$\text{Stack}_i(\omega) = [u_1, u_2, ..., u_m]$$

and r_{i+1} is not loaded,
(1) $\text{dist}_s(r_{i+1}, i + 1) > m$
(2)   With LRU, r_{i+1} is loaded and $\text{dist}_s(r_i, i + 1)=1$.
(3)   Since all stack algorithms are demand algorithms, $\text{dist}_s(r_j, i)=\text{dist}_s(r_j, i + 1)$ for $r_{i+1} \ne r_j$.
(4)   For r_j such that $\text{dist}_s(r_j, i) > \text{dist}_s(r_{i+1}, i)$ the $\text{dist}_s(r_j, i)$ will be unchanged.

Thus, the stack distance describes how stack algorithms adjust the stack as the reference stream is processed (see Figure 7.20). When a page is selected by the algorithm, it is placed on top of the stack, with all pages between the top and the referenced page moving down one position.

Notice that any algorithm that has the inclusion property will also be a stack algorithm. While LRU places pages on the top of the stack on the basis of most recent usage, other algorithms use a similar mechanism with a different policy. Consider LFU as another example: The m most frequently used pages will appear at the top of the stack independently of the physical page frame allocation. LFU is also a stack algorithm.

Stack algorithms display behavior that is important to the system designer. One needs to be assured that if more resources are allocated to a process then performance

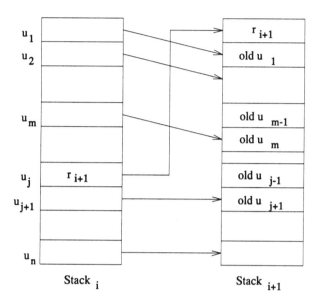

Figure 7.20 Stack Motion When r_i Is Referenced

will improve rather than possibly decay. The correlation holds for stack algorithms, but not for others. Similarly, stack algorithms are more easily analyzed than many nonstack algorithms. For example, one can calculate the cost of page fetches with a single pass over the reference stream for a stack algorithm, since it is easy to predict the number of page faults by simulating the stack. Also, by using the stack distance one can predict performance improvement that can be obtained by adding memory to the system.

LRU Implementations

Over time, LRU has become one of the most popular of the static memory demand paging algorithms, primarily because the idea of locality is a reasonable predictor for program behavior, producing good performance by LRU on a wide variety of page references streams.

To implement LRU, it is necessary to keep an accounting of the most recent use of each page frame. This essentially requires that the page table incorporate another field for the time of last reference (where the "time" can be the virtual time, that is, the index of ω). Of course, this is costly to implement, since it introduces another page table memory write and requires virtual time maintenance. Also, the replacement algorithm must search the entire memory to find the maximum time since the page was referenced.

Since LRU is a stack algorithm, one can reflect the order of use by using a stack to track the page frame usage. Each time a page is referenced, the page is moved to the top of the stack. Implementing this in software will require considerable list maintenance for each page reference.

Since both of these approaches require specialized hardware to accommodate LRU, it may be possible to minimize the hardware, yet still approximate the LRU algorithm.

Suppose that the page table incorporated a single *reference bit* for each page table entry. If the address translation hardware were to set the reference bit each time that the corresponding page were read or written, then it would be easy to determine which pages had been referenced since, all the reference bits were cleared. Now, suppose all bits are initially cleared and then cleared again after being examined during page fault processing. Then it is possible to determine which pages have been referenced since the last page fault (although the order of referenced pages is lost). This will enable one to implement an inexpensive approximation of LRU.

The reference bits can be extended to a shift register in which the least significant bit is the reference bit, and the more significant bits are set by shifting the register contents to the left periodically. Now, more history is saved, although the precision of the history depends on the period between shift operations.

Part of the cost of a page fault is that of writing a page from primary memory onto the secondary memory. The page table can be incorporate a *dirty bit*, that is cleared when a page is loaded, but set whenever the page is written. If the page is selected for replacement and if the dirty bit is clear, then the page has not been written since it was loaded. Therefore, the copy to secondary memory can be avoided because the page frame image is the same as the page image on the secondary storage.

Performance

Performance is an obvious worry in paging systems. First, the overhead for individual page fault handling can be excessive. Second, it is clear from the simple examples that a mismatch between the process's locality and the size of the location space can be disastrous, causing the primary memory to be loaded every few instructions. This phenomenon, called *thrashing*, can slow down the process's execution time by orders of magnitude.

Each page fault will introduce considerable overhead, say R units of time. The time for page fault processing is added to the total execution time; if $|\omega| = t$ and there are f page faults, then the total execution time is

$$T_{exec} = t + f \cdot R$$

or the average amount of overhead per instruction is

$$\frac{T_{exec}}{t} = \frac{t + f \cdot R}{t} = 1 + \frac{f}{t} \cdot R$$

The fraction f/t is the fraction of page references that result in a page fault. If the fraction and R are small, then the cost of page faults will be absorbed over the full execution without undue degradation. As either grows, paging becomes ineffective since the overhead time dominates the total time to run the process.

The value of R depends on the nature of the secondary storage, the page size, the replacement policy overhead, and numerous other factors; the transfer time between primary and secondary storage will tend to dominate for most implementations, since the transfer ordinarily involves mechanical movement.

Suppose that h(k) is the cost of secondary memory transfers of k pages. Then h(0) = 0, and we can assign h(1) = 1, meaning that a single-page transfer requires one unit of time in some unspecified time unit. Now $h(k) \geq h(1)$ since k pages will require more time than one page. Let $|\omega| = t < \infty$. Then the cost of loading pages is

$$C_{load}(m, \omega) = \sum_{i=1}^{t} h(|X_i|)$$

For demand paging algorithms, $|X_t|$ is 0 or 1. So

$$C_{load}(m, \omega) = \sum_{i=1}^{t} |X_i|$$

Since

$$h(1) = 1 = T_{latency} + T_{transfer}$$

then

$$h(k) = T_{latency} + k \cdot T_{transfer}$$

This implies that h(k) < k for loading from rotating secondary storage. And for semiconductor secondary storage or storage technology that minimizes latency, h(k) = k. Replacement cost is always less than loading costs (usually a fixed fraction of the cost), presuming that the paging mechanism incorporates a dirty bit. Thus the cost analysis for loading is the dominant cost of the paging algorithm.

Theorem 7.1. For any given paging algorithm implemented in a system where $h(k) \geq k$, there is a demand paging algorithm with paging loading cost that does not exceed the original algorithm. ‖

Argument
Suppose the general algorithm generates memory state sequence

$$S_0, S_1, ..., S_t,...$$

and the demand algorithm generates memory state sequence

$$S_0', S_1', ..., S_t', ...$$

where

$$S_t = S_{t-1}$$

and

$$S_t' = S_{t-1}' \bigcup X_t' - Y_t'$$

Denote the set of pages placed by the general algorithm at time t, but not yet placed by the demand algorithm at time t ("deferred placements") as P_t. Similarly, denote the set of pages replaced by the general algorithm at time t, but not yet replaced by the demand algorithm at time t ("deferred replacements") by R_t. Now

$$S_t' = S_{t-1}' \bigcup R_t - P_t$$

and

$$P_t = (P_{t-1} \bigcup X_t - Y_t - (S_{t-1}' \bigcup \{r_t\})$$

This follows since X_t is the set of pages fetched by the general algorithm but not necessarily by the demand algorithm, and Y_t is the set of pages placed by the general algorithm but not necessarily by the demand algorithm; S_{t-1}' is the set of pages placed by the demand algorithm before time t, and r_t is a page that might have been replaced by the general algorithm and is staged to be replaced by the demand algorithm, but is now being requested by the page reference stream.

$$X_t' = \begin{cases} r_t & \text{if } p_i \text{ is loaded in } b_j \text{ at time t} \\ \varnothing & \text{otherwise} \end{cases}$$

$$Y_t' = \begin{cases} \varnothing & x_t' = \varnothing \text{ or } |S_{t-1}'| < m \\ y & \text{if } p_i \text{ is loaded in } b_j \text{ at time t} \\ \text{for some } y \, \varepsilon \, R_{t-1} \bigcup Y_t \end{cases}$$

where $S_t' = S_{t-1}' \bigcup X_t' - Y_t'$; also $R_t = (R_{t-1} \bigcup Y_t - X_t) \bigcap S_t'$.

Now, every page placed by the demand algorithm must also have been placed by the general algorithm. Therefore,

$$\sum_t |X_t| \geq \sum_t |X_t'|$$

And for the general algorithm, we have

$$\begin{aligned} C_{load}(m,\omega) \quad &= \sum_t h(|X_t|) \\ &\geq \sum_t |X_t| \\ &\geq \sum_t |X_t'| \\ &= C_{load}(m, \omega) \text{ for the demand algorithm} \end{aligned}$$

Finally, over the years considerable empirical data have been gathered concerning the performance of various paging algorithms and implementations. While these observations do not provide bounds on performance, they do reflect the performance of various replacement strategies for various processes. The general findings can be characterized by plotting the *fault rate* versus the location space size (see Figure 7.21). The fault rate is the number of faults per page reference; thus, is equivalent to the f/t fraction used above.

First, it has often been observed that, for all page reference streams and all algorithms, thrashing will typically occur for m < n/2. Conversely, as m → n, the

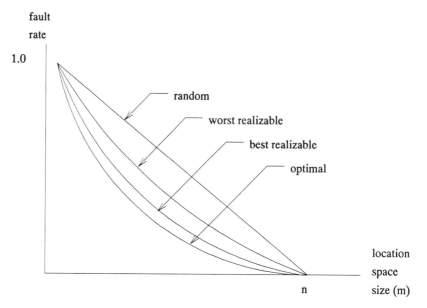

Figure 7.21 Empirical Observations

performance of all algorithms converges to Belady's optimal algorithm. That is, the amount of memory allocated to the process is as least as important as the algorithm. This leads one to consider better ways of matching the primary memory needs of a process to the allocation.

7.4.4 Dynamic Allocation Algorithms

Contemporary operating systems are primarily multiprogramming operating systems, even in a network or shared memory environment. As a result, the primary memory is shared among several different processes at any given time. The paging algorithms discussed above all assumed that the memory allocation was static, that is, a process requested some amount of primary memory when it was started, and that amount did not change during the computation, even if the process went through phases in which it required a large location space and other phases where its memory requirements were modest.

Empirical observations of static paging algorithms reflect a dramatic degradation of performance when the general effective CPU utilization is plotted against the degree of multiprogramming in a uniprocessor system (see Figure 7.22). While one might expect the effective CPU utilization to increase to some point due to overlap of the CPU with I/O activity, one would also expect the overhead to gradually begin to dominate and cause the utilization to degrade. The observations show that systems ordinarily deteriorate rapidly after some degree of multiprogramming is reached, the degree depending on the characteristics of the processes that are in execution. After considerable experimentation, researchers gradually arrived at an explanation for this dramatic degradation: As the degree of multiprogramming increases with a fixed amount of primary memory in the machine, the size of the location space for each process decreases. Reconsidering the examples for the static replacement algorithms, it is apparent that each algorithm fails when the amount of primary memory allocated to the process is less than the set of pages being referenced at a relatively high rate within a part of a program. And this causes the process to thrash, since it constantly replaces a page that will be needed right away.

The thrashing phenomenon led researchers to consider dynamic page frame allocation algorithms. A dynamic allocation algorithm is designed to adjust to these varying memory requirements by adjusting the location space size as a function of the phase in which the process is currently executing.

Suppose that there are k processes sharing the primary memory. Let $m_i(t)$ represent the amount of memory allocated to process i at time t, that is, $m_i(0) = 0$. Then

$$\sum_{i=1}^{k} m_i(t) = m$$

at time t.

Given that $S_0(m_i) = \emptyset$, the memory state for process i at time $t \geq 1$ can be derived from the memory state at time $t - 1$ for an arbitrary parameter, τ:

$$S_t(m_i) = S_{t-1}(m_i) \bigcup X - Y$$

$$X = \begin{cases} r_t & \text{if } dist_b(r_t) < \tau \text{ and } r_t \text{ not in } S_{t-1}(m) \\ \emptyset & \text{otherwise} \end{cases}$$

$$Y = \begin{cases} y & \text{if } dist_b(y) \geq \tau \text{ and } y \in S_{t-1} \\ \emptyset & \text{if otherwise} \end{cases}$$

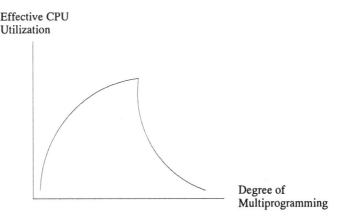

Figure 7.22 Thrashing

The Working Set Algorithm

The working set algorithm was the first widely known algorithm to address thrashing by employing dynamic page frame allocation.

Definition 7.8. Define the amount of memory allocated to process i at time t, $m_i(t)$, by

$$X \neq \varnothing \text{ and } Y = \varnothing => m_i(t) = m_i(t-1) + 1$$

$$X = \varnothing \text{ and } Y = \varnothing => m_i(t) = m_i(t-1)$$

$$X = \varnothing \text{ and } Y \neq \varnothing => m_i(t) = m_i(t-1) - 1$$

The resulting $S_t(m_i)$ is called the working set for process i at time t with window size τ. ∥

The premise of the *working set algorithm* is that the parameter τ (called the *window size*) determines the number of references that should influence the number of pages required by the process on the basis of the locality displayed in the window. For example, if a process only uses 3 pages for 10,000 references, then it should only have 3 page frames allocated to it. But if it uses 20 pages within the last 10,000 references, then it should have 20 page frames in its location space.

Suppose that the reference stream used to illustrate static allocation algorithms were processed with the working set algorithm with $\tau = 3$. Then, as illustrated below, the algorithm would experience 16 page faults.

Page Frame	ω 0 1 2 3	0 1 2 3	0 1 2 3	4 5 6 7
0	x* x x	x* x x	x* x x	
1	x* x x	x* x x	x* x x	
2	x* x x	x* x x	x* x x	
3	x* x x	x* x x	x* x x	
4				x* x x
5				x* x x
6				x* x
7				x*

Notice that the number of pages allocated varies from zero when the process begins to a maximum of $\tau = 3$ page frames. The performance of the working set algorithm could be increased considerably by adjusting the window size to $\tau = 4$, which is just large enough to address the locality for this reference stream, and results in 8 page faults (the minimum since there are 8 pages in the name space).

Page Frame	ω 0	1	2	3	0	1	2	3	0	1	2	3	4	5	6	7
0	x*	x	x	x	x	x	x	x	x	x	x	x				
1		x*	x	x	x	x	x	x	x	x	x	x	x			
2			x*	x	x	x	x	x	x	x	x	x	x	x		
3				x*	x	x	x	x	x	x	x	x	x	x	x	
4													x*	x	x	x
5														x*	x	x
6															x*	x
7																x*

In both these examples, the maximum page frame allocation was τ. For more window sizes that exceed the locality sizes, the page frame allocation will be less than τ.

Definition 7.9. The *working set principle* states that a process, i, can be loaded and active only if $m_i(t) \geq |S_t(m_i)|$; otherwise, the process should be blocked [5]. ‖

Thus the working set algorithm relies on locality (and on a good choice of τ).

The working set algorithm is the basis of many contemporary paging systems. While it relies on knowledge of the backward distance to determine membership in the window, it captures the idea of locality and minimum memory required to run the process. The independent variable in the working set is the window size, and this is determined by the characteristics of the process.

Page Fault Frequency Algorithm [3]

From the example, it is clear that the working set algorithm is susceptible to thrashing in those cases where τ is too small. The *page fault frequency* algorithm attempts to infer the length of the locality by detecting times when the process begins to experience a high rate of page faulting. When the page fault frequency surpasses a threshold value (a parameter to the algorithm), it allocates additional page frames to the process. Conversely, if the process has not experienced a page fault for a relatively long time, then the algorithm will reduce the page frame allocation for the process.

Clock Algorithms

Clock algorithms were introduced as an approximation of the working set algorithm, providing similar performance but allowing for a simpler implementation. The idea for the clock algorithm is to think of a process's page frames being arranged in a circular list, like the numerals on a clock. A single pointer addresses one of the page frames at a time. When a page needs to be replaced, the pointer is advanced to the next page frame and it is considered for replacement.

If each page frame contains a reference bit, then the algorithm could check the bit, clearing it after checking. If the reference bit were set, then move to the next frame, otherwise, replace the page. Such an interpretation causes the clock algorithm to behave like a global memory LRU algorithm.

Suppose that the algorithm keeps a variable named **last_ref** for each page frame. Now, if the reference bit were set, then **last_ref[frame]** is set to the current virtual time for the process that is using it, $T_{processi}$. If the reference bit were not set, then if

$$T_{processi} - \textbf{last\_ref[frame]} > \tau$$

the page loaded in the frame is replaced. Thus, the **last_ref** is an approximation to the time of last reference rather than the actual time. However, this strategy approximates the working set algorithm (and is called *WSClock*).

7.4.5 Combining Paging and Segmentation

There is nothing to preclude a system from employing both paging and segmentation. In such a system (for example, Multics), segments are assumed to be rather large, (larger than a page frame). The paging system supports the segmentation system by allowing segments to be paged. That is, a missing segment fault will not cause the entire segment to be loaded, but only relevant pages.

7.5 FURTHER READING

Knuth, Volume 1, describes free list management and main memory allocations strategies [8]; while this work is old, it is still complete.

Virtual memory has been studied intensively since the late 1960s, beginning with important work at MIT on CTSS and Multics [5, 12, 13]. Early work all focused on local memory strategies [1], while later work addressed various global strategies [2, 3, 15]. Chapter 6 of Coffman and Denning's book [4] and Chapter 5 of Maekawa, Oldehoeft and Oldehoeft's book [11] provide very complete discussions of paging. Alternative discussions of contemporary virtual memory implementations, including hardware considerations, are given in the books by Levy and Eckhouse [10], Hennessy and Patterson [7], and Leffler and others [9].

Segmentation techniques are not as widely used as paging techniques, although several aspects of segmentation appear in contemporary architectures. The Burroughs machines [14] are successful commercial machines that make extensive use of segmentation, while the Multics system is the most complete implementation [13]. Fabry provides an excellent discussion of the issues in shared segments in his discussion of capability-based segments [6].

REFERENCES

1.   L. A. Belady, "A Study of Replacement Algorithms for Virtual Storage Computers," *IBM Systems Journal 5*, 2 (1966), 78-101.
2.   R. W. Carr and J. L. Hennessy, "WSClock -- A Simple and Efficient Algorithm for Virtual Memory Management," *Proceedings of the Eighth ACM Symposium on Operating Systems Principles*, December 1981, 87-95.
3.   W. W. Chu and H. Opderbeck, "The Page Fault Frequency Replacement Algorithm," *AFIPS Proceedings of the Fall Joint Computer Conference 41* , 597-609.
4.   E. G. Coffman and P. J. Denning, *Operating Systems Theory*, Prentice Hall, Inc., Englewood Cliffs, NJ, 1973.

5.   P. J. Denning, "Working Sets Past and Present," *IEEE Transactions on Software Engineering SE-6*, 1 (January 1980), 64-84.

6.   R. S. Fabry, "Capability-Based Addressing," *Communications of the ACM 17*, 7 (July 1974), 403-412.

7.   J. L. Hennessy and D. A. Patterson, *Computer Architecture: A Quantitative Approach*, Morgan Kaufmann Publishers, Inc., San Mateo, CA, 1990.

8.   D. E. Knuth, *The Art of Computer Programming Volume 1 Fundamental Algorithms*, Addison-Wesley Publishing Co., Reading, MA, 1969.

9.   S. J. Leffler, M. K. McKusick, M. J. Karels, and J. S. Quarterman, *The Design and Implementation of the 4.3 BSD UNIX Operating System*, Addison-Wesley Publishing Co., Reading, MA, 1989.

10.   H. M. Levy and R. H. Eckhouse Jr., *Computer Programming and Architecture: The VAX, Second Edition*, Digital Press, Bedford, MA, 1989.

11.   M. Maekawa, A. E. Oldehoeft, and R. R. Oldehoeft, *Operating Systems Advanced Concepts*, Benjamin/Cummings Publishing, Menlo Park, CA, 1987.

12.   R. L. Mattson, J. Gecsei, D. R. Slutz, and I. L. Traiger, "Evaluation Techniques for Storage Hierarchies," *IBM Systems Journal 9*, 2 (1970), 78-117.

13.   E. I. Organick, *The Multics System: An Examination of Its Structure*, MIT Press, Cambridge, MA, 1972.

14.   E. I. Organick, *Computer System Organization*, Academic Press, New York, NY, 1973.

15.   B. Prieve and R. S. Fabry, "VMIN -- An Optimal Variable-Space Page Replacement Algorithm," *Communications of the ACM 19*, 5 (May 1976), 295-297.

EXERCISES

(1)   Figure 7.6 describes the basic mechanism used in many 16-bit microprocessors for mapping CPU addresses into memory addresses. Many of these systems have compilers that will allow a code, data, or stack segment to exceed 64K locations. Explain the actions that the compiler must take to support this capability.

(2)   Suppose that a swapping system contains N regions of sizes $M_1, M_2, ..., M_N$. The context switching time is related to the the the time to perform disk input/output (see Section 6.1). Suppose that the time to transfer a program loaded into memory partition M_i to or from the disk is

$$T_i = f(|M_i|)$$

Derive an expression that can be used to choose the time quantum for a round robin time quantum. You may assume that the time quantum is the same for every region.

(3)   Suppose that a multiprogrammed batch system employs a medium term scheduling policy in which it has fixed-size regions R_0 = 20KB, R_1 = 30KB, R_2 = 30KB, and R_3 = 50KB. The batch stream shown in Figure 7.23 is to be scheduled into the memory. Assume that a job is scheduled into the smallest region that will satisfy its memory requirements. How long will it take the system to process the batch stream?

(4)   Suppose that a multiprogrammed batch system employs a medium-term scheduling policy in which it has fixed-size regions R_0 = 20KB, R_1 = 30KB, R_2 = 30KB, and R_3 = 50KB. The batch stream shown in Figure 7. 23 is to be scheduled into the memory. Assume that a job is scheduled into any available region that will satisfy its memory requirements. How long will it take the system to process the batch stream?

(5)   Suppose that a multiprogrammed batch system employs a medium-term scheduling policy in which it has fixed-size regions R_0 = 20KB, R_1 = 30KB, R_2 = 30KB, and R_3 = 50KB. The batch stream shown in Figure 7. 23 is to be scheduled into the memory. Assume that a job is scheduled into the largest available region that will satisfy its memory requirements. How long will it take the system to process the batch stream?

Job	Memory (KB)	Time in the Region (seconds)
1	18	10
2	29	5
3	10	20
4	33	15
5	14	15
6	49	10
7	19	5
8	16	10
9	21	15
10	31	10

Figure 7.23 A Sample Batch Stream

(6)   Suppose that a multiprogrammed batch system employs a medium-term scheduling policy in which it has fixed-size regions R_0 = 20KB, R_1 = 30KB, R_2 = 30KB, and R_3 = 50KB. The batch stream shown in Figure 7. 23 is to be scheduled into the memory. Suppose that a job is scheduled into any region that will satisfy its memory requirements, provided that no larger jobs that would fit in the partition would be blocked. How long will it take the system to process the stream?

(7)   Why is it necessary for the descriptor segment to be locked into primary memory in a segmented virtual memory system?

(8)   Write a detailed (one-page) pseudocode description of the operation of a missing page fault handler.

(9)   Let ω = 2, 3, 4, 3, 2, 4, 3, 2, 4, 5, 6, 7, 5, 6, 7, 4, 5, 6, 7, 2, 1 be a page reference stream. Given a page frame allocation of 3 and assuming the primary memory is initially unloaded, how many page faults will the given reference stream incur under Belady's algorithm?

(10) Let ω = 2, 3, 4, 3, 2, 4, 3, 2, 4, 5, 6, 7, 5, 6, 7, 4, 5, 6, 7, 2, 1 be a page reference stream. Given a page frame allocation of 3 and assuming the primary memory is initially unloaded, how many page faults will the given reference stream incur under LRU?

(11) Let ω = 2, 3, 4, 3, 2, 4, 3, 2, 4, 5, 6, 7, 5, 6, 7, 4, 5, 6, 7, 2, 1 be a page reference stream. Given a page frame allocation of 3 and assuming the primary memory is initially unloaded, how many page faults will the given reference stream incur under FIFO?

(12) Let ω = 2, 3, 4, 3, 2, 4, 3, 2, 4, 5, 6, 7, 5, 6, 7, 4, 5, 6, 7, 2, 1 be a page reference stream. Given a window size of 6 and assuming the primary memory is initially unloaded, how many page faults will the given reference stream incur under the working set model?

(13) What class of devices is applicable for the theorem that shows that there is a demand paging algorithm that is at least as efficient as any arbitrary algorithm? Explain the rationale for your answer.

(14) Construct a formal argument that LFU (with an LRU tie breaker) is a stack algorithm.

(15) Show that LFU with an arbitrary tie breaker rule is not a stack algorithm.

(16) Write a solution to the problem specified in Exercise 2.12 for a shared memory machine that supports spin locks. The solution to this problem must use the kernel's shared memory and spin lock routines. For this solution, do not use exec, that is, fork child procedures that simply call a procedure in the same file to do their work. Experiment with various values of N between 1 and 8 for n = 64 trapezoids. Plot the respective times versus N.

8

PROTECTION

8.1 FUNDAMENTALS

The class of computers and computer networks that concern us in this book may be shared by a community of different human users, either simultaneously or at different times. The system is not only intended to provide computational services, it is also intended to act as a mechanism for long-term information storage. Since machines are shared among users and since each user is entitled to save information in the system, it is necessary for the system to be able to control the nature of one user's access to another user's information.

System resource protection is a complex issue, involving organizational administrative policies, moral issues, and physical security as external issues, that is, outside the purview of the operating system. These external security approaches may or may not preclude the case that an unauthorized human user can even have physical access to a computer system. In general, we do not address these issues in this book, except to assume that unauthorized human users are able to physically access the computer system.†

---

† It is difficult to solve the problem in an uncontrolled external environment. Security violators are not subject to "rules of the game." Consider single-user UNIX workstations. These systems are often administered by a central organization, with the workstation's "owner" acting as an ordinary user. That is, the owner logs into the machine with no special administrative privilege, since that privilege enables the user to either inadvertently or purposely destroy system files (that cause the operating system to behave as intended by the administrator, for example, /dev files). By providing the administrators with the "root" log in while the owner uses an ordinary user log in, the policy can be implemented, unless the user turns off the power to the machine and then turns it back on with the machine directed to boot up in single-user ("root") mode. Any person that wishes to become "root" may simply cycle power on the machine. This flaw was quickly recognized on most workstation

The operating system is the system agent with which each user interacts when he initiates a session with the system. It is encumbent on the operating system to verify that the user is authorized to use the system; this aspect of protection is generally known as user *authentication*. If a system could be unequivocally correct in its authentication of users, then many aspects of protection would be solved. That is, any action caused by that user would be known to be the full responsibility of that user, and not of some other user masquerading as the intended user. In general, unequivocal authentication is not possible.

Once a user has access to the system, an internal identification can be used to represent the actions of that user. When the user initiates the session, a process is created under the ownership of the user, that is, the process is "owned" by the user (as indicated by the internal user identification in the process descriptor). Any subsequent action by the process is assumed to be in behalf of the specified human user; the process has become an internal agent of the external user. In particular, if the process is allocated resources (for example, files or CPU time), then it is assumed that they belong to the user. And if the process creates another process, then the new process is also ultimately the responsibility of the user (even though the newly created process may or may not be characterized as the "child" of the original process). Because of this fundamental relationship between the user and the processes, it is convenient to simply blur the distinction and identify the internal surrogate processes with the human user.

Users are allocated resources in the system, both in the short term (while the user is logged into the machine) and the long term (while the user is not logged into the machine). Resources can be allocated to a user on an exclusive or shared basis. Exclusive allocation is intended to mean that no other user (process) is allowed access to the resource while it is allocated to the owner. Shared allocation implies that other user (processes) may also have access to the resource while the original owner has access. For example, a memory segment can be allocated exclusively to a process, or it may be shared among a set of processes.

It is the need to support both exclusive and shared access policies simultaneously that challenges the protection system designer. If the system were to only support exclusive access, then the designs to absolutely prevent one process from accessing another's resources are not difficult, for example, consider the base and limit registers for protecting memory. Or if all access were shared among all processes, the problem would be simple, for example, any process could read and write any memory location. The system must provide a means by which a user can control the nature and amount of sharing to his allocated resources. This is the fundamental challenge to operating systems protection.

The discussion of protection is organized by first providing additional background material in the remainder of this section. Then we describe several issues and solutions involved with authentication and with resource sharing. The remainder of the chapter describes two abstract models of protection, the access model and the flow model, and concludes with a survey of mechanisms for implementing protection policies.

UNIX machines, and was remedied with a log in session for the system when it is powered up, but the example makes the point that one cannot depend on simple assumptions such as "the operating system is in control..."

8.1.1 Policy and Mechanism

It is useful to distinguish between policies and mechanisms for accomplishing some goal. Protection systems are especially sensitive to the distinction between the two, although the difference between them is also significant in many other parts of the operating system.

> **Definition 8.1.** A *mechanism* is a set of components used to implement any of a different set of strategies.
>
> A *policy* is a particular strategy that dictates the way that a mechanism is used to achieve specific goals. ∥

Thus a policy dictates the manner in which a mechanism is used, and a mechanism is used to support a policy. For example, a particular communication policy might be that no two processes are allowed to share resources except by exchanging messages. A communication mechanism would be required to support message passing, perhaps by copying messages from one process's address space to the other's address space.

Protection is one aspect of a system's overall security policy. A system's security policy addresses all forms of operation related to the use of the system as it is intended by some high-level position. For example, the system's security relates to the external factors such as moral issues, legal issues, trustworthiness of users and administrators, and authentication of users. To implement the overall security policy, the system must provide mechanisms to protect user's resources from unauthorized use. That is, *protection* refers to a mechanism for enforcing a *security* policy.

It is easy to see that establishing precise policy is difficult (similar to establishing iron-clad requirements for software, in general). One can also observe that policy design and implementation touch on many different disciplines in addition to computer science, for example, organizational psychology, government, and law enforcement.

8.1.2 Authentication

The user identification and password are widely used in operating systems as a form of *authentication*. The user's identification specifies a claim to the rights that the human has to resources in the machine, and the password is the means by which the operating system authenticates the claim that the human user has the rights associated with the identification.

The operating system can take additional measures to ensure itself that the human user is the person he claims to be. Such authentication might use techniques similar to those used by a bank that allows one to transfer funds by telephone. The user may be asked to provide arbitrary additional information besides the password. Contemporary protection systems may even resort to methods such as fingerprint or eye scan identification.

Authentication has received considerable attention in the popular press since cases in which users have managed to *penetrate* a system without authorization are easily understood as a crime in our society. In some cases, penetration is accomplished via the log in route, and in other cases, it may occur in more surreptitious ways such as via a file transfer connection.

Penetration techniques are often characterized in the protection literature as masquerading or clandestine software.

Masquerading

The simplest form of masquerade occurs when a legitimate user identification and password are shared among different human users, perhaps because the external security mechanism is violated (a user leaves his identification and password in a public place, or the user's identification is well known and the password is easily guessed).

A slightly more sophisticated penetration technique is to use one computer to simulate a user: It is not difficult to guess the user identification for some user on a machine, since it is generally used as an electronic mail address and is published. The masquerading computer establishes a connection to the authentication process and rapidly and systematically tries many different passwords for the known user identification. The authentication process can detect the penetration attempt when it observes repeated failure of a user to supply a password; the authentication procedure can count successive failures and terminate the connection if some threshold is surpassed.

A more subtle form of masquerade can take place in file transfer (electronic mail) connections. File transfer fundamentally requires that one computer be able to transfer information into another system's file space, that is, the transmitting computer must be able to gain access to the receiving computer before it can cause the file to be stored. Thus, the file transfer port must also incorporate an authorization mechanism to verify that the transmitting computer has the right to store the file. In many systems, this authentication mechanism is not very sophisticated, since extensive authentication will increase the overhead involved in file transfer. This propensity to use simplified authentication mechanisms provides a loophole that can be used by a *worm* program. The worm masquerades as an incoming file transfer or electronic mail message, allowing the remote machine to gain entrance to the local machine.

Clandestine Modules

A penetrator may be able to circumvent the external protection mechanism and have a clandestine module installed in the operating system, perhaps as a bug fix or as an added feature. The clandestine module will correct the error or add the feature, but also leave undetected loopholes for the penetrator to use at some later time.

Virus programs are often a form of clandestine software, since they enter the system hidden within some other software module and then wreak havoc at a later time.

The clandestine software may also be used by one user to violate another user's resources, and in this case the software is typically called a *Trojan horse* (see additional discussion below).

8.1.3 Managing Resource Sharing

This aspect of protection is concerned with protecting one process from the actions of other processes; the object of the protection is the set of resources associated with the process, for example, the memory and files allocated to the process.

In this context, a process may have different types of access to some set of resources. For example, in Figure 8.1 process B has "type 1" *rights* to process A's W resource, "type 2" rights to X, "type 3" rights to Z, and no rights to resource Y. The various types of rights may correspond to "read" access, "execute" access, or some other type, depending on the nature of the resource.

As with authentication, researchers have characterized several different protection issues and have attempted to design policies and mechanisms to address them (not always successfully).

The Confinement Problem. This aspect of protection refers to the case where a process wishes to limit the dispersion of information to some particular environment. That is, the challenge is to contain all rights to resources to some set of processes.

The Trojan Horse Problem. The Trojan horse was mentioned in the context of clandestine authentication software; it also appears in resource sharing systems. A service program written by one user is used by a client process; when the client process is executing the service program, it uses its own rights. The service program behaves like a Trojan horse if it takes advantage of the client process's rights to access resources (in its own behalf) using the temporarily obtained rights. (There are several variants of the Trojan horse problem.)

Sharing Parameters. A process's resources may be violated if the process allows other processes to call procedures within its address space. For example, suppose a process calls a procedure in some other process's address space, and the procedure modifies parameters that are passed into the procedure so that, when the caller regains control, variables in its address space have been changed by the called procedure.

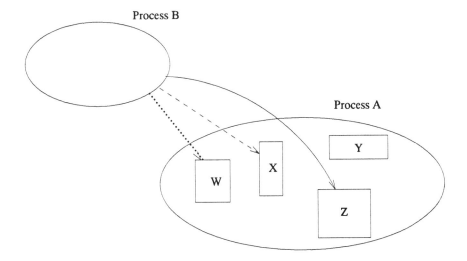

Figure 8.1 Controlled Resource Sharing

This can be avoided by restricting the ability of the called procedure to alter important parameters. For example, if a parameter should not be changed by the called procedure, then it should be passed by value, not by reference. That is, the problem can be eliminated by avoiding sharing of common information, but by sharing copies of common information.

Allocating Rights. A protection system may allow a process to provide another process specific rights to use its resources. In some cases, the first process needs to be able to revoke those rights at any time, that is, rights are only temporarily allocated by one process to another.

A more subtle problem may occur if a process provides rights to another process, and then the third process passes the rights onto other processes (without the knowledge nor permission of the resource owner). Some protection systems disallow rights propagation without the explicit permission of the resource owner.

Finally, there is a class of protection systems that attempts to solve the *mutually suspicious subsystems* problem. Two subsystems are made up of multiple programs — and possibly of multiple processes. The subsystems need to share information, but neither can be sure that the one will honor the information and rights of the other. In this circumstance, one subsystem may temporarily obtain data or rights from the other when the second subsystem requests service from the first. A more subtle form of the problem can occur if one subsystem is able to use the rights of a second subsystem to gain unauthorized access to the second subsystem's resources when the second requests service from the first.

Memory Protection

Historically, considerable effort has gone into protection mechanisms for memory objects. Allocatable units of memory are objects, for example, a word, a partition, a page, a page frame, or a segment. The IBM System/360 and other machines of the era used a set of *memory locks* on small groups of bytes. Suppose that memory were allocated in 16-byte atoms, each atom having an associated 4-bit *lock* register, and each process descriptor included a 4-bit *key* setting. Provided that the process descriptor and locks can only be set while the system is in supervisor mode, the memory access hardware can be made to shift byte addresses right 4-bits to obtain an index into a lock table. The contents of the lock table entry are compared to the key; if the key does not match the lock, then the memory access is an access violation, resulting in a trap to the system. This mechanism will only support a 16-process security policy, since there are only 16 allowable key-lock combinations. It also disallows any form of sharing by the operating system or among user subjects. This can be remedied by reserving patterns for special usage, for example, one key pattern might be a "master key" for any subject with supervisor rights. The corresponding lock pattern may mean "unprotected" memory accessible by any subject. Supervisor access and sharing can be implemented, although the sharing mechanism is weak.

In Chapter 7, virtual memory mechanisms were introduced to augment a process's address space. Virtual memory mechanisms are also useful for implementing impenetrable barriers between processes. A virtual memory defines a process's address space; if a process is unable to access physical memory without using the memory mapping mechanism, then address space isolation is guaranteed by correct management of each process's mapping tables. The problem is not so much in guaranteeing isolation as it is in allowing limited forms of sharing (see the discussion of shared segments in Section 7.3).

In the case of shared segments, each descriptor contains space for rights information that can be checked whenever the segment is made known to or loaded by a process. In the case of segments, the protection flags stored in the segment descriptor correspond to the protection bits in a file (see the next subsection).

File Protection

File protection mechanisms have been prevalent for several decades. (Multics segment protection is an extension of more conventional file protection mechanisms.)

The UNIX file protection mechanism and policy are simple, yet provide a good example of the ideas behind file protection. Every UNIX user is identified by a *user identification* (UID). He is also a member of a group of users, noted by the *group identification* (GID). The UID and GID for a process are part of the process's descriptor, thus it is easily checked by any system program when the process changes its protection rights, attempts to access a file, and so on.

Every UNIX file is created with a UID, GID, and an 11-bit access control flag as shown in Figure 8.2. The D-bit is set if the file is a directory. The three 3-bit user, group, and world fields are used to control access to the file by the owner of the file (process UID matches the file UID), other members of the group name for the file (process GID matches the file GID), and any other process. The respective r bit represents read access, the w bit represents write access, and the x bit represents execute access. If a process that is in the file owner's group wishes to execute the file, then the x bit must be set in the group field of the mask.

The owner of a file (and the "root" user) is allowed to set the file protection bits to any desired pattern. The UNIX security policy also attaches related semantics to files that contain directories, although there are extensions to address a process's ability to manipulate files in the directory.

The setUID bit is used for temporarily increasing a process's rights when the process is executing a trusted software module. Since UNIX does not depend on the kernel being implemented with processes, the system facilities are invoked through procedure call. A process executing a user program, in user space, calls a system program, causing the process to change from the user's rights to the kernel's rights. Each program is stored in a file, and each file has the 11-bit mask described above. If the setUID bit is set, then when a process executes the program loaded in the corresponding file, the process temporarily assumes the UID of the process that owns the file, that is, the UID stored in the file descriptor. When the process ceases executing the program, then it resumes its previous UID. The result is that a file can be constructed so that, when a process executes the code in the file, it has the rights of a system process; when it returns, it reverts back to its original rights.

	owner			group			world			
D	r	w	x	r	w	x	r	w	x	setUID

Figure 8.2 UNIX File Protection Mask

8.2 THE LAMPSON PROTECTION MODEL

In the early 1970s, researchers began to develop fundamental protection mechanisms that are widely used in today's systems. The Lampson model of protection was influential in this early development [10], and it and its extensions are described in this section.

In general, there are active parts of the system, such as processes, that act on behalf of other processes or human users. For the moment we will call all such active elements processes, although we will refine that definition below. The passive elements of the system are accessed by active elements, for example, a memory page, a file, or a message queue; the passive elements are referred to as *objects* in the literature.†

Processes may need to change the set of rights they have to objects, depending on the particular tasks they are doing. The UNIX file system uses the setUID bit in a binary file to allow a process that executes the file to temporarily assume rights appropriate for accessing system tables or otherwise manipulating system resources. The particular set of rights that a process has at any given time is referred to as a *protection domain*, and the *subject* is a process executing in a specific protection domain.

The Lampson model is built on a formal model of a system, subjects, objects, and mechanisms that specify the dynamic relationship among the subjects and objects.

> **Definition 8.2.** A *protection system* is composed from a set of passive objects, active subjects, and a set of *rules* specifying the policy. The protection system represents the current object accessibility by subjects by keeping a current *protection state*. The system guarantees that the protection state is checked for each access of an object by a subject. The protection system transitions from state to state by exercising rules in the system. ‖

A protection system is a mechanism that records the current definition of protection domains, that executes a set of policy-specific rules, and is itself secure (see Figure 8.3).

The protection state is conceptually represented by an *access matrix* mechanism. The access matrix, A, has one row for each subject and one column for each object (every subject is also an object since processes need to be able to exercise control over other processes). The entry in A[S, X] is a string, α, describing the access rights held by subject S to object X.

Each access consists of the following steps (see Figure 8.4):

---

† The name conflict between "protection objects" and "object-oriented programming objects" is unfortunate, but we have chosen to use the term here since it is prevalent in the protection literature. Protection objects are not to be thought of as full objects with inheritance, although they may behave like abstract data types.

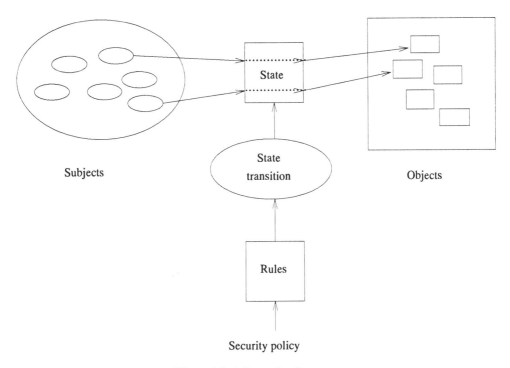

Figure 8.3 A Protection System

(1)   Subject S initiates α access to object X.
(2)   The protection system supplies (S, α, X) in behalf of S, that is, S cannot forge a subject identity since the system supplies the identity.
(3)   The *monitor* of X interrogates A[S, X].

$$\alpha \in A[S, X] \Rightarrow \text{the access is valid}$$
$$\alpha \notin A[S, X] \Rightarrow \text{the access is invalid}$$

This mechanism can be used to implement many different policies. Suppose that a simple system were composed as follows:

$$\text{subjects} = \{S_1, S_2, S_3\}$$
$$\text{objects} = \text{subjects} \bigcup \{F_1, F_2, D_1, D_2\}$$

where F_1 and F_2 are files and D_1 and D_2 are devices. Figure 8.5 is an example protection state for the system. Each subject has **control** privilege to itself. S_1 has **block, wakeup,** and **owner** privileges over S_2 and **control** and **owner** privileges to S_3. File F_1 can be accessed by S_1 with **read*** or **write*** access; S_2 is its owner, and s_3 has **delete** access.

If S_2 attempts **update** access to F_2, then it initiates the access, causing the protection system to create a record of the form (s_2, **update**, F_2). The record is given to the

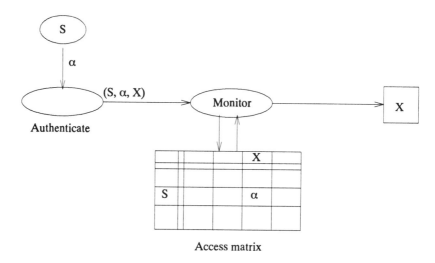

Figure 8.4 Representing the Protection State

	S_1	S_2	S_3	F_1	F_2	D_1	D_2
S_1	control	block wakeup owner	control owner	read* write*		seek	owner
S_2		control	stop	owner	update	owner	seek*
S_3			control	delete	execute owner		

Figure 8.5 A Protection State

monitor for F_2, which interrogates $A[S_2, F_2]$. Since **update** $\in A[S_2, F_2]$, the access is valid and the subject is allowed to update the file object.

If S_2 attempts **execute** access to F_2, then it initiates the access, causing the protection system to create a record of the form (S_2, **execute**, F_2). The record is given to the monitor for F_2, which interrogates $A[S_2, F_2]$. Since **execute**$\notin A[S_2, F_2]$, the access is invalid and the violation is reported to the operating system.

Changing the Protection State

The protection system uses policy rules to control the means by which it alters the protection state. A policy can be partially specified by choosing the type of accesses that can appear in the matrix and then completed by specifying a set of rules for protection state transitions.

Graham and Denning provide an example set of rules in [7] that describes how rights can be passed to other subjects (see Figure 8.6). These rules are consistent with the access types shown in Figure 8.5.

The * is called a copy flag; an access right is not to be transferred from one process to another unless the right belongs to the process executing the transfer **and** the copy flag is set for that particular access right. In Figure 8.5, S_1 can transfer either **read** or **read*** access to S_2 or S_3 for F_1 because S_1 has the copy flag set on the **read** access (by rule 1 in

Rule	Command by S_0	Authorization	Operation
1	transfer$\{\alpha \mid \alpha*\}$ to (S, X)	$\alpha* \in A[S_0, X]$	$A[S, X] \leftarrow \{\alpha \mid \alpha*\}$
2	grant$\{\alpha \mid \alpha*\}$ to (S, X)	"owner" $\in A[S_0, X]$	$A[S, X] \leftarrow \{\alpha \mid \alpha*\}$
3	delete α from (S, X)	"control" $\in A[S_0, S]$ "owner" $\in A[S_0, X]$	delete α from row S
4	$w \leftarrow$ read(S, X)	"control" $\in A[S_0, S]$ "owner" $\in A[S_0, X]$	$w \leftarrow A[S, X]$
5	create object X	none	add column X; $A[S_0, X] \leftarrow$ "owner"
6	delete object X	"owner" $\in A[S_0, X]$	delete column X
7	create subject S	none	add row S; create object S $A[S, S] \leftarrow$ "control"
8	delete subject S	"owner" $\in A[S_0, S]$	delete row S delete object S

Figure 8.6 Policy Rules

Figure 8.6). By rule 2, a subject can grant any access — with or without the copy flag set — provided that the subject owns the object.

The copy flag and the rules are designed to prevent indiscriminate propagation of access rights among subjects. A right can be copied when the owner passes on the copy flag; the copy flag can be transferred from one process to another, or the right can be transferred to a subject with the copy flag cleared.

Notice that we have used the transfer rule as a nondestructive copy rule; another policy might require that the transfer be destructive, that is, when a nonowner subject transfers an access to another subject, it loses its own access. Such a policy might be useful to closely guard the dissemination of rights by the owner subjects.

The delete rule is used to revoke a right for an object from another subject. The authorization required for deletion is that the subject that invokes the delete rule either has **control** over the subject that is losing the access, or it **owns** the object. With this set of rules, if a subject is the **owner** of another subject, then it also has **control** over the subject.

The last four rules describe the means for adding subjects and objects to the access matrix.

The protection system model can be used to address several of the protection problems mentioned earlier in the chapter. The model explicitly addresses problems in sharing parameters, independently of whether the policy wishes to allow subjects to share copies of objects or the objects themselves. It also handles rights allocation in a reasonable manner. For example, dynamic rights revocation can be handled by altering the access matrix at any time, causing a subject's access to an object to be revoked between successive access operations. Propagation of rights can be controlled by using the copy flag.

The protection system also addresses the mutually suspicious subsystem problem. Figure 8.7 illustrates one half of the solution — indirect address by one subsystem to the private object(s) of the other: The object is protected by a "gatekeeper" subject under the control of the ultimate object's owner (that is, the ultimate owner need only have owner access over the gatekeeper subject, which provides implicit ownership of the object). The owner can revoke the untrusted subsystem's access to the gatekeeper subject at any time, and the gatekeeper can authenticate each access from the untrusted subject. Clearly, the "untrusted subject" in the figure may not trust the "owner subject," giving rise to symmetric indirect access to gatekeeper subjects; this would provide a solution to the mutual suspicion problem.

The confinement problem poses a more difficult problem; it is desirable to be able to restrict subjects' ability to propagate rights and information. Because read access (even obtained using indirect access) provides the ability to copy information, it is difficult to allow an untrusted subsystem, for example, a Trojan horse, to provide service while ensuring that it does not retain rights nor information. In general, this requires that the suspicious subject be guaranteed to be *memoryless* or *confined* with respect to its ability to retain information (or to leak it to other subjects). In [9], Lampson examines properties of confined programs more carefully, and concludes that there are different classifications of such programs: ones that are memoryless or fully confined, and ones that may leak varying amounts of information using channels (*legitimate channels*, *storage channels*, and *covert channels*). Tsai, Gligor, and Chandersekaran revisit the covert storage channel problem in a more recent study [21]. If the untrusted subject is not memoryless, then the confinement problem cannot be solved.

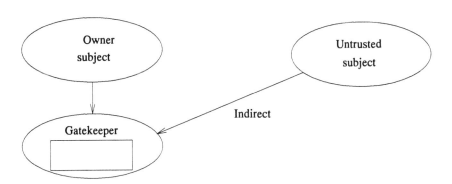

Figure 8.7 Indirect Access

8.3 THE FLOW CONTROL MODEL

The flow model is built around the premise that rights and information flow from subject to subject, and that the system can implement a protection policy by identifying and controlling the flow. (The approach is patterned after government security models.) Both parts of the model rely on partial orderings of rights, organized as a lattice.

Access flow is represented by assigning levels of ability to subjects and objects: Each object is signed a *classification level* reflecting the importance of ensuring protection for the object, for example, **unclassified** or **secret**. Each subject has a corresponding *clearance level*. The classification and clearance levels are also called *security levels*. Each subject and each object belong to one or more *compartments* corresponding to groups of entities that need to interact with one another. An entity's *security class* is an ordered pair (L, C), where L is a security level and C is a compartment. A protection policy is specified by defining security classes and their interrelationship, in general as a lattice (such that each pair of security classes has a least upper bound and a greatest lower bound). The flow control mechanism relies on a total order among the security level of the subjects and objects, and a separate partial order on the compartments: Subject S can access object X if and only if:

(1)   Subject S has a clearance that is at least as high as object X ($L(S) \geq L(X)$), and

(2)   The compartment containing S is contained in the compartment containing X, ($C(S) \subseteq C(X)$).

The use of clearance levels and compartments is inspired by government security models. There are two aspects of authorized access: first, the subject must have a sufficiently high clearance level (the first condition), and second, it must "have a need to know," reflected by being within a compartment.

Figure 8.8 illustrates a possible scenario for a system. Subjects are named A, B, ..., M; objects are named Q, R, ..., Z. Subjects and objects are divided into compartments, with compartment I containing compartments II and III. A, B, and Q are level I; C, D, and E are at level II, and so on. A and B can access Q, but no other subject is permitted to do so. E can access S, T, and U at level 2; it can also access V and W at level 3, and Y and Z at level 4. C can access S and U at level 2, V and W at level 3, and Z at level 4.

Access Flow

Controlling access flow is analogous to dictating the nature of state changes in the access matrix for the Lampson model, that is, the current protection state as determined by the flow model can be represented by an access matrix, and it can be changed through some fixed set of rules similar to the exemplary ones provided above.

For example, suppose we are given the rights:

Read. The subject can read the object, but not write it.

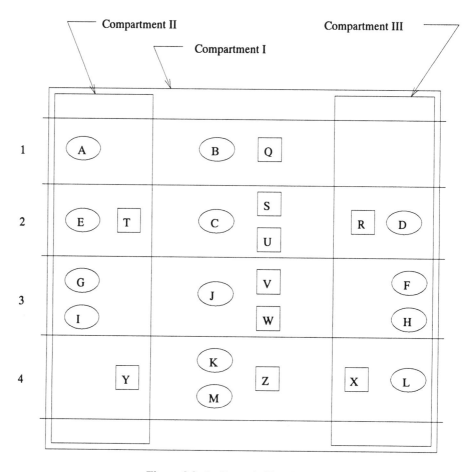

Figure 8.8 An Example Flow Model

Append. The subject can add information to the object, but not read it.

Read-write. The subject can read and append the object.

Execute. The subject can execute the object, but neither read it nor write it.

Control. The subject can pass attributes other than control to other subjects.

Suppose that the system requires that a subject can read an object only if the security class for the subject, S, is greater than or equal to the security class of the object, X $[L(S) \geq L(X)]$, and that a subject can append to an object only if the security class of S is less than or equal to the security class of X $[L(S) \leq L(X)]$, that is, a subject cannot both read and write an object unless the security classes are equal $[L(S) = L(X)]$. Under these conditions, a subject can gather information from a lower security level, but cannot divulge it to any object unless it is more secure.

Figure 8.9 illustrates the policy described in the previous paragraph [11]. The figure omits the authorization necessary for a subject to be able to execute the rule. The authorization must enforce the general flow model property and the two conditions described in the previous paragraph, for example, a subject cannot increase the security level higher than its own security level using rule 7.

In terms of access rights management, the flow model bears many similarities to the Lampson model, although it relies on the partial ordering among clearances and compartments for determining rules for changing the protection state. More significant differences exist in the control of information flow.

Rule	Command by S_0	Operation
1	get(α, X)	S is preparing to α-access X
2	release(α, X)	α is removed from A[S, X]
3	give(α, S′, X)	A[S′, X] ← α
4	rescind(α, S)	delete α from A[S', X]
5	create object(X)	activate object X
6	delete object(X)	deactivate object X
7	change security level(X, i)	L(X) ← i

Figure 8.9 Policy Rules

Information Flow

Information flow among components can be either explicit or implicit. *Explicit* information flow is easily identified by assignment, a writeable parameter from a procedure call, or an input statement. Implicit information flow is more subtle: If a statement such as

$$\text{if}(a = 0)\text{then } b \leftarrow c;$$

appears in a program, then it is possible to assert that, after the execution of the statement, $a = 0$ implies that b has the same value as c (by explicit information flow). Notice also that it may now also be possible to infer the value of the variable a by comparing the values of b and c; this is an example of *implicit* information flow.

Denning [3] specifies three requirements for information flow to be secure, within the environment of the general flow model:
(1)   A statement of the form $y \leftarrow f(x)$ is secure if the explicit information flow from x to y satisfies $L(x) \leq L(y)$.†
(2)   A conditional statement of the form

$$condition \Rightarrow \{S_i\};$$

is secure if each of the S_i are secure and implicit flow from the condition is secure; that is, $L(condition) \leq L(S) = \{S_i\})$.‡
(3)   A program is secure if each statement is secure.

Secure information flow verification becomes intimately involved with the analysis of the programs in which the assignment and conditional statements appear. If security levels are statically assigned to subjects and objects, then the information flow can be analyzed at compile time; otherwise, it will be necessary to verify security at run time.

8.4 PROTECTION MECHANISMS

In the previous sections we described general problems and approaches to implementing protection policies, focusing on the definition of protection mechanisms. In this section, we address the design and implementation of some of these mechanisms.

Implementing the Access Matrix

A protection mechanism is fundamentally based on the means used to save the protection state, to query the state to validate ongoing access, and to change the state. In both models of protection, the access matrix has been used as the abstract representation of the state. Let us first consider implementations of the access matrix.

---

† Since f may be a function of many variables, the level of y must be greater than the levels of each of the arguments of f; this requires that the properties of the least upper bound of the x objects in the lattice must be used to test the order of levels.

‡ Since S may be compound statement made up of S_i the security level of each S_i must be greater than the level of the conditional variables as they are embedded in the lattice. Thus, the security level of the conditional must be less than the greatest lower bound of the security levels of the S_i.

First, the access matrix must be represented in some secure storage medium that can only be read and written by selected processes. Second, it must be possible to route all accesses through the protection system (this may not actually be done for all accesses, but it should be possible). Such routing will ensure that the current protection state will be used to validate each access. Third, the protection system can authenticate the source of each request by a subject, rather than being passed the identity as a parameter through a procedure call. The monitor must be a protected process that can implement the rules. It must not be possible for other subjects to compromise the monitor, for example, by sharing its resources. (Of course, the rules may be logically faulty, allowing another subject to "fool" the monitor into providing unintended access to an object, but that is a policy bug, not a mechanism bug.)

The access matrix itself can be implemented in any of a number of ways. For most collections of subjects and objects, the matrix will be sparse. This suggests that efficient implementations use lists of entries rather than storing the matrix in a rectangular array. For example, the list can contain an entry of the form $(S_i, O_j, \alpha$ set$)$ if α set is the set of strings that are logically stored in $A[S_i, O_j]$. The trade-off is the usual one for sparse matrices; the length of the list is proportional to the number of entries in the matrix (that is, full matrices produce unwieldy lists).

The matrix could be partitioned into column vectors, with each vector being stored as a list of rights to the object it is protecting (the null entries from the matrix are not stored). Now the monitor for the object can easily search the list whenever S_i attempts an access to the object. That is, the vector is an *access control list* for the given object. UNIX employs this technique for protecting files (see above).

Similarly, compressed rows of the access matrix can be associated with the subjects. Whenever the subject initiates the access, the protection system checks the list to see if the subject has the right — capability — to access the designated object. Thus, access rights are allocated to the subject much like a ticket to an event; in the extreme, if the subject does not possess a capability in its list, then it may not even know the name of the object. When the access matrix is stored in this manner, it is called a *capability list*.

Access control lists and capabilities are the most widely used implementations. Capabilities have many other interesting properties and have generally gained in popularity in contemporary distributed systems, so we expand our discussion of them below. Access control lists are discussed in the context of the Multics protection domain implementation.

8.4.1 Protection Domains

Supervisor Mode

The basic von Neumann machine does not offer sufficient hardware mechanisms to support the implementation of many software protection mechanisms. An early extension to the architecture is the idea of two instruction sets for different classes of processes. A system process can operate with the *supervisor* instruction sets and all other processes must use the *user* instructions. The supervisor instruction set is a superset of the user instruction set. Typically, the CPU will contain a 1-bit *mode* register that can be set to indicate which instruction set it is to use when it interprets a program. The supervisor instruction set includes an instruction to set the bit to user mode, but the user mode does not include an equivalent instruction; the mode bit is set from user to supervisor state through an operating system call instruction (trap), an interrupt, and so on. In the context of the flow model, all programs that operate in the supervisor mode have a higher security level than those that operate in the user mode.

This basic mechanism enables one to construct operating systems processes that can control devices, page tables, and the like, and precludes any user process from doing so since instructions that access these registers and devices are omitted from the user instruction set. The vast majority of contemporary architectures that support multiple users or wish to isolate the input/output instructions from the user programs incorporate the supervisor and user modes. UNIX implementations rely heavily on the existence of the two modes to distinguish between a process executing in kernel mode and in user mode. (Notice that in such an architecture it is easy to write single-process operating systems by simply allowing the single process to operate in supervisor mode.)

Figure 8.10 is a visualization of two protection domains in which the inner domain represents programs that are executed with the supervisor mode enabled. Programs that operate in the inner domain have additional logical rights in addition to the extended instruction set, that is, if p is a process, then subject $S_1 = (p, user)$ has different rights than does $S_1 = (p, supervisor)$. Information in each domain is ordinarily stored in files (or segments), where the file descriptor describes the domain in which the contents are either executed or used (see the discussion of the setUID bit, above). Thus, programs and data reside in a domain.

Protection Rings

The generalization of the two-level domain implied by the two-mode CPU is a set of N concentric rings called the "onion skin" or *ring* architecture for protection (see Figure 8.11). The Multics protection system is organized as N = 8 rings of protection in which rings R_0 through R_3 correspond to the inner domain of Figure 8.11, and rings R_4 through R_7 are used by applications. Thus, i < j implies that R_i has more rights than R_j in Multics. Ring R_0 is the minimal kernel of the Multics system and is the only ring that uses the hardware supervisor mode; all outer rings, R_i (i > 0), support programs in user mode.

In Multics, segments (as opposed to files) reside in a ring. The protection mechanism provides a means by which a process can safely change domains, that is, cross rings. If the segment is being executed in R_i, then it can call any procedure in R_j (j ≥ i) without special permission. Upon calling an outer ring, the Multics segmentation mechanism will

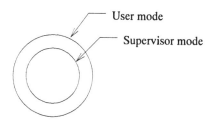

Figure 8.10 A Simple Ring Architecture

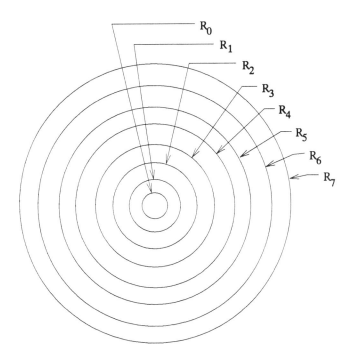

Figure 8.11 The Multics Ring Architecture

ensure that the return and parameter references (which will be an inner ring reference) will be allowed.

Inner ring calls can only be accomplished through published ring *gates* (monitored procedure entry points). Each attempted inner ring crossing will cause a trap to the operating system (using techniques similar to those described for missing segment traps in Chapter 7). The operating system verifies the nature of the call, for example, inner or outer ring crossing. If the ring crossing is inward, then the caller must meet more requirements before the call succeeds.

Each segment has an access control list; it describes the allowable reference access rights (read, write, execute, or append permissions) and a *ring bracket* triple, (R_L, R_M, R_H) specifying rings from which the segment can be called. The *access bracket* for the segment is the pair (R_L, R_M); when the segment is called from outer ring R_i with $R_L \leq R_i \leq R_M$, then the procedure is allowed to read or execute the bracket with no additional checking. The segment is executed in the original ring R_i.

The *call bracket* is determined by the pair (R_M, R_H) identifying a set of concentric rings immediately outside (less trusted than) the access bracket. If the segment is called from a process in the call bracket, the operating system turns control to a gatekeeper associated with the gate entry point. The gatekeeper can authenticate the incoming call to decide if the call should be completed or not. The segment executes in the caller's ring.

The Multics ring structure does not support inner ring data accesses, only procedure calls. Data kept in inner rings can only be accessed using a corresponding inner ring access procedure (compare with the discussion of allowing an untrusted subject to access an object). Whenever a process calls inward, then it changes domains — becomes a different subject. An alternative view is that the operating system has temporarily *amplified* the rights of the process as long as the process executes procedures in the inner ring domain; when the process returns to an outer ring, it will change domains and will resume its previous set of rights.

The ring structure is very general, but it requires considerable hardware and software support. A wide variety of policies can be implemented in ring structures, although the ideas have not often been found to be cost effective in commercial systems (but see the next subsection).

Contemporary Rings

Ring structures are also used in contemporary computer architectures, for example, the Intel 80386 microprocessor incorporates a four-level structure with some similarities to the Multics structure. In this case, there are three levels of instruction sets: level 2 and 3 instructions are the normal application program instruction set, although noncritical portions of the operating system code execute at level 2. Level 1 instructions include input/output instructions, and level 0 instructions are allowed to manipulate segmented memory (using a *global descriptor table*) and to perform context switching.

The architecture is intended to support memory segment manipulation at level 0, while input/output operations operate at a lower clearance level (higher ring number). The main body of the operating system operates at level 2, where its segments are protected by the ring structure, that is, level 3 processes cannot easily gain access to information stored at level 2 (similar to the Multics ring usage).

8.4.2 Capabilities

Capabilities are widely used in contemporary operating systems as a mechanism to employ protection and to span address spaces among subjects. In Chapter 13, we describe several uses of capabilities in specific operating systems.

> **Definition 8.3.** A *capability* is a unique, global name for an access right to an object in a system. ‖

Thus, "read access to sector i on disk k" is a capability, as is "write access to virtual address i in process j's address space." In the context of the protection models, a row in the access matrix is a list of capabilities of the form (object, α access).

A capability is used for two purposes: It is a global address of a resource; second, possession of the address is considered to be sufficient verification that the subject has access to the described object. Since possession of a capability represents that authentication has already taken place, capability-based systems are more efficient than access-control systems. The uses suggest certain properties of capabilities:

(1)   The values taken on by a capability must be derived from a large name space.
(2)   Capabilities must be unique, and not reused once they have been assigned.

(3) Capabilities need to be distinguishable from spurious names (for example, ordinary integers or pointers).

There are two basic approaches to implementing capabilities: They may be wholly implemented within the operating system's address space, or the hardware platform may incorporate specialized support for capabilities.† A capability can be represented internally as a typed scalar value, for example, as a record of the form

```
struct capability
{
            type    tag;
            long    addr;
}
```

So that if c is a capability then c.tag = **capability** and c.addr is the global address. A subject can access an object only if it has a capability with c.addr that addresses an "entry point" to the resource corresponding to the type of the access. The object monitor that receives an access request (with an associated capability) need only verify that c.tag is a **capability** to be assured that the access is valid.

Each subject needs to be able to obtain and use capabilities, but not to be able to generate them. If the subject's capabilities are all maintained in the operating system's space, then the subject is unable to create a data structure that resembles a capability without the intervention of the operating system. However, the subject can use its capabilities (stored in the operating system space) for accessing objects. Notice that in the case that capabilities are exclusively managed by the operating system the tag field in the data structure can be eliminated, since type is implied by the use of the capability, for example, in a segmented virtual memory system, all capabilities are stored in a subject's capability segment.

Tags can be implemented in hardware by associating a tag with units of memory, usually words, for example, see the Burroughs computer architectures [17]. The tag field in the word can be set to **capability** or **other** by a supervisory mode instruction (ordinarily, the tag field can also only be read by a supervisory mode instruction, the object's protection monitor). While it is sufficient for the tag to be a 1-bit flag, tagged architecture machines typically incorporate n-bit tags to allow the software to distinguish among 2^n different classes of memory contents.

Example 8.1: Hydra [1]

Hydra was an experimental operating system built for a research multiprocessor called the c.mmp multiprocessor. A fundamental goal of the operating system was to separate policy and mechanism from one another throughout the system (also see the discussion of Hydra in Chapter 13). This separation was especially important in the protection scheme, which was based on capabilities. The system was designed to allow user-space programs to determine the protection policy for information storage, particularly the file and directory system. The base mechanism is designed to allow policy-level solutions to mutual suspicion, confinement, and dynamic rights revocation.

---

† As a practical approach, capabilities can also be selected randomly from a very large name space. This results in capabilities being unique with high probability, but without guarantee.

Hydra protection mechanisms are based on five principles [1]:

(1) Information can be encapsulated into objects that can be used to validate access.

(2) Objects are typed and recognize certain predefined operations.

(3) Objects are accessed using capabilities. (A capability differs from the definition given earlier in the chapter in that it uniquely identifies an object, but may contain many different access types.)

(4) A subject should have a minimal set of access rights required to complete the desired processing.

(5) Object operation implementations are private to the object.

Each Hydra object is composed of a pair: (C-list, data part). The C-list is manipulated only by the kernel, eliminating the need for the capability to include a tag-wield. In particular, a *local name space* (LNS) is an object type that represents an executing program with a particular set of capabilities (protection domain). Whenever the executing program attempts to access any resource (another object), the LNS must contain an appropriate capability. The kernel supports indirect references through objects by allowing an object to use the capabilities of an intermediate object, provided that the intermediate object authenticates the indirect usage; the kernel also allows the initiator to specify a path of capabilities through objects to avoid manual authentication.

There are a few built-in object types (for example, **procedure, semaphore,** and **process**), while the kernel is prepared to handle arbitrary object types defined in user space. Each object has a subset of operations, named *k-calls*, that are implemented within the kernel: **get/put/add data** k-calls manipulate the data part of an object, and **load/store/append/delete/copy/create** k-calls manipulate the C-list part of an object. The **store** and **append** k-calls use a mask to control propagation of rights (compare with the copy flag in the access matrix). These operations are the fundamental tools that are used by a user-space program to specify a policy. Each k-call is guaranteed to execute completely before another k-call is initiated on any processor; (**load; delete**) and (**store; delete**) k-calls can be treated as transactions through specific higher-level k-calls.

Sharing is accomplished through the dispersion of capabilities by an LNS object. The k-calls allow the responsible LNS to copy capabilities to other LNSs and to revoke capabilities if the policy requires it.

The kernel supports two types of rights: generic and auxiliary rights. Generic rights can be applied to any object, while auxiliary rights are defined for particular object types. The kernel employs a 24-bit rights mask to identify rights. Generic rights have fixed positions in the mask, while auxiliary rights are assigned meaning according to objects (and the policy for managing object access). The kernel simply checks the bit map for appropriate settings when testing a capability for rights.

Objects are defined by implementing a subsystem composed of a set of procedures and a C-list. The subsystem defines a new type for the object, which can be instantiated as needed. Subsystems are the extending mechanism that allows one to define a policy as an object, where the object can be invoked from other objects, yet still have a specific set of amplified rights while it executes. The kernel manages the creation of the object, the type and rights checking, and the amplification when an object is invoked; the particular actions specified by the object are determined by the subsystem definition.

8.4.3 Cryptography

Protection mechanisms inevitably have parts of their design during which crucial information is temporarily unprotected, for example, when information (an access matrix entry, a capability, or raw data) is transferred from one part of the system to another. As a final "line of defense," cryptographic techniques can be used to convert the *clear text* (or *plain text*) to *ciphered text* to protect it whenever it is potentially exposed.

The basic technique is that an encryption function, f, and a decryption function, g = f⁻¹, are defined such that

$$g(key', f(key, clear\_text)) = clear\_text$$

where *key* contributes to the evaluation of the function. The encryption function acts as a lock, and the encryption key is used to lock translation of the clear text into ciphered text. A different key, *key'*, is used to translate the ciphered text back into clear text.

There are two strategies for constructing encryption and decryption mechanisms: designs in which the ciphering mechanism itself provides security, and designs in which the mechanism is public but the keys are complex and secret. In the first case, the f and g functions are complex (making it difficult to guess how the translation is accomplished); in the second case, the keys are complex (making it difficult to "guess" a key).

There are a class of *symmetric* encryption techniques in which the encryption key is the same as the decryption key. This form of encryption is useful if a trusted subsystem performs both the encryption and decryption of information. For example, the user authentication system might use this technique for saving passwords. When the user declares a password, the operating system uses its private key for encrypting the data and storing it in a password object. At authentication time, the operating system uses its key to decode the entry in the password object to compare it to the password supplied by the user.

Asymmetric encryption and decryption are required in cases where different subjects perform the encryption and decryption. Each may then have a private key, suitable for encrypting or decrypting, depending on the rights of the subject. This form or cryptography is required in general protection policies.

8.5 FURTHER READING

Protection and security are complex areas of computer and social sciences. Because of the importance of computers as resources and repositories of information, there is potentially considerable vulnerability in private, corporate, and government sectors. This has raised the public's general interest in computer security and protection, for example, in "hacker" cases [20] and "worm" cases [8, 22].

We have barely touched on the most important issues and approaches. The interested reader is encouraged to explore the literature in the area, perhaps starting with survey papers (for example, [11]) and following with books (for example, [2]).

Capabilities are now widely-used in various operating systems. Fundamental work on capabilities appears in Dennis and Van Horne's early work [4], followed by the classic paper by Fabry [6]; Schroeder, Clark, and Saltzer illustrate the use of capabilities in Multics [19]. Hydra was briefly reviewed in the body of the chapter; the Cambridge CAP system is another operating system that makes extensive use of capabilities [15, 16].

Cryptography has stimulated an almost entirely separate body of research literature, since it has other applications besides those related to computer security. The interested reader may wish to review Lempel's survey paper [12] in addition to Denning's book [2].

Additional discussion of internal protection (within the tighter context of operating systems) can be found in Chapter 8 of Maekawa, Oldehoeft, and Oldehoeft [14]. The most complete description of implementation is Organick's presentation of Multics [18]. Dewar and Smosna describe the Intel 80386 ring protection mechanism in Chapter 3 of [5].

Lunt and others provide a current discussion of the application of the security and protection techniques to relational databases [13].

REFERENCES

1. E. Cohen and D. Jefferson, "Protection in the Hydra Operating System," *Proceedings of the Fifth ACM Symposium on Operating Systems Principles*, November 1975, 141-160.

2. D. E. Denning, *Cryptography and Data Security*, Addison-Wesley Publishing Co., Reading, MA, 1982.

3. D. E. Denning, "A Lattice Model of Secure Information Flow," *Communications of the ACM 19*, 5 (May 1976), 236-243.

4. J. B. Dennis and E. C. Van Horne, "Programming Semantics for Multiprogrammed Computations," *Communications of the ACM 9*, 3 (March 1966), 143-155.

5. R. B. K. Dewar and M. Smosna, *Microprocessors: A Programmer's View*, McGraw-Hill Book Co., New York, NY, 1990.

6. R. S. Fabry, "Capability-Based Addressing," *Communications of the ACM 17*, 7 (July 1974), 403-412.

7. G. S. Graham and P. J. Denning, "Protection -- Principles and Practice," *AFIPS Proceedings of the Spring Joint Computer Conference 40* (1972), 417-429.

8. B. Kocher, "President's Letter: Everything Old is New Again," *Communications of the ACM 33*, 3 (March 1990), 261.

9. B. W. Lampson, "A Note on the Confinement Problem," *Communications of the ACM 16*, 10 (October 1973), 613-615.

10. B. W. Lampson, "Protection," *Proceedings of the Fifth Annual Princeton Conference on Information Science Systems*, 1971, 437-443.

11. C. E. Landwehr, "Formal Models for Computer Security," *ACM Computing Surveys 13*, 3 (September 1981), 247-275.

12. A. Lempel, "Cryptology in Transition: A Survey," *ACM Computing Surveys 11*, 4 (December 1979), 285-304.

13. T. F. Lunt, D. E. Denning, R. R. Schell, M. Heckman, and W. R. Shockley, "The SeaView Security Model," *IEEE Transactions on Software Engineering 16*, 6 (June 1990), 593-607.

14. M. Maekawa, A. E. Oldehoeft, and R. R. Oldehoeft, *Operating Systems Advanced Concepts*, Benjamin/Cummings Publishing, Menlo Park, CA, 1987.

15. R. M. Needham and R. D. H. Walker, "The Cambridge CAP Computer and its Protection System," *Proceedings of the Sixth ACM Symposium on Operating Systems Principles*, November 1977, 1-10.

16. R. M. Needham and A. J. Herbert, *The Cambridge Distributed Computing System*, Addison-Wesley Publishing Co., Reading, MA, 1982.

17. E. I. Organick, *Computer System Organization*, Academic Press, New York, NY, 1973.

18. E. I. Organick, *The Multics System: An Examination of Its Structure*, MIT Press, Cambridge, MA, 1972.

19. M. D. Schroeder, D. D. Clark, and J. H. Saltzer, "The MULTICS Kernel Design Project," *Proceedings of the Sixth ACM Symposium on Operating Systems Principles*, November 1977, 43-56.

20. C. Stoll, "Stalking the Wily Hacker," *Communications of the ACM 31*, 5 (May 1988), 484-497.

21. C. Tsai, V. D. Gligor, and C. S. Chandersekaran, "On the Identification of Covert Storage Channels in Secure Systems," *IEEE Transactions on Software Engineering 16*, 6 (June 1990), 569-580.
22. "Special Section on the Internet Worm," *Communications of the ACM 32*, 6 (June 1989), 677-710.

EXERCISES

(1) Consider a variant of the k-bit key and lock scheme described for memory protection in Section 7.1 in which a process can access memory blocks for which every bit position set to 1 within the lock is also set to 1 in the process's key.
   (a) How many unique locks are in the system?
   (b) Characterize all keys that can access a memory block with the lock 01100110 for k = 8.
   (c) Show how this mechanism can be used to allow a process B to keep some memory blocks private, to share some with process A, and to share others with process C (but for which A and C do not share any memory blocks).

(2) Explain how the UNIX file protection mechanism could be used to allow any process to read and modify a system file using special commands named get_special and put_special.

(3) Given the protection state shown in Figure 8.5 and the set of policy rules shown in Figure 8.6. Without changing the protection state, is it possible for S_1 to **block** S_3?

(4) Given the protection state shown in Figure 8.5 and the set of policy rules shown in Figure 8.6. Show a sequence of rule applications that will change the protection state so that S_3 has **write** access to D_2.

(5) Draw a diagram similar to Figure 8.7 that shows how to solve the mutually suspicious subsystem problem.

(6) Using the flow control protection mechanism, what resources can subject E access in the diagram below? What subjects have access to object V.

(7) Argue for conditions under which the access control method is superior to the capability list approach for implementing the access matrix.

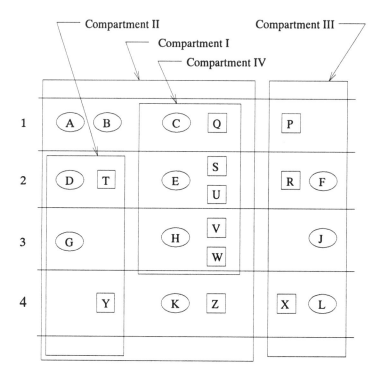

Figure 8.11 An Example Flow Model

9

FILE MANAGEMENT

The previous chapters have concentrated on various properties of processes and have largely ignored the problem of providing information to processes from sources external to the machine or writing information from a process to the external world. The system is configured with input/output devices to accomplish these operations.

Input/output devices can be characterized as storage devices or communications devices: *Storage devices* are used to store data while the computer is powered down; thus, storage devices can be used to keep archival information and to transfer bulk information from one machine to another. *Communications devices* are used to enter data into the machine, to print or display data, and to transmit data from one machine to another. In this chapter, we focus on storage devices and the *file system* abstraction. In Chapters 10 through 12, we address communication devices as they are used for interconnecting distinct computer systems.

9.1 STORAGE DEVICES

An input/output abstract machine hierarchy is shown in Figure 9.1. At the bottom of the hierarchy are physical storage devices, such as tape drives, magnetic disk drives, and optical disk drives.

Devices perform their operation according to certain specific commands, such as "move the read/write head" for a disk drive. While it would be possible for every program to control the device at this fine grain, the tasks are easily committed to hardware implementations that provide a simpler interface, hence the second-level abstract machine (the *device controller*). This abstraction allows the device user to control the operation of the device at a much higher level, such as "write a block of data" or "rewind the tape."

| File systems and other abstractions |
| Device drivers |
| Device controllers |
| Devices |

Figure 9.1 The Input/Output Abstract Machine Hierarchy

The device driver/controller interface is a hardware/software interface. The *device driver* encapsulates many of the device-dependent specifics within a single program that can be invoked by many different processes. That is, different device drivers (for different devices) can provide a similar interface so that a higher-layer machine need not be overly concerned with the details of the particular device.

A number of different abstractions may exist above the device driver interface, although the file system abstraction dominates (there are operating systems that do not support files, for example, recall the discussion of the Multics virtual memory system). We now turn to a brief discussion of storage devices and device drivers before focusing on file systems.

9.1.1 Storage Device Characteristics

Storage devices are either *sequential devices* or *rotating devices*. Both types of storage device perform *block* input/output operations, that is, an operation will read or write a fixed-sized block of contiguous bytes. The size of a block is device dependent, thus the device driver must be specific to the type of device.

Sequential Devices

Sequential storage devices physically store information on some recording medium as a sequence of bytes. Magnetic tape is the prevalent sequential storage medium in today's systems.

Tape drives are engineered to read or write a block of bytes from or to a tape on an individual operation. Thus, the driver will perceive a tape drive as a block device. Each block is called a *physical record* on the tape, and sequential blocks are separated by inter-record gaps that are required to compensate for the inertia encountered to start and stop the tape drive on block input/output operations.

Information stored on a tape drive can be accessed rapidly if the process that reads the tape intends to read all the information on the tape in the order that it is stored on the tape. That is, the significant delays in such an operation are those related to reading and writing a physical record (a function of the physical motion of the tape across the read/write heads).

If the process only desires certain information on the tape, then it must cause the tape drive to position the tape so that the correct information is over the read/write heads (this is called *seeking* to the correct block address on the tape). This can be a very slow operation, measured in tens of seconds, generally making tape prohibitive for anything but sequential access.

Buffering with Sequential Devices

Device input/output operation will incur a number of costs related to data copying. In a read operation, the data are copied from the device into a buffer on the controller. Before the driver can access the data, it must copy the information from the buffer to memory (even if *direct memory access* is used by the controller, a measurable amount of time is required to move the data from the controller's buffer to the memory). The device itself is idle during the controller-to-driver copy operation, since it cannot be involved in another operation while shared memory is being used by the software and the hardware process (why?).

Many controllers are built to compensate for this bottleneck by *double buffering* the data. The controller contains enough memory to buffer two input (and two output) blocks of information. While information is being copied from the first block into the driver's memory, the device can be filling the second buffer. When the next block of information is to be assimilated by the driver, it addresses the second buffer; now the first buffer can be used by the device. The effect is that all controller-to-driver copy operations can be overlapped with device operation.

Sequential devices are accessed serially, so when a process reads block i from the device, it will either discontinue reading the device or read block i + 1 next. Since the process is generally accessing the block byte by byte, there may be an opportunity for the driver to incorporate its own double buffering to support the application process.

When the process has read all the information stored in buffer 1 into block i, it can switch to buffer 2 to continue reading information for block i + 1 of the byte stream. As the process reads buffer 2, buffer 1 can be filled with block i + 2 by the driver.

While hardware double buffering is used to overlap the operation of the device and the controller, software double buffering is used to overlap the operation of the driver and the controller.

Speed mismatches will be more evident between the driver and the controller than between the controller and device. Suppose that we extended the driver so that it has n buffers. Then the tape driver program could race ahead of the process up to n - 1 blocks. If the process should suddenly begin to consume bytes at a high rate, then the process would not be slowed down waiting for blocks to be read into the driver.

Buffering is only useful if the I/O requests occur in bursts. If the process is consistently emptying buffers more rapidly than they can be filled, then having n buffers will not improve the performance at all; the system will operate consistently with parts of two blocks being loaded at a time — the block being consumed by the process and the block being read into a buffer. Double buffering would be useful, but more buffers would be wasted.

Rotating Media

Rotating disks are currently the most prevalent form of storage device on computers. Rotating media also employ a block read/write interface between the controller and the device, also propagated to the driver/controller interface. Rotating media have an advantage over sequential media in that different parts of the media can be accessed in random order.

The random access nature of rotating media allows one to make free use of a **seek** command on the media, unlike the situation in sequential media. However, it ordinarily discourages the use of the device as a sequential storage medium, that is, contiguous blocks on the device need not hold logically contiguous blocks of information. If the operating system intends to provide a device interface similar to the one described for sequential devices, then another layer of abstract machine will have to be interposed between the device driver and the application process: The file system is such an abstract machine.

Once an operating system incorporates a file abstraction for rotating media, it can be used for sequential media as well; the resulting abstract machine provides a uniform interface to all the storage media (with different performance aspects on different classes of devices). In general, the file management abstract machine will be the "user" of the rotating media device drivers.

The storage technology used in disks includes both magnetic and optical approaches. The magnetic disk uses the same approach as in a magnetic tape, although the "patch" of recording surface is positioned under the read/write head in a different manner than with tapes. Optical disks use light to detect storage patterns on the disk surface, while the alignment of areas of the disk under a read head is accomplished in the same manner as it is with magnetic disks.

9.1.2 Device Drivers

The device driver is the first layer of software to interact with devices. Thus, the device driver is executed as a part of a process, either in the operating system or as a part of a user-level application program. The controller operation is algorithmically specified, possibly with parallel operation in distinct parts of the controller. The driver process must synchronize and interact with the controller process in order to complete an input/output operation. Thus, a significant part of the driver/controller interface is intended to synchronize the software and hardware processes in order to accomplish information sharing.

Device driver interface specifics are determined by the computer architecture, the device characteristics, and the operating system architecture. The general form can be described as follows: The driver is broken into two procedures: The *driver* initiates the input/output operation and the *interrupt handler* completes it. The state of any particular input/output operation is maintained by the operating system in between the execution of the two parts.

Whenever a process requests an input/output operation on a particular device (for example, **get/put_byte**), the first part of the device driver starts the device (see Figure 9.2). It writes the status of the operation into the *device status table*. At this point, the first part of the driver has completed its job and terminates (the calling process is blocked if the operating system provides a synchronized interface to the application process).

When the device completes its operation, an interrupt occurs, signifying that event occurrence. The system interrupt handler determines the cause of the interrupt and then invokes the handler part of the driver. The handler determines the state of the input/output operation by reading the device status table and then completes the operation and notifies the original process of the completion.

The synchronization technique between the application process and the hardware process is simplified in this example. The application process and the device share a binary semaphore, S, that is set to 1 when the device is idle. Each application process performs a procedure call on the driver, which results in execution of P(S) for the

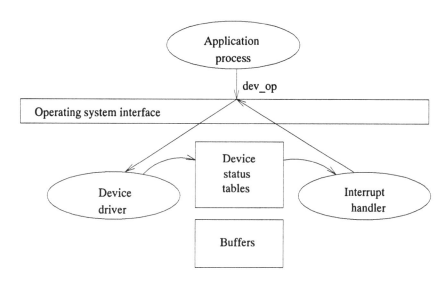

Figure 9.2 Implementing an Abstract Machine Interface to Devices

corresponding application; only one process will succeed in the call, with all subsequent processes blocking on the semaphore. The driver uses another semaphore (actually, pragmatic interfaces use a pair of semaphores) called **idle**, which is implemented in hardware within the device controller. The driver signals the controller to execute the command by performing P(**idle**). Meanwhile, the handler is blocked on the **interrupt_flag** semaphore for the device. When the controller completes the operation, it performs a V(**interrupt_flag**), signaling the handler to complete the input/output operation. The handler will return control to the application process and then perform V(S) to allow the driver to initiate another input/output operation.

Drivers for block-oriented media must also *pack* and *unpack* information before it is used by the calling process. Thus, if a process performs byte-stream-oriented operations on a block device, then the driver must read the corresponding block from the device and store it internally in a buffer. The driver will keep a logical index into the buffer to correspond to the byte stream seen by the process; when a new block is read from the tape, the pointer will address the first byte in the block. As the process continues to call for bytes, the pointer will be advanced through the loaded block. When the pointer reaches the end of the block, another block is loaded from the device. Write operations proceed similarly.

There are several other device-specific details that must be handled by the driver or the operating system. For example, the driver may also provide performance enhancements such as optimized access on rotating storage and/or implement various buffering strategies.

9.2 FILE IMPLEMENTATIONS

Low-level input/output systems provide a uniform interface to software that is intended to make input/output operations simple. However, the interface can be simplified even more by embracing other paradigms; for storage devices the abstraction is usually files (of course, virtual memory is another abstraction).

A trivial file abstraction allows an application process to refer to a logically contiguous collection of bytes using a character string name and information-oriented operations. The information stream may be stored sequentially on a tape or as some random collection of disk sectors. The file system will map the file name into some collection of blocks on the storage device and provide an interface to allow the file users to reference information as a byte stream.

The simple file system may also support a higher-layer abstract machine that implements *structured files*, as opposed to streams of bytes (see Figure 9.3). Such files can be accessed as collections of records.

9.2.1 Low-level File Systems

The low-level file system is intended to provide a simple means by which applications can read and write information on storage. The goal is to allow applications to access some named list of blocks to be accessed as if they contained a sequence of bytes (see Figure 9.4). (The discussion assumes that the storage device is a rotating storage device rather than a sequential device such as tape. Sequential device management is a subset of the management required for rotating storage devices.) To accomplish this task, it is necessary for the low-level file system to provide facilities for allocating and deallocating blocks from the storage device, for constructing collections of blocks, for packing and unpacking bytes to and from the blocks, and for allowing the application to access specific bytes in the stream.

We can start the discussion by describing a typical interface that the low-level file system provides to its clients:

Definition 9.1. A *byte-stream file* is a named sequence of bytes, indexed by the nonnegative integers. Access to the file is defined by a nonnegative integer pointer, called the *read/write head*, which indexes a corresponding byte in the file.

Structured file system
Low Level file system
Device drivers
Device controllers
Storage devices

Figure 9.3 The File System Abstract Machine Hierarchy

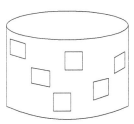

Figure 9.4 Low-level File System Architecture

Operations on the file are:

open (file_name). This operation is used to bind a character string to a byte-stream file and to prepare the file for reading or writing. It sets the read/write head to zero.

close(file_ID). This operation releases the internal state used by the file system to manage the byte-stream input/output.

get_byte(). This operation returns the byte currently addressed by the read/write head and increments the read/write head by 1. If there are no additional bytes in the file, then an error condition is returned.

put_byte(datum). This operation writes a designated value at the byte position currently addressed by the read/write head and then increments the read/write head by 1.

seek(head_position). This operation changes the value of the read/write head to a new value specified as a parameter. ‖

The low-level file system uses device drivers to allow it to read and write blocks on storage devices. The file system must implement the remaining functionality within its abstract machine: It must map a file name to a collection of logically contiguous blocks on the storage devices. It must be able to allocate and deallocate unused blocks from the storage medium. It will use the drivers to read and write blocks and then pack and unpack the byte stream from the collection of blocks. It must be able to recover from spurious errors caused by machine crashes.

Block Management

Mapping the file name to a collection of blocks is a *directory* operation, that is, there must be a data structure that is used to keep track of the various files that might be stored on a particular device. That data structure is called a directory; since directories apply to both low-level and structured files, they are discussed separately below.

The **open** command results in a *file descriptor* being identified that describes the general status of any input/output operations on the file. In particular, it describes the current read/write head position in the file, the access protection on the file, the owner of the file, and miscellaneous other information that the file system designer may choose to include. The file descriptor will also describe the collection of blocks that are used to store the byte stream.

Each file is made up of one or more physical blocks. The first portion of the byte stream is loaded in the first *logical block* of the file, the second portion of the stream is loaded into the second logical block, and so on. Thus, if n physical blocks are used to store the byte stream, then one can refer to logical block 0, logical block 1, ..., logical block n - 1.

The collection of physical storage blocks that contains the logical blocks can be managed using at least three different mechanisms: as a *contiguous* set of blocks on the secondary storage device, as a *list* of blocks interconnected with links, or as a collection of blocks interconnected by a file *index*. The file descriptor will take on a different format for each of the block allocation strategies.

The contiguous block allocation strategy maps the n logical blocks into n contiguously addressed physical blocks. This allocation strategy allows the driver to read or write an entire file in a short amount of time, since the file system will pass a set of disk requests to the driver for blocks that are located adjacent to one another. The requests will cause minimal head movement on the device. A typical file descriptor for contiguously allocated blocks would contain the information indicated in Figure 9.5.

Contiguous allocation does not provide for dynamic file sizes, since it maps the logical structure directly to the physical structure. If a file is stored in some contiguous set of blocks and data are added to the end of the file, then either the next contiguous physical block on the storage device must be made available or the file must be copied to a larger group of unallocated contiguous blocks.

Whenever the file system intends to allocate n blocks to a file, it must find n contiguous physical blocks on the file system. Presuming that space is available on the storage device, it will be necessary to choose some set of m unallocated blocks (m ≥ n). Several substrategies are used in this case, the most popular being *best-fit*, *first-fit*, and

Head position	125
Owner	225
Access	read, write
...	...
First block	2035
Number of blocks	7

Figure 9.5 File Descriptor of Contiguously Allocated Blocks

worst-fit. These strategies are analyzed at length in data structures books. It is sufficient for our purposes to recognize that the best-fit algorithm chooses the set of contiguous blocks such that m-n is minimal. The first-fit algorithm chooses the "first" collection in a linear search of the collections where m ≥ n. And the worst-fit algorithm selects the largest collection that will contain n blocks and then partitions it into two parts containing n blocks (for the file) and a new collection of m - n unallocated blocks.

Contiguous allocation strategies will tend to *externally fragment* the physical disk space into small sets of contiguous blocks that are too small to contain most files.

Linked lists of blocks use explicit pointers among an arbitrary set of physical blocks that make up the file. Logical block i + 1 need not be physically located near logical block i, since block i will contain a header that contains a link that addresses the physical block that contains logical block i + 1 (see Figure 9.6). While it is only necessary that the list be a one-way linked list, two-way linked lists are used to enhance performance (during seek operations).

Linked list allocations have the property that random access of bytes in the stream will tend to be slow. That is, the seek operation will be costly in this block allocation scheme, since it requires list traversal (which potentially requires that many blocks need to be read during the seek).

Indexed allocation requires that a unique block in the file act as an index for all the other blocks that are used to store data. In the simplest case, the file descriptor and the index are combined within a block (see Figure 9.7).

Files may require more or less than the n blocks shown in Figure 9.7. If the file requires much fewer than n, then the space in the index table will be wasted. If most files are less than n, then the accumulation of wasted space may be significant. This loss of space, called *table fragmentation*, can be serious if the mismatch in sizes is significant or if there are many small files.

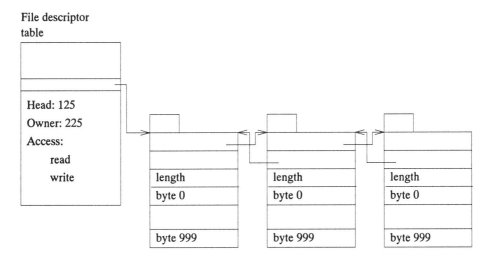

Figure 9.6 File Descriptor for Linked Blocks

Head position	125
Owner	225
Access	read, write
...	...
Block 0	2035
Block 1	5819
...	...
Block n-1	1627

Figure 9.7 File Descriptor for Indexed Blocks

If a file requires more than n blocks, then it will be necessary to extend the index by adding one or more blocks to contain additional index pointers. This can be done by using a linked list scheme for the index blocks.

Implementing the Byte Stream

If the application program were to perform a **put_byte** with the file descriptor in the state shown in Figure 9.5, 9.6, or 9.7, then the contents of byte 125 would be overwritten. To accomplish this, the file system would read the block that contained byte 125, overwrite the byte, and then rewrite the block to the disk. This would require two calls to the disk driver and two disk input/output operations. The file system may delay the write-back operation until it is absolutely necessary (the file system runs out of buffer space or the file is closed); then if the next operation were an operation on any byte in the loaded block (for example, byte 126 if the file were being accessed sequentially), the physical block would already be loaded into the file system's memory, and a disk read operation could be avoided and the write operation could be amortized over several byte operations.

Suppose that the read/write head is positioned at the end of the file and that a write operation is requested. It is then necessary to obtain another block to link into the list following the current last block of the file. In this case, it will be necessary for the file system to obtain a new block and add it to the logical end of the list of blocks.

Managing Unallocated Blocks

When the file system is created, it must know which blocks on the disk can be allocated to files. One obvious way to handle the collection of blocks that are unused is to initialize them into a dummy link-allocated or indexed file called the *free list*. That is, the free list has exactly the same format as a conventional file, except that there is no information stored in any of the blocks. Now, whenever a block is needed for some real file, it can be detached from either end of the free list file and attached to the real file.

The free list will tend to be very large — containing every unallocated block on the disk. This tends to make the indexed implementation impractical for the free list; instead, the linked list strategy is widely used.

While this is a general mechanism, a simpler one will suffice (and is particularly effective for contiguous allocation strategies). Suppose that the file manager keeps a bit map corresponding to the disk block allocation. The ith bit is set if the ith block is allocated, and reset otherwise. This table can be kept in memory, since it only requires one bit per block of secondary storage. When there is a requirement for a free block, the bit map is read to locate a storage block (there is an assumption that the machine instruction set can perform bit masking operations at high speeds). The block can be attached to the requesting file with one device input/output operation.

Example 9.1: UNIX Files

UNIX files are byte-stream files. A UNIX file has no type, so the bytes may contain object code, ASCII characters, or any other encoding chosen by a higher-layer abstract machine. It is up to the application to determine the manner in which it treats the information in the file, that is, as binary or encoded information.

A UNIX file descriptor is called an *inode*, and it has a format roughly corresponding to that shown in Figure 9.8. The inode is loaded (from the storage device) into the file system memory when the file is opened; it remains there until the file is closed. (Thus, if the machine halts while a file is open, then the inode on the disk will differ from the one in main memory if there have been any block changes on the file. The result will be an inconsistent file system, since the blocks have been allocated, but the inode was not rewritten to be consistent with the allocation on the disk.)

The first 12 blocks of a file are indexed directly from the inode, using the "Block i" fields. Since many UNIX files have been observed to be small [5], this is an efficient mechanism for addressing the blocks.

If a file is larger than 12 blocks, the file system allocates an additional index block and links it into the "Single Indirect" pointer of the inode. Suppose that a block can store 1000 disk addresses; then the Single Indirect block will be used as an extension of the inode to provide pointers to an additional 1000 disk blocks. Thus, blocks 0 through 11 are accessed via the pointers in the inode, while blocks

...
Block 0
Block 1
...
Block 11
Single indirect
Double indirect
Triple indirect

Figure 9.8 UNIX i-Node Information

12 through 1011 are accessed indirectly through the single indirect block (see Figure 9.9). Using this strategy, it is possible to have very large files, and as files grow larger the access times get slower.

UNIX files are logically a stream of bytes, therefore, they are likely to be accessed serially. UNIX implementations generally use this observation to enhance performance by buffering ahead on read operations and behind on write operations.

A More Functional Byte-stream File System

If a text editor application were to use the byte-stream file system as defined, it would not be very useful, since the file system effectively only allows bytes to be added or deleted to or from the end of the file. To insert an "extra" byte at position i, all bytes with an index that is greater than or equal to i must be moved, that is, to have their index incremented. Deleting a character will cause a similar problem.

Suppose that Definition 9.1 were enhanced by adding two operations:

Definition 9.2.
insert_byte(datum). This operation is a special form of put_byte that inserts a byte at the current head position, increasing the index of all following bytes in the file.

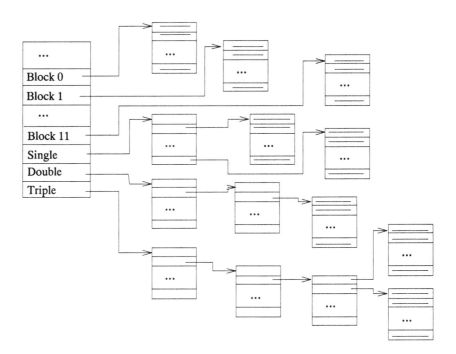

Figure 9.9 UNIX File Blocks

delete_byte(). This operation deletes the byte under the read/write head and decrements the index of all following bytes in the file. ∥

This file system is more general than the file system described in the previous section, since bytes can be added to (deleted from) any part of the file. An abstract machine that supports these additional operations is more complex than the previous one, since it must manage the indexes as described above. Blocks will have to be allocated or deallocated from any point in the block list or index, not just at the end of the list (we ignore the possibility of contiguously allocated blocks here). Since such insertions and deletions are not likely to correspond to the length of a block, it will be necessary to either compact bytes after each such operation or to allow blocks to be partially filled at any given time.

If bytes are compacted after every **insert_byte** or **delete_byte**, then the file will have to be read and rewritten for all bytes that have a higher-number index that the point of insertion or deletion. This solution is generally not acceptable (a file copy between byte editing operations).

Suppose that the file system maintains blocks that are only partially filled. In this case, characters can easily be added at any point in the file by simply obtaining a block from the free list, adding it to the collection of blocks that constitute the file, and then adjusting the location of a small number of bytes between the newly allocated block and its neighbors. In indexed files, this implies that the index itself must be rewritten.

The byte-stream file system with insertions and deletions tends to use more physical space than the pure byte-stream file system. Whenever bytes are inserted or deleted from the interior of a file, then there will be unused space in blocks. This is another form of *internal fragmentation* of the disk space.

Fragmentation losses can be recovered by compacting the file. This requires that the file be copied to a new collection of blocks, such that the new file completely fills each block in the logical order that it appears in the fragmented file.

9.2.2 Structured Files

Low-level file systems are a useful abstraction from device drivers, but they can be made more useful by supporting additional functions that will be commonly used by client processes at higher layers.

Record-oriented Files

An electronic mail system will typically need to store messages and folders of messages. A mail message will be processed by many different programs, for example, an editor, a mail transport program, a mail receipt program, a mail posting program, and a mail browsing program. Thus, it is convenient to incorporate global mailing information into well-defined parts of the message, that is, the mail message will look like a record with fields (compare with Pascal records and C structures). A mail folder will ordinarily be a file containing several such records (of course we could put one message in file and then use a directory structure to organize groups of messages, although this would be slow).

Each mail program will need to replicate this record structure in a consistent manner. This can be accomplished by building an abstract machine (perhaps as a library) on top of a byte-stream file or by reimplementing a file system that can handle collections of records directly on the device drivers.

Definition 9.3. A *structured sequential file* is a named sequence of *logical records*, indexed by the nonnegative integers. Access to the file is defined by a nonnegative integer pointer, called the *read/write head*, which indexes a corresponding record in the file. Operations on the file are:

open(file_name). This operation is used to bind a character string to a byte-stream file and to prepare the file for reading or writing.

close(file_ID). This operation releases the internal state used by the file system.

get_record(size). This operation returns the record (of the specified size) addressed by read/write head.

put_record(record, size). This access function writes the designated record at the current position of the read/write head. ∥

The structured sequential file system can be implemented on top of the byte-stream file system with insert and delete capability. Since records may be of variable sizes, the file system must manage memory to minimize fragmentation. Since the lower file system has no knowledge of "records," it cannot make well-informed decisions about disk block allocation based on record properties.

The structured sequential file system could also be implemented directly on the device driver abstract machine. This will not solve the fragmentation problem, but it may make it tractable. The problem becomes that of finding a good strategy for storing logical records inside of physical records (physical storage blocks).

Suppose that there is a request to add a logical record to the end of a file. If logical records are fixed size, say k units in length, and a block will accommodate K units of information, then j records can be stored in a physical block ($j*k \leq K$). If $j*k = K$, then there is no danger of internal fragmentation and no need for packing records into physical blocks. But suppose that $j*k < K$ or that records have varying sizes; then it will be necessary to either accept the fragmentation losses or to pack records such that a record is distributed over two distinct blocks. If the logical record is larger than a physical block, then distribution is inevitable.

Just as with byte-stream file systems, many applications will need to insert and delete records at points other than the end of the file. The file system capability will have to be extended in a manner similar to the byte-stream extension.

Accessing Records

In some record-oriented file structures, the record types are built into the file system itself. In these cases, the access functions can be designed and implemented at the time the file system is designed and implemented.

For example, a file system may support strings of characters where a record is a string. Now, a **put_record** operation would write a (variable length) array of bytes corresponding to a string to the storage device.

A more functional file system supports abstract data types: The application programmer is allowed to define his own format for logical records and the access routines for reading and writing the records.

The file system must support the idea that the application can export access routines to the file system so that the get and put operations call the application's routines. As the abstract data types become more sophisticated, the file system begins to look like a database system.

Example 9.2: Electronic Mailboxes

For example, one might define an electronic message to have the form shown in Figure 9.10. A mailbox is a collection of such records. The **put_record** operation should append a mail **message** to the end of the mailbox file, and the **get_record** should retrieve the message that is "under" the read/write head.

Figure 9.10 also shows examples of tailored access routines for the message record type. We assume that the get and put routines can be written in terms of the **get_/put_byte** routines.

```
struct message            /* The mail message */
{
       address to;
       address from;
       line   subject;
       address cc;
       string      body;
};

get_record(length)
int length;
{
       struct message *msg;

       msg ← allocate(sizeof(message));
       msg.to ← get_address();
       msg.from ← get_address();
       msg.cc ← get_address();
       msg.subject ← get_line();
       msg.body <- get_string();
       return(msg);
}

put_record(msg)
struct message *msg;
{
       put_address(msg.to);
       put_address(msg.from);
       put_address(msg.cc);
       put_line(msg.subject);
       put_string(msg.body);
}
```

Figure 9.10 Electronic Mail Example

Other File Structures

File systems can also provide more specific structures that are intended to decrease the access time to various records in the file, that is, the file does not appear as a sequential file at the abstract machine interface.

For example, the abstract machine designer may provide an index of the records in the file based on values in some key field in each record. To find a record in the file, the access procedure performs a search on the index (instead of on the records), obtains a pointer into the portion of the file that contains records, seeks to the record, and then completes the access, (see Figure 9.11). These *indexed sequential files* are widely used in business computing for files with very large numbers of records, particularly if the records are often referenced in a nonsequential manner.

The index search can be made to be relatively fast: It is possible to keep the index sorted (and loaded in primary memory when the file is opened). Now the pointer can be found in $O(\log_2 n)$ probes into the index.

Many applications require very large indexed sequential files. Such indexes may be too large to load into the primary memory when the file is opened. Thus, it is necessary to load only portions of the index at a time. Since the key values are sorted, it is possible to store the keys and pointers into "volumes" of the index, where the sorting

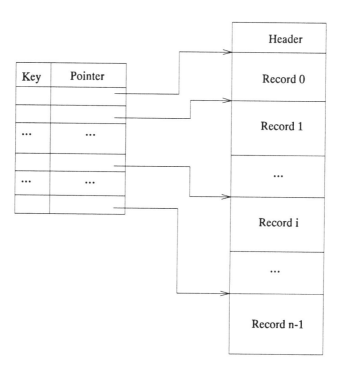

Figure 9.11 Indexed Sequential Files

order is preserved across volumes. This will require that a small volume index be provided to address subindexes; the access procedure will use the volume index to determine the subindex that contains the desired key value; it will then load the target subindex, obtain the pointer, and then access the desired record.

Indexed sequential files can be generalized to support multiple key fields, each with its own index into the records. The storage requirements are increased, and the overhead to manage the indices increases substantially since record deletions can cause dangling pointers in an index.

Suppose that each record has a relatively degenerate structure, for example, a word processing document may contain a stream of characters with embedded formatting records. Each "word" and each formatting command are a record. The obvious key value for a record is either the word itself or the formatting command type. The index might contain one entry for every word and formatting command type that appear in the file. While we inherently assumed that key values are unique above, it is clear that this application would allow a particular key to have many pointers. Such a file organization is called a *fully inverted file*. In such files, the size of the index is a major factor; building and maintaining the index can also be quite expensive. An inverted file is also obviously very expensive to update. However, an inverted file can be extremely useful for "intelligent" access of the file.

9.3 DIRECTORIES

Directories are the mechanism by which the file system manages the files as a whole. Thus, a directory must provide a mechanism by which it can map external names (such as strings of characters) into file descriptors. The directory system will support naming strategies and higher-level mechanisms and policies for organizing collections of files.

File manipulation commands, such as copying files, deleting files, and listing the names of files, are implemented within the directory system.

The simplest form of directory is a *device directory* for a single storage device (or removable medium for a device). The device directory is a structured index of the files that are stored on the device. The degenerate structure is a sorted linear list with elements of the form (**file_name, file_descriptor_location**) (compare with the indexed sequential file structure in Figure 9.11).

Example 9.3: MS-DOS Directories and Files

MS-DOS is intended to operate from a distinguished device, called the *default drive*. All file names are assumed to be located in the device directory on the default drive. If a file is to be referenced on a different device, then the file name includes a drive specifier. Thus, the MS-DOS directory is a collection of device directories, each prefaced by the name of the device and a colon, thus, file **statistics** on a diskette in drive b is referenced as **b:statistics**.

Each device (or diskette) contains a *File Allocation Table*, which acts as an index to disk blocks assigned to any particular file (see Figure 9.12). There is one entry per disk block on the device; the entry is a pointer to the disk block that contains the next logical record in the file. Thus, the directory is a collection of file descriptors with a pointer to the File Allocation Table entry of the first logical block in the file. Unused blocks are marked in the File Allocation Table as being *free*.

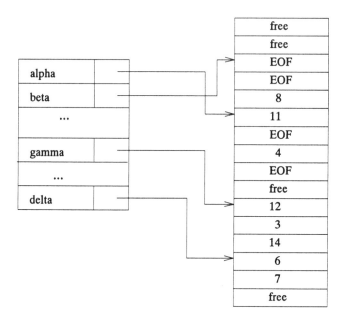

Figure 9.12 DOS Files

The device directory in Figure 9.12 represents a device that contains four files named **alpha**, **beta**, **gamma**, and **delta**. File **alpha** contains three blocks (numbers 5, 11, and 3). There are four free blocks (numbers 0, 1, 9, and 15).

Directory Structures

Since the purpose of the directory is to provide a table of contents of the files in a device, there are several alternatives for choosing the data structure to represent the table of contents. For example, it may be a linear list of file names, sorted by name, by size, by last access time, or by some other criterion. Such a directory is said to support a *flat* name space, since every file appears in a single directory.

It is possible to abstract the idea of a device directory so that the directory is simply a collection of files (without requiring that the collection be every file on the device).

A *hierarchical* name space uses a tree data structure for organizing the file descriptors. In hierarchical file systems, a *root directory* points to other directories and files, that is, a directory is allowed to hold a "file descriptor" for a subdirectory. The subdirectory, in turn, points to lower-layered subdirectories or to files.

The simplest form of hierarchical directory is a tree data structure; every directory or file is pointed to by exactly one superdirectory (except the root, which has no predecessor).

Tree-structured hierarchical directories are widely used in different operating systems, since they allow one to recursively partition the files into collections. Such partitions correspond to directories for individual users, for particular systems applications, and for other users. Once the file system has been partitioned to support individual users, each user can use the tree-structuring mechanism to partition his own collection of files.

Suppose that two users, each with his own directory and subdirectories, wished to share a file (or subtree of files through some directory). In this case, it is convenient to allow the two users' directories both to point to the shared subdirectory. However, the resulting structure is no longer a tree, but is a graph. Whenever sharing is allowed, the file system must be designed to ensure that files are deallocated when all references to them have been deleted. (This is commonly accomplished by including *references counts* for all directories that point to a particular subdirectory or file.)

Graphs may be cyclic or acyclic. Directory structures based on acyclic graphs will share many properties with the more constrained tree, for example, a recursive search for a file in a subdirectory tree will terminate in an acyclic directory structure, but may not terminate in a cyclic directory structure. Many hierarchical file systems support acyclic directory systems, but few support cyclic structures.

Opening a File in a Tree Directory

Tree-structured directories are common in contemporary computer systems. A file name in a tree structured directory can be either relative to some base directory or absolute, that is, relative to the root of the tree. For example, UNIX file names that begin with a "/" are absolute file names describing the names of directories along a path from the root to the desired file. An absolute file name such as "/usr/gjn/books/opsys/chap9" indicates that the root directory contains an entry describing a directory named "usr", which contains an entry describing a directory named "gjn", and so on through "books" and "opsys" to the file named "chap9". If the base directory were "/usr/gjn", then the same file could be referenced using the relative path name "books/opsys/chap9".

When a file is opened, a descriptor for the file must be found in the directory that contains the file. In the previous example, before "chap9" could be opened for reading or writing, the system would need to find the file descriptor in "/usr/gjn/books/opsys". And before the entry can be found in "opsys", the directory descriptor for "opsys" must be found in "books". Thus, when the file is opened using an absolute file name, the open routine must first search the root directory to find the entry for the first-level directory ("usr" in our example). This results in the first-level directory being opened and searched for the second-level directory, and so on.

Typical implementations of file systems allow each directory to be implemented using the same basic storage facilities as an ordinary file. That is, the information stored in the directory is saved in a list of blocks managed through a file descriptor. As a result, the open procedure requires at least one (and probably several) disk read operation for each directory that appears in the path name.

Opening a file thus requires time and effort proportional to the length of the file (path) name, independent of whether or not the path is relative to a base directory or an absolute name.

Directories for Systems with Multiple Devices

In modern computer systems — even personal computers — it is common for the system to be configured with more than one storage device. For example, MS-DOS machines commonly have two floppy disk drives and/or a Winchester disk.

As we saw in Example 9.3, the interface between devices in MS-DOS is not very smooth, that is, a different naming mechanism is used to name a device than is used to name a file in a directory. Full functional file systems manage multiple devices such that the user of the abstract machine need not be aware of physical location of files, nor even the device on which a file is stored. Ordinarily, these file systems do not allow an individual file to have blocks on different devices, but they will support the idea of a directory having files on different devices.

9.4 FURTHER READING

Device management is perhaps the most well established subdiscipline in operating systems. There is little active research in the area, except in the case of networks. Tanenbaum's book provides a lucid description of device management in UNIX-like systems [9]. Milenković discusses generic device management [4].

Shaw has an extensive discussion of buffering algorithms that may be implemented in device drivers or other low level software [7]. Teorey and Pinkerton's paper is one of the most complete discussions of disk request scheduling [10].

There are several excellent discussions of the UNIX file system, including the one given in Chapter 12 of Silberschatz and Peterson [8], as well as the original discussion [6]. Ousterhout and others have also performed a detailed performance analysis of the file system [5]

Tremendous strides have been made with secondary storage management technology in database research. For example, databases typically make extensive use of b-trees for organizing hierarchical information so that it can be rapidly retrieved (see [1]). There is a large overlap of database and operating systems research in these areas (as well as in concurrency control), for example, see the classic work on relational databases [3]. Chang and Mergen describe low-level operating systems support in the storage management mechanism to support database usage [2].

REFERENCES

1.   R. Bayer and E. McCreight, "Organizations and Maintenance of Large Ordered Indexes," *Acta Informatica 11*, 3 (1972), 173-189.

2.   A. Chang and M. F. Mergen, "801 Storage: Architecture and Programming," *ACM Transactions on Computers 6*, 1 (February 1988), 28-50.

3.   J. N. Gray, "Notes on Data Base Operating Systems," in *Lecture Notes in Computer Science*, vol. 60 , Springer-Verlag, New York, NY, 1978, 393-481.

4.   M. Milenković, *Operating Systems Advance Concepts*, McGraw-Hill Book Co., New York, NY, 1987.

5.   J. Ousterhout, H. Da Costa, D. Harrison, J. Kunze, M. Kupfer, and J. Thompson, "A Trace-Driven Analysis of the UNIX 4.2 BSD File System," *Proceedings of the Tenth ACM Symposium on Operating Systems Principles*, December 1985, 15-24.

6.   D. M. Ritchie and K. Thompson, "The UNIX Time-Sharing System," *Communications of the ACM 17*, 7 (July 1974), 365-375.

7.   A. C. Shaw, *The Logical Design of Operating Systems, First Edition*, Prentice Hall, Inc., Englewood Cliffs, NJ, 1974.

8.   A. Silberschatz and J. L. Peterson, *Operating System Concepts, Alternate Edition*, Addison-Wesley Publishing Co., Reading, MA, 1988.

9.   A. S. Tanenbaum, *Operating Systems: Design and Implementation*, Prentice Hall, Inc., Englewood Cliffs, NJ, 1987.
10.   T. J. Teorey and T. B. Pinkerton, "A Comparative Analysis of Disk Scheduling Policies," *Communications of the ACM 15*, 3 (March 1972), 177-184.

EXERCISES

(1)   Using C-like pseudo code, describe a device driver, interrupt handler, and device status table to implement

> open(device)
> close(device)
> get_block(device, buffer)
> put_block(device, buffer)

Because this specification of the problem ignores many details of a real system, it will be necessary for you to make some assumptions about the hardware and operating systems environment; you may use any system as a guideline for your assumptions, but be sure to specify all assumptions that you make in your solution.

(2)   Write an expression in terms of the time to perform input/output operations, $t_{I/O}$ and the compute time, $t_{compute}$ that describes the expected time to run a program that uses a device that incorporates double buffering.

(3)   Suppose that a disk free space list indicates that the following blocks of storage are available: 13 blocks, 11 blocks, 18 blocks, 9 blocks, and 20 blocks.

(a)   There is a request to allocate 10 contiguous blocks to a file. Using the *first-fit* allocation strategy, which block would be allocated to the file?

(b)   There is a request to allocate 10 contiguous blocks to a file. Using the *best-fit* allocation strategy, which block would be allocated to the file?

(c)   There is a request to allocate 10 contiguous blocks to a file. Using the *worst-fit* allocation strategy, which block would be allocated to the file?

(4)   How many device operations (for example, disk sector reads) are required with the linked list approach to implementing a free list? Do two-way linked lists decrease the number of device operations?

(5)   How many device operations are required with the bit map approach to implementing a free list?

(6)   Suppose a UNIX file system inode contains 15 pointers to other disk blocks: 12 to direct blocks and 3 to indirect blocks. What is the maximum number of blocks that can be addressed in a file assuming that a block can contain 1000 disk addresses?

(7)   Suppose we have a file system based on the indexed allocation strategy for managing blocks. Assume that each file has a directory entry giving the file name, first index block, and the length of the file. The first index block, in turn, points to 249 file blocks and one pointer to next index block. If we are currently at logical block 2010 and want to access logical block 308, how many physical blocks must be read from the disk? Explain your answer.

(8)   Measurements of UNIX file usage indicate that the vast majority of the files are approximately 1 MB in length. What are the conditions under which this favors the UNIX file organization?

(9)   Early versions of the MS-DOS file system had a limitation of approximately 40 MB of addressable space on a disk drive. Based on the description of the directory and files, provide some conjectures for the limitation.

(10) UNIX contains a utility named **fsck** that reads the disk and attempts to reconstruct a file system. Offer an explanation about the assumptions one would need to make for **fsck** to be able to operate, and explain how it might work.

10

NETWORKS

10.1 NETWORK COMPUTATIONAL ENVIRONMENTS

Communications devices are used to connect terminals, printers, and sometimes other computers to a computer. They are *character* devices in that information is transferred between the controller and the device as individual characters. In some cases, the driver/controller interface is also a byte-oriented interface, while in others the controller implements packing and unpacking so that the device appears to be a block device to the driver.

In contemporary devices, it is usually cost effective to place a speial-purpose processor in the controller to manage the controller/device interface. In such controllers, the detailed device command algorithms are encoded as instructions for the special-purpose processor. A side benefit of such controllers is that they are "programmable" from the driver side.

The simplest form of controller programming is setting parameters in the controller, such as the speed at which the controller/device interface should transfer information (typically between 300 and 19,200 bits per second), the type of parity protocol, and so on.

Typical communications devices are serial asynchronous lines (RS-232 and RS-422), serial synchronous lines (IBM Bisynchronous and 3270 protocols), and parallel asynchronous lines (used on personal computer line printers).

Drivers for such controllers do not include packing and unpacking algorithms, buffers, or performance optimization functions; they are simple drivers that manage parameter setups and synchronization between the software and hardware processes.

10.1.1 Communication Networks

Computer communication networks provide a mechanism by which a process on one computer can communicate with a processor on a physically distinct computer. The nature of the communication supported by a computer network is far more general than the input/output for conventional devices.

Networks employ simple communications devices such as those described above as well as more sophisticated controllers and drivers to support relatively complex abstract machine hierarchies. The hardware/software interface is implemented between the driver and controller; however, the controller is attached to some shared communication medium rather than to a traditional storage device or terminal. Of course, this view describes each *host*'s view of the intercommunication network (see Figure 10.1).

While there is no seek nor latency optimization to be done by the driver, there are different problems that must be handled by the driver and operating system, primarily relating to the (un)reliability of the subcommunication networks that carry information among the host machines.

The amount of processing that must be done to support reliable network operation and to perform other network-specific device activity (such as routing) is very large. This leads to two problems unique to networks: how to design the algorithms to be used to control the network, and how to implement the resulting designs in a device architecture that relies on drivers to encapsulate the details.

10.1.2 Layered Network Architecture

Layered architectures are widely used to partition the functionality of the network. Standards organizations have defined layered architectures for employing network devices to

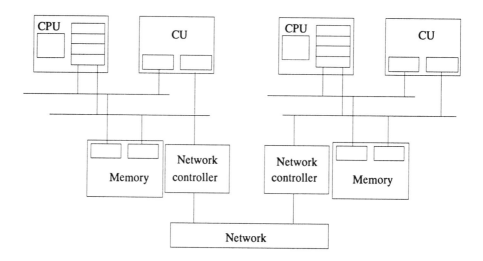

Figure 10.1 Network Devices

achieve machine-to-machine intercommunication (for example, see the International Standards Organization Open Systems Interconnect architecture, also called the *OSI model* [19,21], and the IBM System Network Architecture model, also called the *SNA model* [5]).

Because they are open systems, we describe network devices and the related services in terms of the ISO OSI reference model (see Figure 10.2).

While many details of the various layers are undefined, there is wide agreement about the overall model and the general layer definitions:

Physical layer. This layer of the protocol defines the manner in which signals will be transmitted among host machines on a network. The network device is responsible for generating and receiving these signals. This is analogous to the RS-232 standard for communications devices.

Data link layer. This layer partitions a stream of bytes from the physical layer into a *frame*. It implements error and flow control on frames. This is generally implemented in the network controller hardware.

Network layer. This layer encapsulates frames into *packets* that can be transmitted from one host machine to another using a high-level addressing and routing scheme. If the network uses an *internet* protocol (see below), then that functionality will appear here. While some of this layer is hardware, much of it is software in contemporary implementations.

Transport layer. This layer implements reliable packet delivery for its users. That is, it will fragment and regenerate a stream of bytes from a collection of packets that is transmitted over a network layer. The transport layer must also aid the network layer in maintaining its routing tables.

Session layer. This layer provides additional services to the byte stream, such as high-level naming, and bidirectional transmission services. The session layer begins to be less well defined than the lower layers, except for particular applications.

Presentation layer. This layer handles tasks such as character mapping and number conversion.

Application layer. Functionality implemented at this layer of the architecture is application specific.

Application	Application
Presentation	Presentation
Session	Session
Transport	Transport
Network	Network
Data link	Data link
Physical	Physical

Figure 10.2 The ISO OSI Reference Model

The layered communication architectures can be implemented over simple communications devices or over special network devices. The data link layer will still produce frames for use by the network layer independent of the choice of a physical layer.

If the low-level protocols are implemented on a communication device rather than a network device, then the primary difference will be performance. This follows since the communications devices are all character oriented, while network devices are block oriented.

In the remainder of this chapter, we describe various functions and issues that arise in using network devices. We examine the higher layers of the network in the next two chapters.

10.2 LOW-LEVEL PROTOCOLS

10.2.1 Physical Layer Protocols

The physical layer is intended to transmit and receive signals among some set of host machines. That is, the physical layer is used to pass information from a sending machine to some designated receiving machine in the network.

Physical layer protocols can support *local area networks* (LANs), *metropolitan area networks* (MANs), or *wide area networks* (WANs). The differences among the groups are typically related to speed versus distance trade-offs in the signaling mechanism, for example, telephone lines and satellite transmission can be used to span great distances, but they cannot be used to transmit information at a very high rate of speed. LANs are used in small geographical areas, such as a college campus; MANs are used in a large metropolitan area, such as a city of 2 million people; WANs are used for computer communications for larger distances.

A number of different technologies are used at the physical layer, most aspects of which are beyond the scope of this book. One aspect that we wish to discuss is the *topology* of the physical network, since it has considerable influence on the design of the higher layers. We assume that the physical layer of the network supports multiple host machines each of which can access the physical medium (twisted pairs of wires, coaxial cable, fiber optics, radio broadcast, and so on).

A *fully connected* physical network provides an explicit, point-to-point physical connection between each pair of host machines. Thus, if there are n host machines, then each host must have n - 1 input/output ports (such as communication devices) in order to implement the physical layer of the network (see Figure 10.3). There will be n·(n - 1)/2 connections in the resulting network. Fully connected networks do not scale upward very easily, since the number of connections in the network increases as the square of the number of hosts. To build large networks, other topologies need to be employed at the physical layer.

The physical layer may be a *broadcast* medium, meaning that whenever a signal is transmitted, all hosts receive the signal. Radio transmission is an obvious example of such a medium. Such an implementation usually incurs regulatory restrictions that limit its applicability; it is also relatively insecure, since it is easy to "intercept" signals. However, it provides the same capability as a fully connected topology.

A *star* network topology is composed of n point-to-point connections for an n-host network (see Figure 10.4). The central node is a controller for the network; when host i

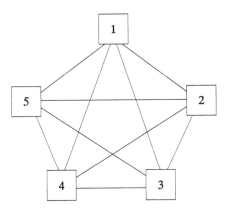

Figure 10.3 Fully Connected Network Topology

wishes to transmit information to host j, it sends the information to the central node (with instructions to route the information to host j).

The *digital switch* is often used to implement the centralized controller in a star topology (see Figure 10.5). The digital switch has n input hosts and (the same) n output hosts. An input host establishes a "circuit" by sending information to the switch indicating that it wishes to transmit information to a prescribed host; the switch incorporates that information into an internal table. Then, whenever the input host places a unit of information, for example, a byte, in its transmit register, the switch will move the information to the appropriate host's receive register. The digital switch multiplexs across all transmitter registers, moving information to receiver registers, in a round robin fashion. A unit of information is transmitted once every n time units.

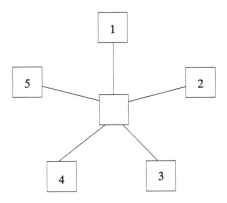

Figure 10.4 Star Network Topology

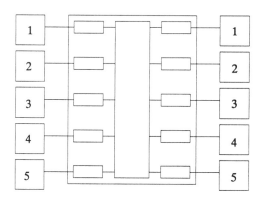

Figure 10.5 Digital Switch Network Topology

Each host machine in a *ring* network has connections with two other host machines, a "left" and a "right" neighbor. A host machine may either absorb a signal that is passed to it from a neighbor or pass it on to the opposite neighbor (see Figure 10.6). *Unidirectional* rings can only pass information in one direction, that is, from the left neighbor to the right neighbor, or vice versa. *Bidirectional* rings allows hosts to pass information in either direction. Each individual link in the ring can use the same technologies as those used in communications devices.

Multiaccess bus physical layer topologies employ a common signaling medium, but logically behave like the broadcast topology (see Figure 10.7). That is, information is transmitted from one host to another by placing it on the shared medium, along with an address designator. The receiver scans the shared medium and retrieves information

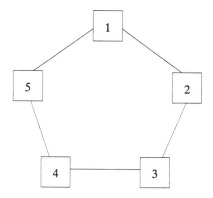

Figure 10.6 Physical Ring Network Topology

addressed to it. In this topology, much of the physical layer protocol will address issues such as synchronous versus asynchronous operation, centralized versus decentralized allocation of the shared medium, and so on. Reliability and contention are the major issues for the multiaccess bus topology. The physical level implementation has an enormous effect on the performance of the higher-layer protocols. For example, the multicast and broadcast physical layer implementations are quite amenable to a network layer broadcast command, whereas others may not be.

10.2.2 Data Link Layer Protocols

Data link layer protocols partition a stream of bytes at the physical layer into groups of bytes called frames. A frame has a header and a trailer that specify various information about the frame, such as the destination of a frame, the transmitter of a frame, the type of the frame, the number of data bytes, and a checksum (see Figure 10.8).

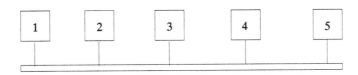

Figure 10.7 Multiaccess Bus Network Topology

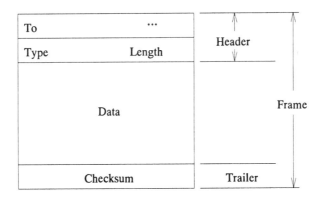

Figure 10.8 Example Data Link Layer Frame

The view of the network above the data link layer is that it will allow host i to send a *typed frame* to host j. The data link network also supports *flow control* and *error control*.

Error control is intended to assure that the contents of a frame are delivered in the same state as they were transmitted. This is usually accomplished by taking a checksum of the header and data (or sometimes just the data) and then writing it in the trailer of the frame. The receiver computes the corresponding checksum upon receipt of the frame; if the computed checksum value is different from the transmitted checksum, the frame is assumed to have not been received properly. The frame is rejected, that is, it is treated as if it were never transmitted at all. The implication is that the data link layer does not implement a *reliable* network, since some frames may be lost.

Flow control is used to control the rate at which packets flow between any pair of host machines. Since the data link layer supports the idea of frames flowing from one host to another, there is the implication that a receiver host must be able to accept frames when they are transmitted. There are several reasons why a host may not be able to accept incoming frames: first, the frame may have been sent to a nonexistent host or one that is currently powered down. Second, the receiving host network device driver will probably be interrupt driven; if the interrupts are disabled, then incoming frames will be lost. Third, the network device driver accepts frames ultimately intended for any process located at the host; this will require that the driver contain its own buffer space to hold incoming frames until the receiver process requests them (from the local operating system). If the buffer space is full, then the receiver machine will be unable to accept a frame without overwriting frame buffer storage.

Thus, the receiver needs to be able to control the rate at which frames are transmitted to it, particularly from some single transmitter. The simplest protocol for accomplishing flow control is the *stop-and-wait* protocol, summarized in Figure 10.9. In terms of IPC primitives, the stop-and-wait protocol corresponds to a synchronous send operation. The synchronization is accomplished with the special type packet, ACK, with no data field. The "time-out" is used to prevent the sender from waiting forever if the outgoing data frame or the incoming ACK frame is lost; if the sender does not receive an ACK before the time-out expires, then the sender may assume that the transmission has failed. That is, the data link layer does not assume that frames can be transmitted reliably.

The *sliding window protocol* is a generalization of the stop-and-wait protocol that allows a transmitter to have up to approximately N frames in transit before it receives an ACK. Whenever the data link layer intends to transmit some number, n, of frames to another machine, it may be slowed down by the physical layer or by a slow receiver (there is no way for the transmitter to distinguish between the two).

Assume that the data link layer assigns numbers to the set of frames. The data link transmitter maintains a pair of pointers, S_U and S_L. S_L points to the lowest numbered frame that has been transmitted but for which no ACKnowledgment has been received, and S_U is the first frame not yet sent. Thus, all frames between S_L and S_U, called the *current window*, are in transit.

The receiver maintains a similar pair of pointers, R_U and R_L. R_L points to the next frame that the receiver is expecting to receive, and R_U is set to $R_L + n$ (the receiver window size). The receiver is prepared to accept any frame that lies within its window; if a frame arrives with an address outside the window, then the receiver knows that it has a spurious frame and that there has been a transmission error.

```
Sender transmits a frame;
Sender sets a time-out on the transmission;
Sender waits for an ACKnowledgment;

...

if (Sender receives ACKnowledgment) continue;
if (frame times-out)
     Retransmit timed-out frame;
```

(a) Transmitter


```
Receiver accepts the frame;
Receiver transmit the ACKnowledgment;
```

(b) Receiver

Figure 10.9 Stop and Wait Flow Control

The sliding window algorithm is shown in Figure 10.10. The transmitter can proceed up to approximately N frames ahead of the last ACKnowledged frame; when it hits the boundary of the transmit window, it will quit transmitting until it either times out on old transmissions or until ACKnowledgments are received. When frames are rejected on the receiver end, then the transmission will eventually time out.

10.2.3 Commercial LANs

The Ethernet

The *Ethernet* was introduced by DEC, Intel, and Xerox in 1980 [4] and subsequently modified slightly and embraced by the IEEE as a standard [6]. The Ethernet incorporates the physical and data link layer protocols for a local area network. Information is delivered in packets (equivalent to data link frames) with a sustained signaling rate of 10 million bits per second. At the physical layer, the topology is a multiaccess bus; packets are placed on the bus by the sender, and one or more receivers can retrieve the packets by reading the bus. In this sense, the Ethernet is logically a broadcast medium, similar to radio broadcast used in the predecessor Aloha net [1].

The unique aspect of the Ethernet is that it incorporates decentralized control of the shared bus, using *carrier sense, multiple access protocol with collision detection* (CSMA/CD). The LAN is not guaranteed to be reliable, that is, the physical and data link layer protocols may occasionally drop packets due to unusual circumstances.

Whenever a sender wishes to transmit a packet, it first listens to the shared medium (the multiaccess bus); if another host is currently transmitting, then the sender defers, waiting for a clear carrier to transport the packet. When the carrier is sensed, the sender begins to transmit the packet, reading the shared medium as it writes it.

```
while (S_U-S_L<max_transmit_window_size)
{
      Sender transmits frame S_U;
      Sender sets a time-out on the transmission;
      increment S_U;
};

  ...

if (Sender receives ACKnowledgment)
      Adjust S_L;
if (frame times-out)
{
      Reset S_LandS_U;
      Retransmit all frames from the timed-out frame onward;
}
```

(a) Transmitter

```
      Accept the frame;
      if (R_L≤receive_frame_number≤R_U)
      {
              Adjust R_LandR_U;
              Transmit the ACKnowledgment
      }
      else
              Reject frame;
```

(b) Receiver

Figure 10.10 Sliding Window Flow Control

There is a race condition among senders. Suppose that senders at physical extremes of the shared bus simultaneously begin to transmit. Each will sense carrier and begin to send. Eventually, the signals will begin to interfere with one another, that is, there is a *collision* among the signal. Each sender will eventually detect this occurrence since it is reading each bit as it places it on the shared medium, that is, there is decentralized *collision detection*.

The time frame in which the race can occur is the amount of time required for a signal to propagate from one end of the shared medium to the other and back again (why?). This time is called the *slot time*; if a sender attempts to transmit a packet, then it must monitor the transmission for at least the slot time to guarantee that the race condition does not occur and that the packet will not experience a collision.

At this point, the individual sender recognizes that the shared medium has been inadvertently allocated to two senders and that at least one of the senders needs to defer to the other. The idea is to resolve this competition for the shared medium using a decentralized algorithm. Each sender will *backoff* for some interval of time and then attempt to obtain the shared medium again. To prevent the reoccurrence of the collision after the backoff time has passed, each sender chooses a random amount of time for its own backoff. Thus, if two senders collide, then one will backoff for X time units, and the other will backoff for Y time units, where X and Y are likely to be different since they were chosen randomly. It is clear that the time units should be slot times, since these are the lowest time units in which one can detect collisions. Therefore, X and Y can be small integers that are multiplied times the slot time.

As contention for the shared medium increases, the chance of collision increases. And the chance of two or more senders choosing the same backoff time increases the longer that the net remains in a saturated condition. Ethernet uses a *binary exponential backoff* algorithm to address this problem. On the first collision, a sender backs off 0 or 1 slots; on the second collision, it backs off 0, 1, 2, or 3 slots; and on the ith successive collision, it backs off between 0 and $2^i - 1$ slots. Thus, the more often that a sender fails (due to collision), the longer potential period of time it will defer before attempting to retransmit.

The IEEE 802.3 (Ethernet) LAN is widely-used in distributed systems, since it is relatively fast and economical. It does not address higher layer protocols, but provides a sound data link layer on which one can implement other protocols.

Token Ring LANs

The IEEE 802 Token Ring and Token Bus LAN have evolved from an IBM SNA variant and a manufacturing standard protocol, respectively [6]. At the physical layer, this LAN may be a bus, star, or ring operating at signaling rates of up to 16 Mbs. However, the signaling strategies used in IEEE 802.4 (Token Bus) and 802.5 (Token Ring) are different from that used in IEEE 802.3.

At the data link layer, each host is assigned a logical address from a set of N nonnegative numbers. Host i can receive packets from host i - 1 (modulo N) and send packets to host i + 1 (modulo N). The placement of the host on the physical layer medium is independent of the logical address assigned to a host. Thus, the data link layer implements a logical ring topology on a somewhat arbitrary medium.

When host i intends to send a packet to host j, it waits for host i - 1 to provide it with an explicit signal that that bus is available; this signal is the *token*. There is only one token in the logical ring at any given time. When host i receives the token, then it has exclusive access to the shared medium, so it attaches the packet to the token and transmits it to host i + 1. Host i + 1 will determine that the medium is being used (host i+1 is not enabled to transmit), then determines if it is the intended receiver of the packet. If it is, it retrieves the packet and forwards the token without the attached packet to host i + 2. The packet continues around the ring until it is received by host j.

The token ring also employs decentralized control, but in a regular manner. The Ethernet allows any host to obtain the shared medium as often as it likes, while the token ring enforces fairness by passing the token around the ring. When the Ethernet detects a collision, it must recover from the situation; collisions do not occur in token rings.

However, the token ring depends upon each host behaving properly. If host i crashes, then the ring must be reconfigured so that host i - 1 will send tokens directly to host i + 1, and host i + 1 must accept such packets. If host i happens to have the token when it crashes, the net is debilitated.

The token ring can be made more robust by having each host keep track of the time at which it last saw the token. If the token does not arrive in a sufficiently long time (how long?), then the host may assume that the token is lost and propagate a new token. Of course, this causes a race condition: Two or more hosts may decide that the ring has crashed and attempt to introduce a new token. We leave it as an exercise to design a recovery approach for introducing a single new token.

10.3 MID-LEVEL PROTOCOLS

A typical implementation of the abstract machine hierarchy for network input/output operations is shown in Figure 10.11. The data link layer is partially implemented in the device controller and partially in the driver. The physical layer is implemented in the controller and the device itself. The mid-layer protocols provide device independence to applications, while high-layer protocols extend services for programming convenience. In this section we discuss the mid layer protocols, and in the next section we describe some high-layer protocols.

The transport and network layers correspond to the file system in terms of abstract machine hierarchy, although there are designs of the ISO OSI protocol in which parts of these layers are implemented in the network device driver or controller.

Just as file systems provide an abstraction of storage device input/output operations, the mid-layer protocols provide abstractions for network input/output.

10.3.1 The Network Layer

The purpose of the network layer is to allow information to be distributed over logical networks in which frame addresses are generalized to accommodate different data link layer address spaces. In general, network level addressing will allow the logical network to be the composition of several individual networks or to allow the network to incorporate *routing* techniques for transmitting information of a partially connected network of hosts.

High-layer protocols	Application
	Presentation
	Session
Mid-layer protocols	Transport
	Network
Device drivers	Data link
Device controllers	Data link
	Physical
Communication devices	Physical

Figure 10.11 The File System Abstract Machine Hierarchy

The frame that is used by the data link layer encapsulates a block of data; the network layer reads and writes the data link data block with a specific template, yielding a *packet* that is wholly enclosed within a frame (see Figure 10.12). When a host's data link layer transmits a packet, it encapsulates it in a frame. When the data link layer receives a frame, it decapsulates the packet and passes it to the network layer.

Packet addresses are interpreted by network layer protocols; they use a different name space than appear in frames. A frame address must specify a specific host address that can receive information directly from the sending host. When a host receives a frame, the network layer may choose to *forward* the packet to another host by again encapsulating it in a frame and sending it to another host. This enables one to achieve the logical effect of a fully connected network across a set of individual networks.

For example, if host A in Figure 10.13 intends to transmit information to host G, it could encapsulate a packet for G in a frame and send it to host B; when host B receives the frame, it looks at the address in the enclosed packet and determines that the packet should be forwarded to host E. Thus, host B's data link layer reencapsulates the packet in a frame and sends it to host E. Host E follows the same process, but at the time it forwards the packet, it will have to decide whether to *route* the packet to host C or to host F (both will work, but one will result in fewer intervening *hops* than the other in the ultimate delivery of the packet to host G). Eventually, the data link layer at G will receive the frame, decapsulate it, and recognize it as a packet for itself.

Routing in partially connected networks is commonly used in WANS, since the cost of a fully connected network over large geographic areas is usually prohibitive. The *ARPAnet* [19] is the forerunner of such networks, and much of today's knowledge about

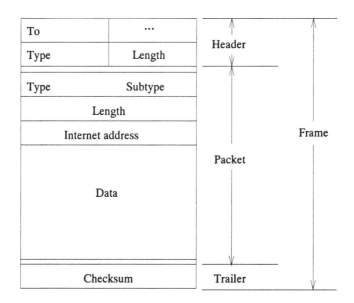

Figure 10.12 Example Network Layer Packet

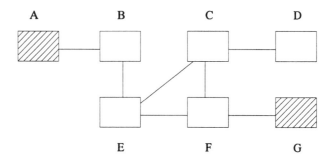

Figure 10.13 Routing in a Partially Connected Network

network architecture is a direct result of experience with the ARPAnet. The ARPAnet network and data link layers are implemented in a special-purpose computer called an *interface message processor*, or simply *IMP* (see Figure 10.14).

As LAN technology has become cost effective, individual nodes in a WAN can become a collection of hosts with their own local communications mechanism (see Figure 10.15). The IMP appears to be a normal host machine to the other hosts on a particular LAN, but retains its routing function at the WAN level. Such a machine is called a *gateway* machine to distinguish it from an ordinary IMP in an ARPAnet-style WAN.

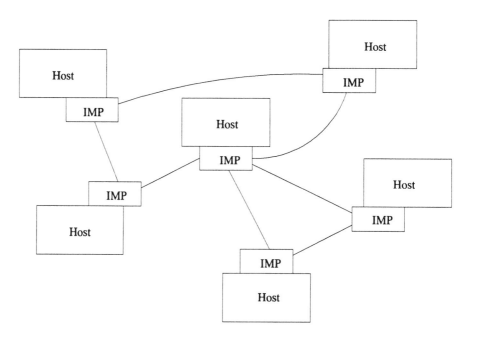

Figure 10.14 Routing in the ARPAnet

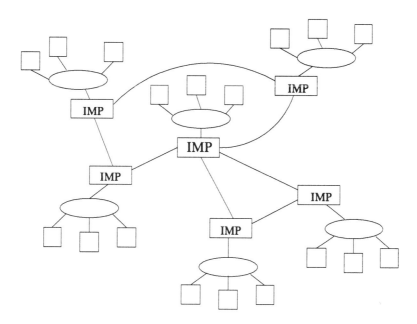

Figure 10.15 Interconnected LANs using a WAN

The IMP-style gateway has two forms of routing to perform: First, it must perform routing in the WAN network, and second, it can be used to forward packets from an ordinary host machine on a LAN into the WAN. The packet can then be transmitted across the WAN to some other IMP-style gateway to another LAN; the packet can then be routed into the remote LAN and delivered to a host machine that resides there. The second form of routing is between hosts on distinct LANs. The WAN is used to make a network of LANs, called an *internet*.

The internet architecture can also be used to interconnect many geographically close LANs without actually using a WAN, as shown in Figure 10.16. In the figure, 3.5 IMP-style gateways have been collapsed into one LAN gateway, and 2.5 IMP-style gateways are collapsed into a second gateway. Some of the WAN-level routing from the previous configuration is performed entirely within a gateway, while other routing is done in the host machines themselves. That is, if a host on the network with two gateways intends to send a packet to a host on a different network, then the packet needs to be sent to the gateway that services the destination LAN.

The primary task of the network layer is to handle routing. The particular style of routing depends on the style of the network, but the basic tasks remain the same:
(1) The sending host must use a local routing table to select a destination for the first hop in the route to the ultimate receiver.
(2) The sender transmits the frame to the intermediary.
(3) The intermediary determines if the encapsulated packet should be routed on, using its routing table, or if it has reached its destination.

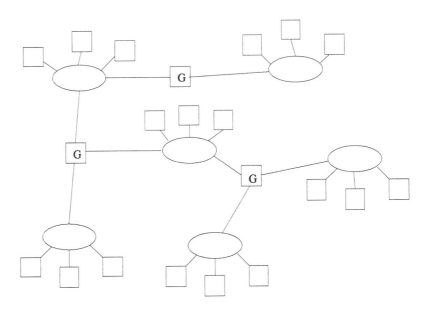

Figure 10.16 A LAN Internet

The internet can become large, suggesting that routing tables become large. If each host has to keep a routing table for all other hosts on the network, then the size requirement may make it impossible for a host to be part of the internet. Of course, any host is not likely to need to communicate with all other hosts on a very large network; the host could keep a subset of the destination hosts in its routing tables, provided that there is some mechanism by which a host can add entries to its local routing table if needed.

Can the same strategy be applied to a gateway machine? That is, is it possible for a gateway machine to perform internet routing when it has only an incomplete routing table? The answer is yes, provided that all the topology of the network appears in some collection of gateways, and the gateways provide a protocol among themselves for ensuring that all information is kept and can be shared on demand.

As the internet grows, the overall reliability of the net decreases. That is, if a gateway (or other host) has a reliability of 0.999, then the overall reliability of n machines as a collection is 0.999^n. A combination of reasonably reliable machines will become unreliable if *every* machine must be up at any given time. When a machine is taken down (crashes, goes down for maintenance or repair, and the like) the routing tables must be changed in the internet, since they are inaccurate. Thus, *routing table maintenance* is a critical aspect of the operation of the internet.

The name space used at the network level is ordinarily different from the one used at the data link layer. Since the names are intended to apply to any host in the internet, the naming scheme can be simplified by using hierarchical names: The net name is at the top of the hierarchy, followed by the host name within a particular net. Additionally, host machines are assumed to be multiprogrammed; therefore, the transport layer will use a third level of the hierarchy to identify a process communication port, called a *socket* in the ARPAnet world. Thus, an internet name is a three-component name of the form (*net, host, socket*), contrasted with a single-component data link address space.

The LAN internet topology has become common in the commercial world. It also provides an opportunity for interconnecting different types of LANs, for example, Ethernet and Token Ring. Since each gateway acts as a host for two or more LANs, it must include physical and data link layer protocols for the respective LANs. However, when a packet from one LAN is passed to another LAN within the gateway, the packet may have to be reformatted or otherwise converted to match the destination LAN protocols. As a result, gateway machines are required to perform *protocol translation* in addition to *media translation*.

It is possible to use the features and functions of the network layer as the basis of application programs. While this does not strictly conform to the OSI model, it is nevertheless done. These applications view the network as an *unreliable packet network* that does its best to deliver packets. Users of the unreliable packet network must compensate for situations in which packets might be lost at some lower layer (for example, checksum errors and full buffers in the data link layer). The application programs must also compensate for the possibility that a stream of packets could be delivered out of order (for example, sequential packets were routed through the internet on different paths). One example of an application in which the unreliable packet network is sufficient is some voice applications; if a packet is dropped, the receiver can sometimes interpolate the missing information or simply omit it. A remote disk application is another example, discussed below.

Since there are applications that can use the network layer directly by adding a programming interface to the packet network, the notion of *datagram* has come to be widely used. A datagram is a block of information that can fit wholly within a single packet. The network layer can deliver individual datagrams to arbitrary hosts on the (inter)net without using extra protocol software that ensures reliable delivery.†

In the UNIX world, the *de facto* standard has become the Internet Protocol (IP) as the network layer implementation [11]. The popular abstract machines that use IP are the Transmission Control Protocol (TCP) [13] and the datagram interface to the internet, the User Datagram Protocol (UDP) [12]. While TCP is clearly a transport layer protocol, UDP could be classified as a network layer protocol or a transport layer protocol.

10.3.2 The Transport Layer

The transport layer is intended to provide a reliable, end-to-end mechanism for transmitting bytes of information from one host to another. The session layer and above should not care that the network is a packet network or need to know about routing, or any other functions implemented at the lower layers.

Network packets are analogous to telegrams in the sense that each is separately addressed and sent to the receiver. Reliability could be achieved by using a communication model that bears more resemblance to telephony than to telegraphy. The telephone uses the notion of *circuit* for communication; a sender establishes a circuit by placing a call to the receiver. Once the circuit has been established, it is unnecessary to precede

---

† The ARPAnet IP protocol includes a packet fragmentation facility that guarantees reliable delivery of a packet, as if it were not fragmented for delivery.

each piece of information with a destination address, since the circuit already specifies who the sender and the receiver are for any piece of information that is to be transmitted.

In packet networks, it is possible to establish *virtual circuits* through the network. A virtual circuit establishes a fixed route through the network for a fixed sequence of packets. If the sender and receiver agree to establish a virtual circuit between them, then the sender can transmit a byte stream across the virtual circuit without even being concerned about packet boundaries.

Opening a virtual circuit requires that the sender and the receiver agree to exchange information. The sender and the receiver are assumed to communicate via specific ports (sockets in the discussion of the network layer); any process that intends to communicate with other processes must establish a socket so that other processes have an "end" on which to connect the virtual circuit. After both processes have created a socket, one of them must establish the virtual circuit by setting up its end and then causing something on the remote end to accept the request to connect the virtual circuit to the specified socket.

If the virtual circuit crosses a gateway, it will be important to preserve the route; therefore, the gateway must keep a table of virtual circuits that pass through it. Whenever a packet is to be delivered along the given virtual circuit, the gateway will use the state information in the table to ensure that packets traverse the same route for each packet of a given virtual circuit.

Virtual circuits use handshaking protocols similar to those discussed for flow control (stop-and-wait and sliding window protocol). Such protocols ensure that packets do not get dropped, since lost packets will cause retransmission. Notice that the sliding window protocol at the transport layer refers to a stream of packets between *ports* (process "mailboxes"), rather than between host machines. Thus it is conceivable that a sliding window protocol might be used at the data link level and again at the transport level.

When a pair of processes are through with a virtual circuit, they must "tear it down," since network resources are required to keep the virtual circuit in tact.

In UNIX, and to a some extent in the more general OSI world, TCP is the prevailing transport layer implementation. It provides virtual circuit capabilities that enable a sending process to establish a connection to a remote machine and to exchange information (bidirectional) over the connection. Communication over TCP is reliable, so it has become widely used in many different applications such as window systems, remote file systems, and mail systems.

10.4 NAMING

We have previously discussed one form of name space conversion, that of translating data link layer names into internet names. The mechanism for identifying specific objects in a network is more complex than this mapping; we discuss the generalization in this section.

Each process executes in its own *name space*, that is, a collection of names of various objects it can reference. A process can only reference an object by using its name. Memory locations are obvious elements of the name space; but names may also refer to devices or communication ports for other processes. To ensure that the objects that appear in the name space will be protected from unsupervised reference by other processes, the name space is made private to the process (see Chapters 7 and 8). That is, no other process can reference objects in a process's name space without the explicit permission of the operating system and/or the process, since the names are private to the owning process.

An analogy for a process's name space might be the set of telephone extensions for the various telephones within a corporation. Similar to names in a process's name space, names reference various kinds of objects: some names refer to people while others refer to answering machines, FAX machines, computer modems, or simply a telephone in a conference room. The extension numbers — names — are used to call within the PBX system, as 3-, 4-, or 5- digit numbers. If a telephone subscriber intends to reference a name outside the corporation's name space, then a different set of names (from a different name space) must be used.

Processes can only share information by sharing names from some global name space. Suppose that processes A and B each have their own name space, and both desire for B to be able to use name X in A's name space (see Figure 10.17). Then the operating system must provide some way to export a name from A's space, and for B to be able to import and reference X.

Continuing the telephone analogy, if two corporations intend to communicate with one another, then it must be possible for a person in one corporation to identify a unique name (telephone number) in the name space of all corporations that intend to communicate with one another. If the two corporations are in the same area code, then the shared name space that encapsulates both corporate name spaces is the 7-digit telephone number. PBX manufacturers have simplified the name space management by mapping parts of the corporate name space into the area code name space, that is, by prefixing the corporate name with a global identifier for the corporation. While an internal extension may be 2-7581, the corporate name within an area code might be 492-7581. Notice that a PBX may not allow an outside call to be routed directly to some internal extensions and may not allow external calls to originate from every internal extension; that is, not all internal names appear in the global name space.

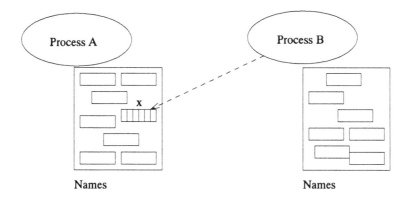

Figure 10.17 Sharing Names

Now reconsider the set of name spaces that must be managed in an internet to provide orderly communication among a set of processes (see Figure 10.18). Each process exists in a name space established by the programming language and the operating system. The process uses the notion of a socket to send (or receive) information to (or from) other similar name spaces.

The first part of name management is to make oneself known to the internet. The internet uses a name space of the form

<net, host, socket>

to identify a process's socket within a host machine's name space, within a network's name space. Now, for a process to introduce itself to the internet name space, it must bind its local name space address for the socket into the internet name space (via the data link layer to the physical subcommunication network). The effect is that the process and the internet name space agree to share this part of the process's name space.

In the telephone analogy, this corresponds to the PBX administrator setting the operating profile so that an internal telephone extension can place and receive external calls. There is no logical requirement that the external telephone number be a superset of the extension number, except for simplicity in naming.

Next, a process that intends to initiate communication with another process must presume that the remote process has bound a socket to the internet name space (with a previously agreed upon name). The initiating process can then use internet facilities to bind the remote socket internet name into its own address space at a socket, allowing it to reference the remote process's address space using the socket.

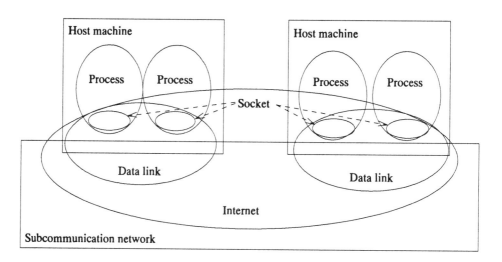

Figure 10.18 Naming Domains

This corresponds to one corporate telephone subscriber placing a call to an "external" telephone number in another corporation.

This general problem of correlating names across various domains is called the *naming problem*. There are several complex issues related to naming: First, there is some disagreement about *naming conventions* — how external names should be formed, as relative names or as absolute names. While most agree that the names should be *shared dynamically* (to allow named resources to be moved in the network), there are several design choices related to exporting/importing the name. We consider these issues next.

10.4.1 Naming Conventions

Names provide one level of indirection between the point of reference for the object and the place where it is located (that is, each process actually operates in an *address space*, for which each object's address is derived from its name). Therefore, a name must be *bound* to an address before it can actually be used. (In the telephone system, telephone numbers must ultimately translate to circuits and telephone handsets.) Static binding means that the name is translated to the address, probably at compilation time, while dynamic binding means that the name is bound after the program has been compiled. (See the discussion in Chapter 7.) By using names, a process is provided with a layer of transparency between itself and the object. As a result, objects can move while their names stay the same.

There are two general schemes for assigning names to objects in a network: absolute and relative names. An *absolute* name is associated with an object, independently of the current location of the resource and independently of the current location of the entity that references the object. An absolute name can be passed as a parameter from one process to another.

If one were to use Social Security numbers to identify people for telephone conversations, then it might be possible for a subscriber to use a 9-digit number to place a call to a particular person independently of where the person currently is located. If the receiver were home, then the home phone would receive the call; if the person were on an airplane, then the airplane phone would receive the call. (There are some obvious technical problems to overcome before absolute naming can be used in the telephone system.)

A *relative* name is bound to an object depending on the location of the process that uses the name. For example, UNIX files names are either absolute or relative; an absolute file name describes the path from the root of the file system to the file. A relative file name maps to different files, depending on the current directory of the user that uses the relative file name. Thus, relative names are ambiguous when taken out of context; before the name can be bound, it must be *disambiguated* by incorporating the knowledge about the place of reference into the name. Relative names cannot be passed across name spaces without including disambiguating information with the name.

Telephone systems use relative names: Extension numbers are usually 5-digit numbers, while those within an area code are 7-digit numbers. The first two digits disambiguate the local extension. Similarly, the area code (and country code for international calls) provides additional disambiguation information. Thus, part of the naming problem is closely related to name space design.

10.4.2 Sharing Names

For a process to introduce an external name to its name space, it must have some *name registry* available to it. The name registry is a directory of names and locations for external names in various name spaces. A process can make a name external by making the name known to the name registry, and it can import names by requesting the name and location from the name registry.

In the telephone system, if one subscriber intends to place a call to a different subscriber, then the initiator must know the telephone number — the name — of the recipient of the call. In some cases, the calling subscriber simply knows the name of the recipient (unless the recipient moves). Otherwise, the recipient must use the name registry (directory assistance) to bind the name (the number of the receiver) to an internal address (the receiver's telephone).

The name registry is essentially a database that is accessed by a key name. The database can be implemented as a centralized facility — a *name server* — or as a fully decentralized set of duplicate tables — every process containing the full registry. The latter approach is difficult to maintain and will not scale well. The former approach relies on centralized information. A middle approach is to use the name server, with the information in the name server distributed across a network (either by partitioning or by replication). The name server will ordinarily be in its own name space, therefore, a process must use a *well-known name* to request the service of the name server.

This is analogous to the universal number for directory assistance in the telephone system; that is, (area code) 555-1212 is the number for directory assistance within any area code.

Partitioned name servers imply that each name server be able to either respond to a name request or be able to route the request to a sibling name server, which will be able to respond to the request (recursively). Replicated name servers require that the information stored in the set of name servers be consistent at some well-chosen granularity in time.

10.5 THE CLIENT-SERVER MODEL

We are now ready to introduce a general distributed computation paradigm, one that relies on the network layer facilities, including the name service.

The *client-server* model of computation is a popular distributed programming paradigm in which one process, the server, is a persistent process that provides a specified service to any other process, a client, that desires the service. Several contemporary products employ the client-server model, including file servers and print servers.

The client-server model is asymmetric, as suggested by the name. The persistent server "always exists in the network," passively waiting for requests for activity, while client processes decide when to utilize the server. A server is a slave process that solicits work, while a client is a master process that requires services.

The server is initiated as an autonomous process in a network of machines. The basic structure of a server process is shown in Figure 10.19. The structure suggests a datagram interface, since the server is able to accept requests from any particular client, service it, and then accept a request from a different client.

```
{
        initialize;
        while (TRUE)
        {
                wait_for_request(...);
                service_the_request(...);
        };
}
```

Figure 10.19 Server Structure

If requests take a relatively long time to satisfy, for example, because it is necessary to establish a virtual circuit between the client and the server before the service can be provided, then the server will be monopolized by one client at a time. Often the machine that implements the server would be able to support more than one request for service at a time (through multiprogramming) provided that the services did not interfere with one another.

The model can be expanded to allow this multiprogramming. Suppose that the server is initiated with a special *listener* process whose only job is to accept service requests and to delegate them to other processes that perform the actual service. Now the server processes take the form shown in Figure 10.20.

Each client request results in the creation of a unique server process connected to the client with a virtual circuit. The client can exchange information with the server at its leisure without blocking other clients from the service.

In this model, a machine is likely to have several processes executing identical procedures on a shared data structure (that is, the data structure that describes the state of the global service). Context switches among the server processes can become the dominant processing task on the server machine. This scenario has encouraged the use of the *threads* or *lightweight processes* introduced in Section 2.4.1. Threads are processes that do not have full resources allocated to them; instead, they operate on resources owned by an encapsulating process that represents the server. Since threads have fewer resources, they can be multiplexed much more rapidly than regular processes.

In Figure 10.20, the client process initiated service by sending a message to a "well_known_socket" address in the network. That is, the client program was required to know the socket name in order to initiate a service request. Since the address is "well-known," it is either hard-coded into the procedure or it is obtained from a user. How would the user have known the address? Probably by looking up the address of the service in some name service.

If the address is compiled into the procedure, then the service cannot move around the network. The processes that execute the procedure will not be able to obtain service from alternative sources.

If the address is stored in a name service, then the binding of service name to service address can be delayed until the moment that service is required. The user can look up the service address in the directory and specify the address at the time that the request is made. If the server is unavailable, then the directory can be changed to reflect an alternative address where similar service may be obtained.

```
listener()
{
   socket client, server;
   virtual_circuit virt_circ;

   initialize;
   while (TRUE)
   {
      client ← wait_for_request(well_known_socket);
      server ← create_socket();
      virt_circ ← accept_virtual_circuit(client, server);
      create_process(server, ..., virt_circ, ...);
   };
}

server(..., virt_circ,  ...)
{
   while (service_is_required)
   {
      read(virt_circ, ...);
      service_the_request(...);
      write(virt_circ, ...);
   };
   close_virtual_circuit(virt_circ);
}

listener();
```

Figure 10.20 Server Structure

When the client process intends to request a service, it uses the name server to map the service name into an address where the service might be obtained, that is, the name server keeps a current directory of services in which it can look up mappings. Now the client schema appears as shown in Figure 10.21.

Example 10.1: Berkeley UNIX Sockets

The Berkeley Software Distribution of UNIX includes a communication package for managing the network at the network and transport level, called the *socket* package. The socket package is used to support pipes, virtual circuits, and datagrams. It allows the programmer to use various protocols with each communication model, for example, TCP is the default protocol used with a virtual circuit.

The **socket** system call causes a port to be created for the calling process. Parameters to the socket call specify the name space to be used (for example, UNIX names and IP names), the nature of communication that will occur on the port (for example, datagrams or virtual circuits), and the protocol to be used with the port (there may one or more protocols that can be used with the port type).

```
{
      message *msg;
      socket client, server;
      virtual_circuit virt_circ;

      ...
      send_datagram(NAME_SERVER, "service name");
      msg = receive(NAME_SERVER);
      server = msg.server_address;
      client =create_socket();
      virt_circ = open_virtual_circuit(client, server);
      while (...)
      {
            write(virt_circ, ...);
            read(virt_circ, ...);
            process;
      };
      close_virtual_circuit(virt_circ);
      ...
}
```

Figure 10.21 The Client Process Schema

The **bind** system call is used to assign a symbolic name to a port. For example, if the port is in the UNIX name space, then bind will create a file name by which another process can reference the port.

The **connect** call is used to initiate a virtual circuit connection. The call will result in the opposite end of the virtual circuit being located (provided that it has been bound to some name in the name space accessible to the calling process; see **bind**). Of course, there are many circumstances under which **connect** will fail, such as the name not appearing in the name space.

The **listen** call is executed by a process that intends to accept a **connect** request for a virtual circuit. The effect of the call is to specify the maximum number of pending connections that the process is willing to support at any given time. That is, each incoming **connect** needs to be queued until the listening process is able to accept the connection. If the process that is being connected to has not done a **listen**, then the queue is zero length, and the attempted **connect** from other processes will be rejected.

accept is a blocking read on socket, waiting for an incoming **connect** message. A successful **accept** creates a new socket and returns it to the calling program; the ends of the virtual circuit will be the new socket on the end that executed the **accept** and the original socket on the end that executed the **connect**. The process can then continue to **accept** connection requests on the original socket while a virtual circuit is established on the new socket.

Figures 10.22 gives the skeleton of an example that establishes a virtual circuit between a master process and a slave process using the BSD socket package [17]. In this example, the UNIX name domain is used. The slave process "listens" for a request to connect on one socket, **skt**, yet establishes its end of the virtual circuit on another end, **new_skt**.

```
master()
{
   int skt;
   struct protoent *protocol;
   struct sockaddr_in *name;

/* Create the socket */
   protocol = getprotobyname("tcp");
   skt = socket(AF_UNIX, SOCK_STREAM, protocol->p_proto);
/* Connect to the slave */
   if (connect(skt, &name, sizeof(name)))
   { /* Failed connection */
      recover();
      exit(0);
   };
/* Communicate with the slave process */
   ...
/* Tear down the circuit */
   close(skt);
}

slave()
{
   int skt, new_skt;
   struct protoent *protocol;
   struct sockaddr *address;
   struct sockaddr_in *name;

/* Create the socket */
   protocol = getprotobyname("tcp");
   skt = socket(AF_UNIX, SOCK_STREAM, protocol->p_proto);
/* Bind the socket to an external name */
   bind(skt, &name, sizeof(name));
/* Mark the socket as a listener ... */
   listen(skt, 5);
/* ... then complete the rendezvous */
   new_skt = accept(skt, &address, sizeof(address));
/* Perform tasks for the master */
   ...
/* Close this end of the connections
   close(skt);
   close(new_skt);
}
```

Figure 10.21 BSD Socket Slave Example

10.6 FURTHER READING

Tanenbaum's network book [19] and Davies and others [2] are extensive treatments of network protocols. The essential elements of network protocols are also discussed in Tanenbaum and van Renesse's survey paper [18] and Zimmerman's summary of the ISO OSI model [20]. Similar material can be found in DesJardins and Foley [3]. The IBM SNA network protocol is discussed in a wide variety of IBM documents, including [5].

Metcalfe and Boggs paper on the Ethernet [9] is a classic discussion of the CSMA/CD protocol. The IEEE refinement of the actual Ethernet protocol appears in [6]. Quarterman and Hoskins have written an interesting survey of various networks [14].

Most papers about files systems have a discussion of naming. There is a particularly good discussion of naming in the paper by Oppen and Dalal [10]. Schwartz, Zahorjan, and Notkin describe extended name services in heterogeneous networks of systems [16].

In this chapter, we have briefly described how sockets are used in the BSD UNIX to accomplish IPC across name spaces. Additional details can be found in [8]. The book by Leffler and others contains even more extensive information about the mechanisms [7]. AT&T System V.3 includes an alternative mechanisms for dealing with network (called *streams*), described in the paper by Ritchie [15].

REFERENCES

1.　N. Abramson, "The Aloha System," *AFIPS Proceedings of the Fall Joint Computer Conference 37* (1970).

2.　D. W. Davies, D. L. A. Barber, W. L. Price, and C. M. Solominides, *Computer Networks and Their Protocols*, John Wiley & Sons, New York, NY, 1979.

3.　R. DesJardins and J. S. Foley, "Open Systems Interconnection: A Review and Status Report," *Journal of Telecommunication Networks 3*, 3 (1984), 194-209.

4.　*The Ethernet: A Local Area Network Data Link Layer and Physical Layer Specification*, Digital Equipment Corporation, Intel Corporation, and Xerox Corporation, September 1980.

5.　*An Introduction to Advanced Program-to-Program Communication (APPC)*, IBM International Systems Center, IBM Corporation, Technical Bulletin GG24-1584-0, July 1983.

6.　*Local Network Standards Committee: A Status Report, Draft B*, IEEE Project 802, October 1981.

7.　S. J. Leffler, M. K. McKusick, M. J. Karels, and J. S. Quarterman, *The Design and Implementation of the 4.3 BSD UNIX Operating System*, Addison-Wesley Publishing Co., Reading, MA, 1989.

8.　S. J. Leffler, R. S. Fabry, W. N. Joy, and P. Lapsley, "An Advanced 4.3BSD Interprocess Communication Tutorial," in *Unix Programmer's Manual Supplementary Documents 1*, Computer Systems Research Group, Computer Science Division, Department of Electrical Engineering and Computer Science, University of California, Berkeley, April 1986.

9.　R. M. Metcalfe and D. R. Boggs, "Ethernet: Distributed Packet Switching for Local Computer Networks," *Communications of the ACM 19*, 7 (July 1976), 395-404.

10.　D. C. Oppen and Y. K. Dalal, "The Clearinghouse: A Decentralized Agent for Locating Named Objects in a Distributed Environment," *ACM Transactions on Office Information Systems 1*, 3 (July 1983), 230-253.

11.　J. Postel, "Internet Protocol: DARPA Internet Program Protocol Specification," RFC No. 791, September 1981.

12. J. Postel, "User Datagram Protocol," RFC 768, USC Information Sciences Institute, August 1980.

13. J. Postel, "Transmission Control Protocol: DARPA Internet Program Protocol Specification," RFC No. 793, September 1981.

14. J. S. Quarterman and J. C. Hoskins, "Notable Computer Networks," *Communications of the ACM 23*, 10 (October 1986), 932-971.

15. D. M. Ritchie, "A Stream Input-Output System," *AT&T Bell Laboratories Technical Journal 63*, 8 (October 1984), 1897-1910.

16. M. F. Schwartz, J. Zahorjan, and D. Notkin, "A Name Service for Evolving, Heterogeneous Systems," *Proceedings of the Eleventh ACM Symposium on Operating Systems Principles*, November 1987, 52-62.

17. *Networking on the Sun Workstation*, Sun Microsystems, Inc., Document Number 800-1345-10, September 1986.

18. A. S. Tanenbaum and R. van Renesse, "Distributed Operating Systems," *ACM Computing Surveys 17*, 4 (December 1985), 418-470.

19. A. S. Tanenbaum, *Computer Networks, Second Edition*, Prentice Hall, Inc., Englewood Cliffs, NJ, 1988.

20. H. Zimmerman, "The ISO Model for Open Systems Interconnection," *IEEE Transactions on Communications COM-28*, 4 (April 1980), 425-432.

21. "Status of OSI (and Related) Standards," *ACM SIGCOMM Computer Communications Review 20*, 3 (July 1990), 83-99.

EXERCISES

(1) Suppose that the sliding window protocol uses modulo N arithmetic for assigning numbers to frames. How many frames may the transmitter have outstanding at any given moment?

(2) The slot time in an Ethernet is the time required for a signal to pass from one end of the shared medium to the other and back again. Prove that this is a sufficient amount of time in which the race condition could occur.

(3) Explain why the Ethernet has a minimum size data field.

(4) Suppose that a host in a logical (data link layer) token ring LAN has detected that the ring has crashed since the token has not been received in a sufficiently long time. What is the minimum amount of time that a host should wait? Explain your answer.

(5) Design an algorithm that each host can execute that will reestablish a logical token ring with a single token once the a host has decided that the token is lost.

(6) Consider the scheme for employing only partially complete routing tables in each node and gateway of the ARPAnet. Explain why, if the union of all the information in the partial routing tables is complete, consistent, and stable, routing will operate correctly. State all assumptions that you make about gateway behavior.

(7) Provide an example that illustrates how routing may fail if an internet's routing tables are in flux.

(8) Implement a skeletal "talk" facility between two processes. The facility is assumed to be asymmetric in the sense that one of the processes acts as an *initiator* and the other behaves as a *receiver*. The initiator begins the talk session by requesting a virtual circuit with the receiver (that is, the initiator takes the role of client and the receiver takes the role of server). Use the BSD socket interprocess communication mechanism with internet address domain as the IPC mechanism. Each process should provide a single tty window for both sending and receiving; precede outgoing messages with a > symbol and incoming messages with a < symbol.

Your system should be demonstrable on two processes on the same machine, for example, between processes in two different windows or across machines, without changing the code. Specify the socket address at run time. Use socket numbers that are not likely to be duplicated by someone else that is also working on the same problem in the same name space.

(9) Implement a simple producer-consumer pair of processes in which the producer begins with a fixed set of buffers. As long as it contains a buffer, the producer can send a "widget" to the consumer in a datagram, decrementing the number of buffers for each widget sent. When the consumer receives the widget, it sends a datagram back to the producer (simulating a buffer being returned). The returned datagram causes the producer to increment the number of buffers available. You are only simulating buffers transmission, using datagrams to synchronize the two processes. Use the BSD socket datagrams and UDP with internet address domain as the IPC mechanism. Print information on stdout of each process to illustrate the synchronization.

Your system should be demonstrable on two processes on the same machine, for example, between processes in two different windows or across machines, without changing the code. Specify the socket address at run time. Use socket numbers that are not likely to be duplicated by someone else that is also working on the same problem in the same name space.

(10) Write simplified versions of BSD *connect*, *accept*, and *listen* (called *CONNECT*, *ACCEPT*, and *LISTEN*) that use BSD SOCK_DGRAM sockets to establish a virtual circuit. Also, write specialized versions of *read* and *write* (*READ_VC* and *WRITE_VC*) to read and write byte streams from and to the virtual circuit. Use UNIX *bind* and all datagram facilities as you require. Do not worry about reliability in this problem, focus on designing and establishing the connection and on packing and unpacking datagrams that you use to carry your stream information.

11

DISTRIBUTED
STORAGE

Distributed programs rely on the operating system to provide facilities for synchronizing and communicating information among the constituent parts of the computation. Contemporary operating systems employ the ISO OSI reference architecture to implement communication at the upper layers of the network protocol stack. This development has evolved from file systems to accomplish synchronization and communication to more specialized approaches. Because of the evolution of the techniques from traditional communication applications to file systems to distributed synchronization, it is useful to study communication prior to synchronization. This chapter addresses distributed file systems and distributed memory, and the next one focuses on synchronization.

Global file systems enable a new level of cooperation among processes on individual machines. No application machine is responsible for managing the global files, since a new network resource has been added to the system to handle this function. The overall organization absorbs the cost and the benefit of the globally accessible information.

In this chapter we examine remote disk and file systems for network configurations as well as distributed virtual memory.

11.1 SHARING INFORMATION ACROSS THE NETWORK

Contemporary application software makes extensive use of the file system abstraction and the virtual memory abstraction to use primary and secondary memory (Figure 11.1).

In the conventional memory model, the application program is written to distinguish between information stored in the secondary storage as files and information stored

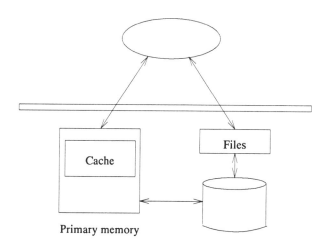

Conventional Memory

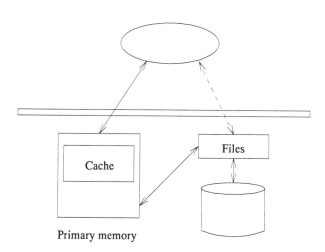

Multics Memory

Figure 11.1 Using Memory

in directly executable (primary) memory. Interestingly, Multics smeared the distinction by having the segmentation mechanism use the file system to extend the directly executable name space to include all the memory.

The task in distributing storage to remote machines is to extend the conventional memory model so that it enables an application program to reference local memory in the usual manner and to reference memory on a remote machine using the conventional model or some modest extension (Figure 11.2).

Several approaches are used to design distributed storage: one class is based on distributing the file abstraction, another class focuses on distributing the directly executable memory abstraction, and a final class does not attempt to make remote memory transparent — adding a new abstract machine to the memory interface.

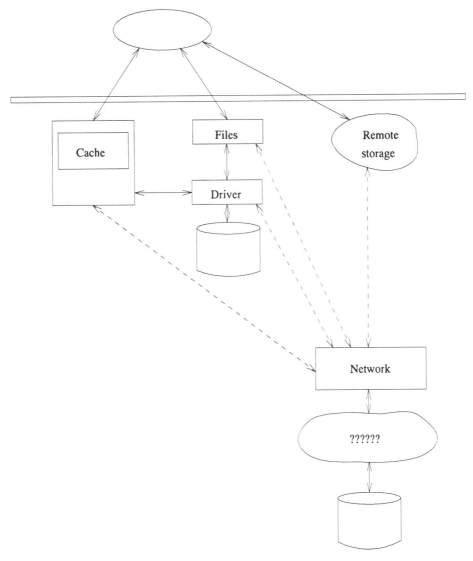

Figure 11.2 Using Memory

11.1.1 Extending the File System Model

The file model was discussed in Chapter 9, characterized as the abstract machine modules shown in Figure 11.3. Data stored on a disk are organized as named collections of information. A file can be created by one application and then shared with different applications at a later time.

In a physical network of computers, the file is a natural unit of information sharing across individual sites. That is, a process on one machine can create information and then write it to a file; then the process on another machine can cause the file to be transferred across the network to its own machine where it can be read like any other local file. Transport layer protocols can be used to move the file between the two machines.

Since the file system is an abstraction of a storage device, that is, it is a convenient mechanism for reading and writing information from the storage device, it is also a useful model of operation for reading and writing information across the network. That is, the file is stored on one machine, yet records in the file are read and written by an application process on a distinct machine. This can be accomplished by partitioning the functionality shown in Figure 11.3 so that part of it is implemented on a local client machine with the application and part of it is implemented on a remote server machine.

There are several strategies for implementing remote files: One is to partition the functionality with a network interface between the file system code and the disk driver. That is, the server machine implements a *remote disk* that client applications access via the network, using commands similar to those ordinarily existing at the interface to a local disk driver. In this case, a machine references the globally shared facility in units of virtual disk pages, that is, a client process reads and writes disk blocks from and to a disk server.

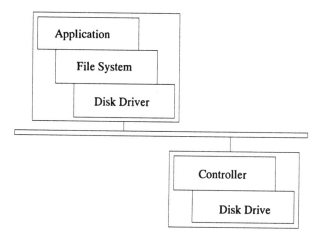

Figure 11.3 Relationship Among Files and Devices

A higher-level partition might be to divide the file system software into two parts, running one part on the local client machine and the lower part on the *remote file server* machine. In this case, the client-server interface is determined by the precise point at which the partition is made; one could generally expect that the interface would be similar to the application-file system interface, that is, a client process reads and writes byte streams from the remote file server.

A third strategy is to create the partition at the application-file system interface. The file server is a complete file system that provides service at the level of full file operations, such as copy a file or delete a file. These file systems support the client machine by caching copies of files into the client's machine and then managing the copies to ensure consistency among the them.

11.1.2 Extending the Executable Memory

Finally, just as virtual memory systems are abstractions of file systems, distributed memory is a generalization of distributed files. In distributed memory systems, information is shared at the primary memory level rather than the secondary memory level.

Basic distributed executable memory models extend the memory interface by adding new functions. A simple example of this type of extension is the Sequent multiprocessor **shmalloc** system call described in Chapter 7. Other approaches allow the programmer to explicitly map the location of memory fragments to specific nodes in a network.

Distributed virtual memory concentrates on using the existing primary memory interface for manipulating remote memory. The operating system obscures the physical location of the memory from the processes using it.

11.2 REMOTE DISK SYSTEMS

Hardware platform evolution continues toward personal workstations supporting networked and distributed computing. To be effective, each workstation must be able to support a minimum amount of computation, including bitmapped screen interfaces, network communications, and multiprogramming in behalf of the single user.

There are few software environments that can be created to support the station hardware without relying on a mass storage system. However, disk drives are relatively expensive compared to the cost of most other parts in the workstation. And since the workstation is likely to be physically placed in the immediate vicinity of the user, the noise and heat emitted from a disk drive are annoying factors associated with the workstation. If the workstation could be built without a rotating disk drive, it would be more economical and less of an annoyance to its users.

Manufacturers can easily build systems without a disk drive, but can nontrivial software be supported by such a machine? With multiprogrammed workstations, it is clear that the operating system and applications require access to large amounts of memory such as can be provided by a disk drive.

Suppose that a large disk were installed on a server machine, and other client machines shared the disk by using a network to reference the disk (see Figure 11.4). The client machine will incorporate a local *virtual disk* driver to replace the conventional local disk driver. The virtual disk driver software interface is the same as a local disk driver, allowing client software to reference the virtual disk as if it were local.

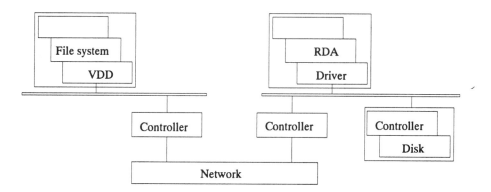

Figure 11.4 A Shared Remote Disk Server

The virtual disk driver, VDD, encapsulates each disk command into a network packet and then transmits it to the surrogate remote disk application, RDA, on the disk server machine (see Figure 11.5). The surrogate application unpacks the disk command from the network packet and generates a request to its local disk (the shared disk), based on the command it received. Thus, a **read** command includes the command and a virtual disk address; the RDA translates the virtual disk address to a local disk address and issues a disk **read**. Similarly, a **write** command packet includes the command, a disk block, and the virtual address.

```
Client System                Server System

   ...
disk_op(details);
VDD: Pack params;
VDD: Send request;           NET: Receive request;
                             NET: Deliver to remote disk;
                             RDA: Unpack params;
                             RDA: Generate local disk I/O;
                                ...
                             RDA: I/O op complete;
                             RDA: Generate reply;
VDD: Receive reply;          RDA: Send reply;
VDD: Unpack params;
VDD: Return to client;
   ...
```

Figure 11.5 Diskless and Disk Machine Interaction

When the disk server's local disk operation completes, the RDA encapsulates the result of the operation — a **write** completion notification or a disk block in the case of a **read** — and sends it to the VDD on the client machine. The client VDD unpacks the result and returns it to the local application (for example, the local file system).

Recall the nature of the interface to a disk driver; since disks are block-oriented devices, units of transfer are disk pages. Suppose that a sector will fit wholly within a single network packet, with a small amount of extra space for the command and address; then it would be possible to transmit a disk sector between the diskless machine and the disk machine using a single packet. This observation opens the possibility of using the packet level of service, especially since it delivers a substantially higher level of performance than virtual circuit protocols.

The remote disk architecture is simple, but potentially suffers from two problems: performance and reliability. Each disk access will incur two network packet transmissions in addition to a conventional disk access operation on the server. Can disk servers be made to perform at acceptable levels by employing fast-access disk machines on a local area network, compared to the performance of a low- or medium-speed local disk access? Since LANs have considerably lower reliability that computer buses, will they be sufficiently reliable to carry disk access requests and responses, especially using packet-level protocols? Will a client machine be permanently blocked or lose data stored on a disk if the disk server crashes while being used by the client?

These are the fundamental issues addressed in contemporary remote disk server designs. We discuss each below.

11.2.1 Reliability

Contemporary network protocols provide a datagram level of service at nearly the same performance cost as a packet level (data link layer) delivery mechanism. Datagrams differ from packets in that a datagram may be fragmented and reconstituted within the sender and receiver data link layers. Datagrams are guaranteed to be reliable *within* the individual datagram; however, the entire datagram may be lost, or datagrams may be delivered in a different order than they were transmitted. Remote disk servers may be implemented with packets or datagrams.

Suppose that a virtual disk sector, ordinarily the same size as a physical disk sector on the server, fits wholly within a packet. Then the protocol used to support remote disk access need not be concerned with out-of-order delivery. (Out-of-order delivery would ordinarily only occur if the protocol used an internet; because of the unpredictability of response time for passing through one or more gateways, remote disk protocols typically restrict the configuration so that the disk server and the client machine are supported by a common LAN. Thus, out-of-order delivery is not likely to occur in the configuration in any case.) Now reliability is related to two issues: ensuring that a disk command eventually gets executed *one or more times*, and synchronizing the operation of the client and the server should one or the other crash during a disk request.

Reliable Command Execution

Disk commands are restricted to a small number of operations: block **read** and **write**, track **seek**, and similar disk commands (for example, to park the read/write heads). The **seek** command should be employed by the server's disk driver to control the head movement as a function of a local disk management strategy. Since a client machine shares the disk with other clients, the client should not be allowed to execute the **seek** command (or any of the other miscellaneous commands). Thus, the VDD is really required only to transmit **read** and **write** commands.

Suppose that a client issued a **read** command and either the packet containing the command were lost before it was delivered to the server or the result was lost after the server had completed the **read**. If the VDD employed a time-out mechanism when it issued the **read** packet, then either the result would be returned or the time-out would eventually expire (in the case that one of the packets had been lost). Suppose that the VDD simply reissued the **read** request; then the second request would produce the same end result as the first request had it succeeded. If the command packet had been lost on the first attempt, then the read never actually occurred at the server; the second, or any subsequent, attempt would cause the server to read the disk and return the result.

Even if the command packet had been delivered and the result packet had been lost, subsequent **read** operations do no harm and will return exactly the same result as the first time (provided the sector is not being written by some other client). The **read** operation is said to be *idempotent,* meaning that it can be executed repeatedly and still produce the desired result.

A disk **write** operation is also idempotent. If the command packet is lost or it succeeded and the acknowledgment packet was lost, then a subsequent write will still result in the same block being written to the remote disk.

If the remote disk server can be constructed so that all commands issued by a client are idempotent, then the client-server interface can be constructed using acknowledgment and time-outs.

Crash Recovery

Suppose that the disk machine crashed during some session of reads and writes on the disk, that is, while a file is open on the client machine. Eventually, the disk server will recover and be able to respond to requests, even though while it is down the client machine is unable to proceed past a blocking read.

Notice that the client machine and the server machine are not relying on either being in a particular state in order for operation to be correct, that is, the server machine has no knowledge of *why* the diskless machine wants to read or write any particular sector. Compare this to the observation that a disk driver on a local machine has no knowledge of which files it is reading or writing, and in fact this allows the disk driver to optimize seek times by satisfying disk requests in an arbitrary order. The state of any file operation is maintained wholly within the client machine; the server machine is a *stateless* servant of the diskless client machine. Therefore, crash recovery in the disk machine need not know about open files, since that information is maintained elsewhere.

11.2.2 Performance Issues

Remote disk systems potentially introduce significant overhead to ordinary storage input/output operations. A read or write operation to a local disk will require two context changes (from a processor executing in user space to the disk driver in systems space, and back again), in addition to the time to physically access the rotating storage device. A remote disk access adds the time to encode and decode parameters, in addition to the time to transmit two network packets. At the server, the client's request must also compete with requests for other clients, since the disk server will be shared.

WFS Performance

The Woodstock File Server (WFS) is an early *page-level file server* that incorporates the design described for disk servers in addition to minimal locking operations [31]. In WFS, the shared disk is a relatively high performance disk compared to local disk drives configured into each workstation. With this configuration, the developers compared the time to read and write a disk page on the local disk with the corresponding time on WFS. While a local sector read required an average of 60 ms, a WFS sector read required an average of 48 ms if only one client was currently using the server, 76 ms if two clients were using the server, and 100 ms if three clients were using the server. Similarly, a local write required an average of 47 ms and a remote write required an average of 73 ms, 109 ms, and 150 ms for loads of one, two, and three clients, respectively. (The increased time for writes is incurred at least in part from the WFS server policy of reading a page to validate it prior to writing it.)

While these measurements essentially ignore the relative disk access times for the local and remote disk, they provide significant empirical data to support the feasibility of remote disk servers, that is, remote disk access for the single user case is actually *faster* than accessing the (slow) local disk. They also identify the potential for rapid degradation on overloaded disk servers.

More Performance Observations

Lazowska and others conducted a considerably more extensive study of remote disk performance for three different implementations (commercial and research systems) [16]. The study uses a queueing network model to predict performance for diskless workstation configurations. Measurements are taken to characterize critical parameter values for the queueing model and to assist in building an accurate model. The model takes many factors into account, including a characterization of the load, the effect of buffer space, transfer block size, network protocols, and network packet size, in addition to various policies related to functions such as prefetching and caching.

Four major conclusions result from this study:

(1)   A shared disk server is feasible for supporting several diskless workstations. The models predict (and the measurements support the observation) that the disk server will be quite competitive with local disk access for lightly loaded servers. Even if the server load is allowed to grow by increasing the number of workstations using the server with a relatively fixed profile of disk demand, the server's performance does not degrade significantly. The critical resource in the observed system was found to be the server CPU.

(2)   Network protocols *must* provide for volume transfers at every level. Disk access tends to have relatively high latency delays, yet rapid transfer times once the access actually starts. Large block transfers amortize the latency delays across many bytes, reducing the average time per byte transferred. Because of layering techniques within the network and between various software layers within the client and the server, there is considerable potential for fragmentation or other

mismatches of block sizes. These mismatches tend to reintroduce the latency delays.

(3)   Concentrating on the server performance is likely to be more effective than concentrating on improving clients' performance. The configuration is likely to benefit by adding CPU cycles, additional disk, or additional buffer memory to the server. The client machine can benefit by adding memory or by providing a local disk for caching (see below).

(4)   "Network contention should not be a performance problem for a 10-Mbit network and 100 active workstations in a software development environment" (page 266 of [16]).

11.3 REMOTE FILE SYSTEMS

A file is organized as a linear sequence of records. In the degenerate case, each record is a byte. Software reads and writes the mass storage system by reading and writing records from the sequence.

As described in Chapter 9, a file is implemented as a descriptor and a collection of disk blocks. While there are different strategies for implementing the stream of blocks, linked lists are the most widely used sequential file systems, resulting in information distribution on disk blocks such as shown in Figure 11.6. Suppose that this file segment were implemented on a remote disk server. If an application wishes to access record i, then a single remote disk access is sufficient. However, records i + 1 to i + 3 each require that two disk blocks be accessed to retrieve the record. Similarly, traversal of a file will require sequential access of the file blocks and, consequently, multiple network accesses to the remote disk.

Suppose that the server were given enough knowledge so that it could traverse linked lists of disk blocks. Then, even though the server would still be required to perform multiple disk accesses, the network traffic could be reduced considerably, resulting in more efficient record access on the disk. (This is a pedagogical illustration, not normally implemented in commercial file servers.)

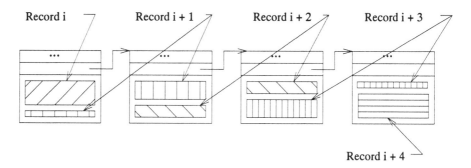

Figure 11.6 Logical Records in a File

Recall the steps for opening a file in a tree-structured directory. The path name through the tree specifies a sequence of directories that must be searched in order to find the file descriptor for the target file (at a leaf node of the directory tree). As pointed out in Chapter 9, a path traversal can result in reading a significant number of disk blocks, since each directory level will ordinarily involve at least two read operations. When these operations are carried out over the network to a remote disk, the resulting load on the server and the delay for network transmission can become extreme. One alternative might be to implement the open routine entirely within the server.

This is the basic rationale for remote file systems. While remote disks are simple and relatively efficient, there are cases where a client machine needs to do several reads with a relatively small amount of computation between each read (for example, to look up a pointer in a block). If such operations could be implemented in the server, then an overall increase in efficiency should result due to the elimination of network delays.

11.3.1 Remote File System Organization

A remote file system differs from a remote disk system in that some of the semantics of the file and directory system are implemented within the server as well as the client machine. The server provides shared files, accessible from each of the client machines. As part of the file service, the server may provide concurrency control and file protection.

Many contemporary network file systems are implemented in the context of UNIX file systems, for example, AT&T Remote File System [24] and Sun's Network File Systems [25, 28]. Thus, our discussion is based around many UNIX file system concepts. In particular, we assume that the file system is hierarchical — tree-structured except for the case when a file is linked into more than one directory — and that files are named according to path names in a tree or graph structure.

Files may be referenced on remote servers in two general ways: superpath names and remote mounting. Superpath names expand the normal UNIX absolute path names to include a level above root. Names in the high level are machine names. Two forms of superpath names are used:

$$pawnee:/usr/gjn/book/chap11$$

and

$$/../pawnee/usr/gjn/book/chap11$$

(The latter name is intended to mean "start at this machine's root, go up one level, and then choose the machine name and the absolute path name on the machine.) This technique causes the application software to distinguish between local files and remote files, since remote file names have the superlevel.

UNIX file systems include a mechanism for incorporating subfile systems within the root file system. By performing a **mount** operation, a subtree can be appended to an existing hierarchical directory system (see Figure 11.7).

The **remote mount** approach allows the **mount** operation to extend across the network, interconnecting the logical tree in one machine into the tree structure on another machine. The **remote mount** command shown in Figure 11.8 mounts directory b in machine A at mount point (directory) x in machine B. Thus /a/b/c in machine A refers to

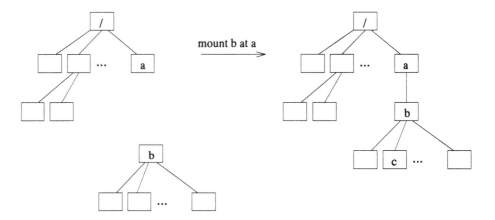

Figure 11.7 The UNIX mount Command

the same file as /x/b/c when referenced in machine B. Notice that this approach causes processes on each machine to see a different topology of the network file system, although local and remote files have the same form.

The issue of determining remote names also arises in remote file systems. For a file system to be remotely mounted or otherwise referenced from a client machine, it may be necessary for the name to be *advertised* in a global name space (see the discussion of naming in Chapter 10). Remote file systems ordinarily operate in a network configuration that includes a name server that implements the global name space.

Opening a file system on a remote file server may be a relatively complex and time-consuming operation. Suppose that a file name is specified as a network reference,

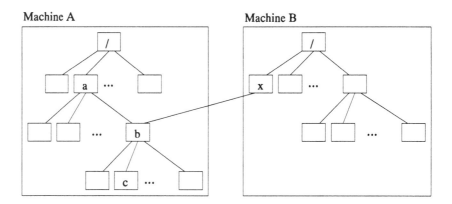

Figure 11.8 A Shared Remote Disk Server

using remotely mounted file systems. In general, the open command causes a serial search of each directory in the path name (see Chapter 9). At each level of the search, there is the possibility of encountering a remote mount point (see Figure 11.9). Each subsequent directory search may cause the remainder of the path name to be passed to a new file server to complete the command. For example, if a process in machine B attempted to open /x/b/c/d/e, the open request would have to be processed in all three machines in order to locate the file descriptor for the leaf node file.

In UNIX file systems, a successful file open operation will result in the file descriptor being loaded into the client's memory (refer to Chapter 9). This is likely to also be required in most systems, since the current state of the file is saved in the descriptor. If two different client processes open the same file, then each will have a cached version of the open file descriptor. Depending on the operating system policy, it may be acceptable to allow both systems to have the file open for writing at the same time (this is acceptable in UNIX). This situation illustrates the necessity for storage locks to control concurrent access to a file that has multiple open operations, at least one of which allows writing. For example, the AT&T RFS system provides a mechanism for locking, while the Sun NFS does not.

There are many strategies for implementing the file read and write operations once a file has been opened. The AT&T RFS approach and the Sun NFS approach illustrate contrasting strategies.

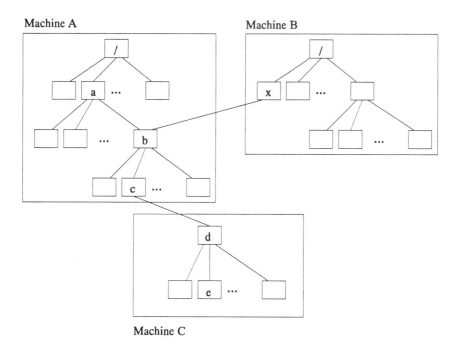

Figure 11.9 Opening Remote Files

Example 11.1: AT&T RFS [24]

A goal of RFS is to make remote file access be as similar to local file access as possible. Each network *domain* (portion of a larger network) includes a central name server that registers advertised file systems within the domain. (RFS does not support interdomain remote file operations.) The RFS client looks up a file system name in the name server then remotely mounts the file system in the client's file name space. Upon completing the first **remote mount** between a client and a server, a virtual circuit is established between the two machines. Subsequent **remote mounts** use the existing virtual circuit by multiplexing.

User-level software makes calls on the kernel file system in the same manner for local and remote files. However, the kernel is modified so that inodes are replaced by a *file system switch*, FSS. The FSS supports multiple file system implementations: Ordinary inodes, and inodes that refer to remote files (see Figure 11.10). References to local files are switched to the local inodes, while references to remote files are handled by an RFS inode type. An RFS inode's device-dependent portion does not refer to disk blocks, but references a remote inode on the server. Kernel software that encounters an RFS inode uses a *remote procedure call* mechanism to complete the operation on the server machine (remote procedure calls are described in Chapter 12). An RFS inode and a corresponding inode are created upon the execution of an **open** call.

The **read** and **write** commands result in a request being sent to the server (containing a buffer of data in the case of **write**). Thus, block pack and unpack are implemented in the server.

The server processes each command as a transaction, that is, it either completes the command or does no part of the command. Furthermore, transactions are processed serially within the server, preventing critical sections across command executions. (However,

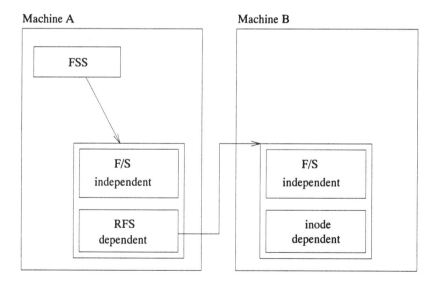

Figure 11.10 RFS FSS and Rnodes

multiple servers can exist on a machine, and these servers must use mutual exclusion operations.) The user-level software masquerades as the client process by using the client's uid, gid, and so on. It then performs the file operation on behalf of the client in the server machine.

Both the client and the server contain part of the inode, including file and record locks. If the server crashes while the client has a file open, then the server must be able to recover the state that existed at the time of the crash. Otherwise, the client may believe a file is locked while the server recovers with the file unlocked. The virtual circuit mechanism signals the client machine if the server crashes. The client kernel marks the appropriate RFS inode, and then notifies the application process of the remote file failure. The application is responsible for its own recovery policy. The server maintains a per client record for each inode in stable storage, which is used in the case of either a client or a server crash.

The RFS developers do not report on the performance of RFS.

Example 11.2: Sun NFS [25, 28]

NFS provides similar service to RFS, although it uses a different approach for recognizing remote file operations and for communication between the client and the server.

NFS also uses the remote mount model to address file naming and to provide some location transparency. However, the name server in the Sun systems does not support a software register operation. Instead, names are manually registered in the name server by a system/network administrator. This allows the NFS name server to provide network names to facilities that are installed by the system administrator, but makes it more difficult for application programmers to add their own distributed subsystems to the network.

Client-server interoperation also uses remote procedure call, but with an underlying datagram protocol rather than a virtual circuit. (The remote procedure call procedure itself provides a specialized reliability protocol.)

The Sun kernel also alters the file system interface used by application programs. Sun's goal was to support heterogeneous file systems, even within the client machine. Therefore, a new *virtual file system*, VFS, is implemented in the kernel (see Figure 11.11). VFS employs different system calls than ordinary UNIX files and also replaces the inode (visible to application programs) with a *vnode*. The vnode acts somewhat like the RFS FSS in the sense that it allows the kernel to support different file system implementations, for example, it may point to a local UNIX file descriptor (inode), to a small computer file system such as DOS files, or to a remotely mounted file system. The client-resident portion of the remote file system makes remote procedure calls on the server in much the same manner as RFS.

A major difference in RFS and NFS is in the management of state and recovery. NFS is designed as a stateless file server (compare with remote disk servers). Each server command is atomic and will either run to completion or have no effect on the server's data. As a result, NFS can use datagrams rather than the less efficient virtual circuit protocol. With a stateless protocol and idempotent operations, either the client or the server can crash without affecting the operation of the other (besides inordinate delays).

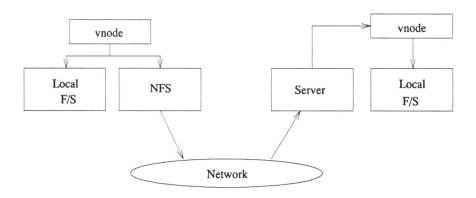

Figure 11.11 NFS VFS and Vnodes

The Sun developers report that by using read-ahead and write-behind buffers at both the client and the server machine (with a large, fast disk) they were able to run benchmarks on NFS that surpassed the performance of a file system with a local SCSI disk drive.

Example 11.3: The Sprite File System [21, 22]

The Sprite researchers have built their file system to take advantage of two empirical observations about the use of UNIX file systems: High-performance local file systems make extensive use of buffering between the user-level process and the disk, and the amount of physical memory that can be used for buffering has a large effect on the performance.

In a remote file system, the buffering can take place at the client and/or the server machine; typical implementations employ buffering at both places (see Figure 11.12). (Because disk blocks are buffered across the network, the literature commonly refers to this form or buffering as *caching*.) In addition to reducing the effective access time within the file, caching in the shared server case can give the server more freedom in moving the disk head (head optimization), and it can reduce contention on the network.

The Sprite Network File System operates much like the Sun NFS, the differences being primarily in the mechanism for caching files. Since Sprite exploits caching techniques, it must go to extra effort to ensure coherency among the cached copies of the file. Second, Sprite employs dynamic space allocation for each cache, in which the cache allocation strategy is intertwined with the virtual memory mechanism.

Sprite uses a delayed write-back policy whenever a client writes into its cache. That is, instead of immediately flushing the cached information to the server and through the server cache onto the disk, writes are accommodated when there is "idle" time. This allows the client write operations to complete without waiting for the server disk write to complete, and it sometimes economizes in writes in the case where data are deleted shortly after they were written. In the delayed write-back case, it may not yet have been written to the disk. Sprite uses a 30-second delay on write-back operations and then has another 30 seconds to actually accomplish the action.

Client   Server

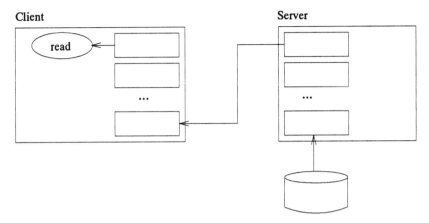

Figure 11.12 Sprite File Caching on Read

Some file servers only support *sequential write sharing*; in this scheme, multiple clients are precluded from having any file open in which any one of the clients has write permission. If a file is written and then closed, the caches are flushed, and any subsequent open will operate on the data created by the write.

Concurrent write sharing is a more flexible approach in which several clients may have the same file open for reading or writing. In this case, newly written data must eventually be propagated to the reader clients in a timely fashion. Sprite supports both sequential and concurrent write sharing.

Sequential write sharing ensures that tardy cache blocks from a previously opened file do not interfere with a new open. The more difficult problem of pending write-back blocks from some other client are handled by forcing the tardy writer to update the server's disk image if an open arrives before the write-back has completed.

Concurrent write sharing is handled by simply disabling caching if any client has a shared file open for writing.

The Sprite researchers report that their experiments with the file system have resulted in attractive performance comparisons. Clients that use caching have a 10% to 40% speedup over clients that do not use caching. Also, using caching, diskless clients ran a set of benchmarks less than 12% more slowly than workstations with disks. Based on the utilizations observed in the experiments, the conjecture is that in a typical configuration of clients (running "average" programs) a server ought to be able to handle up to 50 client machines. More detailed reports of the performance experiments and results appear in [21].

11.4 FILE CACHING SYSTEMS

The third class of sharing allows entire files to be automatically copied from the server to the client, and then returned to the server when the client closes the file. Thus, client machines are ordinarily expected to include at least a small disk.

File-level caching improves the overall performance by eliminating individual disk block or file block updates across the network. All changes are made to the local copy before it is rewritten to the server.

File-level caching still allows the consistency problem to exist, except it now occurs on a file-by-file basis. The literature in this area characterizes files as being *immutable* or *mutable* meaning that the file may not be changed by the client when it has been copied, or it may be changed, respectively. There are two prominent (experimental) file systems that use file-level caching: the Cedar File System and the ITC File System. They differ in the way that they address consistency in mutable files.

Example 11.4: The Cedar File System [13]

The other distributed file systems described in this chapter have all been used in the context of UNIX. The Cedar File System, CFS, exists in the Cedar Programming Environment; thus, its interface differs from the other example file systems. The Cedar Environment is intended to support group programming, so it focuses on mechanisms to allow an individual programmer to have a private name space of files and to be able to integrate the files into the shared name space. The private name space is implemented within each programmer's workstation, and shared files are kept on file servers. When the client wishes to use a shared file, a copy is made on the local disk (so that a copy exists on a server and in the client). The shared copy has a global name and the local copy has a private name. A client can maintain a large number of local names that do not have any physical file at the client machine. When the local name is used, for example, in an **open** command, then the local name will be used to obtain a copy of the remote file and be bound to the copy.

The file server supports only immutable files. An immutable file cannot be written, and it has a unique name; the name is intended to reflect the *version* of the information stored in it. Thus, an immutable file can be copied to a local file system, but it cannot be written back to the server. If it changes, then the client must create a new version of the file and save it on the server. Consistency is not an issue, since files are immutable. Software in the Cedar Environment ordinarily creates new versions of files even in the local file system.

The challenge changes from consistency strategies to version management. The first aspect of version management is the naming convention. Each file is suffixed with a version number, for example, "/ivy/Cedar/CFS/CFSNames.mesa!5" is a name for version 5 of the file with the base name of CFSNames.mesa. CFS automatically uses the lowest version number for some operations, for example, **delete**, and automatically uses the highest version number for other operations, for example, **open**.

CFS does not focus on economizing disk space. Therefore, versions are saved on the server as complete new copies. To prevent the disk space from filling instantaneously, a *keep* parameter is used as the number of most-current versions of a file to retain; all older versions are discarded when a new version is stored in the server.

CFS was designed specifically to support Cedar programmers. The *DF system* uses the CFS to support configuration management within a client workstation. It allows a programmer to use a set of local names that are bound to shared files whenever that is necessary. In most cases, these files will be immutable since they are the environment for files containing software being developed. In the case of mutable files, the version written back to the server is the copy that other programmers will want when they act upon the given file.

Example 11.5: The Andrew Vice/ITC File System [14, 20, 26, 27]

The Andrew project is a distributed computing environment under development at Carnegie-Mellon University in the Information Technology Center. The file system for the environment is sometimes called the *Andrew File System* and sometimes the *ITC File System*. *Vice* is the name for the collective servers that implement the file system.

The file system works on the principle of file-level caching, presuming that each client machine contains a disk. The motivation for file-level caching is to minimize network traffic and disk head contention at the server. Cached files are not necessarily immutable, so the file system incorporates a mechanism to ensure consistency among the cached copies. While our earlier motivation has generally been to distribute more of the work of the file system into the server, the Andrew File System is designed with the idea that the server will be shared by many clients, thus, it should only do the minimum necessary to ensure safe sharing. The high-level goal of the file system is to incorporate acceptable performance in conjunction with scalability.

Early versions of the system only cached files into the client, but later versions also cached directories and symbolic links. Because each client machine employs BSD UNIX, a file that has been opened and cached onto the client's disk is also cached into the client's memory (at the block level). File changes are reflected back to the server only when the file is closed; directory changes are written through to the server.

Because the client contains a disk, a closed file may be resident on the disk. When the client opens the file, it assumes that the local copy (if it is present) is consistent. The server is responsible for notifying the client of inconsistencies for all files that are cached onto the client's disk, using a *callback* mechanism. As a result, the server need not receive open validation requests of locally cached files. If the client machine crashes, then it is assumed that all its local files may be inconsistent. Therefore, it generates a cache validation request for each file on its disk.

The consistency mechanism requires that the client and the server each maintain state about the file system. This forces the server to use callback each time the file is written at the server location and to incorporate a crash recovery scheme.

11.5 DISTRIBUTED MEMORY

Distributed file systems rely on the familiar model of files for sharing information among processes. Files were designed to allow sharing over time, that is, one process used the file exclusively, and then another process could use it later when the first process had closed it. Considerable effort has gone into distributed file system design to allow copies of a file to be simultaneously open by more than one process and in keeping the copies consistent with one another.

Distributed memory systems are intended to achieve the same general effect, but with a tighter coupling among the processes than is typical of file-oriented interaction. Two or more processes share information by sharing parts of their own address spaces (see Figure 11.13). No file paradigm is used to structure the sharing; all protocols related to information structure are handled by common data structure agreement among the processes.

There are several fundamental issues for distributed memory systems:

(1)   **Transparency**. How much knowledge should the process need to keep about the location and implementation of the shared part of the address space?

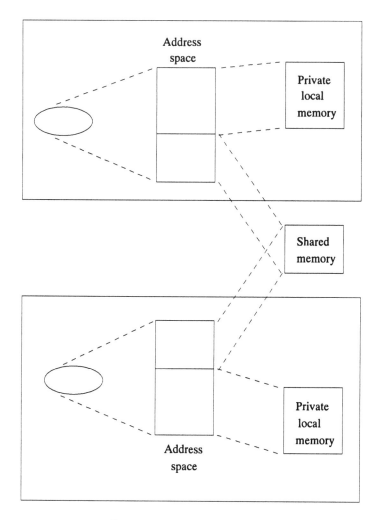

Figure 11.13 Distributed Memory

(2) **Units of sharing**. Should pages or segments of the address space be shared?
(3) **Managing names**. Information will have to be imported and exported by naming the unit to be shared. How should this be handled?
(4) **Efficiency of the underlying implementation**. Assuming that the two processes and their address spaces are on different machines; what are efficient implementations of the remotely stored shared memory?

Research in distributed memory approaches is still very active. There is no general agreement as to the best way to resolve these issues. The observations presented in this section reflect several of the more promising research directions in the area.

11.5.1 Remote Memory

Remote memory systems focus on the interface to the memory. For example, the programmer explicitly identifies parts of the program that are to be mapped to shared memory, while all other parts are mapped to the resulting process's private local memory. This suggests that the programming language be extended and that the programmer identify shared data structures at compile time, for example, by declaring a data structure and marking it as **shared**. In some cases, the programmer will also control the topology of the resulting graph of shared memory segments, that is, not only will the data structure be marked as shared, but it will also be mapped to a virtual processor. In this manner, the programmer can provide enough information to the run-time system so that it will know the identity of processes that share any particular segment of the memory and be able to map that to a location that will minimize network traffic.

The operating system for remote memory systems will provide a relatively simplified communication model, similar to that used to support block-oriented remote file systems. Using the client-server model, shared memory can be implemented at any node in the network as a server that communicates with any client requests much as a block-oriented file server might behave. The remote memory server must be able to accept blocks for storage, advertise the name in the global name space, authenticate users of the name space, allow efficient access (for example, by caching copies of the shared memory segment), and preserve the coherency of the data.

Because the implementation of the shared memory is not transparent, it is possible to apply special semantics to data stored in the shared memory. Data consistency can be "defined away" by specifying that data stored in the shared memory are not guaranteed to be consistent with other copies. Coherency can then be guaranteed by adding a synchronizing mechanism in those cases where it is needed. Furthermore, it is possible to introduce new abstract data type semantics that conform to applications needs (as opposed to general-purpose use). For example, the computation can be built to rely on 1-producer, n-consumers such that a single producer generates information in the shared memory, and n copies can be consumed before the data no longer exist in the memory.

The criticisms of general remote memory systems are primarily with the level of transparency. The distribution of the memory is specific, providing the programmer with maximum flexibility in tuning the access, but requiring that the remote memory be treated differently from local memory. Two different models that make distributed memory transparent are gaining in popularity: distributed objects and distributed virtual memory.

11.5.2 Distributed Objects

Object-oriented programming has become a popular model for defining computations. While objects are defined as independent abstract data types, they also tend to implicitly rely on the idea that a thread of control passes from one object to another. Thus, implementations tend to be in terms of processes, with the thread of control moving from object to object.

However, each object maintains its own address space, with the union of all objects constituting the computation's address space, that is, the object names provide visible names for the name space. Provided that object names can be managed across a network, the object model is a viable means for transparently representing distributed computations with inherently distributed memory.

Objects are difficult for an operating system to manage efficiently since they can be very small (an integer is an object) or very large (a bitmap image is an object). With distributed memory, the difficulty is to be able to move objects around on the network so that when an object is being heavily used by another object, the two are loaded on the same machine. Thus, object mobility is a key issue in implementing distributed objects. While similar to load balancing, object mobility differs in the sense that only portions of address spaces are moved (the portion that is internal to the object), with the object names being maintained in a global address space.

Emerald is a combination language and system to support object mobility [15]. While the Emerald designers accept the idea that implementation of small and large objects might be different, they believe that these implementation differences should not be apparent at the object interface. As a consequence, Emerald provides a single object interface for local and distributed objects. The compiler distinguishes between the two implementations; it generates code that allows large objects to be migrated at run-time.

The Emerald implementation distinguishes global objects from local objects and generates an object descriptor that can incorporate a global name. If the object is remote, then the descriptor will contain enough information for a local message to be forwarded to the object. Since objects migrate and since they are dynamic, the descriptor must also keep reference counts so that the descriptor space can be recovered. Global object forwarding addresses may potentially exist on several machines, depending on the ability of the system to track an object's movement.

11.5.3 Distributed Virtual Memory

Shared remote memory inherently has an aspect of abstraction to it, since it is memory that is treated as if it were local memory while it is implemented on a remote machine. Virtual memory incorporates a memory mapping mechanism as an inherent part of its operation. It is natural to employ part of the mechanism to implement distributed memory.

Virtual memory references differ from physical memory references in that each virtual address is mapped to a physical address prior to being used by the physical memory module. In distributed virtual memory, a virtual address may be mapped to a local physical memory location or into a shared virtual memory space as shown in Figure 11.14. When a private page is loaded into the process's primary memory, it is obtained from the process's unshared secondary memory image. When a shared page is loaded, it is obtained from a remote, shared secondary storage image.

A fundamental problem in distributed virtual memory design is in maintaining consistency among the loaded pages and the shared secondary images on the various machines. The challenge in distributed virtual memory is to design the memory mapping manager so that is correct and efficient. Both centralized and distributed algorithms exist for the memory mapping manager.

Multiprocessor cache coherency solutions are not generally feasible for distributed virtual memory, since they rely on the existence of a shared bus among the caches (see the discussion of snooping caches in Chapter 1). A paging cache coherence solution must take the *page synchronization* and the *page ownership* strategies into account when providing a solution.

Page synchronization can use an *invalidation* approach or a *write-broadcast* approach to assure that when a process writes to a cached page, coherency is maintained

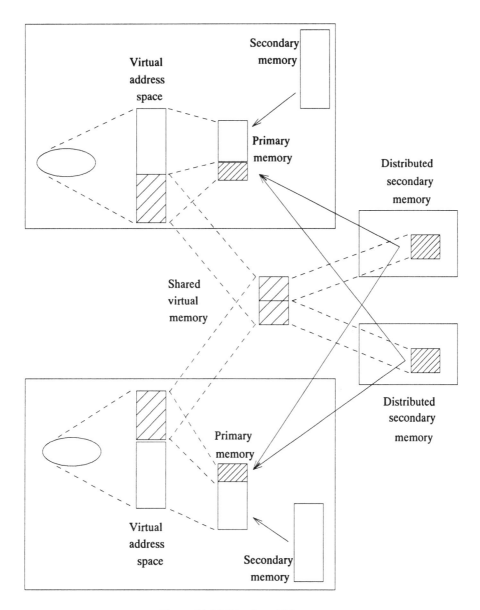

Figure 11.14 Distributed Memory

across all other processes that are using the page. Each page has one "owner" processor for a writable page in the invalidation approach; that is, the "owner" contains the last process to write to the page. A write fault first causes all cached copies of the page to be invalidated, and then the processor that caused the fault changes its access to the page copy to write; now the processor "owns" the page and proceeds with the write operation.

A read operation removes "ownership" from the current owner, that is, no processor is the owner if the last operation was a read.

The write-broadcast approach differs from the invalidation approach in that a write fault causes the faulting processor to update all copies of the cached page before proceeding. Unfortunately, write-broadcast requires special hardware support and is also not an efficient strategy since the owner must participate in each conflict.

Paged ownership can be either *fixed* or *dynamic*. In the fixed ownership case, a page is always owned by the same processor (thus, fixed ownership conflicts with the strategy for managing page synchronization using the invalidation approach). In the case of a write-broadcast page synchronization approach, fixed ownership requires that the owning processor be interrupted for each page write operation.

Dynamic ownership can be implemented by a centralized or a distributed memory manager, in conjunction with an invalidation page synchronization mechanism. The centralized memory manager approach relies on a single copy of the memory manager existing on a particular processor in the network. It keeps global information as to the current access rights, ownership, and locks that exist in the network. As with other centralized approaches, it is relatively simple to implement, but tends to be a bottleneck and a crucial single point in the network.

Distributed managers can use a strategy in which the set of shared pages is statically partitioned and allocated to different managers, or message broadcasting techniques are used on the network (compare with snooping caches in the multiprocessor case).

Distributed virtual memory approaches continue to be a topic of contemporary research, but even experimental implementations provide encouraging performance. It appears that this approach will dominate in distributed storage as applications move to tighter coupling and away from traditional input/output models.

11.6 FURTHER READING

Svobodova has written a comprehensive article that appears in *ACM Computing Surveys* and addresses many of the file server issues described here as well as others [30].

Cheriton and Zwaenepoel also conducted performance studies of diskless workstations prior to that work reported in the body of the chapter [9].

Finally, there are a number of good papers about individual file and disk servers in addition to the papers cited in the body of the chapter, including Alpine file system [5], Apollo Domain file system [17], Cambridge File Server and the Xerox Distributed File Server [19], Masscomp EFS [10], the Newcastle Connection [6], and Swallow [23].

Distributed memory is less widely studied than are file systems. There are several interesting distributed memory papers, including the Linda system [7], the Amber system [8], the Mirage system [12], and general observations by Stumm and Zhou [29].

Distributed objects have also grown in importance with the growing popularity of object-oriented programming. The Emerald system has been mentioned in the chapter; Presto [3] and distributed Smalltalk [1, 2] are related projects that focus on issues related to distributing objects.

Much of the leading work in distributed virtual memory is due to Li [18] (and our discussion of distributed virtual memory follows the introductory part of this paper). Subsequent papers on NUMA organizations also employ distributed virtual memory techniques, for example, see [4] and [11].

REFERENCES

1. J. L. Bennett, "Distributed Smalltalk," *Proceedings of the 2nd ACM Conference on Object-Oriented Systems, Languages, and Applications*, Orlando, FL, October 1987, 318-330.

2. J. K. Bennett, "Distributed Smalltalk: Inheritance and Reactiveness in Distributed Systems," Department of Computer Science, University of Washington, Ph.D dissertation, December 1987.

3. B. N. Bershad, E. D. Lazowska, and H. M. Levy, "Presto: A System for Object-Oriented Parallel Programming," *Software -- Practice and Experience 18*, 8 (August 1988), 713-732.

4. W. J. Bolosky, R. P. Fitzgerald, and M. L. Scott, "Simple But Effective Techniques for NUMA Memory Management," *Proceedings of the Twelfth ACM Symposium on Operating Systems Principles* , December 1989 , 19-31.

5. M. R. Brown, K. N. Kolling, and E. A. Taft, "The Alpine File System," *ACM Transactions on Computer Systems 3*, 4 (November 1985), 261-293.

6. D. R. Brownbridge, L. F. Marshall, and B. Randell, "The Newcastle Connection," *Software -- Practice and Experience 12*, 12 (December 1982), 1147-1162.

7. N. Carriero and D. Gelernter, "The S/Net's Linda Kernel," *ACM Transactions on Computer Systems 4*, 2 (May 1986), 110-129.

8. J. S. Chase, F. G. Amador, E. D. Lazowska, H. M. Levy, and R. J. Littlefield, "The Amber System: Parallel Programming on a Network of Multiprocessors," *Proceedings of the Twelfth ACM Symposium on Operating Systems Principles* , December 1989 , 147-158.

9. D. R. Cheriton and W. Zwaenepoel, "The Distributed V Kernel and Its Performance for Diskless Workstations," *Proceedings of the Ninth ACM Symposium on Operating Systems Principles 17*, 5 (July 1983), 129-140.

10. C. T. Cole, P. B. Flinn, and A. B. Atlas, "An Implementation of an Extended File System," *USENIX Proceedings*, June 1985, 131-149.

11. A. L. Cox and R. J. Fowler, "The Implementation of a Coherent Memory Abstraction on a NUMA Multiprocessor: Experiences with PLATINUM," *Proceedings of the Twelfth ACM Symposium on Operating Systems Principles* , December 1989 , 32-44.

12. B. D. Fleisch and G. J. Popek, "Mirage: A Coherent Distributed Shared Memory Design," *Proceedings of the Twelfth ACM Symposium on Operating Systems Principles* , December 1989 , 211-223.

13. D. K. Gifford, R. M. Needham, and M. D. Schroeder, "The Cedar File System," *Communications of the ACM 31*, 3 (March 1988), 288-298.

14. J. H. Howard, M. L. Kazar, S. G. Menees, D. A. Nichols, M. Satyanarayanan, R. N. Sidebotham, and M. J. West, "Scale and Performance in a Distributed File System," *ACM Transactions on Computer Systems 6*, 1 (February 1988), 51-81.

15. E. Jul, H. Levy, N. Hutchinson, and A. Black, "Fine-Grained Mobility in the Emerald System," *ACM Transactions on Computer Systems 6*, 1 (February 1988), 109-133.

16. E. D. Lazowska, J. Zahorjan, D. R. Cheriton, and W. Zwaenepoel, "File Access Performance of Diskless Workstations," *ACM Transactions on Computer Systems 4*, 3 (August 1986), 238-268.

17. P. J. Leach, P. H. Levine, B. P. Douros, J. A. Hamilton, D. L. Nelson, and B. L. Stumpf, "The Architecture of an Integrated Local Network," *IEEE Journal on Selected Areas in Communication SAC-1*, 5 (November 1983), 842-857.

18. K. Li and P. Hudak, "Memory Coherence in Shared Virtual Memory Systems," *ACM Transactions on Computer Systems 7*, 4 (November 1989), 321-359.

19. J. G. Mitchell and J. Dion, "A Comparison of Two Network-Based File Servers," *Communications of the ACM 25*, 4 (April 1982), 233-245.

20. J. H. Morris, M. Satyanarayanan, M. H. Conner, J. H. Howard, D. S. H. Rosenthal, and F. D. Smith, "Andrew: A Distributed Personal Computing Environment," *Communications of the ACM 29*, 3 (March 1986), 184-201.

21. M. N. Nelson, B. B. Welch, and J. K. Ousterhout, "Caching in the Sprite Network File System," *ACM Transactions on Computer Systems 6*, 1 (February 1988), 134-154.

22. J. K. Ousterhout, A. R. Cherenson, F. Douglis, M. N. Nelson, and B. B. Welch, "The Sprite Network Operating System," *IEEE Computer 21*, 2 (February 1988), 23-36.

23. D. P. Reed and L. Svobodova, "SWALLOW: A Distributed Data Storage System for a Local Network," *Local Networks for Computer Communication*, 1981, 355-373.

24. A. P. Rifkin, M. P. Forbes, R. L. Hamilton, M. Sabrio, S. Shah, and K. Yueh, "RFS Architectural Overview," *Proceedings of Communix 86*, June, 1986, 35-43.

25. R. Sandberg, D. Goldberg, S. Kleiman, D. Walsh, and B. Lyon, "Design and Implementation of the Sun Network File System," *USENIX Proceedings*, June 1985, 119-130.

26. M. Satyanarayanan, J. H. Howard, D. A. Nichols, R. N. Sidebotham, A. Z. Spector, and M. J. West, "The ITC Distributed File System: Principles and Design," *Proceedings of the Tenth ACM Symposium on Operating Systems Principles*, December 1985, 35-50.

27. M. Satyanarayanan, "Scalable, Secure, and Highly Available Distributed File Access," *IEEE Computer 23*, 5 (May 1990), 9-21.

28. M. Stein and S. Ahnger, "Tutorial #M5: The Network File System," *Usenix Technical Conference and Exhibition*, June 1987.

29. M. Stumm and S. Zhou, "Algorithms Implementing Distributed Shared Memory," *IEEE Computer 23*, 5 (May 1990), 54-64.

30. L. Svobodova, "File Servers for Network-Based Distributed Systems," *ACM Computing Surveys 16*, 4 (December 1984), 353-398.

31. D. Swinehart, G. McDaniel, and D. Boggs, "WFS: A Simple Shared File System for a Distributed Environment," *Proceedings of the Seventh Symposium on Operating Systems Principles*, December 1979, 9-17.

EXERCISES

(1) The WFS developers have indicated some performance numbers comparing remote disk read and write operations with local disk read and write operations. Explain why these numbers may be misleading.

(2) Lazowska and others [16] reported that network protocols must provide for volume transfer at every protocol level. The discussion of this observation indicates that large block transfers amortize the latency delays across many bytes. Provide some rational argument for this statement.

(3) Lazowska and others' study [16] also indicates that overall disk server performance is more likely to be increased by concentrating on the server rather than on the clients. Provide a rational argument for this statement.

(4) Explain why diskless workstation and server configurations generally do not use the internet.

(5) The network software on some commercial microcomputers uses the Ethernet along with a number of different protocols, including the ISO Internet Protocol (IP) and the the User Datagram Protocol (UDP). Suppose that we transmit 512 1 KB packets from one machine to another as fast as possible. Measurements indicate that a workstation with a 16.67 MHz clock can transmit the packets to a workstation with a 25 MHz clock at a rate of 171 packets/second. The transmission in the opposite direction was observed to occur at a rate of 256 packets/second. Provide a possible explanation for these phenomena, and argue the plausibility of your explanation.

(6) In Section 11.3, the pedagogical example suggested that a server could have knowledge of logical records stored within a file (or files). Discuss some of the issues that must be addressed in a server that supported such an interface.

12

DISTRIBUTING FUNCTIONALITY

Network file services are systems-level applications, generally implemented using low- and mid-level network protocols, in part due to performance constraints, and in part due to the fact that file and disk servers were implemented prior to the existence of any substantial amount of higher-layer network protocols. Over time, file services will increasingly migrate up the protocol stacks to provide extended interfaces and functions and to use the higher layer services.

The distributed memory view of distributed computing has resulted in definite advances in the effective use of networks of machines. However, there is another perspective on distribution that concentrates on distributing function rather than storage. (Some might argue that distributed objects employ both views.) This perspective is less well developed than the distributed storage perspective, but some aspects of it are rapidly emerging as fundamental approaches to distributed systems. One result of the early stage of its development is that the relevant topics do not necessarily flow together nicely; they appear as a potpourri of important tools that are used in distributing a computations functionality.

The tools used in designing distributed function systems include the *high-layer protocols*, *process synchronization* tools, *transactions and concurrency control*, *distributed deadlock*, *interprocess communication*, and *remote procedure call*. In this chapter, we describe each of the tool classes.

12.1 HIGHER-LAYER NETWORK PROTOCOLS

The OSI model is not precisely defined above the transport layer, although there are notable exceptions that define a vertical slice of the protocols, for example, the X.400 mail protocol, the FTAM file transfer protocol, and the X.500 resource directory. Instead, the state of the art is in experimentation with various approaches to using networks to support distributed functionality of one form or another.

Distributed functionality (or *distributed computation*) refers to the case where a computation is implemented in such a manner that parts of the computation are executed on different machines (usually as processes), in which the parts use the network for communication and synchronization. In general, a distributed operating system is required to support distributed computations (although this is not strictly required). Since the operating system must provide tools to accommodate various computing paradigms and to simplify the task of implementing a distributed computation, it generally uses the technology in its own implementation.

There are many different paradigms for building distributed computations, for example, the client-server model is one paradigm and remote procedure call is another. In all cases, the computation is partitioned into a set of *schedulable units of computation* (which we will continue to call processes), each potentially being placed on a distinct machine. The challenge of the distributed application programmer is to partition the functionality of the computation so that it meets desired requirements (such as performance requirements or so that local computation is performed at the physical location of external resources). It is beyond the scope of this book to study partitioning strategies; however, it is the job of the operating system to support any strategy that the application programmer should choose.

The distributed processes will need to share information and to synchronize with one another, just as they do in a local memory environment. The minimum amount of support that the operating system needs to provide is the ability to exchange signals so that these operations can accomplish synchronization.

The simplest distributed applications can communicate using files and a network file transfer protocol or a network file system. Whenever a sending process wishes to transmit information to the another process, it opens a file, writes the information to the file, closes it, and then sends the entire file to the receiving process using a transport level file transfer protocol. Electronic mail systems are typically built using this level of interaction among processes.

Another application area that illustrates a closer coupling between a pair of processes is a remote terminal facility. A number of operating systems support various kinds of virtual terminal. A simple variant is for one machine to implement a simple terminal emulator, connecting the terminal emulator to the host machine using the network (instead of a point-to-point communication line). Such an application is not effective using a file transfer mechanism, but the virtual circuit mechanisms are adequate.

Facilities for supporting bitmapped terminals (workstations) require more sophistication, since the amount of data transmitted for display is prohibitive for terminals with nontrivial resolution and/or color. The terminal's device driver is distributed between the host and the terminal itself (implying local storage and computational facilities in the terminal). This simplifies the amount of work done in the host and increases the amount of work done in the terminal. Contemporary window systems make wide use of this approach (for example, see the X window system [13]).

The higher layers of the network protocol stack implement *sessions* and *presentation*. The distributed applications themselves reside above the presentation layer of the ISO reference model.

12.1.1 Sessions

The session layer is not well-defined in the ISO protocols. However, there are several examples of functions that might exist within the session layer.

The transport layer provides a mechanism for introducing virtual circuits and naming, but none to assist an application in managing a set of sessions. For example, suppose that a process, p_0, were required to exchange information among some set of other processes, $\{p_1, p_2, ..., p_n\}$. Furthermore, suppose that the processes used virtual circuits to support the communication. Then the application process will either use a blocking read on the various virtual circuits or will have to poll each of them to determine when p_i is transmitting a message to p_0.

The UNIX **select** system call is an example of such a mechanism. Each BSD UNIX virtual circuit is established as a socket of type virtual circuit. The socket is mapped into a file descriptor, which is accessed by the process using file input/output read and write operations. To prevent polling, yet be responsive to incoming messages, a process can call **select** with "read," "write," and "exception" masks, requesting that the kernel indicate which of the specified file (socket) descriptors are ready for reading or writing or have a pending exception. The process performs a **select**, and then either ignores the virtual circuits or begins processing information based on the state returned by **select**.

Of course, UNIX incorporates various calls to read and write virtual circuits, and these might also be characterized as session layer functions.

12.1.2 Presentation

The presentation layer is concerned with correct translation of data from the "network" format to the format that the application process is expecting. For example, data may be transmitted as some form of binary encoding to assist in byte-level error recovery, while the application is expecting ASCII characters. Then the Presentation Layer is responsible for translating the ASCII to the special encoding upon transmission and decoding the data before they are delivered to the receiver.

Network representations are desirable for error detection and recovery and to establish an external data representation that is independent of any particular host's internal representation. Sun Microsystems has been a leader in this area by establishing an external data representation, called *XDR*, for intercommunication among different types of machines. Any host machine can translate internal data into XDR and send it over the network, while any other host can then translate the standard XDR representation into its internal representation.

XDR implementations define several built-in conversion routines for scalar values, for example, **xdr_int** and **xdr_string**. The transmitting process uses the built-in routines to convert scalars and combinations of the scalar routines to encode records. The presentation layer software at the receiver location uses decoding routines to convert the XDR to the local internal form.

12.2 PROCESS SYNCHRONIZATION

Distributed computation is based on the idea of partitioning a computation into parts, scheduling the parts on separate processors, and supporting synchronization and communication among them. Chapter 4 describes several mechanisms for accomplishing synchronization; most of these mechanisms implicitly rely on the existence of a shared memory for the processes.

Semaphores are the classic mechanism for synchronization. However, each process must be able to read and write the memory that contains the semaphore in speeds on the order of the CPU cycle time. Monitors also rely on shared memory in which each process can execute when it obtains the monitor.

Even in shared memory hardware systems, semaphores can cause considerable difficulty. Since shared memory machines commonly include a cache memory between the CPU and the bus (see Chapter 1), a semaphore is likely to be loaded into the cache, particularly in the case where the multiprocessor incorporates spin locks. When a process releases the semaphore, it writes the corresponding memory cell. This will invalidate each cache memory that contains a process that is blocked on the semaphore. The result will be contention at the bus and memory and the reloading of the caches. Soon thereafter, one of the processes will obtain the semaphore, writing a new value to its cache and again invalidating the caches of all other processes.

Semaphores can be implemented in an abstract shared memory on a network. An abstract shared memory simulates a shared physical memory. That is, some location in the network implements the physical memory and all other processes access the memory through network operations. Now, either semaphores are a special operation on the shared memory, that is. the semaphore algorithms are implemented at the site of the physical memory; or the physical memory is accessed using a network operation, not really viable due to the network overhead; or the shared memory is cached to the location of each process, corresponding to the same situation as occurs in shared memory multiprocessor caches.

One alternative to the dilemma is to reconsider event ordering as a means to accomplish synchronization (see Chapter 4). It is generally sufficient to be able to establish an order among the set of all event occurrences in the individual processes to accomplish coordination of their behavior. And the techniques used establish the synchronization are more amenable to network based implementation than are semaphores.

Before reconsidering ordering among events, we will provide some background information by considering a special case of event ordering, that of implementing a global clock.

12.2.1 Global Clocks

A simple communication problem is to be able to synchronize the local clocks on a set of distinct machines in a network. Each clock is driven by its own crystal, and crystals can vary slightly in their frequency (for example, two crystals of the same rated frequency may vibrate a different number of times in one week's time). As a result, a clock will "drift" from the true time if it is not periodically reset. The network is a natural mechanism to use to synchronize all host clocks. Unfortunately, we know that, if we use a low-level protocol to pass the synchronization signal to all the hosts, some of them may not receive the information due to the unreliability of the low-level network. The high-level network can be made reliable, but not punctual (since the reliability is ensured through retransmissions if necessary).

Clock synchronization can be approximated by a number of different techniques, ranging from voting on the correct time, to setting the time based on a single, efficient signal. It is also possible to achieve much of the effect of clock synchronization by focusing on event ordering in a distributed system.

Suppose that we have a community of processes in execution on distinct machines and that processes transmit messages to one another whenever there is a need to share information or synchronize their operation. A global clock is needed to determine *when* some event occurred and, in particular, to determine if some event occurred before or after some other event. That is, one would like to have a *total order* on the set of all events that may occur in a distributed system. But, since it may be impossible to determine which event occurred first, one can establish a *partial order* and then use it to establish a *possible* total order of events that is consistent with an observed behavior (or set of constraints).

Definition 12.1. The relation $<\cdot$ is the smallest relation satisfying:

(1) e_i and e_j are events in the same process and $e_i <\cdot e_j \Rightarrow e_i$ occurs before e_j.
(2) e_i is the transmission of a message and e_j is the receipt of the message $\Rightarrow e_i <\cdot e_j$.
(3) $e_i <\cdot e_j$ and $e_j <\cdot e_k \Rightarrow e_i <\cdot e_k$.

If neither $e_i <\cdot e_j$ nor $e_j <\cdot e_i$, then e_i and e_j are *concurrent*. ‖

Figure 12.1 represents the progress of p_0, p_1, and p_2. Events e_{0i} represent the sequential occurrence of events within process p_0. Since e_{01} occurs before e_{02},

$$e_{01} <\cdot e_{o2}$$

In the figure, the directed edges from one event to another represent the transmission of a message from one process to another, with the sending event at the tail of the edge and the receiving event at the head of the edge. So e_1 represents the event corresponding to p_1 sends a message to p_0, and e_{02} represents the reception of the message by p_0. This situation is denoted by writing $e_{11} <\cdot e_{02}$.

The $<\cdot$ relation is similar to the precedence relation used in Chapter 3, except that now we are looking at event occurrences rather than process execution. In our previous discussion of precedence, we did not allow processes to have multiple events for synchronization; instead, processes were separated such that an event either marked the initiation or termination of a process. The $<\cdot$ relation can be used to describe serialization among synchronizing events.

Definition 12.2. (Lamport's Clock Condition) Let C be a function that assigns a nonnegative integer value to each event e_i. For events e_i, e_j

$$e_i <\cdot e_j \Rightarrow C(e_i) < C(e_j) ‖$$

The clock condition describes proper global operation for event occurrences that have precedence. Now we need to relate the global operation with event activity within the intercommunicating processes: Let $\{p_0, p_1, ..., p_{n-1}\}$ be a set of processes, each with a number of internal events. And, let C_i be a local clock that maps any event that occurs in p_i into a nonnegative integer.

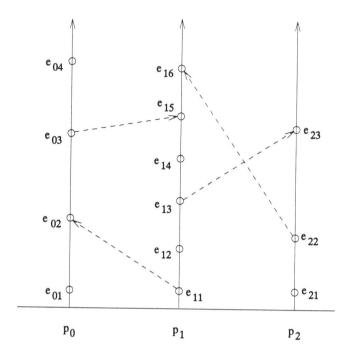

Figure 12.1 Space-Time Diagram for Three Processes

Suppose that:
(1)   If e_j occurs before e_k in p_i, then

$$C_i(e_j) < C_i(e_k)$$

(2)   If e_s is a send event by p_i and e_r is a receive of that message by p_j, then

$$C_i(e_s) < C_j(e_r)$$

These conditions allow the clock condition to hold between two distinct processes. That is, the synchronizing operation between the two processes preserves the partial order across a pair of processes.

Figure 12.2 is the previous state-time diagram with the introduction of clock values for each process. Each event within a process must have at least one clock tick between itself and adjacent events. Similarly, any directed edge that represents message sending must cross a line that connects similarly indexed clock ticks within each process.

Now, define the local clock function for a process so that it is guaranteed to assign strictly increasing integer values to events that occur in sequence in a process. Let C_i be a register within p_i:
(1)   Increment C_i between event occurrences.
(2)   If event e_s sends message m from p_i, then associate a *time stamp*

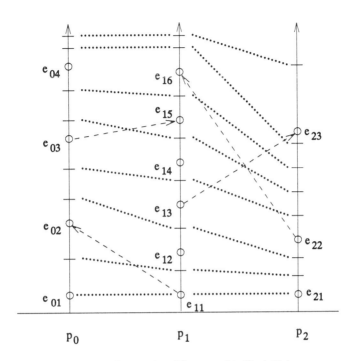

Figure 12.2 Space-Time Diagram with Clock Values

$$T_m = C_i(e_s)$$

with the message. When p_j receives m, it sets C_j to be some value that is greater than or equal to its current values and greater than T_m.

That is, p_j's clock will be synchronized with p_i's clock when a message is sent from p_i to p_j. Now we have an implementation of the clock condition across multiple processes.

The space-time diagram shown in Figure 12.2 represents the logical progress of the three processes. It suggests one consistent view of the total order of events in the distributed system. However, Figure 12.3 also represents an acceptable view, one that suggests that the local clocks are closely synchronized in real time. Thus, the clock condition illustrates the correct operation of a set of processes without really specifying the strict order in which all events *must* occur.

The partial orderings on the events in the distributed system can be converted to a total ordering by using the partial ordering of the local clocks in conjunction with an arbitrary ordering on processes (to resolve ties that exist among the local events). Now every event in the system can be said to occur before or after any other event. If the events are related by message passing, then the partial order determines that part of the total order; if the events are unrelated (happen at the same time), then the order among processes breaks the tie.

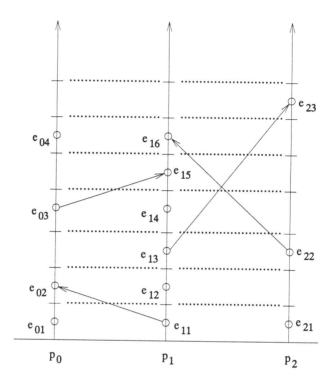

Figure 12.3 An Alternate View of the Space-Time Diagram

Lamport also describes applications of his global clock algorithms to distributed systems and to physical clocks. Considerable more detail can be found in [10].

12.2.2 Eventcount and Sequencers Revisited

In Chapter 4, eventcounts and sequencers were introduced as an alternate mechanism (to semaphores) for synchronization. Eventcounts represent the number of **advance** calls on the eventcount, and sequencers represent the number of **ticket** calls. Eventcounts are defined to allow simultaneous calls, while **ticket** calls are fully serialized. Eventcounts are read using the **read** or **await** calls, and **ticket** returns the current value of the sequencer.

Eventcounts and sequencers accomplish synchronization by focusing on the order of related events rather than through a mutual exclusion mechanism. As a result, they can be implemented in a network environment without relying on an implementation of shared memory. The approach is built on the idea of global clocks described above.

12.3 INTERPROCESS COMMUNICATION

In contrast to synchronization, IPC requires that information be exchanged (in addition to the implicit synchronization of synchronous send and blocking receive operations).

Multiple-process computations in a multiprogramming (uniprocessor) environment essentially simulate the true distributed environment provided by a network of distinct machines. As a result, the extension of the the IPC abstract machine interface from the multiprogramming environment to the network environment is generally not significant.

The specific difference between multiprogramming IPC and network IPC naming interfaces is in the need for name registering and binding (as described in Chapter 10). Multiprogramming IPC name space spans are handled within the shared operating system, while network-based IPC requires explicit services to accomplish these tasks.

The basic issues for the actual exchange of information are related to datagrams and sockets. The IPC mechanism might be built on a message paradigm or on the notion of communication links; if messages have restrictions on their sizes, then they can ordinarily be implemented directly on datagrams. But if the messages sizes are essentially unrestricted, or if the mechanism uses links, then it will ordinarily require that IPC be supported by virtual circuits.

Once the intername space interface is designed, the major problem in network IPC becomes the efficient and reliable implementation of the abstract machine. Here we see considerable effort expended at constructing efficient implementations. For example, both the V Kernel and Mach (see Chapter 13) place considerable emphasis on this aspect of their design and implementations.

12.4 TRANSACTIONS AND CONCURRENCY CONTROL

12.4.1 Transactions

Transactions are widely used in distributed databases to address the problem of multiple processes updating storage that has multiple parts (see Chapter 2). They are also useful in systems that are susceptible to crash or in which the consequences of an unfortuitous crash are catastrophic. In general, the problem arises because a process may begin to update a set of fields in a record while another process is already updating the record. If the second process interrupts the first or if it updates the fields in a different order than the first, the resulting record may have some fields reflecting the update from one of the processes while other fields reflect updates by the other. If the system crashes in the middle of a transaction, the effect may be the same as the concurrent access problem.

Transactions on multiple resources require that the system provide a mechanism to allow a process to either complete a set of changes to the set of resources or have the effect of incremental changes be ignored if the transaction does not complete. In the former case, the transaction is *committed*, and in the latter case the transaction is said to have been *aborted*. Thus, a transaction can be thought of as a set of small operations that are themselves executed atomically.

There are many occasions when operating systems use transactions to coordinate the operation of processes. For example, remote file systems use transactions for most forms of caching at the page level, block level, and file level, since movement of information requires that client and server state have multiple fields updated at any given time.

The transaction's individual steps are initiated by a *start_transaction* symbol and terminated by either an *abort* or a *commit* operation, depending on whether the transaction is to be fully completed or the interim data should be reset to the state there were in when the *start_transaction* occurred.

Transaction implementation effectively checkpoints the state of the relevant resources when a transaction is initiated. The operations within the transaction are executed on a copy of the resources or on the original resources provided that the checkpoint information can be used to restore the resources to the state that existed at the checkpoint. In databases, the transaction is *rolled back* to the original state; in general computations, the effective rollback may be accomplished in an arbitrary manner. If another transaction is started when one is in progress, then the state must be checkpointed carefully so that the effect of the first transaction is preserved if it commits.

If the transaction is aborted, then the resource state is restored on the basis of the checkpoint information. If it is committed, then the copy of the changes becomes the master version, and the checkpoint information can be released.

12.4.2 Concurrency Control

Concurrency control enables a set of processes to interleave a set of transactions on a set of shared resources, providing the same result as if each process were given exclusive control of all related resources for the duration of a transaction. Thus, concurrency control guarantees logical *serializability* of a set of transactions, even though the operations within the transactions may be interleaved.

Resource *locks* are the most widely used mechanism for implementing concurrency control. When a transaction changes a part of the resource, it can lock the resource for the duration of the transaction. Subsequent processes that attempt to alter that part of the resource will be unable to do so until the first transaction completes.

The *two-phased locking* protocol ensures that a set of transactions will produce correctly serialized results. During the first phase, the transaction acquires locks but does not release any, and during the second phase, it releases locks and does not acquire any. In the degenerate case, all acquisitions take place when the transaction is initialized and all releases take place when the transaction terminates.

Two issues that arise from indiscriminate use of locks are related to the size of a "part" of the resource and deadlock. If the resource is a file, then should the lock apply to a disk page, a logical file block, or to the entire file? Different researchers make strong arguments for each case. The arguments revolve around the trade-off of the number of locks to manage versus the amount of concurrent access that can be supported across transactions.

Deadlock can occur if transactions happen to lock parts of the system's resources while requesting other parts. In cases where the two-phased locking approach forces each transaction to acquire all its locks when it is initiated, it is possible to allow the concurrency control mechanism to explicitly avoid deadlock. Otherwise, it will have to employ one of the techniques described in Chapter 5, for example, enforcing the order in which each transaction acquires locks, detection, or time-out (preemption).

Concurrency control revolves around a logically centralized lock manager. If the resources are distributed on a network, then the lock manager must be able to obtain state from each of the constituent nodes. Because of the relative speed of network communication compared to multiprogramming (or shared memory) environments, distributed concurrency control based on locking will encourage the use of locks that control relatively large units of resource.

Just as time-stamping and event ordering can be used to solve general process synchronization problems, they can also be used to address serialization. Locks are used to arbitrate conflicts at run-time, while the time-stamping approach establishes an order of serialization a priori. Each transaction is assigned a time-stamp when it is initiated, then these time-stamps are used to determine the order in which conflicting operations from the two transactions are to be executed. The difficulty is the same as in general synchronization; if the transactions originate on different machines, then their time-stamp values must have been derived from a global clock rather than a local one.

12.5 DISTRIBUTED DEADLOCK DETECTION

We have mentioned deadlock in the context of transactions and concurrency control. Contemporary distributed systems must provide general solutions to deadlock, since the increasing number of resources and processes makes deadlock more likely, and since there is generally no centralized mechanism that can observe deadlock in the case that resources are geographically separated.

While distributed programs tend to perform best if they use only local resources, the nature of partitioning (for performance and for sharing of scarce or expensive resources) implies that processes will utilize remote resources. Each site in a distributed system is only able to obtain knowledge about the state of remote resources through message-passing mechanisms. Consequently, it is difficult for any single process to know the instantaneous state of all resources in the network.

Because of the importance of messages in distributed systems, *communication deadlock* is sometimes distinguished from resource deadlock. Communication deadlock occurs when a set of processes are deadlocked waiting for messages rather than for general resources. This form of deadlock is insidious, since it may make it impossible for an independent detection algorithm to detect the state of blocked processes.

Detection is the favored approach for addressing deadlock in distributed systems. Prevention algorithms tend to require that resource request patterns be regular; this is untenable in a general network of machines with diverse applications. Avoidance algorithms rely on keeping the entire system in a safe state; it is a message-intensive operation to implement such an approach for each resource allocation in the network. Detection is left as the only viable alternative, usually running as a background activity in the network.

A deadlock detection algorithm must be able to construct a resource graph for the network and then analyze it for cycles; and in the case of consumable resources (for example, messages), it must conduct additional analysis as described in Chapter 5.

The resource graph can be built using a centralized, distributed, or hierarchical algorithm. Centralized algorithms maintain the resource state graph at a single site; the challenge is for the analysis site to be able to obtain a reliable view of the state. Distributed algorithms maintain the state graph across the network; the challenge is to conduct the analysis of the graph as a distributed algorithm. Hierarchical approachs logically partition the network and then conduct analysis within the partition as a first step and analysis across the partitions as a second task; this approach effectively uses a combination of centralized and distributed approachs.

The centralized approach requires that the detection site have complete knowledge of the network's resource state. Thus, each request, acquisition, and release operation must result in a message being (reliably) sent to the centralized site. The detection site continuously processes messages, updates the resource graph, and conducts analysis of it. This approach tends to be expensive in message traffic (a virtual circuit must exist between the site and each other site in the network). It also requires that the detection site be completely reliable, since if the site crashes there is no detection in the system.

There are several different distributed detection algorithms, each of which rely on the state of the network being obtained through a circulating "token" that obtains information at each node that it visits, and also disseminates knowledge about other sites. Depending on the exact nature of the information held in the token, the deadlock may be determined at a link in the token path traversal, or the token may be required to traverse a cycle through the network, and once the cycle is completed, the originating node can detect the deadlock.

12.6 REMOTE PROCEDURE CALL

One traditional way of passing information among different modules is to use procedure call mechanisms with parameter passing. *Remote procedure call* (RPC) protocols are a means by which a programmer can call a procedure that is loaded on a different machine. RPC is a specialized form of interprocess communication in which the initiating program performs a send operation immediately followed by a blocking read operation. The receiving program performs a blocking read until it receives the message sent by the "caller" process; it then provides the service and returns a result by sending it to the original process. From the original process's point of view, the IPC behaves as if it were a procedure call.

An RPC implementation should allow a programmer to write calling and called application procedures such that the calling procedure is executed on one machine and the called procedure is executed on another. Since RPC is intended to resemble ordinary procedure call as closely as possible, there are several issues that need to be addressed by any RPC implementation; specifically, the syntax of the call should be the same as for any local call in the high-level programming language. While it may be difficult for the semantics of the call to be exactly the same, for example, call-by-name parameter management, most semantics should also be the same in both cases. The recipient of the RPC will need to execute in an environment that is similar to the one in which the call was made. While it is usually not possible to create the dynamic stack in the called procedure's address space, the parameter and return mechanism interface should be the same as for a local implementation.

RPC implementations take the general form shown in Figure 12.4. The client machine consists of the client application code, a client stub, and the transport mechanism, while the server machine implements a transport mechanism, server stub, and the server code. The transport mechanism implements network message passing. While the requirements are for reliability, actual implementations tend to use a datagram protocol with a special-purpose RPC protocol for reliability. The stub modules are used to encode and decode parameter lists on call and return. The server process is a surrogate calling process for the client.

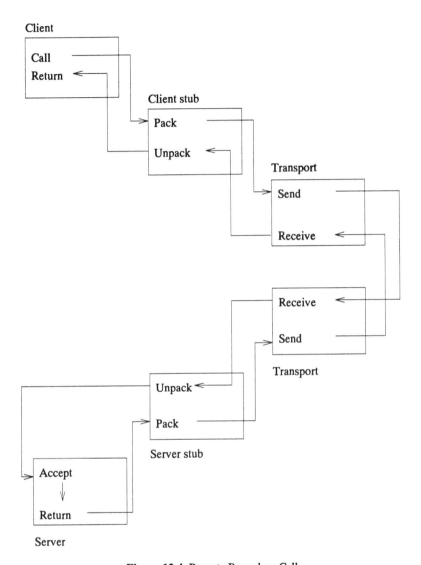

Figure 12.4 Remote Procedure Call

It must be possible to write the client software so that the remote procedure call has the same syntax as a local call, with the location of the procedure being determined at link time. This suggests that the client software will need to be statically bound to a local procedure, which can span address spaces (over the network) to communicate with the server. The client stub is the intermediary; it is statically linked into the calling program, but will use run-time information (including a name service) to communicate with the server.

How can the client stub be generated automatically? Contemporary programming languages employ procedure interface modules that define the calling sequences of all procedures. A module that implements a procedure is said to *export* it, and modules that use a procedure are said to *import* it. The interface module provides sufficient information to generate the client stub, since it identifies the symbolic procedure name and parameters; a stub compiler can use the interface module to generate calls to the local transport mechanism to accomplish the interchange of calls and returns and to package the parameters into appropriate network messages. At run-time, the client stub will use a name server to locate the server and then will exchange messages with the server as required.

On the server side, each module that exports a procedure must be prepared to accept remote calls. This requires that the server contain a surrogate calling procedure (that is, a surrogate calling *process*) that will accept call requests from the client stub and make the local call. The server stub is generated using interface modules and the export directives in procedures that are implemented in its address space. The server registers each procedure with the name server, enabling the client stub to locate the procedure at call time. Registration includes adding the name to the name server and mapping internal identifiers to the procedure. At call time the client stub will pack the calling parameters into a message and then send it to the network port specified by the name server. The transport portion of the server will deliver the message to the server stub, which will unpack the parameters, identify the procedure to be called, and call it. When the procedure returns (with results), the server stub packs the results and returns them to the client stub. The client stub unpacks the results and returns to the caller.

Parameters that are passed as call-by-value are easy to handle with the above mechanism. Parameters that are passed by name or reference are difficult to handle since they suggest that the client and server stubs be required to evaluate parameters passed to the server. Different remote procedure packages use different approaches to this latter problem. However, each will require network traffic between the client stub and the server stub.

Remote procedure calls are useful for distributing processing across different machines, but they do not encourage parallel computation. When a caller invokes a remote procedure, it blocks during the remote procedure execution.

However, remote procedures are widely used in contemporary distributed applications, since they implement a traditional programming model with little thought about distribution strategies. For example, both Sun NFS and AT&T RFS are implemented on top of remote procedure call facilities.

12.7 FURTHER READING

Reed and Kanodia introduce eventcounts and sequencers in [12]. This paper also slightly redefines the Lamport clock condition and uses it to argue the correctness of eventcounts and sequencers in distributed systems.

Jefferson and his coworkers have developed an alternative method for managing global time among a set of distributed host machines. The *time warp* approach takes the (optimistic) assumption that the processes are nearly synchronized, and that event synchronization messages that arrive "out of order" are the exception rather than the rule. In this case, the time warp approach rolls back all processes to an earlier time if a synchronizing message arrives after a process had assumed that none would arrive. See [7] for details.

Atomic transactions and concurrency control are the subject of considerable literature in distributed databases. The classic paper on the topic is by Eswaran and others [5]; Bernstein and Goodman also provide an extensive review of the issues [1]. Database books also address these issues in a complete framework; for example, see Ullman [17] or Korth and Silberschatz [9]. In the operating systems literature, Lampson and Sturgis describe the two-phase commit protocol [11], and Svobodova surveys concurrency control in her paper about file and disk servers [15].

There are two more recent survey papers concerning distributed deadlock detection: Knapp provides an extensive survey focused on databases [8], and Singhal broadens the discussion to distributed systems in general [14].

Remote procedure call has been around for several years [18]. The technique has become considerably more popular with the continued performance enhancement at the lower network layers. Fundamental improvements in the technology appear in the papers by Birrell and Nelson [4] and Gifford and Glasser [6]. Lazowska and his colleagues have focused on remote procedure call in heterogeneous environments [3] and to support "lightweight procedures" [2]. Tay and Ananda have published a comprehensive bibliography on various specific remote procedure call designs [16].

REFERENCES

1. P. A. Bernstein and N. Goodman, "Concurrency Control in Distributed Database Systems," *ACM Computing Surveys 13*, 2 (June 1981), 185-221.
2. B. N. Bershad, T. E. Anderson, E. D. Lazowska, and H. M. Levy, "Lightweight Remote Procedure Call," *ACM Transactions on Computer Systems 8*, 1 (February 1990), 37-55.
3. B. N. Bershad, D. T. Ching, E. D. Lazowska, J. Sanislo, and M. Schwartz, "A Remote Procedure Call Facility for Heterogeneous Computer Systems," *IEEE Transactions on Software Engineering SE-13*, 8 (August 1987), 880-894.
4. A. D. Birrell and B. J. Nelson, "Implementing Remote Procedure Calls," *ACM Transactions on Computer Systems 2*, 1 (February 1984), 39-59.
5. K. P. Eswaran, J. N. Gray, R. A. Lorie, and I. L. Traiger, "The Notions of Consistency and Predicate Locks in a Database System," *Communications of the ACM 19*, 1 (November 1976), 624-633.
6. D. K. Gifford and N. Glasser, "Remote Pipes and Procedures for Efficient Distributed Communication," *ACM Transactions on Computer Systems 6*, 3 (August 1988), 258-283.
7. D. R. Jefferson, "Virtual Time," *ACM Transactions on Programming Languages and Systems 7*, 3 (July 1985), 404-425.
8. E. Knapp, "Deadlock Detection in Distributed Databases," *ACM Computing Surveys 19*, 4 (December 1987), 303-328.
9. H. F. Korth and A. Silberschatz, *Database System Concepts*, McGraw-Hill Book Co., New York, NY, 1986.
10. L. Lamport, "Time, Clocks and the Ordering of Events in a Distributed System ," *Communications of the ACM 21* , 7 (July 1978), 558-565.
11. B. Lampson and H. Sturgis, *Crash Recovery in a Distributed Data Storage System*, Xerox Palo Alto Research Center, April 1979.
12. D. P. Reed and R. K. Kanodia, "Synchronization with Eventcounts and Sequencers," *Communications of the ACM 22*, 2 (February 1979), 115-123.
13. R. W. Scheifler, *X Window System Protocol, Version 11*, MIT Laboratory for Computer Science, Cambridge, MA, 1986.

14. M. Singhal, "Deadlock Detection in Distributed Systems," *IEEE Computer 22*, 11 (November 1989), 37-48.

15. L. Svobodova, "File Servers for Network-Based Distributed Systems," *ACM Computing Surveys 16*, 4 (December 1984), 353-398.

16. B. H. Tay and A. L. Ananda, "A Survey of Remote Procedure Calls," *ACM SIGOPS Operating Systems Review 24*, 3 (July 1990), 68-79.

17. J. D. Ullman, *Principles of Database Systems, Second Edition*, Computer Science Press, Rockville, MD, 1982.

18. J. White, "A High-Level Framework for Network-Based Resource Sharing," *Proceedings of the National Computer Conference*, 1976, 561-570.

EXERCISES

(1) Write pseudocode definitions of a client stub and a server stub.

(2) Explain how client and server stubs could be algorithmically generated for a language that uses interfaces specifications (for example, C++).

(3) Using an RPC package, write a program that generates data and three remote procedures in a common module on a remote machine. The first remote procedure should open a UNIX file for writing, the second remote procedure should store the data in an open file, and the third procedure should close the specified file.

   The main program must generate a structure, say something like a record containing a field of type **timeval** [see **gettimeofday**(2)] and a char[N] (for some small, fixed N). An example record might look like

```
{
        {
                123454678;
                9012345;
        };
        "This is record 1"
}
```

   The first remote procedure should have a string argument that names the file to be opened, and the third remote procedure should have an argument that specifies which file is to be closed. The program should call the "store" remote procedure once for each record it generates, passing the record as a parameter; the remote procedure should then store the record at the end of the specified file.

(4) This problem assumes that something similar to the Sun RPC package is available to you. Using the Sun low-level remote procedure call facilities (in particular, the callback facility), write a main program that calls a remote procedure of the form

```
timer(increment, number_of_ticks);
int increment, number_of_ticks;
```

   When "timer" is called on the remote machine, have it send a message to a callback procedure; the message should be time-stamped with the result returned by *gettimeofday*, and identify the remote machine and process identifier. The callback procedure should write the data to stdout. After the remote procedure has sent the data to the callback procedure, it should *sleep* for "increment" seconds and then transmit another message with the same format as the first message. Perform the sleep-transmit loops "number_of_ticks" times; then have the remote procedure return with a final message of the same form as the callback messages.

13

CASE STUDIES

13.1 OPERATING SYSTEM REQUIREMENTS

In the previous chapters we discussed many aspects of contemporary operating systems as individual topics. However, an operating system is an integrated collection of elements that collectively provides resource management services to the system's users. In this chapter we review several different architectural strategies for composing the elements into a system.

13.1.1 Operating System Tasks

Device Management

Device management, including device drivers, was discussed at some length in Chapter 9. While the remainder of the operating system needs to interact with the device driver component, there is little argument that this aspect of the system needs to be kept separate to allow devices to be added to the machine without recompiling the operating system.

Device input/output operations usually write and read primary memory, using direct access techniques. This influences the memory management policy used in the operating system.

Since device operations usually involve mechanical motion of some type, device management is critically related to process management. The relationship exists when the device I/O is initiated and when it is terminated, that is, interrupts prevail as the signaling mechanism for I/O completion.

File System

The file system and implementations were discussed in Chapters 9 and 10. There is considerably less agreement about the coupling of the file system to the operating system nucleus than is the case with devices. Some operating system architects prefer that the bulk of the file system be implemented within the nucleus, while others put a minimum amount of the file system in the nucleus and then extend the functionality with application programs.

File system implementations have become a high-visibility issue in recent years due to the requirement for distribution in a network environment (as remote disks, remote file systems, and distributed databases). Related to the need for distribution is the need for an operating system to support a network file system in which the collection of subfile systems is heterogeneous. For example, a network may need to support both UNIX and DOS computers, each with their own file systems to be shared by different users and processes on the network.

The file system is tied closely to the device management and memory management portions of the system.

Memory Management

There is considerable discussion of memory management architecture in Chapter 7. Most contemporary operating systems employ some form of virtual memory, primarily paging. LRU approximations and working set variants, for example, WSClock, are the most widely used (as static and global strategies, respectively). Small computers continue to use address translation mechanisms to enlarge their address space.

The difficult issue in operating system architecture is to determine the interrelationship of the virtual memory system with the process management part of the system. There is little agreement about the "correct" approach to this problem. And the requirement for distributed virtual memory makes this issue even more difficult.

Process Management

Processes were introduced in Chapter 2 and then refined in Chapters 3 and 4. The CPU and memory are the key high-speed resources in a computer system; thus, process management and memory management are critical parts of the operating system design. An approach that best supports this interoperation is a fundamental factor in the operating system architecture.

13.1.2 An Informal Taxonomy of OS Types

A number of approaches can be taken for configuring the components of an operating system, ranging from a monolithic to a functionally distributed system. Some popular approaches can be characterized as follows:

Monolithic Organization. At one end of the spectrum is the monolithic organization in which the system is viewed of being composed of user programs and a system program. The system program, \ither zero or one process, implements all the functions of the operating system.

Modular Nucleus. A modular nucleus architecture is one step in sophistication up from the monolithic nucleus. Here, the system is composed from some small set of modules, isolating some parts of the implementation from other parts.

Extensible Nucleus. These operating systems are built as minimal operating systems that can be extended to meet specific requirements. The base system provides fundamental mechanisms, and the extensions are tailored to time-sharing, batch, real time, or other classes of service.

Layered Architectures. These architectures are also modular, but with a particular set of constraints on how the modules are interconnected. The layered architecture uses abstraction to manage the detail among the modules.

Message-passing Operating Systems. These operating systems are designed to support application processes that intercommunicate exclusively using messages. Ordinarily, the processes communicate with the operating systems using messages; however, the system itself may be implemented as a community of processes. These operating systems are also ordinarily characterized as network or distributed systems.

Network Operating System. A network operating system is not so much an architecture as a class of operating systems used to control a network of local memory computers. Often, such operating systems are also used for a stand-alone machine.

Distributed Operating System. These operating systems also represent a class of architectures used to implement operating systems for a multiprocessor or a network of machines. Distributed operating systems are distinguished from network operating systems by their goal of completely hiding the hardware architecture from the application software.

In the remainder of this chapter, we provide several examples to illustrate each of these organizations. Our intent is not to build a taxonomy of these operating systems; rather, it is to illustrate various operating systems types. As a result, we may use a particular example to illustrate a type characteristic when in fact the operating system could as easily be characterized in some other way, for example, we use Eden to illustrate modular designs while it is also a distributed operating system.

13.2 MONOLITHIC ORGANIZATIONS

Monolithic organizations are classic organizations for any program implementation, since they require the least amount of analysis prior to implementation and since they tend to be very efficient if well implemented.

Classic program partitioning is often based on data structures. The operating system data structures include resource queues, process descriptors, file descriptors, device descriptors, event queues (semaphores), deadlock information, virtual memory tables, and the like. That is, each concept that we have discussed requires some form of storage to track the state of the system, and the operating system must keep that state current so that it can base its policy decisions on correct assumptions.

Partitioning the program on the basis of the use of data structures can be very difficult (see Figure 13.1). For example, it is tempting to encapsulate scheduling information in a module that allocates the CPU to waiting jobs; however, the scheduler will also need to know the swapping state of a process before it can make an intelligent scheduling decision. Similarly, the swapper must know about pending input/output operations that involve memory buffers before deciding to swap out a process.

While it is clear that one can find partitions that minimize the amount of interpartition communication, the minimum may be unacceptable. That is, a partitioned operating system might be too inefficient for a machine with limited computing or information transfer bandwidth; the performance factor overwhelms the software engineering design aspects of the solution.

Example 13.1: The UNIX Kernel [1]

The UNIX kernel is a monolithic kernel, originally designed as an interactive, time-sharing operating system for small DEC minicomputers (PDP 11). The designers of UNIX were participants in the Multics project, so their design decisions were undoubtedly influenced by the limited bandwidth of the hardware platform on which the kernel needed to be implemented.

UNIX earned visibility in 1973 [43] with its simple file system, pipes, clean user interface (the shell), and extensible design. The UNIX kernel was intended to provide basic machine resource management, with the ability to easily extend the operating system to

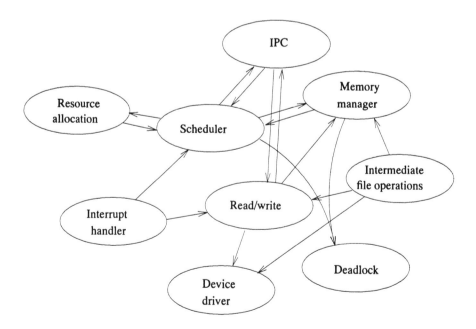

Figure 13.1 Functional Overlap

accomplish specific computation. That is, UNIX had limited goals with respect to services for application programs, reasoning that the application programmers for the system would be the developers themselves. It was also recognized that the kernel would need to be reconfigured often to accommodate new devices. Therefore, in light of limited bandwidth from the hardware platform, the best engineering trade-off would be to build the kernel as a monolithic software module that could implement process management, memory management, and a minimal file system (see Figure 13.2).

The early kernel had two important interfaces: to the application programmer and to the devices. The device/kernel interface relied on device drivers having fixed entry points whose location was placed in the /**dev** pseudo directory. The kernel used the fixed "names" to look in /**dev** and to call the I/O initiation part of the device driver. The interrupt handler provided the second part of the interface between the device and the kernel.

The kernel/application interface was originally small and clean. This fit with the philosophy that the kernel was a minimal operating system to manage critical resources, while the bulk of the file system would be implemented in user space as library routines.

The kernel implemented process and memory management and a minimal file system. Early UNIX provided a process model based on **fork, exec, wait**, and interprocess communication using pipes. The kernel implemented scheduling, pipes, interrupts, and the process-spawning mechanism. There were no other IPC mechanisms in the kernel (for example, semaphores, and shared memory).

Memory management was accomplished using the three-segment (text, data, and stack) model in conjunction with swapping. The swapping strategy was intimately intertwined with the scheduling subsystem. Later versions of UNIX incorporated virtual memory; contemporary implementations (while still monolithic) typically utilize paging.

The kernel file system provided disk block management, including free-list and i-node management. The actual read/write operations were primarily implemented in device drivers.

The original UNIX kernel was small, efficient, and monolithic. Designing the kernel as a monolith made perfect sense with the constraints and goals listed above: since the kernel was to have a minimum of functionality, it was unnecessary to employ a partitioned approach. It was feared that a modular kernel implementation would have resulted in an inefficient implementation.

Applications	Utilities	Commands
Device drivers	Monolithic kernel - Process management - Memory management - File system	

Figure 13.2 The UNIX Architecture

UNIX is still widely used today, often for relatively large systems. It has been expanded, ported, and reimplemented many times since its inception, always retaining the monolithic structure. In the 1980s, almost all UNIX implementations had moved from swapping systems to paging systems. Process management has been upgraded to address multiprocessor and distributed hardware configurations. Network and graphic devices have proven to be a difficult problem for the monolithic approach, since they tend to require considerable attention, that is, they may need to be implemented in the kernel. Today's UNIX kernel is huge and complex. Most implementations are difficult to modify due to the close coupling of various parts of the kernel. Many of the reasons for using a modular approach rather than a monolithic approach now exist in UNIX environments, and few of the reasons justifying the monolithic approach still dominate in these machines. However, the UNIX application program interface has become well entrenched, even to the point of becoming an open systems standard [18].

13.3 MODULAR NUCLEUS

A modular program is one in which the functionality is partitioned among logically independent components with well-defined interfaces among the related modules.

In contrast to monolithic designs, the operating system is implemented with program modules and/or processes. Here the engineering trade-off of function encapsulation versus performance swings toward functional encapsulation.

As with all such software architectures, the modular nucleus is considerably easier to maintain and modify than is the monolithic approach. Data abstraction allows modules to hide implementations of data structures, thus supporting local modification. The cost of modularization is potential performance degradation compared to monolithic implementations and the difficulty in constructing good partitions.

As a side benefit of modularization, the system can be implemented as abstract data types or objects. This allows the modules to be implemented as monitors, thus providing a high-level synchronization mechanism within the operating system.

The Eden distributed operating system is a modular operating system built on the object-oriented model. Eden is described in the section on distributed operating systems, below. A testimony to the modularity of the Eden design is that it was implemented on three different hardware platforms in three years. Each implementation differed radically from the others, the first being accomplished using Ada and the Intel iAPX 432 microprocessor, the second using the VAX with Pascal (and VMS features), and the third using a network of VAX machines and an extension of Concurrent Euclid (simulated on top of UNIX processes). Implementations differed in that, for example, synchronization was accomplished using the hardware in the first implementation, VMS IPC in the second implementation, and monitors in the third implementation.

Example 13.2: The MINIX Kernel [51]

Tanenbaum has designed and implemented a kernel, *MINIX*, that is compatible with the UNIX Version 7 monolithic kernel system call interface. While it can be viewed as a layered architecture (see below), it also illustrates the approach used to implement the same interfaces as a monolithic system using a modular approach.

The MINIX operating system architecture is illustrated in Figure 13.3. The kernel is implemented as a collection of system processes (called *tasks* in MINIX) that provide a user/kernel interface that is the same as the UNIX system call interface, thus, although the kernel is implemented with processes, it appears to be a collection of procedures.

The kernel is designed as three layers of modules, the lower two layers of which are a nucleus. The lowest layer is one module that implements system tasks. It must manage task descriptors, task scheduling (as opposed to UNIX process scheduling), small messages among tasks, and interrupts.

Input/output and kernel state maintenance are handled by specialized task modules (similar to device drivers) located in the second layer. Device tasks are multiplexed by the process management module and encapsulate the information for each device — one per task. The "system task" manages the kernel state (as opposed to the device states managed by the other tasks). All tasks interact using the message facility provided in the lowest layer.

The memory manager and file system modules are client processes that use the services of the system tasks. They are not critical parts of the MINIX nucleus, although they implement functions that are in the UNIX kernel. Whereas modules in the lower two layers manage resources, the memory manager and file system generally implement the specifics of system calls. For example, the memory manager implements **fork** and **exec**, and the file system implements **open**, **read**, and **mount**. (Tanenbaum notes that, since the file system is actually implemented as a server process with all communication via messages, it will also operate as a file server on a remote machine with minimal changes.)

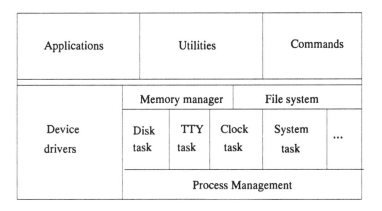

Figure 13.3 The MINIX Architecture

13.4 EXTENSIBLE NUCLEUS

There is a class of operating system architectures that can be viewed as platforms for building a tailored operating system. The platform is a general-purpose foundation for function-specific parts of the architecture, (compare with the lower two layers of the MINIX implementation of the UNIX kernel.)

The philosophy behind this approach is that the operating system can be implemented in two parts: a *policy-dependent* (hardware-independent) part and a *hardware-*

dependent (mechanism-dependent) part. The hardware-dependent part provides a low-level *virtual machine* with memory and process management, usually with only the bare essentials for device management. The policy-dependent part reflects the requirements of the operating systems, for example, time-sharing, multitasking, and real time.

This architecture is used to solve two different problems in operating systems: It allows policy-dependent variants of an operating system to be built on a single hardware platform (Figure 13.4). Secondly, it allows a specific policy-dependent part of the operating system to be portable (Figure 13.5). The RC 4000 nucleus and the IBM VM system were driven by the former area. MINIX relies more on the latter reasoning for virtual machine support.

The Hydra multiprocessor operating system is perhaps most widely known for its crisp identification of policy-mechanism separation. However, both the Intel iMAX operating system and Mach go to considerable effort to support the same kind of philosophy. The RC 4000 operating system kernel and Hydra are discussed in this Section, and Mach is described in Section 13.6.

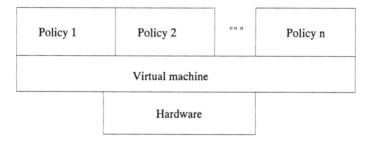

Figure 13.4 Multiple-policy Support

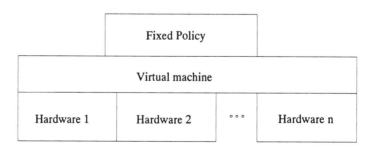

Figure 13.5 Portable Operating System Support

Example 13.3: The RC 4000 Nucleus [9]

The RC 4000 was a multiprogrammed computer manufactured in the late 1960s by A/S Reg-necentralen (Copenhagen). The goals for the RC 4000 were that it be useful for a variety of different applications ranging from time-sharing to process control (real time) support. As a means to accomplish the goal, an abstract machine called the *monitor* or the *nucleus* was built to manage resources in the machine, but not to implement any particular operating system policy. That is, the nucleus was not useful to support application programs without the remainder of the operating system being built as a higher-level abstract machine that used the nucleus.

The monitor implements preemptive scheduling, initiation and control of processes, IPC, and initiation of device input/output operations. The monitor has no inherent strategy for resource allocation nor for process management policy; those features are implemented above the nucleus (see Figure 13.6).

The nucleus mechanism assumes that process creation implies a hierarchy, that is, whenever a process initiates another process, the new process is a child of the first. An operating system built on top of the nucleus is like any other process in terms of resource management; it receives resources when it is created, and any processes that it creates are its children. The operating system is responsible for the resources held by the processes within its hierarchy.

Not only are the resource and process policies deferred to "applications," but any application process can be created or destroyed during the nucleus's normal operation, allowing operating systems to be dynamically created and destroyed.

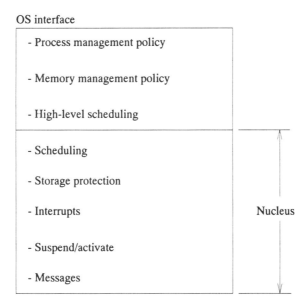

Figure 13.6 The RC 4000 Nucleus

IPC facilities include messages, queues, and four primitives to **send message**, **wait message**, **send answer**, and **wait answer**, (see Figure 13.7). Each process is allocated a fixed number of message buffers when it is created (given to the process by the parent, from the parent's own allocation of buffers). The **send message** primitive copies a message into a particular buffer and delivers it to the queue of the specified receiver. If the receiver has performed a **wait message**, then it will be blocked awaiting the incoming message; the sender proceeds after the message is delivered to the queue whether or not the receiver was waiting.

When the receiver succeeds with the **wait message** call, it is provided with the name of the sender, the contents of the message, and the address of the buffer. The buffer will be used to return an answer to the sender. The sender proceeds asynchronously until it needs the answer, at which time it calls **wait answer**. If no answer has been delivered to the sender's queue, then it blocks until one arrives. When the answer arrives, the data are copied into the sender's address space and the buffer is released to the sender's free pool.

The mechanism supports a form of IPC that is similar to remote procedure call, with the exception that the caller can proceed to some later point where it accepts the return. The number of messages that a sender can have pending depends on the number of message buffers that the process's parent allocated to it.

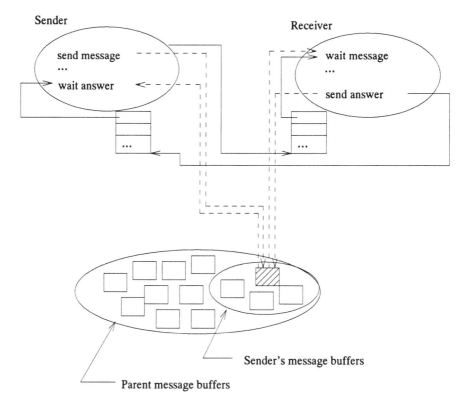

Figure 13.7 RC 4000 Message Passing

This explanation also describes the general mechanism employed by the RC 4000 nucleus for resource and process management. Any process can create children if it has sufficient resources to support them; whenever a child is created, its resources are allocated from the pool previously allocated to the parent.

The RC 4000 nucleus is an early example of a virtual machine operating system. It supports many different higher-level operating systems, by focusing on primitive resource management mechanisms and leaving the policy to the higher-level portion of the operating system. Many contemporary operating systems use the same basic idea of an extensible nucleus.

Example 13.4: The Hydra System [54]

Hydra is an experimental operating system designed at Carnegie-Mellon University, specifically for a research hardware platform called *c.mmp*. Thus, Hydra is a distributed operating system that we use as an example of a system that focuses on the separation of policy and mechanism. Hydra is built as a kernel mechanism of "universal applicability" that can be used to construct an arbitrary set of coexisting operating systems. This can be achieved by following two principles in the kernel design: The kernel must implement protection, but it must not implement policy.

A fundamental decision in the Hydra design is that the kernel should support abstract data types (essentially objects). Each resource managed by Hydra is an abstract data type, called a *virtual resource* in the Hydra literature. This abstraction allows the kernel to provide low-level virtual resource management facilities (to create classes, to create instances, to apply operators to instances, and to perform generic operations to classes), while the particular uses of the virtual resources are deferred to application processes.

The protection mechanism is built around capabilities and rights amplification (see Chapter 8). Each virtual resource (object) is defined in terms of simple data and capabilities to preexisting virtual resources. Whenever a virtual resource provides service, that is, operations are performed on the virtual resource, the encapsulated virtual resources may perform actions that the encapsulating virtual resource is incapable of performing. When a process executes inside the encapsulated virtual resource, it may be able to perform operations that it could not perform when executing outside the encapsulated virtual resource.

Completely separating mechanism from policy is quite difficult; for example, once the capability-based mechanism is chosen to implement protection among kernel objects, an authority-based file system built on top of the kernel would be influenced by the capability design and implementation. Even so, the separation of policy and mechanism is a major design goal, and it is reflected in the implementation of the kernel [26]. The results of this research have undoubtedly influenced several other contemporary operating systems.

A policy program implements a virtual resource using the kernel mechanism and physical resource (see Figure 13.8). The virtual resource is a user-level program rather than a kernel program, allowing the management of the virtual resource to be tuned to the specific needs of a set of applications.

The cost of the flexible policy approach is performance and security. The separation of policy and mechanism suggests implementations that require context switching between user space and kernel space as the virtual resource is used, and cause severe performance degradation; "slow" policy implementations also aggravate the problem. Since user-level programs can be added any time after the kernel has stabilized, bugs can be introduced at any time. This requires that the kernel provide protection barriers around policy modules. Also, virtual resources cannot be permitted too much control over their corresponding

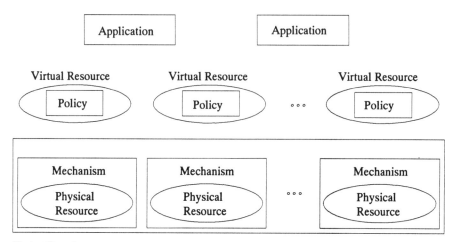

Figure 13.8 Virtual and Physical Resources

physical resources, since they may monopolize physical resources at the expense of other virtual resources.

Hydra compromises on performance and protection principles by using the principle of *policy/mechanism separation*. While policies are encoded in user-level code, the kernel mechanism uses two approaches: It may provide a protected image of hardware operation, allowing a policy module to perform protected manipulation of the physical hardware. Second, families of policies may be implemented in the kernel, with individual policies determined by parameter values set at the user level.

Reference [26] describes three examples of how the kernel is used to implement the policy/mechanism separation: scheduling, paging, and protection. The scheduling and paging implementations use parameterization, and the protection approach uses clear separation.

As an example of the parameterization approach, consider scheduling: Each process operates in conjunction with a scheduling policy module (implementation of a virtual CPU resource). It is possible for several such policy modules to exist at any given time, allowing various scheduling policies to be enforced for different subsets of processes. Each process has a mask that specifies its priority, processor mask (specifying a subset of acceptable CPUs in c.mmp), time quantum, and maximum current page set size. The kernel scheduler is a priority scheduler that uses these parameters in dispatching processes to CPUs.

The Hydra protection approach uses full separation of policy and mechanism (see Chapter 8). In the context of this discussion, we observe that each process interacts with a protection policy module (within the relevant virtual resource). The protection policy uses the parameterized policies for scheduling and paging that are implemented within the kernel; as a consequence, this aspect of protection is specified wholly within an address space of a process. The difficulty is in assuring that procedures are invoked appropriately, since this amounts to interaddress-space operation. The kernel provides an environment in which it can support negotiation between a process and its policy module, guaranteeing that the result of the negotiation is acceptable. For example, a process that is blocked on a semaphore can be restarted by a policy module before or after the process becomes unblocked. If the process is restarted with the semaphore still set, then it would presumably believe that it had successfully obtained the semaphore when it had simply been restarted by the policy module. In this case, the negotiation between the process and the policy module is degenerate; the kernel guarantees the acceptability of the outcome of the negotiation by returning a error from the P call for all abnormal restarts by the policy module.

13.5 LAYERED OPERATING SYSTEMS

Layered architectures are a fundamental technique for dividing complex systems into manageable parts. We have used the technique to describe software/hardware hierarchies in computer systems (see Chapter 1); layered architectures are the means by which network protocols are defined (see Chapter 10); and they are used in operating system architectures (even in several of those that we have used as examples of other organizations).

The intellectual challenge to layered architectures is determining the order of the layers as well as the content. That is, how can the functions shown in Figure 13.4 be partitioned into layers such that functions in layer i cannot use the facilities layer i + k. This suggests that it would be possible to redraw the figure as an acyclic graph, with no circular dependencies among the modules. It also suggests that the modules identified in the figure would need to be refined to eliminate cycles in the graph.

One variant to pure layering is illustrated by the MINIX example above: The kernel uses layers in which there are two types of processes — ordinary processes and system tasks. This provides the opportunity to use one form of task to implement general processes. While it tends to proliferate levels (complicating the interlevel logic and potentially introducing inefficiencies), it is a useful general technique.

While the principle of the layered operating system is well accepted, few contemporary operating systems are actually able to adhere to the principle (however, the general idea is pervasive). We review the classic layered operating system, THE. Interesting refinements to the THE ideas are used in Venus [27] and in Saxena and Bredt's work [45].

Pilot is a more recent operating system that employs the layered approach. It employs the idea of multilayers to implement fundamental functions. For example, the virtual memory manager is built on the file manager and parts of the swapper; the file manager is built on the swapper and parts of the filer, the swapper is built on the filer, and the filer is built on the Mesa support abstract machine.

Example 13.5: Dijkstra's THE System [14]

Dijkstra's experimental layered operating system was developed at the Technische Hogeschool Eindnoven (THE), hence the unusual English name. The goal of THE is to design and implement a provably correct operating system. The layering approach provides a model for isolating various aspects of the operating system, proving properties about that portion of the system and then using it to implement other aspects of the system.

The THE layering is summarized in Figure 13.9. Level 1 implements processes, scheduling, and the synchronization mechanism among them. This allows the memory management system to use processes in its implementation, but disallows the possibility that the scheduler could use information about memory management in making its decisions. As a result of this organization, the scheduler could potentially dispatch processes that have been swapped out of the memory.

The higher levels of THE have more relevance to machines in the 1960s than to contemporary machines. The operator console does not use the normal input/output buffering and device driver mechanisms, instead using its own. However, both can rely on virtual memory.

13.6 MESSAGE-PASSING OPERATING SYSTEMS

Message-passing operating systems incorporate at least one, and possibly several, processes. Application processes communicate with one another and usually with the operating system process(es) by exchanging messages. The MINIX operating system is an example of an operating system that provides a system call interface, yet it is implemented as a collection of communicating processes.

Message-based operating systems are useful models for network and distributed operating systems, since they establish the operating system as a distinct, autonomous computational entity with an interface that can exist across machine boundaries. Of course, it is still possible to use a system call *interface* to the operating system while the implementation uses processes, as done with network UNIX implementations, but this is a less natural approach than to propagate the message-passing interface to the application processes.

There are several experimental message-passing operating systems, some of which are described under other characterizations. The Mach kernel is an excellent example.

Example 13.6: RIG, Accent, and Mach

Mach [3] is descended from the Accent operating system [40], which is descended from the RIG system [24]. Each of these systems focuses on an efficient IPC facility to support communities of processes. RIG was less concerned with the distribution of the processes across a multiprocessor or network of hardware machines than were the two successors.

Level 5	User programs
Level 4	Input/output management
Level 3	Operator console
Level 2	Memory management
Level 1	CPU scheduling and semaphores
Level 0	Hardware

Figure 13.9 Dijkstra's THE Layered Architecture

RIG used the ideas of messages and ports to support IPC, originally within a multiprogramming environment and then on a network of machines. A message is a header and data, while a port is a queue for messages, associated with a process.

The RIG IPC mechanisms were found to be insufficient in terms of the protection on ports (there were no restrictions on which processes could write to a port), failure notification (port numbers allowed dangling references to failed ports), transparency of service (ports were bound to the machine and to the process, making it difficult to move a process), and message size limitations [39].

Accent was developed for a network of Spice workstations, again using messages and ports. Recognizing the shortfalls of RIG, ports were redesigned as capabilities — protected kernel objects — rather than as integer pointers. This solution makes it possible to address the protection, failure notification, and transparency limitation of RIG ports since the operating system must actively manage capabilities.

Message size limitations are addressed through the use of the a new virtual memory design explicitly intended to handle paging and IPC [15]. An Accent message is a header followed by a collection of typed data objects. The length of the message is essentially unrestricted; that is, it must be less than or equal to 2^{32} bytes (the size of a paged address space).

Each process, including the kernel, has its own paged address space managed by the kernel. "Large" messages that are sent to a port on the local machine are transmitted by copying the page table entry rather than the page (see Figure 13.10).

Of course, information in a message may exist in both processes' address space, so a *copy-on-write* technique is used so that the two page tables reference a common message body until one or the other of the two processes writes into its own logical copy; this causes an actual copy of the message data to be created so that each process has its own version.

While the message and port abstraction define IPC behavior independently of process location, the implementation distinguishes between the cases of message sending within a machine and across machines. When a message is sent from a process on one machine to a process on another machine, the message must be copied and transmitted across the interconnecting network on a page by page basis.

Accent was designed specifically for the Spice workstation environment, including the Pascal application programming environment with its own software support libraries. Accent was not designed to be adapted to UNIX applications or to operate efficiently in a shared memory multiprocessor environment. Mach is intended to address these concerns, as well as to refine the message-based IPC mechanism.

Shared memory multiprocessors provide a raw IPC mechanism that supports finer-grained computation than exists on networks of local memory machines. However, process-oriented computational models typically rely on "heavyweight" processes with relatively high context-switching times. Mach refines the idea of a schedulable unit of computation over that used in Accent. It also refines the virtual memory mechanism to better support IPC and to allow the paging policy to be defined as user-state procedures [41].

Mach schedulable units of computations are characterized as *tasks* and *threads*. A task is an execution environment for one or more threads, and a thread (also known as a *lightweight process*) is a sequence of instruction executions within a task. Thus tasks are allocated resources, including paged address spaces, memory, port capabilities, and devices, while the threads that run in a task share these allocated resources. Specifically, threads are able to run in parallel in a multiprocessor environment, using interthread synchronization to coordinate access to resources within the task. This model also supports conventional

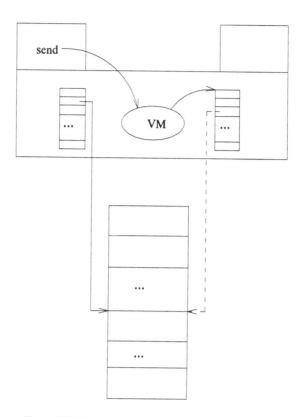

Figure 13.10 Transferring Large Messages in Accent

processes and concurrency appropriate for network-wide concurrency, since a traditional process is a single thread operating in a task. Finally, threads offer the possibility of the application programmer having more control over the scheduling policy, hence making it possible for the parallel programmer to write efficient algorithms [8].

Messages and ports are used to support communication among various units, with the proviso that ports are to be thought of as object references, as in objected-oriented systems, rather than as messages to processes. That is, a port is a reference object for some service and a message is a collection of data objects. Ports are used for thread-to-thread communication (for example, within a task) and for task-to-task communication (for example, across a network).

Tasks can create other tasks, similar to UNIX process spawning; spawned tasks and their parents can share address spaces through inheritance, allowing intertask communication via shared virtual memory. The address space inheritance is controlled on a page level, providing for various sharing policies to enforce protection between the parent and its child.

Mach's virtual memory extends the basic ideas used in the Accent virtual memory, in particular supporting efficient address space transfers within a single machine. In addition, *pagein* and *pageout* functions may be executed in user space rather than in kernel space.

13.7 NETWORK OPERATING SYSTEMS

A network operating system is generally a single-machine operating system that has been adapted for use in a network environment (the Pilot operating system is an exception in that it was developed especially as a network operating system). The modifications can be modest, providing high-speed communications facilities such as file transfer and terminal interconnection ("remote log in"). Or they can be more ambitious, providing IPC, remote file systems, and remote procedure call; many of the more ambitious efforts could be argued to be distributed operating systems rather than network operating systems since they make several aspects of the physical distribution transparent to the application programmer.

The limitations of network operating systems are generally architectural limitations in which the original operating system was designed specifically for a uniprocessor environment, yet it is being used to manage the resources in a multiprocessor or network environment.

The National Software Works was an early attempt at a network operating system (in the ARPAnet context), see Chapter 18 of [13]. Because of the wide use of UNIX on individual time-sharing machines and its evolution as a workstation operating system, it is usually the base operating system for a network extension, for example, SunOS [49] and AT&T System V.3 [2].

Network operating systems do not necessarily attempt to make the location of a file transparent at the operating systems interface. The lack of transparency may require that a user copy a file from a remote machine to the local machine before accessing it, or it may provide remote file facilities in which the separation of the process and the file is obvious. For example, the remote file open command might specify the name of the machine that contains the file; for example,

$$\text{open("pawnee:/usr/gjn/book/chap13", ...)}$$

might be used to reference a file named "/usr/gjn/book/chap13" stored on a machine named "pawnee."

Executing a program at a remote location will require overt action, for example, logging into the remote site and executing the program, or extending the parameters and names for system calls.

Example 13.7: Version 4 BSD UNIX [25, 38]

Previously, generic UNIX systems have been described as an example of monolithic kernels. Version 4 BSD UNIX is also implemented as a monolithic kernel, even though it is also a good example of an uniprocessor operating system that has been extended to a network operating system.

The system incorporates a number of commands that cause execution to take place at remote sites. The **finger** command is used to list information about each person logged into a machine; "**finger** @pawnee" causes the **finger** command to be executed at the remote machine named "pawnee."

Version 4 BSD also includes other useful commands of this type, including **rlogin** to log into a remote machine from the local machine and **rcp** to copy files from a remote machine to the local machine; for example,

rcp "pawnee:/usr/gjn/book/chap13"

will cause the file name "/usr/gjn/book/chap13" located on the machine named "pawnee" to be copied to the current directory on the local machine. The operating system contains a number of other useful remote commands.

Version 4 BSD differs from the pure time-sharing UNIX systems in that it provides specific extensions to support sockets for network-wide IPC, explicit file transfer, and remote log in. Sun Microsystems has extended 4.2 BSD as a commercial version that incorporates a remote file server and a remote procedure call facility.

The fundamental addition to the kernel is the socket facility (discussed in Chapter 10). Sockets are the means by which a process can reference network addresses outside its own address space. Without sockets, there is no adequate naming facility to enable a process to reference other unrelated processes, nor is there a mechanism for sending and receiving messages across the network.

The socket mechanism is also the platform on which Sun builds its Remote Procedure Call (RPC) mechanism. RPC employs sockets with a datagram protocol (optionally, a virtual circuit protocol). The RPC mechanism, in turn, is used to support the Sun Network File System (NFS) and the network-based NeWS window system.

Example 13.8: The Pilot Operating System [42]

Pilot is a single-user, single-language commercial operating system built for Xerox workstations operating in a LAN environment. The assumptions in the design rely on the workstations using various resources on the network during normal operation, including remote files and printers; Pilot also incorporates an extensive network IPC mechanism. The operating system is blended with a robust programming environment, Mesa, allowing conventional operating system functions to be implemented in the run-time environment and the operating system.

The single-user, single-language assumption allows the designers to take a less stringent position with respect to protection than exists in more general-purpose shared machines. The protection mechanisms are *defensive* rather than *absolute*, attempting to address errors rather than malicious attacks. As a result, much of the protection is implemented by the compiler and language rather than by the operating system.

Pilot files do not have hierarchy, that is, there is no tree-structured directory among files. Pilot users can create the illusion of hierarchy through naming conventions. A hierarchical file system could also be built as a user-level program. Each file is accessed using a capability; data are the file is stored in pages that are mapped directly into the virtual memory. Thus, a file can be created and saved on the mass storage system (resulting in the creation and return of a capability for the file) by marking it as a permanent file rather than a temporary one and then by storing the contents into the virtual memory.

The address space for a workstation is shared among all processes on the workstation. It is partitioned into *spaces* so that memory can be allocated and deallocated, to associate a portion of the virtual memory with a file and to provide units of transfer between the secondary and primary store for swapping. This mechanism gives considerable flexibility to the application programmer in controlling the virtual memory policy.

The *stream* facility is used to reference input/output devices as a byte stream (similar to a UNIX file). The stream interface is also superimposed on the network using a Xerox virtual circuit protocol. Thus, IPC can be accomplished by opening a stream between two processes and reading and writing the stream (compare with BSD sockets with virtual circuits).

The Pilot operating system is a revolutionary network operating system, built in a proprietary commercial environment. Many of the ideas from the system have appeared in other systems, particularly those related to the network IPC. However, UNIX is now much more widely used as a network operating system, with many of the Pilot functions being implemented in network UNIX.

13.8 DISTRIBUTED OPERATING SYSTEMS

The state of the art in operating systems is in the design and development of distributed operating systems. Contemporary operating research papers nearly all focus on various aspects of distributed operating systems. While several significant systems have been built, none enjoy wide commercial success.

Tanenbaum and van Renesse identify five issues that distinguish distributed operating systems from network operating systems [52]:
(1)   **Communication primitives**. The issue here is to find alternatives to shared memory synchronization primitives (semaphores and monitors). These issues were addressed in Chapter 12.
(2)   **Naming and protection**. These issues are related to the problem of a process on one machine identifying and communicating with processes on a remote machine. These issues were addressed in Chapter 8.
(3)   **Resource management**. Network-wide resource management is concerned with issues such as scheduling, load balancing, and distributed deadlock detection. Some of these issues were covered in Chapter 12.
(4)   **Fault tolerance**. This area is related to the robustness of a system under isolated failure. This topic is not addressed in this book.
(5)   **Services to provide**. These issues are related to the design and use of file servers, print servers, remote execution facilities, and miscellaneous other facilities.

Notable distributed operating system studies that address at least a subset of this list of issues include Accent [40], Amoeba [30, 50, 52] Argus [28], Cambridge Distributed Computing System [31], Charlotte (also known as ROSCOE) [48], Choices [10], Chorus [44], DEMOS, [6, 37], Distributed UNIX [29], Eden [4], Emerald [21], Firefly [46], Hydra [19, 54], iMAX-432 [22], LOCUS [36, 53], Mach [3], Medusa [33], Psyche [47], Sprite [34], StarOS [19, 20], Tandem NonStop [5], Thoth [12], V kernel [11], and X kernel [17, 35]. Amoeba, the Cambridge Distributed Computing System, the V kernel, and Eden are reviewed in [52]. In the remainder of this section, we review some characteristics of LOCUS, Eden, and the V kernel.

Example 13.9: LOCUS [36, 53]

LOCUS is intended to operate on a network of local memory machines, providing a UNIX-compatible system call interface (it is a procedure-based operating system) that allows a process to reference files at any location on the network without knowing any of their locations, that is, with network transparency to file access. LOCUS is also intended to provide high reliability and availability and good performance. The primary contribution of LOCUS to distributed operating systems technology is in its transparent file mechanism, including the extension to transaction support.

Each machine contains a copy of the LOCUS operating system that can operate as a standalone system or as a component in the distributed system. The system will automatically replicate files at various locations to support reliability, availability, and performance. That is, replicated files that have been moved to a local machine can be accessed more rapidly than remote files; they are also less susceptible to network partitioning errors. LOCUS also supports relocation of processes across the network as a mechanism to support load balancing or to otherwise distribute computation.

The file system is at the foundation of LOCUS. The UNIX file system model is extended by providing a remote mount facility similar to that described in Chapter 11, allowing subtrees to be composed with a local directory as required. The actual location of the remote-mounted subtree is managed by the operating system and is transparent to all applications and users.

Subtrees can be replicated across the network. That is, a subtree may be remote mounted at various host machines and be replicated at any of these machines, as determined by LOCUS. The operating system may choose to replicate a file based on the type of access (for example, files opened for reading can be copied with little penalty) or to increase availability in the event that the network is partitioned by failures. The operating system also inspects the file path in making its decisions about replication, recognizing that all nodes in the path must be within a partition if the network fails. Since directories are generally accessed in read mode, it is natural to replicate directories throughout the network, particularly directories that are located close to the root (since they tend to be updated less than ones that are located close to leaf nodes).

LOCUS incorporates a facility for concurrency control across replicated copies of a file. This is accomplished by separating the file system into a *using site*, a *storage site*, and a *current synchronization site* (see Figure 13.11). A process at the using site performs the **open** operation on a file copy at a storage site by having the operation pass through a single current synchronization site for the particular file. Subsequent **read** and **write** operations result in interoperation directly between the using and storage sites.

The application process references the file using UNIX-like file operations supplemented with **commit** and **abort** system calls. Each system call (performed at a using site) will either be executed locally (if the storage site and current synchronization site are local) or will result in a remote procedure call to the current synchronization site and to the chosen storage site. From the application process's point of view, the operation has the same behavior as a local file operation.

The **commit** and **abort** calls implement transactions on open files. That is, a file may be opened for writing, have records written to it, and then either have the changes committed or aborted through these commands. (The **close** call performs an implied **commit**.)

Remote process creation is accomplished through extensions of the UNIX **fork** and **exec** commands and by adding another call, **run**, to the repertoire. The parent process specifies the location at which a **fork**ed process should run through site information in the process's environment. The **fork** command can be executed at either the local or remote site, with remote execution resulting in the establishment of an environment that is the same as the parent's environment. The process may also be moved when an **exec** is called,

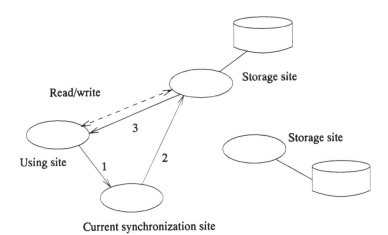

Read/write

Storage site

Using site

3

2

Storage site

1

Current synchronization site

Figure 13.11 LOCUS File Operations

allowing the parent process to cause compatible binary code to be executed at the remote site. For convenience, the remote **fork** and **exec** calls can be invoked using a **run** system call.

The availability and reliability requirements for LOCUS are designed to sustain network failures that may result in the network being partitioned into two or more parts. The system is designed to recover from network partitions, causing new current synchronization sites to be created in each partition that contains shared files and then merging them when the network failure is repaired.

Example 13.10: The Eden System [4]

The Eden operating system is designed to address effective distribution of computation, while also supporting integration among the parts. Eden is based on the idea that application programs will be written in an object-oriented programming language; the underlying system supports object management in a distributed computing environment. As a result, Eden research addresses the programming languages and user-level (library) functions that complement the Eden kernel. This object-oriented position naturally leads Eden to be characterized as a modular operating system as well as a distributed operating system.

Eden research lead to evolutionary research on several subsequent systems, including the Heterogeneous Computer System [32], Emerald [21], and other distributed object-oriented operating systems. The primary contributions to distributed operating systems by this set of research projects are in object mobility in a network environment, remote procedure call (particularly in heterogeneous systems), naming (in the HCS project), and the blend of programming languages and operating systems. In particular, Eden's contribution is primarily in support for distributed objects.

Each distributed application is built as a collection of *Eden objects* (compare with Hydra assumptions). An Eden object differs from an ordinary object first in its size: Eden objects are very large. An Eden object is referenced using capabilities (a unique identifier and access rights), its location is unknown to other objects (location transparency), and it can be dynamically moved across the network (mobility). Objects communicate using message request/reply pairs through a published method interface that specifies the *invocation procedures* for the object; that is, messages are similar to remote procedure calls. An Eden object is implemented as a number of processes, synchronizing among themselves using monitors. A process within an object blocks on invocation of another object, while companion processes may continue to execute. An Eden object can checkpoint itself, creating a persistent, passive representation of the active object. The checkpoint can be used for crash recovery; it is also the mechanism for reading and writing permanent storage. A passive object can be made active by receiving an invocation. Objects are defined in the Eden Programming Language (EPL), which is based on Concurrent Euclid.

Eden objects provide a sound application expression language for distributed environments. The developers describe several types of applications including a mail system, a "transput" facility for moving bulk information among objects (including devices), a file system (since files are not part of the kernel), and an appointment calendar system.

The problems addressed by the kernel are to support large, mobile, secure objects. Large objects may contain many processes; thus the kernel must provide facilities to manage processes within an Eden object, to synchronize processes within an object, and to provide the checkpointing ability. Mobility is made possible through the use of capabilities to reference objects. That is, one object cannot directly reference another, but must use a capability to ask the kernel to reference the object (which also provides a security mechanism). The kernel uses capabilities to provide protection among the objects and to control remote object invocation.

An object invocation contains a capability for the receiving object, along with various parameters. The invocation can be processed at compile time by generating code to pack parameters and by generating stubs for the invoking and invoked objects (see Figure 13.12). The outgoing stub includes a **SynchInvoke** call to the kernel. This call uses the capability to validate the access and to locate the remote object. It then performs a remote call, blocking only the calling process, not other processes in the invoking object. At the invoked object location, a reader process must have been defined to field remote calls and map them into local invocations. The reader performs a kernel **ReceiveOperation** to accept the **SynchInvoke** call provided by the invoking object. It then calls the invoked object stub, passing it return information so that it can return a message directly to the invoking stub process. Prior to returning, the invoked stub invokes the local object using procedure call; upon return, it packs results and returns them to the calling stub.

The Eden kernel is responsible for managing the processes that implement Eden objects (including synchronization), for mapping objects to locations, and for validating capabilities and mapping the references to the correct location.

Library routines are used to provide a procedural interface to the kernel, for example, in managing synchronous invocations, and to perform several standard operating system functions in user space.

The programming language enables the generation of stubs for invocation and for providing synchronization constructs within an object.

Eden was never implemented directly on bare hardware, thus device and resource management was never really implemented in the system. The file system was implemented entirely outside the kernel as a set of objects. Eden illustrates the viability of object-oriented approaches for distributed systems and caused the researchers to focus on efficient object mobility mechanism [21] and more extensive use of remote procedure call, particularly in heterogeneous systems [7].

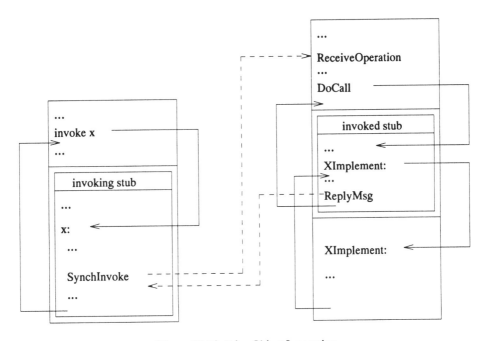

Figure 13.12 Eden Object Invocation

Example 13.11: The V Kernel [11]

Just as Mach has evolved from RIG and Accent, V was influenced by earlier work related to Thoth [12] and to a lesser extent with DEMOS [6, 37]. The V system focuses on the communication aspects of distributed operating systems. V is based on three design tenets:

(1)   Fast communication mechanisms for large amounts of data are the most critical facility for distributed systems.

(2)   Communication protocols, rather than software within operating systems and applications, define the system's abilities.

(3)   The system should be built with a small kernel (replicated at each node) that implements the protocols and services, which will implement a simple network-transparent process, address space, and communication model.

These tenets are used to build a *software backplane* that specifies an operating environment for applications. One should be able to add software to the V system under a similar set of constraints (and with a similar set of services) that a hardware designer works with when designing a board to add to a computer.

The software backplane idea encourages the need for providing shared state throughout the network, for example, shared memory as a mechanism for providing shared state to distributed components. While it is tempting to simply cache pages across the network, using a coherence approach to ensure consistency, this often results in severe contention at the location of the true page image. V looks for alternative means for dealing with consistency, resulting in a *problem-oriented shared memory* (see Chapter 11).

The V designers have also observed that distributed systems are often used similarly by groups of workers, and that there is a higher bandwidth of communication among the group than is needed throughout the network, that is, there is "locality" on the set of processes in a distributed system. This has led to the development of specialized group communication protocols that rely on multicasting.

The V Message Transport Protocol (VMTP) illustrates the philosophy of the V design. A remote **send** operation results in a single client system call (reducing the number of context switches over some implementations); with the single call, the kernel uses the client's buffer space for parameters and results rather than producing its own copies. VMTP recognizes short and long messages; since more than half of the message traffic in a V system fits into 32-byte data blocks, VMTP is optimized to handle small messages differently than long ones (up to 16 KB in length). The resulting mechanism is far more efficient for small messages than would be a generic approach. VMTP is also optimized for request-response (remote procedure call) use. It does not use a virtual circuit; reliability is built into a response packet, eliminating the need for ACKs for this particular class of uses.

VMTP is widely used within V. As a performance optimization, each process descriptor contains a VMTP template with several fields filled in. The overhead in making a remote procedure call is reduced over conventional methods, since there is no need to request buffers space for the message, and the time to fill in the header is smaller.

Groups of processes are identified using the same name space as individual processes; that is, there is no distinction (in the name) between a group and a process. Of course, this implies that names must be mapped to processes so that group members can be identified.

Kernel services include time, process, memory, and device management in addition to the communication services. A kernel service is implemented in a module configured into each V host. Modules are registered with the IPC facility and referenced in the same manner as user-level modules. This allows local requests for service to be handled efficiently within the kernel and without other mechanisms if the request is remote.

13.9 FURTHER READING

Several specific references have been cited throughout this chapter. In addition there are many good textbooks that compare and contrast commercial operating systems, for example, Horner reviews MS-DOS, Macintosh, UNIX, VAX VMS, and IBM operating systems [16], and Keller discusses CP/M, MS-DOS (PC-DOS), UNIX, and IBM VM and MVS (among others) [23].

REFERENCES

1. *AT&T Bell Laboratories Technical Journal*, AT&T, October 1984.
2. *AT&T UNIX System V Technical Seminar*, AT&T, Greensboro, NC, May 1986.
3. M. Acetta, R. Baron, W. Bolosky, D. Golub, R. Rashid, A. Tevanian, and M. Young, "Mach: A New Kernel Foundation for UNIX Development," *Proceedings of the 1986 USENIX*, Atlanta, GA, 1986, 93-112.
4. G. T. Almes, A. P. Black, E. D. Lazowska, and J. D. Noe, "The Eden System: A Technical Review," *IEEE Transactions on Software Engineering SE-11*, 1 (January 1985), 43-59.
5. J. F. Bartlett, "A NonStop (tm) Kernel," *Proceedings of the Eighth ACM Symposium on Operating Systems Principles*, December 1981, 22-29.
6. F. Baskett, J. H. Howard, and J. T. Montague, Task Communication in DEMOS, November 1977.

7. B. N. Bershad, D. T. Ching, E. D. Lazowska, J. Sanislo, and M. Schwartz, "A Remote Procedure Call Facility for Heterogeneous Computer Systems," *IEEE Transactions on Software Engineering SE-13*, 8 (August 1987), 880-894.

8. D. L. Black, "Scheduling Support for Concurrency and Parallelism in the Mach Operating System," *IEEE Computer 23*, 5 (May 1990), 35-43.

9. P. Brinch Hansen, "The Nucleus of a Multiprogramming System," *Communications of the ACM 13*, 4 (April 1970), 238-250.

10. R. Campbell, G. Johnston, and V. Russo, "Choices (Class Hierarchical Open Interface for Custom Embedded Systems)," *ACM SIGOPS Operating Systems Review 21*, 3 (July 1987), 9-17.

11. D. R. Cheriton, "The V Distributed System," *Communications of the ACM 31*, 3 (March 1988), 314-333.

12. D. R. Cheriton, M. A. Malcolm, L. S. Melen, and G. R. Sager, "Thoth: A Portable Real-Time Operating System," *Communications of the ACM 22*, 1 (February 1979), 105-115.

13. D. W. Davies, E. Holler, E. D. Jensen, S. R. Kimbleton, B. W. Lampson, G. LeLann, K. J. Thurber, and R. W. Watson, *Distributed Systems -- Architecture and Implementation*, Springer-Verlag, New York, NY, 1981.

14. E. W. Dijkstra, "The Structure of the THE Multiprogramming System," *Communications of the ACM 11*, 5 (May 1968), 341-346.

15. R. Fitzgerald and R. F. Rashid, "The Integration of Virtual Memory and Interprocess Communication in Accent," *ACM Transactions on Computer Systems 4*, 2 (May 1986), 147-177.

16. D. R. Horner, *Operating Systems Concepts and Applications*, Scott, Foresman and Company, Glenview, IL, 1989.

17. N. C. Hutchinson, L. L. Peterson, M. B. Abbot, and S. O'Malley, "RPC in the x-Kernel: Evaluating New Design Techniques," *Proceedings of the Twelfth ACM Symposium on Operating Systems Principles*, November 1989, 91-101.

18. *IEEE P1003.1 Trial Use Standard*, IEEE P1003 Standards Committee, 1986.

19. A. K. Jones and P. Schwarz, "Experience Using Multiprocessor Systems -- A Status Report," *ACM Computing Surveys 12*, 2 (June 1980), 121-165.

20. A. K. Jones, R. J. Chansler, I. Durham, K. Schwans, and S. R. Vegdahl, "StarOS, a Multiprocessor Operating System for the Support of Task Forces," *Proceedings of the Eighth ACM Symposium on Operating Systems Principles*, December 1979, 77-93.

21. E. Jul, H. Levy, N. Hutchinson, and A. Black, "Fine-Grained Mobility in the Emerald System," *ACM Transactions on Computer Systems 6*, 1 (February 1988), 109-133.

22. K. C. Kahn, W. M. Corwin, T. D. Dennis, H. D'Hooge, D. E. Hubka, L. A. Hutchins, J. T. Montague, F. J. Pollack, and M. R. Gifkins, "iMAX: A Multiprocessor Operating System for an Object-Based Computer," *Proceedings of the Eighth ACM Symposium on Operating Systems Principles*, December 1981, 127-136.

23. L. S. Keller, *Operating Systems Communicating with and Controlling the Computer*, Prentice Hall, Inc., Englewood Cliffs, NJ, 1988.

24. K. A. Lantz, K. D. Gradischnig, J. A. Feldman, and R. F. Rashid, "Rochester's Intelligent Gateway," *IEEE Computer 15*, 10 (October 1982), 54-68.

25. S. J. Leffler, M. K. McKusick, M. J. Karels, and J. S. Quarterman, *The Design and Implementation of the 4.3 BSD UNIX Operating System*, Addison-Wesley Publishing Co., Reading, MA, 1989.

26. R. Levin, E. Cohen, W. Corwin, F. Pollack, and W. Wulf, "Policy/Mechanism Separation in Hydra," *Proceedings of the Fifth ACM Symposium on Operating Systems Principles*, November 1975, 131-140.

27. B. H. Liskov, "The Design of the Venus Operating System," *Communications of the ACM 15*, 3 (March 1972), 144-149.

28. B. Liskov, D. Curtis, P. Johnson, and R. Scheifler, "Implementation of Argus," *Proceedings of the Eleventh ACM Symposium on Operating Systems Principles*, Austin, TX, December 1987, 111-122.

29. G. W. R. Luderer, H. Che, J. P. Haggerty, P. A. Kirslis, and W. T. Marshall, "A Distributed UNIX System Based on a Virtual Circuit Switch," *Proceedings of the Eighth ACM Symposium on Operating Systems Principles*, December 1981, 160-168.

30. S. J. Mullender, G. van Rossum, A. S. Tanenbaum, R. van Renesse, and H. van Staveren, "Amoeba: A Distributed Operating System for the 1990s," *IEEE Computer 23*, 5 (May 1990), 44-53.

31. R. M. Needham and A. J. Herbert, *The Cambridge Distributed Computing System*, Addison-Wesley Publishing Co., Reading, MA, 1982.

32. D. Notkin, A. P. Black, E. D. Lazowska, H. M. Levy, J. Sanislo, and J. Zahorjan, "Interconnecting Heterogeneous Computer Systems," *Communications of the ACM 31*, 3 (March 1988), 258-273.

33. J. K. Ousterhout, D. A. Scelza, and P. S. Sindhu, "Medusa: An Experiment in Distributed Operating System Structure," *Communications of the ACM 23*, 2 (February 1980), 92-105.

34. J. K. Ousterhout, A. R. Cherenson, F. Douglis, M. N. Nelson, and B. B. Welch, "The Sprite Network Operating System," *IEEE Computer 21*, 2 (February 1988), 23-36.

35. L. Peterson, N. Hutchinson, S. O'Malley, and H. Rao, "The x-kernel: A Platform for Accessing Internet Resources," *IEEE Computer 23*, 5 (May 1990), 23-33.

36. G. Popek, B. Walker, J. Chow, D. Edwards, C. Kline, G. Rudison, and G. Thiel, "LOCUS: A Network Transparent, High Reliability Distributed System," *Proceedings of the Eighth ACM Symposium on Operating Systems Principles*, December 1981, 169-177.

37. M. L. Powell and B. P. Miller, "Process Migration in DEMOS/MP," *Proceedings of the Ninth ACM Symposium on Operating Systems Principles*, Bretton Woods, NH, July 1983, 110-119. Published as Operating Systems Review 17(5).

38. J. S. Quarterman, A. Silberschatz, and J. L. Peterson, "4.2BSD and 4.3BSD as Examples of the UNIX System," *ACM Computing Surveys 17*, 4 (December 1985), 379-418.

39. R. F. Rashid, *From RIG to Accent to Mach: The Evolution of a Network Operating System*, Computer Science Department, Carnegie-Mellon University, Pittsburgh, PA, May 1986.

40. R. F. Rashid and G. Robertson, "Accent: A Communication Oriented Network Operating System Kernel," *Proceedings of the 8th Symposium on Operating Systems Principles*, December 1981, 64-75.

41. R. Rashid, A. Tevanian, M. Young, D. Golub, R. Baron, D. Black, W. Bolosky, and J. Chew, "Machine-Independent Virtual Memory Management for Paged Uniprocessor and Multiprocessor Architectures," *IEEE Transactions on Computer Systems 37*, 8 (August 1988), 896-907.

42. D. D. Redell, Y. K. Dalal, T. R. Horsley, H. C. Lauer, W. C. Lynch, P. R. McJones, H. G. Murray, and S. C. Purcell, "Pilot: An Operating System for a Personal Computer," *Communications of the ACM 23*, 2 (February 1980), 81-92.

43. D. M. Ritchie and K. Thompson, "The UNIX Time-Sharing System," *Communications of the ACM 17*, 7 (July 1974), 365-375.

44. M. Rozier, V. Abrossimov, F. Armand, I. Boule, M. Gien, M. Guillemont, F. Herrmann, C. Kaiser, S. Langlois, P. Leonard, and W. Neuhauser, "Chorus Distributed Operating Systems," *Computer Systems 4*, 4 (Fall 1988), 305-370.

45. A. R. Saxena and T. H. Bredt, "A Structured Specification of a Hierarchical Operating System," *Proceedings of the International Conference on Reliable Software*, April 1975, 310-318.

46. M. D. Schroeder and M. Burrows, "Performance of Firefly RPC," *ACM Transactions on Computer Systems 8*, 1 (February 1990), 1-17.

47. M. L. Scott, T. J. LeBlanc, and B. D. Marsh, "Design Rationale for Psyche, a General-Purpose Multiprocessor Operating System," *Proceedings of the ICPP*, August 1988, 255-

262.

48. M. H. Solomon and R. A. Finkel, "The Roscoe Distributed Operating System," *Proceedings of the Seventh ACM Symposium on Operating Systems Principles*, December 1981, 108-114.

49. *Release 3.2 Manual for the Sun Workstation*, Sun Microsystems, Inc., Document Number 800-1364-10, September 1986.

50. A. S. Tanenbaum, R. van Renesse, H. van Staveren, G. J. Sharp, S. J. Mullender, J. Jansen, and G. van Rossum, "Experience with the Amoeba Distributed Operating System," *Communications of the ACM 33*, 12 (December 1990), 46-63.

51. A. S. Tanenbaum, *Operating Systems: Design and Implementation*, Prentice Hall, Inc., Englewood Cliffs, NJ, 1987.

52. A. S. Tanenbaum and R. van Renesse, "Distributed Operating Systems," *ACM Computing Surveys 17*, 4 (December 1985), 418-470.

53. B. Walker, G. Popek, R. English, C. Kline, and G. Thiel, "The LOCUS Distributed Operating System," *Proceedings of the Ninth ACM Symposium on Operating Systems Principles*, July 1983, 49-70.

54. W. A. Wulf, E. Cohen, W. Corwin, A. Jones, R. Levin, C. Pierson, and F. Pollack, "Hydra: The Kernel of a Multiprocessing Operating System," *Communications of the ACM 17*, 6 (June 1974), 337-345.

EXERCISES

(1) Consider the functional blocks and their interconnections that are illustrate in Figure 13.1. Choose a partition of these blocks and then justify your choice with a cogent argument.

(2) Write a program schema for the bounded buffer problem using the RC 4000 IPC primitives.

(3) The Pilot operating system is intertwined with the Mesa programming language. One aspect of this melding of the language and the system is that Mesa supports monitors with Pilot's support. In the semantics of Mesa monitors, a *notify* is viewed as a hint that a condition has been set, rather than as a guarantee that a waiting process will detect the condition change as is the case for the *signal* primitive in the Hoare monitor semantics. What are some advantages of the Mesa semantics compared to Hoare's semantics? What are some disadvantages of the Mesa semantics?

(4) As Mach has become more popular as an operating system kernel, there have been many complaints about the performance of the early multiprocessor versions. Provide some conjectures for why Mach might be slower at the systems call level compared to UNIX.

(5) Many of the designers of UNIX also participated in the Multics project. It is often stated that UNIX was designed to be a simple operating system that used many concepts and ideas from Multics. Draw some comparisons between UNIX and Multics.

(6) The Eden operating system was designed after Hydra had appeared in the literature (and some of the Eden designers had also participated in the Hydra project). Compare and contrast the two operating systems.

(7) Choose a contemporary operating system other than one discussed in this chapter and write a paper summarizing how the system addresses device management, file management, process management, and memory management. It is not necessary for you to provide a critical analysis of the papers that describe the operating system, nor of the operating system itself. Part of the purpose of this exercise is to provide you with an opportunity to explore the technical literature. Do not use another textbook as the primary source of your information. Consult the open technical literature, using liberal citations of that literature in your paper.

14

PERFORMANCE ANALYSIS

Performance evaluation is a large discipline in computer science, with a number of books devoted to subareas: performance measurement, analytic modeling, and simulation modeling. In this chapter we provide a brief introduction to analytic and simulation modeling.

The fundamental external measures of system performance were defined in Section 2.3

Throughput is a measure of the amount of work that the system is able to accomplish per unit time, for example, the throughput might be measured in jobs/hour or interactive requests/minute.

Turnaround time is a measure of the time required for some requested service to be obtained, for example, the response time in a time-sharing system.

Resource utilization is generally of concern to the designer or manager of a system, since it reflects the fraction of the time that the resource is actually being used by the system customers. For example, in a virtual memory system, the primary memory and bus utilization would be important factors in measuring the performance of the system.

Availability is a major concern in some systems, since it is a reflection of how quickly a job can obtain service from the system. Availability is particularly important in real-time applications such as process control systems. High availability generally implies low resource utilization in the system.

Depending on the requirements on the system, different measures may be critical. In real-time systems where performance failure may be catastrophic, utilization and throughput are of relatively low concern, whereas availability and turnaround time are very important. In a general-purpose shared system, it may be an organization goal to keep the capital investment low while providing the best possible service; throughput and utilization are then important factors.

14.1 QUEUEING MODELS

Queueing models are the fundamental analytic models for computer systems. The most simple models address only the basic characteristics of system behavior and then predict potential performance of the system as a function of those characteristics. A queueing model is a performance analyst's first tool for determining the feasibility of a system architecture.

14.1.1 Background

A basic queueing model is shown in Figure 14.1; the most simple model represents nonpreemptive systems in which a *job* arrives at the system, enters a queue to compete for the single server, gains exclusive use of the server for some amount of time and then departs from the system. The preemptive model allows one job to interrupt the service of another, causing the interrupted job to be returned to the queue to await service at a later time.

The queueing model can be analyzed if a few properties are added to the model to specify basic behavior. First, the *arrival pattern* characterizes the pattern in which jobs arrive at the queue. This will describe loading conditions on the system. Whenever one

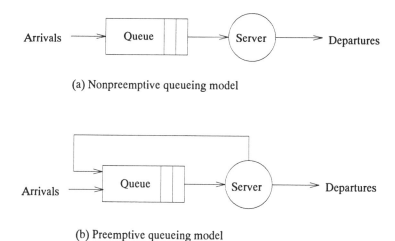

(a) Nonpreemptive queueing model

(b) Preemptive queueing model

Figure 14.1 A Basic Queueing Model

job yields the server, either through preemption or by departing the system, then some other job must be selected from the queue and allocated the server (queueing models generally assume that the server will be busy if there are any jobs in the queue). The *scheduling discipline* characterizes the manner in which jobs are selected from the queue; scheduling disciplines are analogous to the scheduling algorithms discussed in Chapter 6. The *service pattern* characterizes the requests for service by the individual jobs.

Mean Value Models

One characterization of the arrival pattern (and load on the system) is the *mean interarrival rate*, α, in jobs/time. And, similarly, the *mean service rate*, β, in jobs/time is a reflection of the demand on the server being made by each job.

For the mean values to realistically predict the performance of the system, the system must have reached *steady state*, that is, its performance must be observed over a long enough period of time so that α is an accurate reflection of the observed arrival rate, and β is an accurate reflection of the observed service rate.

Using the mean interarrival and service rates, one can compute the mean utilization of the server:

Definition 14.1. Given the rate at which jobs arrive in the system, α, and the rate at which they complete service, β, then the *utilization*, ρ, is the arrival rate times the average service time, that is,

$$\rho = \alpha \times \frac{1}{\beta} = \frac{\alpha}{\beta} \parallel$$

ρ is a useful measure of performance for a system. For example, if $\rho > 1$, then the arrival rate is greater than the service rate, that is, the system will never come to steady state since jobs are arriving faster than they can be serviced. If $\rho < 1$, then the system will reach steady state and ρ represents the fraction of the time that the server will be busy. Notice that if ρ is just slightly less than 1 then the system is stable, but may converge on the steady state slowly.

Mean value models are useful for making quick estimates about the feasibility of a system, but they do not provide enough information to predict the effect of bursts of arrivals or of an occasional job with very large service time. As a result, it is impossible to predict any of the characteristics of the queue length based only on the mean arrival and service rates.

Realistically, jobs are likely to arrive with variations of the time between arrivals, that is, the arrival rate may be sporadic rather than regular. Similarly, the amount of service time that a job requires may be unrelated to other jobs that request service in general-purpose systems. Because of these variations, the arrival rate may exceed the service rate for short periods of time, causing a number of jobs to be queued (if the service rate exceeds the arrival rate for a period of time, then the server becomes idle). That is, the queue is a buffering mechanism between variations in the arrival rate and the service rate. (Remember that if $\rho > 1$ then over time the system will fail, independent of the queue size, since the system simply is subjected to more load than it is capable of handling.)

Better models of the arrival pattern and service pattern are needed to make the performance prediction more accurate.

Probability Distribution Functions

Performance analysts use probability density functions and probability distribution functions as more detailed characterizations of the arrival and service pattern.

> **Definition 14.2.** Let x be a *random variable* on $(0, \infty)$. Then the *probability density function* is
>
> $$f(t) = \text{probability}[x = t]$$
>
> and the *probability distribution function* is
>
> $$F(t) = \text{probability}[x \leq t] = \int_0^t f(x)\,dx \|$$

The reciprocal of the arrival rate is the *interarrival time*. One can plot the probability that the time between the arrival of two jobs is some random variable, x, for $t \in (0, \infty)$, that is, the probability$[x = t]$, which is the density function. Similarly, one can plot the probabilities for the service time, generating a second density function. Density functions are a better mechanism for characterizing arrival and service patterns than mean values, since they represent variance in the expected values rather than just the mean value. Density functions have been used to represent observed arrival and service patterns.

A discrete approximation to the (continuous) density function can be constructed from observed data in the real system. A *histogram* can be used to plot the probability$[x=t]$ for discrete values of t. This is done by defining N ranges on $[0, K)$, $R_0, R_1, ..., R_{N-1}$ such that R_i reflects the probability that the random variable takes on any value in the range $[i \times \frac{K}{N}, i + 1 \times \frac{K}{N})$. For example, the histogram shown in Figure 14.2 indicates that values between 4 and 6 occur most often, with values between 4 and 5 occurring approximately one-fifth of the time and those between 5 and 6 one-sixth of the time.

Suppose that we wished to sample the histogram to obtain a single arrival or service time. Then those values that have high probability should result more often than those values with relatively low probability, that is, about a 20% of the time, we should get a value between 4 and 5, while we should almost never get a value between 9 and 10.

It is difficult to obtain a sample directly from the histogram shown in Figure 14.2; however, suppose that we "integrated" the histogram by changing the bin definition so that bin R_i represented the probability that the random variable takes on any value in the range $[0, i + 1 \times \frac{K}{N})$ (compare with the distribution function definition). The resulting histogram, shown in Figure 14.3, still represents the same arrival or service pattern, but does so using the probability distribution instead of the probability density.

Now consider the *uniform distribution* on the interval $(0, 1)$; that is, any number between 0 and 1 has equal probability of being chosen. Randomly choose some number,

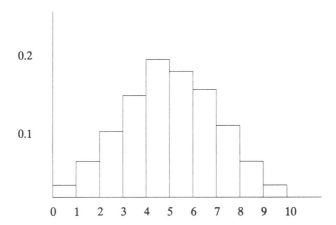

Figure 14.2 A Histogram Representing the Density

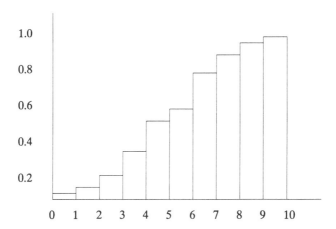

Figure 14.3 A Histogram Representing the Distribution

v, that is in (0, 1) and let v be a probability. Now, we would like to select a number from either histogram that has probability v of being chosen, that is, we want the number, t, such that $f(t) = v$. If we knew the inverse, f^{-1} or F^{-1}, then we could simply compute $f^{-1}(v)$ or $F^{-1}(v)$ to find the proper value of t.

Consider a continuous function that fits the histogram shown in Figure 14.2. The inverse of the function is a mapping but not a function, since $f^{-1}(v)$ may evaluate to two different numbers, for example, notice that $f^{-1}(0.15)$ would evaluate to a value of $t \approx 3.5$ and $t \approx 6.5$ (depending on how the continuous function fit the histogram. But $F^{-1}(v)$ is single-valued, being about 2.5. Furthermore, numbers can now be selected from the distribution function as samples.

While the histogram is intuitive, it is generally not useful for analyzing the queue-ing model since it has no closed mathematical form. There are other continuous func-tions that are far more useful.

There are several widely used distribution functions, briefly described below.

We have mentioned the uniform distribution (on the unit interval) above. The uni-form distribution, of course, can be defined for any range of values.

The *normal distribution* often occurs in nature as a model of "random" occurrences and may be a good model for describing the arrival or service pattern.

The *(negative) exponential distribution* is favored by queueing theorists because it has certain properties that fit well with arrival patterns and because it yields tractable ana-lyses. Assume:

(1)   The number of arrivals during a given interval of time depends only on the length of time and not on the past history of the system.
(2)   For any small time interval, the probability of a single arrival is $\alpha \Delta t$, where α is constant. The probability of more than one arrival is negligble.

Then it can be shown (see [6], pages 446-448) that

$$f(t) = \alpha e^{-\alpha t}$$

and that

$$F(t) = \int_0^t \alpha e - \alpha x dx = 1 - e - \alpha t$$

which has a mean value of $\frac{1}{\alpha}$ (computed as the first derivative of F). This arrival pro-cess is called the *poisson process*. The distribution function, F(t), represents the proba-bility that the interarrival time is less than or equal to t.

While the exponential distribution is popular, the *hyperexponential distribution* function provides a more realistic approximation of observed interarrival times. The hyperexponential distribution is a combination of two individual exponential distributions (with different α parameters). The hyperexponential distribution is given by

$$F(t) = 1 - ae - b\alpha t - (1 - a)e - c\alpha t$$

for $0 < a < 1$ and $0 < b < 1 < c$.

Other distribution functions are useful to represent arrival and service patterns (as well as other "random" phenomena in a system model); for example, see [9].

14.1.2 Analytic Performance Measures

The utilization of the server is one measure of the performance of a system (Definition 14.1), and the average length of the queue is another, a slightly more comprehensive one.

Theorem 14.1. (Little's Law) Let L be the *average length of the queue*; then

$$L = \alpha W$$

where α is the arrival rate and W is the average waiting time for a job. ‖

The reader should consult Kleinrock [9], Volume 1, page 17 for a proof of Little's law. The law is useful, since it relates the length of the queue to the waiting time for each job.

Now we can consider a derivation of the amount of time that a job will have to wait to complete service in a system with the FCFS scheduling algorithm, provided that the system is in steady state.

Theorem 14.2. Suppose that the queueing model has a negative exponential (poisson) arrival pattern with rate α and an arbitrary service pattern described by an arbitrary distribution F(t) with mean $= \frac{1}{\beta}$. Furthermore, suppose that the queueing discipline is FCFS. Then the average waiting time, W, is

$$W = \frac{W_0}{1 - \rho}$$

where W_0 is the expected time to finish the job currently in service. ‖

Argument
Let W_t be the expected waiting time for all jobs in the system with $t \leq$ service time $\leq t + \Delta t$. Then, at the time that a new job arrives,

$$W = W_0 + \sum_i W_i$$

where W_i are the service times of the jobs already in the queue (the scheduling discipline is FCFS).

During W_t, L_t is the expected number of jobs with $t \leq$ service time $\leq t + \Delta t$, which can be written as

$$L_t = \alpha W_t \times dF(t)$$

by Little's law (L = αW), since $\alpha \cdot W_y$ is the number of arrivals and dF(t) is the probability that the service time is in (t, t + Δt). The time to service these jobs is

$$t \times \alpha W_t \, dF(t)$$

Now, to compute W, it is necessary to sum the times over varying t:

$$W = W_0 + \int_0^\infty \alpha t W_t dF(t)$$

and since the queueing discipline is FCFS, W = W_t for some t of a newly arrived job; that is,

$$W = W_0 + \int_0^\infty \alpha t W \, dF(t) = W_0 + \alpha W \int_0^\infty t \, dF(t) = W_0 + \alpha W \frac{1}{\beta} = W_0 + \rho W$$

and therefore

$$W = \frac{W_0}{1 - \rho} \; ‖$$

Response Time in a Time-sharing System

In time-sharing systems, the original model is altered slightly to better reflect arrivals and departures, as shown in Figure 14.4.

Here there are n terminals, where a user enters a request to the system, waits for a response, examines the response, then enters the next request, and so on. The user is said to alternate between a *think state* and a *wait state*. Now, the interarrival corresponds to the amount of time that the user is in think state for one iteration, and the service time is the amount of time that the user is in the wait state.

Theorem 14.3. Given a time-sharing system with n terminals and a single server being scheduled with a preemptive round robin policy. Then the expected ratio of think time to total time is

$$T_{think} = \frac{1 - pr_0}{n\rho}$$

where pr_0 is the probability that no users are waiting. ‖

Argument
T_{think} is the ratio of average interarrival time to the total circulation time; that is,

$$T_{think} = \frac{\frac{1}{\alpha}}{\frac{1}{\alpha} + W}$$

W is the expected wait time, for which we can write a more detailed description. If there are no users waiting, then the request will be served immediately, and this happens with probability pr_0. Thus $(1 - pr_0)$ is the probability that there is at least one user is waiting. Thus, $\beta(1 - pr_0)$ is the average service load in the system.

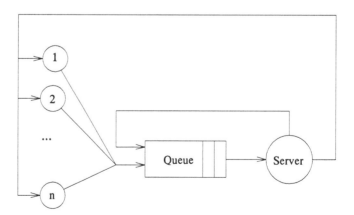

Figure 14.4 A Time-sharing Queueing Model

While a user is in think state, requests will continue to arrive from other users; that is, the average input load while a user thinks is

$$n\alpha T_{think} = n\alpha \frac{\frac{1}{\alpha}}{\frac{1}{\alpha} + W}$$

For the system to be in steady state, the average input load must be the same as the average service load; that is,

$$n\alpha \frac{\frac{1}{\alpha}}{\frac{1}{\alpha} + W} = \beta(1 - pr_0)$$

and, solving for W,

$$W = \frac{n}{\beta(1 - pr_0)} - \frac{1}{\alpha}$$

So,

$$T_{think} = \frac{\frac{1}{\alpha}}{\frac{1}{\alpha} + \frac{n}{\beta(1 - pr_0)} - \frac{1}{\alpha}}$$

$$= \frac{\beta(1 - pr_0)}{n\alpha}$$

$$= \frac{1 - pr_0}{n\rho} \parallel$$

Generalizations

This section contains the most simple analytic models for predicting the performance of systems. More complex models are required for different scheduling disciplines and for different arrival and service patterns, the extensions to the basic model being obvious.

The fundamental model changes for *multiserver* queueing systems such as that shown in Figure 14.5. The analysis becomes more complex with the added detail.

The queueing model may also be extended so that it is a composition of simpler queueing models; such a compound model is called a *queueing network* (see Figure 14.6). Queueing network analysis introduces even more detail, although any given portion of the model may not be difficult to analyze. Contemporary performance tools will analyze a queueing network with a program.

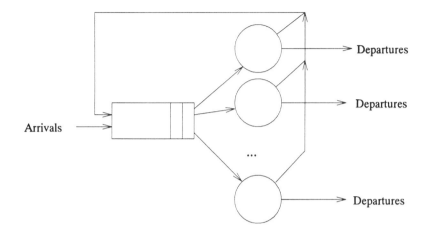

Figure 14.5 A Multiserver Queueing Model

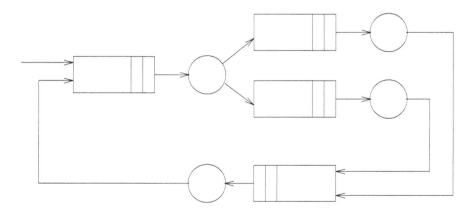

Figure 14.6 A Queueing Network

14.2 DISCRETE EVENT SIMULATION

Simulation is often used to model the behavior of a scheduling system or other complex systems when the level of detail begins to overwhelm the analytic model. A model of a complex system may itself be simple or complex, depending on the requirements for the model. A simple model makes many assumptions about the external stimuli, internal state, internal organization, and internal operation of the *target system*; it also produces a simplified description of the behavior of the system. A model becomes correspondingly more complex as it addresses more and more details of (makes fewer and fewer assumptions about) the operation of the target system. A requirement for more precise predictions of the behavior of a target system suggests that the model will need to incorporate corresponding amounts of detail.

A discrete event simulation program represents the internal organization of the target system with some model of *modules* and an *interrelationship* among the modules; the simulation model then represents the functional behavior of each module within the model organization, with the stimuli/response information defined by the interrelationship. (The model may be hierarchical in the sense that the behavior of a module may be represented by a simulation model.) Thus the level of detail in the model is reflected both by the organization mapping and the modules within the organization.

During simulation execution, a module is activated by applying a stimulus. Activation of the module means that it will cause a series of *events* to occur. Each event changes the state of the module and may also produce a reaction by the module. The reaction will propagate to other modules (as defined by the interrelationship among the modules) and act as a stimulus to these adjacent modules. The representation of the module's behavior will reflect the amount of time required for the corresponding part of the target system to react, and it will produce an appropriate estimate of the reactions to the modeled stimuli. Thus, an event occurrence within a module results in the passage of simulation time and a change in the stimuli for adjacent modules.

While it may be a more simple task to construct a simulation model than to analyze a queueing model, it is also easy to make simulation models that do not adequately represent the target system. Each simulation model must be validated before the results that it produces are useful.

Queueing models need to be analyzed once to obtain a prediction of performance. Simulation models must be executed many times with many different sets of external stimuli. The stimuli must also be chosen carefully to ensure that they represent the conditions under which the target system will operate.

14.2.1 Generating a Simulation Model

Physical Processes: An Abstraction of the Target System

Target systems are composed of many "parts" that may operate concurrently; thus, such systems may be thought of as *parallel systems*. The simulation literature characterizes semiautonomous parts of the physical target systems as *physical processes*. A physical process is made up of a set of events, each of which has some time of occurrence. Furthermore, there is a dependency relation among the set of events within a physical process. Some event occurrences are relevant to the operation of other physical processes, acting as synchronization points among the physical processes. Physical processes are an abstraction from the true components of the target system, since the target system may not even be related to computer components.

A simple abstract machine environment can be used to define how physical processes share information in the target system, in particular, how signals of event occurrences are propagated among relevant physical processes. Abstract parallel machines may be characterized as *shared memory systems* or a *local memory systems*.

Shared memory systems incorporate a common memory among all the physical processes in the system. Any set of physical processes may exchange information by reading and writing information from or to the shared memory locations.

In a local memory architecture, physical processes can only share information by sending messages across a network. As in real systems, the network may be regular and structured, or it may be a logical fully connected network.

The physical process abstract machine represents the means by which parts of the target system intercommunicate. Thus, the collection of physical processes may execute in either a shared memory or message-passing environment.

Logical Processes: An Abstracton of Physical Processes

A collection of physical processes may be represented by a set of *logical processes* to represent the critical parts of the behavior of each corresponding physical process. Logical processes are more abstract models of the active "parts" of the target system in the simulation model; so each physical process maps into a logical process. A logical process is the fundamental schedulable unit of computation in the distributed simulation program. A logical process must model the behavior of the physical process by approximating the state of the physical process and then simulating important event occurrences — those that are relevant to the operation of other physical processes — using the same circumstances that the event would occur under in the physical process. Other events are ignored in the logical process model of the physical process. For local memory physical process systems, logical process events produce simulation messages among the logical processes; for shared memory physical process systems, logical process events invoke read or write operations on the shared memory.

Executing Logical Processes

A simulation program is an application program for the *host environment* or *host machine*. (Entire hardware/software systems have been built explicitly as simulation host machines; for example, see [8, 11].)

The simulation program can be divided into a *simulation application* or simply the *simulation*, and the *simulator kernel*, or simply the *simulator*.

The simulation application is the set of model-specific program statements that represents a particular system being modeled; that is, the simulation application is the program that represents the event occurrences for a logical process. Programs written in a simulation programming language are simulation applications.

A simulation application models the global state of the target system as the composition of all of the logical process states. The simulation application specifies set of events which will cause the state to change.

The simulator kernel is independent of the definition of any individual logical processes, but dependent on the host machine; it is the mechanism that manages the execution of logical processes (and, hence, changes the simulation state), provides simulated time, gathers statistics about the simulation application, and produces summary reports. In general, simulation programming language run-time systems implement the simulator kernel.

Thus, the simulator kernel provides an execution environment for the simulation application much as an operating system provides an execution environment for a conventional application program.

Representing Concurrency in a Simulation

Logical processes represent schedulable units of computation in the simulation. If two parts of the target system may operate concurrently, then their representations must appear in distinct logical processes.

Suppose there is some set of logical processes, $\{LP_1, LP_2, ..., LP_n\}$ that may take place in parallel, then the activation of each logical process, LP_i, is represented by two events, **initiate**(LP_i) and **terminate**(LP_i) (compare with the process moded used earlier in Chapters 3 and 6). During some arbitrary (simulated) time interval, **initiate**(LP_i) occurs for each logical process LP_i, and no **terminate**(LP_i) for any LP_i. At the end of the time interval, the simulator state reflects the simultaneous execution of all n parts of the target system.

Event-oriented Simulation

Simulation applications written as *event-oriented* models are characterized by modules in which events are not analogous to logical process, but are individual parts of the simulation application.

The major components of an event-oriented simulation package are facilities for defining events (one per module), for representing states, for introducing transactions to the model, and for managing the execution of events.

For example, if event A should cause event B to occur after some computed amount of time, then some simulation application module representing the occurrence of event A would include statements such as those shown in Figure 14.7.

The *execute* procedure represents processing performed by the module to redefine the global state of the model. The *cause* statement is a simulation kernel call that schedules event B to occur at some future time.

The simulator kernel has the basic schema shown in Figure 14.8. Although it is not apparent from the pseudocode, *event* is a record that is entered into the kernel's *schedule of pending events* by the *cause* call of Figure 14.7. (Besides the identity of the pending event, the record also specifies the transaction for which the event applies as well as the time at which the event should occur.) The *select_next_event* call retrieves the event from the schedule of pending events that has the minimum time of occurrence, that is, the event that is to occur next. The *evaluate* procedure interprets the simulation application event declaration on the given transaction.

Thus, the fundamental task of the event-oriented simulator kernel is to schedule pending events, to advance the simulation clock, and to dispatch events.

```
execute(details_of_event_A);
cause(event_B, to_transaction-number,
          when_B_is_to_be_executed);
```

Figure 14.7 Simulation Application Schema

```
simulated_time = 0;
while (true) {
        event = select_next_event();
        if (event->time > simulated_time)
                simulated_time = event->time;
        evaluate(event);
}
```

Figure 14.8 Simulation Kernel Loop

Process-oriented Simulation

Process-oriented simulation maps more closely to the logical process model described above. Logical process definitions are defined as *classes* in the simulation application. Causal relationships among the events local to a logical process are represented by sequential execution within the logical process. Simulated time is implemented by interspersing *hold* statements to represent the passage of time between events (compare with the distinction between using precedence and synchronization).

For example, suppose that a logical process represents a situation in which event A causes event B, and event B causes event C, then a class declaration for the logical process might be defined by the code schema shown in Figure 14.9.

As in event-oriented simulation, the *execute* call represents modification of the simulation state. The *hold* call is a kernel call that blocks the logical process until some amount of simulated time has elapsed; then the logical process is rescheduled for execution. Thus, the simulator kernel acts as a scheduler and dispatcher of logical processes.

The *hold* call is often implemented in the same manner as the *cause* and *select_next_event* simulator kernel calls discussed under event-oriented simulation. This follows, since the simulator kernel is generally an ordinary application program running on an abstract machine provided by some real operating system.

For the simulation to execute, it is necessary to create *instances* of the classes, corresponding to individual logical processes. Because the simulation program is now defined as a collection of instances, *messages* are used to represent causal effects among the instances; this, of course, is similar to IPC among operating system processes and messages among objects. As a result, the *execute* steps in the figure may include message *send* and *receive* calls.

```
execute(event_A);
hold(until_B_is_to_be_executed);
execute(event_B);
hold(until_C_is_to_be_executed);
execute(event_C);
```

Figure 14.9 Process-oriented Simulation Application Schema

A simulated transaction is processed by the instances in the model by sending a message to the "first" instance, which models the behavior of the corresponding physical process; the instance will invoke other instances as required (using messages).

The logical processes (instances) are not necessarily the same entities that might be supported by an underlying operating system; however, the simulator will then have to support the usual process management functions to support class instances. In particular, the simulator kernel will need to support instance creation and destruction, instance scheduling, and instance dispatching, in addition to simulated time management.

14.3 DISTRIBUTED SIMULATION

Complex discrete event simulation models (of complex target systems) result in the occurrence of a very large number of events. Supporting a program that implements the discrete event simulation is a computationally intensive task due to the large amount of computation to manage and interpret the various event occurrences in the model and to reflect the changing state in the various modules. It is natural to consider using multiple-processor systems to execute the simulation, either on multiprocessors or on networks of machines.

A parallel or distributed simulation uses logical processes to model the activity of the parts of the target system. Intercommunication among the logical processes depends on the nature of the real machine architecture that hosts the simulation and therefore must make use of the mechanisms used by the host environment for supporting interprocess communication. Thus, a shared memory multiprocessor may be used to simulate a set of physical processes on a local memory system, and vice versa.

Distributing the simulation over a network or a multiprocessor requires that the simulator kernel be distributed, including an effective strategy for dispatching simulation application program execution to the individual processors. Like much other contemporary software, simulation kernels were conceived, designed, and implemented for the single-processor environment. The inherent design of traditional simulation methods depends heavily on the existence of serial operation within the kernel itself, even though it may represent high degrees of parallelism in the target system. Event-oriented simulation has a closer association with serial operation than does process-oriented simulation. Therefore, it is easier to build a distributed simulator around the process-oriented approach than the event-oriented approach. In the remainder of this section, we will assume that the simulation paradigm is process-oriented simulation.

The two simulator kernel tasks that are critical to efficient operation of the simulation system and to the ability to implement the simulator kernel as a distributed program, are management of the logical process schedule (equivalent to managing a schedule of events) and management of the simulated time. In particular, the kernel must ensure that instances are executed from the schedule in proper simulated time sequence and that when logical processes synchronize they do so under a common clock value.

The fundamental bottleneck to the execution of any simulation system is the management of the event schedule. In general, the schedule is maintained as a data structure of event and transaction descriptors, ordered by simulated time. Each new event that is scheduled must be inserted into the data structure, and the execution of each event requires the deletion of the event from the data structure. A straightforward implementation of the event list, as implied above, will require $o(n_2)$ for management of the list (where n is the number of events in the list). Vaucher and Duval [18] describe techniques for reducing the time to manage the event schedule, including sorted trees organizations. The paper also describes *time-mapping algorithms* for organizing the events into lists of lists; this technique is widely used in logic-level simulation [11]; these techniques are more sensitive to the relative consistency of time between events than the number of events. The time mapping algorithms may also be space intensive.

For any distributed implementation of the simulator kernel, it will be necessary to either centralize the event list for the entire simulation or distribute it in such a way that autonomous parts of the simulation application do not interfere with one another.

The simulated time is not difficult to manage in a single-processor host system. A single integer variable local to the simulator kernel represents the simulated time. When the simulator kernel is distributed over multiple processors or a network, considerable more care must be exercised to obtain correct operation of the simulator kernel.

The Conservative Technique [2, 3, 13]

The conservative technique is the earliest and most widely used of the distributed simulation techniques. It assumes that each logical process will be implemented by a real process in the host computing environment, using message-based interprocess communication mechanisms provided by the host environment. (Notice the implicit assumption of large-grained physical processes for local memory systems.) Now, distributed simulation is essentially a problem in synchronizing a set of asynchronous (logical) processes. Thus, there is an assumption that the logical processes will intercommunicate using messages and that the simulation kernel will also be implemented under the local memory assumption.

Since logical processes map into host machine processes, the host operating system manages all local processes directly. A logical process can then be created, destroyed, blocked, and unblocked and be the sender or receiver of messages just like any other process in the host environment. Simulation application programs are generic application programs in the host environment. The kernel only need guarantee that the logical processes agree on simulated time, and that can be done through protocol among the local processes.

Whenever a logical process simulates an event occurrence, it needs to notify certain other processes that the event occurred and the local simulated time at which the event occurred.

Since logical processes may be dispatched to different machines, there may be disagreement about the global time. Using ideas about managing global clocks on networks (see Section 9.2), it is possible to achieve loose synchronization among the logical processes by relying on order of event executions within a logical process. The basic idea is the following: Whenever a logical process executes an event, it sends notification messages to that effect to all other relevant logical processes, with a local time-stamp (simulated time) on the message. If a distinct logical process depends on the event occurrence prior to executing certain of its own events, then the local event cannot be executed until the logical process knows that the predecessor event has already occurred. Therefore, the logical process contains the dependent event blocks until it receives a message from the logical process containing the predecessor event with a time-stamp that is greater than or equal to its local (simulated) time. Thus, the two event occurrences have been synchronized with respect to a global clock rather than with respect to two independent local clocks.

The algorithm for managing the time and for scheduling events that are dependent on external event occurrences becomes more complex when more than one external event is involved. Suppose that LP_i can proceed once it has synchronized with LP_j and LP_k. After some event has occurred within LP_i, then it will signal LP_r and LP_s that they may proceed. Figure 14.10 is a logical process for LP_i.

Other optimizations can also be made by calculating dependencies within a logical process so that it can "execute ahead" of the other logical processes. The reader should consult one of the references to see those details.

A logical process cannot proceed until it receives messages on all of its input channels, for example, LP_i in Figure 14.10 would be blocked until messages had been received on both channels 1 and 2. If the model has channels that are used conditionally, then a receiving logical process could be blocked indefinitely, waiting for input on the aforementioned channel. Thus it is necessary to employ deadlock detection or avoidance algorithms as the simulation executes.

The Chandy-Misra technique is a conservative, message-based technique for implementing distributed simulation. Individual logical processes are blocked until they are certain that additional simulation can be performed without the danger of late-arriving messages invalidating any simulation that has already been accomplished. The technique relies on the physical process abstract machine being a local memory multiprocessor, that is, the technique assumes that the target system can be modeled as a set of physical processes that exchange messages.

14.3.1 Optimistic Simulation [7, 8]

Jefferson and his colleagues have implemented an entire system attuned to distributed simulation (and similar applications) on the Caltech Mark III Hypercube, a local memory multiprocessor. This work is based on Jefferson's research on global clocks for distributed systems, much as Chandy and Misra's work relies on the global clock work. Thus, not surprisingly, it also is built around a framework of logical processes intercommunicating with time-stamped messages.

Whereas the Chandy-Misra technique is conservative about the prospect of late-arriving synchronization messages, the time warp mechanism employs an optimistic strategy; that is, a logical process assumes that it has all relevant (time-stamped)

```
receive(msg1, channel1,...);
receive(msg2, channel2, ...);
simulate_until = minimum(msg1.timestamp, msg2.timestamp);
while (local_time <= simulate_until) {
        hold(until_next_event_is_to_executed);
        execute(next_event);
        send(msg, channel3, time_stamp(), receiver(event_A));
        send(msg, channel4, time_stamp(), receiver(event_A));
};
```

Figure 14.10 Logical Process Schema

synchronization messages in its queue whenever it begins to execute. Of course, sometimes this assumption is incorrect; a late-arriving message indicates to the logical process that it has simulated some activity in the absence of proper information. Therefore, the logical process is rolled back to the point that erroneous processing occurred, that is, to the time-stamp of the late-arriving message. The logical process may have sent erroneous message as a consequence of the optimistic algorithm, so those messages must be invalidated with *antimessages*, one for each erroneous message. Antimessages will propagate the rollback of other logical processes.

The time warp approach makes an optimistic assumption about the completeness of message queues, ie. about the relative synchronous operation among asynchronous logical processes. If it detects an error in the assumption, it uses the antimessages and rollback to recover. The Time Warp Operating System that supports the distributed simulation is designed to use process rollback as the standard method of synchronizing processes.

14.3.2 Comparing the Distributed Simulation Techniques

The section summarizes our comparison, with a few additional observations. First, there are few impartial quantitative comparisons since few have implemented the same simulation using both models; the interested reader should consult the latest Distributed Simulation System Proceedings for the most current results in this rapidly changing field, for example, [15].

As pointed out above, the optimistic technique is optimistic about the probability that the asynchronous logical processes will proceed in relative sychronicity. The conservative technique does not make this assumption and instead goes to great measures to explicitly assure synchronous operation with the time-stamped messages.

The optimistic technique is designed to execute logical processes as soon as it receives any time-stamped message; it does not ensure that messages will be delivered in strictly increasing time-stamp order; thus, the possibility of rollback. The conservative technique is careful to ensure that the timestamps on all messages delivered on a channel are strictly increasing so that when a logical process receives the message, it knows that there will be no "earlier" messages. Thus, whenever a logical process receives a message, it is free to simulate a block of activity that occurs between the last time-stamp time and the time of the time-stamp of the newly received message. Optimistic programs tend to be highly process oriented, while conservative programs (constructed as process-oriented simulations) tend slightly more toward event-oriented simulation.

The conservative technique relies on the interconnection scheme among the logical processes being static (see the example above). The optimistic technique can accommodate a multidrop interconnection. Optimistic simulation can accommodate a wider class of target systems than the conservative approach.

Jefferson points out that the conservative technique is somewhat constraining in terms of canceling pending events [8]. If we assume that a logical process can send a message with a *future* time-stamp on it, then the logical process will have difficulty canceling that message (prior to the sending logical process's time reaching the future time-stamp time). It is not clear that Chandy and Misra ever intended that this situation arise, that is, that future timestamps could be used.

While it is necessary to take deadlock into account under the Chandy-Misra technique, that is unnecessary in the time warp case.

The time warp technique relies on saving antimessages and the rollback state. The Chandy-Misra technique requires very limited amounts of space to save the state of the computation.

Each technique can be expected to be more effective under particular situations. The time warp technique is superior to the Chandy-Misra technique if channels in the network are not used often, if the network among the logical processes is dynamic, and if the size of the computation within the logical processes is well matched. The inverse is true if the logical processes may vary widely in their speed of execution (the amount of time that asynchronous logical processes may drift is large between synchronization points).

14.4 FURTHER READING

Performance analysis is an important topic in computer systems since, ultimately, performance often discriminates between good and unacceptable solutions. There are many good books and papers devoted to the area; we especially recommend the books by Lazowska and others [10] and by Molloy [14].

There are a number of excellent textbooks on analytic modeling. The classic books in the area have been Feller's introduction to probability [6] and Conway, Maxwell, and Miller's book on scheduling theory [4]. The material in these two fundamental books has been upgraded, particularly with respect to computer system analysis, with the more recent two-volume set on queueing theory by Kleinrock [9].

See [12] for a detailed description of the techniques used to accomplish process-oriented simulation. Process-oriented simulation evolved with early object-oriented simulation, most prominent in the work of Dahl and his coworkers [5].

Discussions of distributed simulation have appeared in the literature since the mid 1970s [1-3, 7, 8, 13, 15-17].

REFERENCES

1. R. E. Bryant, "Simulation of Packet Communication Architecture Computer Systems," M.I.T. Technical Report, LCS, Tech. Rep.-188, 1977.
2. K. M. Chandy and J. Misra, "Distributed Simulation: A Case Study in Design and Verification of Distributed Programs," *IEEE Transactions on Software Engineering SE-5*, 5 (September 1979), 440-452.
3. K. M. Chandy and J. Misra, "Asynchronous Distributed Simulation via a Sequence of Parallel Computations," *Communications of the ACM 24*, 4 (April 1981), 198-205.
4. R. W. Conway, W. L. Maxwell, and L. W. Miller, *Theory of Scheduling*, Addison-Wesley Publishing Co., Reading, MA, 1967.
5. O. J. Dahl, B. Myhrhaug, and K. Nygaard, "The SIMULA 67 Common Base Language," Norwegian Computer Center technical report, Oslo, Norway, 1968.
6. W. Feller, *An Introduction to Probability Theory and Its Applications, Volume 1, Third Edition*, John Wiley & Sons, New York, NY, 1968.
7. D. R. Jefferson, "Virtual Time," *ACM Transactions on Programming Languages and Systems 7*, 3 (July 1985), 404-425.
8. D. Jefferson, B. Beckman, F. Wieland, L. Blume, M. DiLoreto, P. Hontalas, P. Laroche, K. Sturdevant, J. Tupman, V. Warren, J. Wedel, and H. Younger, "Distributed Simulation and the Time Warp Operating System ," *Proceedings of the Eleventh ACM Symposium on Operating Systems Principles* , Austin, Texas, November 1987 , 77-93.

9.   L. Kleinrock, *Queueing Systems (Volume 1: Theory, Volume 2: Computer Applications)*, John Wiley & Sons, New York, NY, 1975, 1976.

10.   E. D. Lazowska, J. Zahorjan, G. S. Graham, and K. C. Sevcik, *Quantitative System Performance*, Prentice Hall, Inc., Englewood Cliffs, NJ, 1984.

11.   M. R. Lightner, "Modeling and Simulation of VLSI Digital Systems," *Proceedings of the IEEE 75*, 6 (June 1987), 786-796.

12.   M. H. MacDougall, *Simulating Computer Systems*, MIT Press, Cambridge, MA, 1987.

13.   J. Misra, "Distributed-Discrete Event Simulation," *ACM Computing Surveys 18*, 1 (March 1986), 39-65.

14.   M. K. Molloy, *Fundamentals of Performance Modeling*, Macmillan, 1989.

15.   D. Nicol, ed., *Proceedings of the SCS Multiconference on Distributed Simulation*, The Society for Computer Simulation, January 1990.

16.   J. K. Peacock, E. G. Manning, and J. W. Wong, "Synchronization of Distributed Simulation using Broadcast Algorithms," *Computer Networks 4*, 1 (February 1980), 3-10.

17.   J. K. Peacock, J. W. Wong, and E. G. Manning, "Distributed Simulation Using a Network of Processors," *Computer Networks 3*, 1 (February 1979), 44-56.

18.   J. G. Vaucher and P. Duval, "A Comparison of Simulation Event List Algorithms," *Communications of the ACM 18* (1975).

EXERCISES

(1)   Assume that a system is a single-server queueing system with a poisson arrival pattern with a mean interarrival time of 24 jobs per minute and that each job uses a mean of 1 second (exponentially distributed).
      (a)   What is the mean utilization of the server?
      (b)   What is the expected amount of time that a job will have to wait before receiving service, given the the queueing discipline is First-come, First-served?
      (c)   What is the expected length of the queue?

(2)   Suppose that the average waiting time for a server is determined to be 3 minutes and the arrival rate is observed to be 3 jobs per minute. What is the expected length of the server's queue?

(3)   Suppose that you go to an airline ticket counter that has several ticket agents all servicing a single queue of travelers. You observe that the queue seems to hold an average of 12 travelers and that a new traveler joins the line once every 3 minutes. How long would you expect to wait in the line?

(4)   Suppose that a queueing system with a FCFS scheduler has a poisson arrival pattern with a rate 5 jobs per minute and a service time distribution with a mean service per job of 15 seconds per job. What is the average waiting time for a job?

(5)   Let the name space of a program be N = {0, 1, 2, ..., 31}. Write a program to simulate LRU and Belady's optimal replacement algorithms. Test the algorithms on various reference streams generated as illustrated below.

```
main( )
{
        generate(32, 0, 10500);
        generate(8, 5, 10500);
        . . .
        generate(16, 16, 10000);
}
```

```
generate(locality_length, first_page, number)
int locality_length;
int first_page;
int number;
{
/* Generate number page references in the range
 *         (first_page, first_page+locality_length)
 * from a uniform distribution.
 *
 * Although the example code shows the routine "printing" the
 * page references, you should write your code so that it
 * generates the stream in a more appropriate format.
 */
        for (i=0; i<number; i++)
        {
                printf(random()*locality_length+first_page);
        };
}
```

Prepare a report on your simulation and analysis of the experiment; the report should be a maximum of two typewritten pages stating your assumptions and conclusions for the simulation. You may add up to two additional pages of figures to support and illustrate the points that you make in your conclusion. You are free to use the language and systems of your choice for this assignment: include a listing of your program.

(6)   Write a program to simulate a queueing network system with $1 \leq N \leq 3$ identical processors and $1 \leq M \leq 3$ different I/O devices (see the figure below).

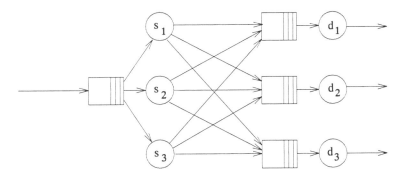

Jobs arrive in the system according to an exponential service time distribution, queue up for a processor, are scheduled to an available server on a FCFS basis, obtain a service time quantum (based on an exponential service time distribution), perform I/O on one of the devices (chosen randomly), and then depart the system.

The interarrival times are specified by an exponential distribution

$$F(t) = 1 - e^{**}(-t/50)$$

The execution time distribution for each task is also exponential and is specified as

$$F(t) = 1 - e^{**}(-t/5)$$

The execution time distribution for each device is also exponential and is specified as

$$F(t) = 1 - e^{**}(-t/10)$$

Notice that you can sample an exponential distribution function of the form

$$F(t) = 1 - e^{**}kt$$

as follows:

a)   Obtain a random number, X, from a uniform distribution of
      numbers between zero and one.
b)   Evaluate $(1/k) * \ln(1 - X)$.

Exercise your model for each configuration until at least 50 jobs have completed processing, for N, M = 1, 2, and 3. Write a concise report on the results of your experiment in the following format:

Part 1: Observed data for each of the following phenomena:
      Length of simulated time:
      Server[i] was {busy|idle} at termination.
      Tasks completed:
      Tasks currently in the queue:
      Throughput rate (tasks/time):
      Average turnaround time:
      Average queue length:
      Maximum queue length:
      Average processor service time:
      Average device service time:
      Percent of time the server[i] was busy:
      Percent of time the device[i] was busy:

Part 2: Conclusions. Write a maximum of three typewritten pages stating your assumptions and conclusions for the simulation. You may add up to two additional pages of figures to support and illustrate the points that you make in your conclusion.

(7)   Write a program to simulate a queueing network system with two identical processors and three different I/O devices (see the figure below).
      Jobs arrive in the system according to an exponential service time distribution, queue up for a processor, are scheduled to an available server using round robin scheduling, obtain a service time quantum, perform I/O on one of the devices (chosen randomly), and then either return to the queue for more service or depart the system. The number of times that a job requests processor service is defined by a uniform distribution between 5 and 15. Assume that each time the scheduler runs it takes 20% of a time quantum.
      The interarrival times are specified by an exponential distribution

$$F(t) = 1 - e^{**}(-t/50)$$

The execution time distribution for each task is also exponential and is specified as

$$F(t) = 1 - e^{**}(-t/5)$$

Experiment with various time quanta and then report your results as in the previous problem.

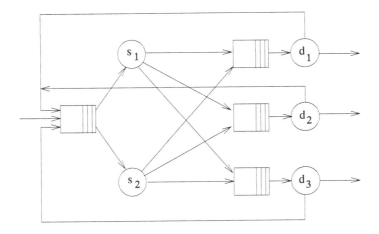

(8)   Consider the simple queueing system shown below:

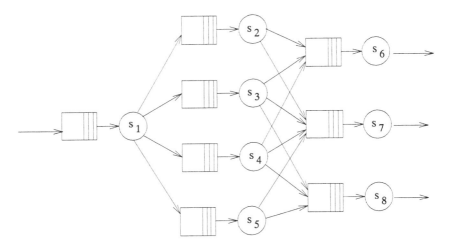

Using the (Chandy-Misra) conservative simulation strategy, implement a distributed simulation of the queueing system. You will have to provide a mechanism to produce arrivals at various simulated times; this should be a procedure or process rather than manual input, since you will likely need to run the simulator for several jobs to see its true behavior. Halting with control-C is acceptable. Use an exponential distribution for the interarrival times. Whenever a server completes and passes a job to some downstream server, choose the particular server randomly with equal probabilities.

Each server should be an LP. Write your servers so that each uses a normal distribution to determine the real time to simulate its activity, but each advances the simulation time by a fixed amount (for that particular server) for each input message. Allow a server to process jobs in parallel so that if two jobs arrive at the same time they will depart at the same time, utilizing twice as much service time at the node (note that you will essentially be simulating nonpreemptive, multiplexed scheduling in this case). Of course this violates the behavior of a true queueing model, but greatly simplifies the behavior of your simulator.

You may wish to debug your distributed simulation on a single machine; however, use network IPC so that it would be possible to run you simulator on multiple machines by parameterization.

Debug your distributed simulation on a single machine; however, use network IPC so that it would be possible to run you simulator on multiple machines by parameterization with changing the code.

Write a report with your listing that describes how your simulation performed. Your program description should not only explain generally how your solution is written, but also must include a report on the simulation itself. Try to use local system facilities to illustrate utilization of simulated resources *and* of the processes that implement the logical processes. It should be possible to read your report and understand both the results of the simulation and also how well the distributed computation that implemented the simulation performed.

(9)   Modify the simulation program described in the previous exercise as shown below.

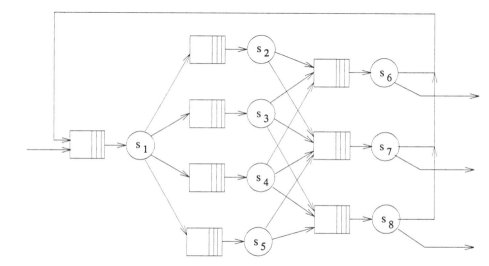

A *null message* can be sent by any logical process whenever it can ensure that it will not send a subsequent message with an earlier time than the time-stamp that appears on the null message (see [13]. Thus, a null message is a form of message that indicates to dependent LPs that the sending LP has advanced the time of its simulation, even though no event occurrence is being transmitted in the message.

Incorporate null messages into each logical process so that it can notify "downstream" logical processes whenever it advances its clock. You will need to initiate each LP by having it send out null messages with time zero to each of its successors.

BIBLIOGRAPHY

"Special Section on the Internet Worm," *Communications of the ACM 32*, 6 (June 1989), 677-710.

AT&T Bell Laboratories Technical Journal, AT&T, October 1984.

AT&T UNIX System V Technical Seminar, AT&T, Greensboro, NC, May 1986.

The Ethernet: A Local Area Network Data Link Layer and Physical Layer Specification, Digital Equipment Corporation, Intel Corporation, and Xerox Corporation, September 1980.

IBM VSE/SP General Information Guide, IBM Corporation, 1986.

An Introduction to Advanced Program-to-Program Communication (APPC), IBM International Systems Center, IBM Corporation, Technical Bulletin GG24-1584-0, July 1983.

Local Network Standards Committee: A Status Report, Draft B, IEEE Project 802, October 1981.

IEEE P1003.1 Trial Use Standard, IEEE P1003 Standards Committee, 1986.

"Status of OSI (and Related) Standards," *ACM SIGCOMM Computer Communications Review 20*, 3 (July 1990), 83-99.

Release 3.2 Manual for the Sun Workstation, Sun Microsystems, Inc., Document Number 800-1364-10, September 1986.

Networking on the Sun Workstation, Sun Microsystems, Inc., Document Number 800-1345-10, September 1986.

Unix User's Manual Reference Guide, 4.3 BSD, Computer Systems Research Group, Computer Science Division, Department of Electrical Engineering and Computer Science, University of California, Berkeley, April 1986.

Abramson, N., "The Aloha System," *AFIPS Proceedings of the Fall Joint Computer Conference 37* (1970).

Acetta, M., R. Baron, W. Bolosky, D. Golub, R. Rashid, A. Tevanian, and M. Young, "Mach: A New Kernel Foundation for UNIX Development," *Proceedings of the 1986 USENIX*, Atlanta, GA, 1986, 93-112.

Agarwal, A., J. Hennessy, and M. Horowitz, "Cache Performance of Operating System and Multiprogramming Workloads," *ACM Transactions on Computer Systems 6*, 4 (November 1988), 393-431.

Agerwala, T. and Arvind, "Data Flow Systems: Guest Editor's Introduction," *IEEE Computer 15*, 2 (Feb 1982), 10-13.

Allchin, J. E. and M. S. McKendry, "Synchronization and Recovery of Actions," *Proceedings of the 2nd Annual ACM Symposium on the Principles of Distributed Computing*, August 1983, 31-44.

Almes, G. T., A. P. Black, E. D. Lazowska, and J. D. Noe, "The Eden System: A Technical Review," *IEEE Transactions on Software Engineering SE-11*, 1 (January 1985), 43-59.

Andrews, G. R. and F. B. Schneider, "Concepts and Notations for Concurrent Programming," *ACM Computing Surveys 15*, 1 (March 1983), 3-43.

Archibald, J. and J. L. Baer, "Cache Coherence Protocols: Evaluation Using a Multiprocessor Simulation Model," *ACM Transactions on Computer Systems 4*, 4 (November 1986), 273-298.

Athas, W. C. and C. L. Seitz, "Multicomputers: Message-Passing Concurrent Computers," *IEEE Computer 21*, 8 (August 1988), 9-24.

Backus, J., "Can Programming Be Liberated from the von Neumann Style? A Functional Style and Its Algebra of Programs," *Communications of the ACM 21*, 8 (August 1978), 613-641.

Baer, J. L., "A Survey of Some Theoretical Aspects of Multiprocessing," *ACM Computing Surveys 5*, 1 (March 1973), 31-79.

Bartlett, J. F., "A NonStop (tm) Kernel," *Proceedings of the Eighth ACM Symposium on Operating Systems Principles*, December 1981, 22-29.

Baskett, F., K. M. Chandy, R. R. Muntz, and F. G. Palacios, "Open, Closed, and Mixed Networks of Queues with Different Classes of Customers," *Journal of the ACM 22*, 2 (April 1975), 248-260 .

Baskett, F., J. H. Howard, and J. T. Montague,Task Communication in DEMOS, November 1977.

Bayer, R. and E. McCreight, "Organizations and Maintenance of Large Ordered Indexes," *Acta Informatica 11*, 3 (1972), 173-189.

Beguelin, A. L., "Deterministic Parallel Programming in Phred," University of Colorado, Department of Computer Science, Ph. D. dissertation, May 1990.

Belady, L. A., "A Study of Replacement Algorithms for Virtual Storage Computers," *IBM Systems Journal 5*, 2 (1966), 78-101.

Bennett, J. L., "Distributed Smalltalk," *Proceedings of the 2nd ACM Conference on Object-Oriented Systems, Languages, and Applications*, Orlando, FL, October 1987, 318-330.

Bennett, J. K., "Distributed Smalltalk: Inheritance and Reactiveness in Distributed Systems," Department of Computer Science, University of Washington, Ph.D dissertation, December 1987.

Bernstein, A. J., "Program Analysis for Parallel Processing," *IEEE Transactions on Electronic Computers EC-15*, 5 (October 1966), 757-762.

Bernstein, P. A. and N. Goodman, "Concurrency Control in Distributed Database Systems," *ACM Computing Surveys 13*, 2 (June 1981), 185-221.

Bershad, B. N., T. E. Anderson, E. D. Lazowska, and H. M. Levy, "Lightweight Remote Procedure Call," *ACM Transactions on Computer Systems 8*, 1 (February 1990), 37-55.

Bershad, B. N., D. T. Ching, E. D. Lazowska, J. Sanislo, and M. Schwartz, "A Remote Procedure Call Facility for Heterogeneous Computer Systems," *IEEE Transactions on Software Engineering SE-13*, 8 (August 1987), 880-894.

Bershad, B. N., E. D. Lazowska, and H. M. Levy, "Presto: A System for Object-Oriented Parallel Programming," *Software -- Practice and Experience 18*, 8 (August 1988), 713-732.

Bic, L. and A. Shaw, *The Logical Design of Operating Systems, Second Edition*, Prentice Hall, Inc., Englewood Cliffs, NJ, 1988.

Birrell, A. D., R. M. Needham, and M. D. Schroeder, "Grapevine: An Exercise in Distributed Computing," *Communications of the ACM 25*, 4 (April 1982).

Birrell, A. D. and B. J. Nelson, "Implementing Remote Procedure Calls," *ACM Transactions on Computer Systems 2*, 1 (February 1984), 39-59.

Black, D. L., "Scheduling Support for Concurrency and Parallelism in the Mach Operating System," *IEEE Computer 23*, 5 (May 1990), 35-43.

Bolosky, W. J., R. P. Fitzgerald, and M. L. Scott, "Simple But Effective Techniques for NUMA Memory Management," *Proceedings of the Twelfth ACM Symposium on Operating Systems Principles*, December 1989, 19-31.

Brinch Hansen, P., "The Nucleus of a Multiprogramming System," *Communications of the ACM 13*, 4 (April 1970), 238-250.

Brinch Hansen, P., *The Architecture of Concurrent Programs*, Prentice Hall, Inc., Englewood Cliffs, NJ, 1977.

Brinch Hansen, P., *Operating System Principles*, Prentice Hall, Inc., Englewood Cliffs, NJ, 1973.

Brooks, F. P., *The Mythical Man-Month: Essays on Software Engineering*, Addison-Wesley Publishing Co., Reading, MA, 1975.

Broy, M., *Control Flow and Data Flow: Concepts of Distributed Programmings*, Springer-Verlag, New York, NY, 1985.

Brown, M. R., K. N. Kolling, and E. A. Taft, "The Alpine File System," *ACM Transactions on Computer Systems 3*, 4 (November 1985), 261-293.

Brownbridge, D. R., L. F. Marshall, and B. Randell, "The Newcastle Connection," *Software -- Practice and Experience 12*, 12 (December 1982), 1147-1162.

Browne, J. C., "Framework for Formulation and Analysis of Parallel Computation Structures," *Parallel Computing 3* (1986), 1-9.

Bryant, R. E., "Simulation of Packet Communication Architecture Computer Systems," M.I.T. Technical Report, LCS, TR-188, 1977.

Campbell, R. H. and R. B. Kolstad, "An Overview of Path Pascal's Design," *ACM SIGPLAN Notices 15*, 9 (September 1980), 13-24.

Campbell, R., G. Johnston, and V. Russo, "Choices (Class Hierarchical Open Interface for Custom Embedded Systems)," *ACM SIGOPS Operating Systems Review 21*, 3 (July 1987), 9-17.

Carr, R. W. and J. L. Hennessy, "WSClock -- A Simple and Efficient Algorithm for Virtual Memory Management," *Proceedings of the Eighth ACM Symposium on Operating Systems Principles*, December 1981, 87-95.

Carriero, N. and D. Gelernter, "The S/Net's Linda Kernel," *ACM Transactions on Computer Systems 4*, 2 (May 1986), 110-129.

Chandy, K. M. and L. Lamport, "Distributed Snapshots: Determining Global States of Distributed Systems," *ACM Transactions on Computer Systems 3*, 1 (February 1985), 63-75.

Chandy, K. M. and J. Misra, "Distributed Simulation: A Case Study in Design and Verification of Distributed Programs," *IEEE Transactions on Software Engineering SE-5*, 5 (September 1979), 440-452.

Chandy, K. M. and J. Misra, "Asynchronous Distributed Simulation via a Sequence of Parallel Computations," *Communications of the ACM 24*, 4 (April 1981), 198-205.

Chandy, K. M. and J. Misra, *Parallel Program Design: A Foundation*, Addison-Wesley Publishing Co., Reading, MA, 1988.

Chang, A. and M. F. Mergen, "801 Storage: Architecture and Programming," *ACM Transactions on Computers 6*, 1 (February 1988), 28-50.

Chang, J. M. and N. F. Maxemchuk, "Reliable Broadcast Protocols," *ACM Transactions on Computer Systems 2*, 3 (August 1984), 251-273.

Chase, J. S., F. G. Amador, E. D. Lazowska, H. M. Levy, and R. J. Littlefield, "The Amber System: Parallel Programming on a Network of Multiprocessors," *Proceedings of the Twelfth ACM Symposium on Operating Systems Principles*, December 1989, 147-158.

Cheriton, D. R., "The V Distributed System," *Communications of the ACM 31*, 3 (March 1988), 314-333.

Cheriton, D. R., M. A. Malcolm, L. S. Melen, and G. R. Sager, "Thoth: A Portable Real-Time Operating System," *Communications of the ACM 22*, 1 (February 1979), 105-115.

Cheriton, D. R. and W. Zwaenepoel, "The Distributed V Kernel and Its Performance for Diskless Workstations," *Proceedings of the Ninth ACM Symposium on Operating Systems Principles 17*, 5 (July 1983), 129-140.

Chu, W. W. and H. Opderbeck, "The Page Fault Frequency Replacement Algorithm," *AFIPS Proceedings of the Fall Joint Computer Conference 41* , 597-609.

Clark, D., "The Structuring of Systems Using Upcalls," *Proceedings of the Tenth ACM Symposium on Operating Systems Principles*, December 1985, 171-180.

Coffman, E. G. and P. J. Denning, *Operating Systems Theory*, Prentice Hall, Inc., Englewood Cliffs, NJ, 1973.

Coffman, E. G., M. T. Elphick, and A. Shoshani, "System Deadlocks," *ACM Computing Surveys 3*, 2 (June 1971), 67-78.

Coffman, E. G. and R. L. Graham, "Optimal Scheduling for Two-Processor Systems," *Acta Informatica 1*, 3 (1972), 200-213.

Cohen, E. and D. Jefferson, "Protection in the Hydra Operating System," *Proceedings of the Fifth ACM Symposium on Operating Systems Principles*, November 1975, 141-160.

Cole, C. T., P. B. Flinn, and A. B. Atlas, "An Implementation of an Extended File System," *USENIX Proceedings*, June 1985, 131-149.

Conway, M., "A Multiprocessor System Design," *Proceedings of the AFIPS Fall Joint Computer Conference,*, 1963, 139-146.

Conway, R. W., W. L. Maxwell, and L. W. Miller, *Theory of Scheduling*, Addison-Wesley Publishing Co., Reading, MA, 1967.

Corbato, F. J., M. M. Daggett, and R. C. Daley, "An Experimental Time-Sharing System," *Proceedings of the Spring Joint Computer Conference 21* (1962), 335-344.

Courtois, P. J., F. Heymans, and D. L. Parnas, "Concurrent Control with 'Readers' and 'Writers'," *Communications of the ACM 14*, 10 (October 1971), 667-668.

Cox, A. L. and R. J. Fowler, "The Implementation of a Coherent Memory Abstraction on a NUMA Multiprocessor: Experiences with PLATINUM," *Proceedings of the Twelfth ACM Symposium on Operating Systems Principles* , December 1989 , 32-44.

Dahl, O. J., B. Myhrhaug, and K. Nygaard, "The SIMULA 67 Common Base Language," Norwegian Computer Center technical report, Oslo, Norway, 1968.

Davies, D. W., D. L. A. Barber, W. L. Price, and C. M. Solominides, *Computer Networks and Their Protocols*, John Wiley & Sons, New York, NY, 1979.

Davies, D. W., E. Holler, E. D. Jensen, S. R. Kimbleton, B. W. Lampson, G. LeLann, K. J. Thurber, and R. W. Watson, *Distributed Systems -- Architecture and Implementation*, Springer-Verlag, New York, NY, 1981.

Deitel, H. M., *Operating Systems, Second Edition*, Addison-Wesley Publishing Co., Reading, MA, 1990.

Denning, D. E., "A Lattice Model of Secure Information Flow," *Communications of the ACM 19*, 5 (May 1976), 236-243.

Denning, D. E., *Cryptography and Data Security*, Addison-Wesley Publishing Co., Reading, MA, 1982.

Denning, P. J., "The Working Set Model for Program Behavior," *Communications of the ACM 11*, 5 (May 1968), 323-333.

Denning, P. J., "Virtual Memory," *ACM Computing Surveys 2*, 3 (September 1970), 153-189 .

Denning, P. J., "Working Sets Past and Present," *IEEE Transactions on Software Engineering SE-6*, 1 (January 1980), 64-84.

Dennis, J. B. and E. C. Van Horne, "Programming Semantics for Multiprogrammed Computations," *Communications of the ACM 9*, 3 (March 1966), 143-155.

DesJardins, R. and J. S. Foley, "Open Systems Interconnection: A Review and Status Report," *Journal of Telecommunication Networks 3*, 3 (1984), 194-209.

Dewar, R. B. K. and M. Smosna, *Microprocessors: A Programmer's View*, McGraw-Hill Book Co., New York, NY, 1990.

Dijkstra, E. W., "Co-operating Sequential Processes," in *Programming Languages*, F. Genuys (ed.), Academic Press, New York, NY, 1968, 43-112.

Dijkstra, E. W., "The Structure of the THE Multiprogramming System," *Communications of the ACM 11*, 5 (May 1968), 341-346.

Dongarra, J. J. and D. C. Sorenson, "SCHEDULE: Tools for Developing and Analyzing Parallel Fortran Programs," in *The Characteristics of Parallel Algorithms*, L. H. Jamieson, D. B. Gannon, and R. J. Douglass (ed.), MIT Press, Cambridge, MA, 1987, 363-394.

Dubois, M., C. Schuerich, and F. Briggs , "Synchronization, Coherence, and Event Ordering in Multiprocessors," *IEEE Computer 21* , 2 (February 1988), 9-21.

Eager, D. L., E. D. Lazowska, and J. Zahorjan, "Adaptive Load Sharing in Homogeneous Distributed Systems," *IEEE Transactions on Software Engineering SE-12*, 5 (May 1986), 662-675.

Ellis, C. A., "On the Probability of Deadlock in Computer Systems," *Proceedings of the Fourth ACM Symposium on Operating Systems Principles* , 1973, 88-95 .

Estrin, G. and R. Turn, "Automatic Assignment of Computations in a Variable Structure Computer System," *IEEE Transactions on Electronic Computers EC-12*, 5 (Dec 1963), 755-773.

Eswaran, K. P., J. N. Gray, R. A. Lorie, and I. L. Traiger, "The Notions of Consistency and Predicate Locks in a Database System," *Communications of the ACM 19*, 1 (November 1976), 624-633.

Fabry, R. S., "Capability-Based Addressing," *Communications of the ACM 17*, 7 (July 1974), 403-412.

Feller, W., *An Introduction to Probability Theory and Its Applications, Volume 1, Third Edition*, John Wiley & Sons, New York, NY, 1968.

Finkel, R. A., *An Operating Systems VADE MECUM, Second Edition*, Prentice Hall, Inc., Englewood Cliffs, NJ, 1988.

Fitzgerald, R. and R. F. Rashid, "The Integration of Virtual Memory and Interprocess Communication in Accent," *ACM Transactions on Computer Systems 4*, 2 (May 1986), 147-177.

Fleisch, B. D. and G. J. Popek, "Mirage: A Coherent Distributed Shared Memory Design," *Proceedings of the Twelfth ACM Symposium on Operating Systems Principles* , December 1989 , 211-223.

Forman, I. R., "On the Design of Large Distributed Systems," MCC Technical Report No. STP-098-86, Rev. 1.0, January 1987.

Garcia-Molina, H., F. Germano, and W. H. Kohler, "Debugging a Distributed Computing System," *IEEE Transactions on Software Engineering SE-10*, 2 (March 1984), 210-219.

Gawrys, G., P. Marino, G. Ryva, and H. Shulman, "ISDN: Integrated Network/Premises Solutions for Customer Needs," *Proceedings of the IEEE International Conference on Communications*, June 1986, 2-6.

Gifford, D. K. and N. Glasser, "Remote Pipes and Procedures for Efficient Distributed Communication," *ACM Transactions on Computer Systems 6*, 3 (August 1988), 258-283.

Gifford, D. K., R. M. Needham, and M. D. Schroeder, "The Cedar File System," *Communications of the ACM 31*, 3 (March 1988), 288-298.

Glaser, H., C. Hankin, and D. Till, *Principles of Functional Programming*, Prentice Hall, Inc., Englewood Cliffs, NJ, 1984.

Goldberg, A. and D. Robson, *Smalltalk-80: The Language and its Implementation*, Addison-Wesley Publishing Co., Reading, MA, 1985.

Graham, G. S. and P. J. Denning, "Protection -- Principles and Practice," *AFIPS Proceedings of the Spring Joint Computer Conference 40* (1972), 417-429.

Gray, J. N., "Notes on Data Base Operating Systems," in *Lecture Notes in Computer Science*, vol. 60 , Springer-Verlag, New York, NY, 1978, 393-481.

Groenbaek, I., "Conversion Between the TCP and ISO Transport Protocols as a Method of Achieving Interoperability Between Data Communication Systems," *IEEE Journal of Selected Areas in Communication SAC-4*, 2 (March 1986), 288-296.

Habermann, A. N., *Introduction to Operating System Design*, Science Research Associates, Inc., Chicago, IL, 1976.

Harel, D., "On Visual Formalisms," *Communications of the ACM 31*, 5 (May 1988), 514-530.

Hayes, J. P., *Computer Architecture and Organization, Second Edition*, McGraw-Hill Book Co., New York, 1988.

Henderson, P., *Functional Programming*, Prentice Hall, Inc., Englewood Cliffs, NJ, 1980.

Hennessy, J. L. and D. A. Patterson, *Computer Architecture: A Quantitative Approach*, Morgan Kaufmann Publishers, Inc., San Mateo, CA, 1990.

Hewitt, C. E. and R. R. Atkinson, "Specification and Proof Techniques for Serializers," *IEEE Transactions on Software Engineering SE-5*, 1 (1979), 10-23.

Hill, M. D. and A. J. Smith, "Evaluating Associativity in CPU Caches," *IEEE Transactions on Computers 38*, 12 (December 1989), 1612-1630.

Hoare, C. A. R., "Monitors: An Operating System Structuring Concept," *Communications of the ACM 17*, 10 (October 1974), 549-557.

Hoare, C. A. R., "Cooperating Sequential Processes," *Communications of the ACM 21*, 8 (August 1978), 666-677.

Holt, R. C., "Some Deadlock Properties of Computer Systems," *Computing Surveys 4*, 3 (September 1972), 179-196.

Holt, R. C., G. S. Graham, E. D. Lazowska, and M. A. Scott, *Structured Concurrent Programming with Operating Systems Applications*, Addison-Wesley Publishing Co., Reading, MA, 1978.

Horner, D. R., *Operating Systems Concepts and Applications*, Scott, Foresman and Company, Glenview, IL, 1989.

Horning, J. and B. Randell, "Process Structuring," *ACM Computing Surveys 5*, 1 (March 1973), 5-30.

Howard, J. H., M. L. Kazar, S. G. Menees, D. A. Nichols, M. Satyanarayanan, R. N. Sidebotham, and M. J. West, "Scale and Performance in a Distributed File System," *ACM Transactions on Computer Systems 6*, 1 (February 1988), 51-81.

Hutchinson, N. C., L. L. Peterson, M. B. Abbot, and S. O'Malley, "RPC in the x-Kernel: Evaluating New Design Techniques," *Proceedings of the Twelfth ACM Symposium on Operating Systems Principles*, November 1989, 91-101.

Hwang, K. and F. A. Briggs, *Computer Architecture and Parallel Processing*, McGraw-Hill Book Co., New York, NY, 1984.

Ingalls, D. H. H., "The Smalltalk-76 Programming System Design and Implementation," *Proceedings of the Fifth Annual ACM Symposium on Principles of Programming Languages*, 1978, 9-16.

Jamieson, L. H., D. B. Gannon, and R. J. Douglass, *The Characteristics of Parallel Algorithms*, MIT Press, Cambridge, MA, 1987.

Jefferson, D. R., "Virtual Time," *ACM Transactions on Programming Languages and Systems 7*, 3 (July 1985), 404-425.

Jefferson, D., B. Beckman , F. Wieland , L. Blume , M. DiLoreto , P. Hontalas , P. Laroche , K. Sturdevant, J. Tupman , V. Warren , J. Wedel , and H. Younger , "Distributed Simulation and the Time Warp Operating System ," *Proceedings of the Eleventh ACM Symposium on Operating Systems Principles* , Austin, Texas, November 1987 , 77-93.

Jennings, D. M., L. H. Landweber, I. H. Fuchs, D. J. Farber, and W. R. Adrion, "Computer Networking for Scientists," *Science 231* (February 1986), 943-950.

Jones, A. K., R. J. Chansler, I. Durham, K. Schwans, and S. R. Vegdahl, "StarOS, a Multiprocessor Operating System for the Support of Task Forces," *Proceedings of the Eighth ACM Symposium on Operating Systems Principles* , December 1979 , 77-93.

Jones, A. K. and P. Schwarz, "Experience Using Multiprocessor Systems -- A Status Report," *ACM Computing Surveys 12*, 2 (June 1980), 121-165.

Jordan, H. F., "The Force," in *The Characteristics of Parallel Algorithms*, L. H. Jamieson, D. B. Gannon, and R. J. Douglass (ed.), MIT Press, Cambridge, MA, 1987, 395-436.

Jul, E., H. Levy, N. Hutchinson, and A. Black, "Fine-Grained Mobility in the Emerald System," *ACM Transactions on Computer Systems 6*, 1 (February 1988), 109-133.

Kahn, K. C., W. M. Corwin, T. D. Dennis, H. D'Hooge, D. E. Hubka, L. A. Hutchins, J. T. Montague, F. J. Pollack, and M. R. Gifkins, "iMAX: A Multiprocessor Operating System for an Object-Based Computer," *Proceedings of the Eighth ACM Symposium on Operating Systems Principles*, December 1981, 127-136.

Karp, R. M. and R. E. Miller, "Parallel Program Schemata," *Journal of Computer and System Sciences 3*, 4 (May 1969), 167-195.

Kay, A. C., "Microelectronics and the Personal Computer," *Scientific American 237*, 3 (September 1977), 231-244.

Keller, L. S., *Operating Systems Communicating with and Controlling the Computer*, Prentice Hall, Inc., Englewood Cliffs, NJ, 1988.

Keller, R. M., "On Maximally Parallel Program Schemata," *Proceedings of the 11th Symposium on Switching and Automata Theory*, October 1972, 33-50.

Kleinrock, L., *Queueing Systems (Volume 1: Theory, Volume 2: Computer Applications)*, John Wiley & Sons, New York, NY, 1975, 1976.

Knapp, E., "Deadlock Detection in Distributed Databases," *ACM Computing Surveys 19*, 4 (December 1987), 303-328.

Knuth, D. E., *The Art of Computer Programming Volume 1 Fundamental Algorithms*, Addison-Wesley Publishing Co., Reading, MA, 1969.

Kocher, B., "President's Letter: Everything Old is New Again," *Communications of the ACM 33*, 3 (March 1990), 261.

Korth, H. F. and A. Silberschatz, *Database System Concepts*, McGraw-Hill Book Co., New York, NY, 1986.

Lamport, L., "Proving the Correctness of Multiprocess Programs," *IEEE Transactions on Software Engineering SE-3* , 2 (March 1977), 125-133.

Lamport, L., "Time, Clocks and the Ordering of Events in a Distributed System ," *Communications of the ACM 21* , 7 (July 1978), 558-565.

Lamport, L., "Using Time Instead of Timeout for Fault Tolerant Distributed Systems," *ACM Transactions on Programming Languages and Systems 6*, 2 (April 1984), 254-280.

Lamport, L., R. Shostak, and M Pease, "The Byzantine Generals Problem," *ACM Transactions on Programming Languages and Systems 4*, 3 (July 1982), 382-401.

Lampson, B. W., "Protection," *Proceedings of the Fifth Annual Princeton Conference on Information Science Systems*, 1971, 437-443.

Lampson, B. W., "A Note on the Confinement Problem," *Communications of the ACM 16*, 10 (October 1973), 613-615.

Lampson, B. W., "Atomic Transactions," in *Distributed Systems -- Architecture and Implementation*, B. W. Lampson (ed.), Springer-Verlag, New York, NY, 1981, 246-265.

Lampson, B. W. and D. D. Redell, "Experience with Processes and Monitors in Mesa," *Communications of the ACM 19*, 5 (February 1980), 105-117.

Lampson, B. W. and R. F. Sproull, "An Open Operating System for a Single-User Machine," *Proceedings of the Seventh Symposium on Operating Systems Principles*, December 1979, 98-105.

Lampson, B. and H. Sturgis, *Crash Recovery in a Distributed Data Storage System*, Xerox Palo Alto Research Center, April 1979.

Lampson, B. W. and H. E. Sturgis, "Hints for Computer System Design," *Proceedings of the Ninth ACM Symposium on Operating Systems Principles*, July 1983, 33-48.

Landwehr, C. E., "Formal Models for Computer Security," *ACM Computing Surveys 13*, 3 (September 1981), 247-275.

Lantz, K. A., K. D. Gradischnig, J. A. Feldman, and R. F. Rashid, "Rochester's Intelligent Gateway," *IEEE Computer 15*, 10 (October 1982), 54-68.

Lauer, H. C., "Observations on the Development of an Operating System," *Proceedings of the Eighth ACM Symposium on Operating Systems Principles*, December 1981, 30-36.

Lazowska, E. D., J. Zahorjan, D. R. Cheriton, and W. Zwaenepoel, "File Access Performance of Diskless Workstations," *ACM Transactions on Computer Systems 4*, 3 (August 1986), 238-268.

Lazowska, E. D., J. Zahorjan, G. S. Graham, and K. C. Sevcik, *Quantitative System Performance*, Prentice Hall, Inc., Englewood Cliffs, NJ, 1984.

Leach, P. J., P. H. Levine, B. P. Douros, J. A. Hamilton, D. L. Nelson, and B. L. Stumpf, "The Architecture of an Integrated Local Network," *IEEE Journal on Selected Areas in Communication SAC-1*, 5 (November 1983), 842-857.

Leffler, S. J., R. S. Fabry, W. N. Joy, and P. Lapsley, "An Advanced 4.3BSD Interprocess Communication Tutorial," in *Unix Programmer's Manual Supplementary Documents 1*, Computer Systems Research Group, Computer Science Division, Department of Electrical Engineering and Computer Science, University of California, Berkeley, April 1986.

Leffler, S. J., M. K. McKusick, M. J. Karels, and J. S. Quarterman, *The Design and Implementation of the 4.3 BSD UNIX Operating System*, Addison-Wesley Publishing Co., Reading, MA, 1989.

Lempel, A., "Cryptology in Transition: A Survey," *ACM Computing Surveys 11*, 4 (December 1979), 285-304.

Levin, R., E. Cohen, W. Corwin, F. Pollack, and W. Wulf, "Policy/Mechanism Separation in Hydra," *Proceedings of the Fifth ACM Symposium on Operating Systems Principles*, November 1975, 131-140.

Levy, H. M. and R. H. Eckhouse Jr., *Computer Programming and Architecture: The VAX, Second Edition*, Digital Press, Bedford, MA, 1989.

Li, K. and P. Hudak, "Memory Coherence in Shared Virtual Memory Systems," *ACM Transactions on Computer Systems 7*, 4 (November 1989), 321-359.

Lightner, M. R., "Modeling and Simulation of VLSI Digital Systems," *Proceedings of the IEEE 75*, 6 (June 1987), 786-796.

Liskov, B. H., "The Design of the Venus Operating System," *Communications of the ACM 15*, 3 (March 1972), 144-149.

Liskov, B., "Primitives for Distributed Computing," *Proceedings of the Seventh ACM Symposium on Operating Systems Principles*, December 1979, 33-42.

Liskov, B., D. Curtis, P. Johnson, and R. Scheifler, "Implementation of Argus," *Proceedings of the Eleventh ACM Symposium on Operating Systems Principles*, Austin, TX, December 1987, 111-122.

Liskov, B., "Distributed Programming in Argus," *Communications of the ACM 31*, 3 (March 1988), 300-312.

Luderer, G. W. R., H. Che, J. P. Haggerty, P. A. Kirslis, and W. T. Marshall, "A Distributed UNIX System Based on a Virtual Circuit Switch," *Proceedings of the Eighth ACM Symposium on Operating Systems Principles*, December 1981, 160-168.

Lunt, T. F., D. E. Denning, R. R. Schell, M. Heckman, and W. R. Shockley, "The SeaView Security Model," *IEEE Transactions on Software Engineering 16*, 6 (June 1990), 593-607.

MacDougall, M. H., "Computer System Simulation: An Introduction," *ACM Computing Surveys 2*, 3 (1970), 191-209.

MacDougall, M. H., *Simulating Computer Systems*, MIT Press, Cambridge, MA, 1987.

Maekawa, M., A. E. Oldehoeft, and R. R. Oldehoeft, *Operating Systems Advanced Concepts*, Benjamin/Cummings Publishing, Menlo Park, CA, 1987.

Mattson, R. L., J. Gecsei, D. R. Slutz, and I. L. Traiger, "Evaluation Techniques for Storage Hierarchies," *IBM Systems Journal 9*, 2 (1970), 78-117.

McQuillan, J. M., I. Richer, and E. C. Rosen, "The New Routing Algorithm for the ARPANET," *IEEE Transactions on Communications COM-28*, 5 (May 1980), 711-719.

Mealy, G. H., B. I. Witt, and W. A. Clark, "The Functional Structure of OS/360," *IBM Systems Journal 5*, 1 (1966), 3-51.

Metcalfe, R. M. and D. R. Boggs, "Ethernet: Distributed Packet Switching for Local Computer Networks," *Communications of the ACM 19*, 7 (July 1976), 395-404.

Milenković, M., *Operating Systems Advance Concepts*, McGraw-Hill Book Co., New York, NY, 1987.

Misra, J., "Distributed-Discrete Event Simulation," *ACM Computing Surveys 18*, 1 (March 1986), 39-65.

Mitchell, J. G. and J. Dion, "A Comparison of Two Network-Based File Servers," *Communications of the ACM 25*, 4 (April 1982), 233-245.

Mogul, J. and J. Postel, "Internet Standard Subnetting Procedure," RFC 950, August 1985.

Molloy, M. K., *Fundamentals of Performance Modeling*, Macmillan, 1989.

Morris, J. H., M. Satyanarayanan, M. H. Conner, J. H. Howard, D. S. H. Rosenthal, and F. D. Smith, "Andrew: A Distributed Personal Computing Environment," *Communications of the ACM 29*, 3 (March 1986), 184-201.

Mullender, S. J., G. van Rossum, A. S. Tanenbaum, R. van Renesse, and H. van Staveren, "Amoeba: A Distributed Operating System for the 1990s," *IEEE Computer 23*, 5 (May 1990), 44-53.

Murata, T., "Petri Nets: Properties, Analysis and Applications," *Proceedings of the IEEE 77*, 4 (April 1989), 541-580.

Needham, R. M. and A. J. Herbert, *The Cambridge Distributed Computing System*, Addison-Wesley Publishing Co., Reading, MA, 1982.

Needham, R. M. and R. D. H. Walker, "The Cambridge CAP Computer and its Protection System," *Proceedings of the Sixth ACM Symposium on Operating Systems Principles*, November 1977, 1-10.

Nelson, M. N., B. B. Welch, and J. K. Ousterhout, "Caching in the Sprite Network File System," *ACM Transactions on Computer Systems 6*, 1 (February 1988), 134-154.

D. Nicol, ed., *Proceedings of the SCS Multiconference on Distributed Simulation*, The Society for Computer Simulation, January 1990.

Notkin, D., A. P. Black, E. D. Lazowska, H. M. Levy, J. Sanislo, and J. Zahorjan, "Interconnecting Heterogeneous Computer Systems," *Communications of the ACM 31*, 3 (March 1988), 258-273 .

Oppen, D. C. and Y. K. Dalal, "The Clearinghouse: A Decentralized Agent for Locating Named Objects in a Distributed Environment," *ACM Transactions on Office Information Systems 1*, 3 (July 1983), 230-253.

Organick, E. I., *The Multics System: An Examination of Its Structure*, MIT Press, Cambridge, MA, 1972.

Organick, E. I., *Computer System Organization*, Academic Press, New York, NY, 1973.

Osterweil, J. P., "A Deadlock Model based on Process-Resource Graphs," M.S. thesis, Department of Computer Science, University of Colorado, 1975.

Osterweil, J. P. and G. J. Nutt, "Modeling Process-Resource Activity," *International Journal of Computer Mathematics 7*, 1 (1979), 21-35.

Ousterhout, J. K., A. R. Cherenson, F. Douglis, M. N. Nelson, and B. B. Welch, "The Sprite Network Operating System," *IEEE Computer 21*, 2 (February 1988), 23-36.

Ousterhout, J., H. Da Costa, D. Harrison, J. Kunze, M. Kupfer, and J. Thompson, "A Trace-Driven Analysis of the UNIX 4.2 BSD File System," *Proceedings of the Tenth ACM Symposium on Operating Systems Principles*, December 1985, 15-24.

Ousterhout, J. K., D. A. Scelza, and P. S. Sindhu, "Medusa: An Experiment in Distributed Operating System Structure," *Communications of the ACM 23*, 2 (February 1980), 92-105.

Patil, S. S., "Limitations and Capabilities of Dijkstra's Semaphore Primitives for Coordination among Processes," MIT Project MAC Computation Structures Group Memorandum No. 57, MIT, February 1971.

Peacock, J. K., E. G. Manning, and J. W. Wong, "Synchronization of Distributed Simulation using Broadcast Algorithms," *Computer Networks 4*, 1 (February 1980), 3-10.

Peacock, J. K., J. W. Wong, and E. G. Manning, "Distributed Simulation Using a Network of Processors," *Computer Networks 3*, 1 (February 1979), 44-56.

Perrot, R. H. and A. Zarea-Aliabadi, "Supercomputer Languages," *ACM Computing Surveys 18*, 1 (March 1986), 11-25.

Peterson, G. L., "Myths About the Mutual Exclusion Problem," *Information Processing Letters 12*, 3 (June 1981), 115-116.

Peterson, J. L., *Petri Net Theory and the Modeling of Systems*, Prentice Hall, Inc., Englewood Cliffs, NJ, 1981.

Peterson, J. L. and A. Silberschatz, *Operating Systems Concepts, Second Edition*, Addison-Wesley Publishing Co., Reading, MA, 1985.

Peterson, L., N. Hutchinson, S. O'Malley, and H. Rao, "The x-kernel: A Platform for Accessing Internet Resources," *IEEE Computer 23*, 5 (May 1990), 23-33.

Peyton Jones, S. L., *The Implementation of Functional Programming Languages*, Prentice Hall, Inc., Englewood Cliffs, NJ, 1987.

Popek, G., B. Walker, J. Chow, D. Edwards, C. Kline, G. Rudison, and G. Thiel, "LOCUS: A Network Transparent, High Reliability Distributed System," *Proceedings of the Eighth ACM Symposium on Operating Systems Principles*, December 1981, 169-177.

Postel, J., "User Datagram Protocol," RFC 768, USC Information Sciences Institute, August 1980.

Postel, J., "Internet Protocol: DARPA Internet Program Protocol Specification," RFC No. 791, September 1981.

Postel, J., "Transmission Control Protocol: DARPA Internet Program Protocol Specification," RFC No. 793, September 1981.

Postel, J. and J. Reynolds, "Telnet Protocol Specification," RFC 854, USC Information Sciences Institute, May 1983.

Powell, M. L. and B. P. Miller, "Process Migration in DEMOS/MP," *Proceedings of the Ninth ACM Symposium on Operating Systems Principles*, Bretton Woods, NH, July 1983, 110-119. Published as Operating Systems Review 17(5).

Prieve, B. and R. S. Fabry, "VMIN -- An Optimal Variable-Space Page Replacement Algorithm," *Communications of the ACM 19*, 5 (May 1976), 295-297.

Quarterman, J. S. and J. C. Hoskins, "Notable Computer Networks," *Communications of the ACM 23*, 10 (October 1986), 932-971.

Quarterman, J. S., A. Silberschatz, and J. L. Peterson, "4.2BSD and 4.3BSD as Examples of the UNIX System," *ACM Computing Surveys 17*, 4 (December 1985), 379-418 .

Randellβ]B., ed., *The Origins of Digital Computers*, Springer-Verlag, New York, NY, 1987.

Rashid, R. F., *From RIG to Accent to Mach: The Evolution of a Network Operating System*, Computer Science Department, Carnegie-Mellon University, Pittsburgh, PA, May 1986.

Rashid, R. F. and G. Robertson, "Accent: A Communication Oriented Network Operating System Kernel," *Proceedings of the 8th Symposium on Operating Systems Principles*, December 1981, 64-75.

Rashid, R., A. Tevanian, M. Young, D. Golub, R. Baron, D. Black, W. Bolosky, and J. Chew, "Machine-Independent Virtual Memory Management for Paged Uniprocessor and Multiprocessor Architectures," *IEEE Transactions on Computer Systems 37*, 8 (August 1988), 896-907.

Redell, D. D., Y. K. Dalal, T. R. Horsley, H. C. Lauer, W. C. Lynch, P. R. McJones, H. G. Murray, and S. C. Purcell, "Pilot: An Operating System for a Personal Computer," *Communications of the ACM 23*, 2 (February 1980), 81-92.

Reed, D. P. and R. K. Kanodia, "Synchronization with Eventcounts and Sequencers," *Communications of the ACM 22*, 2 (February 1979), 115-123.

Reed, D. P. and L. Svobodova, "SWALLOW: A Distributed Data Storage System for a Local Network," *Local Networks for Computer Communication*, 1981, 355-373.

Rifkin, A. P., M. P. Forbes, R. L. Hamilton, M. Sabrio, S. Shah, and K. Yueh, "RFS Architectural Overview," *Proceedings of Communix 86*, June, 1986, 35-43.

Ritchie, D. M., "A Stream Input-Output System," *AT&T Bell Laboratories Technical Journal 63*, 8 (October 1984), 1897-1910.

Ritchie, D. M. and K. Thompson, "The UNIX Time-Sharing System," *Communications of the ACM 17*, 7 (July 1974), 365-375.

Rosen, S., *Programming Systems and Languages*, McGraw-Hill Book Co., New York, NY, 1967.

Rosen, S., "Electronic Computers: A Historical Survey," *ACM Computing Surveys 1*, 1 (March 1969), 7-36.

Rosin, R. F., "Supervisory and Monitoring Systems," *ACM Computing Surveys 1*, 1 (March 1969), 37-54.

Rozier, M., V. Abrossimov, F. Armand, I. Boule, M. Gien, M. Guillemont, F. Herrmann, C. Kaiser, S. Langlois, P. Leonard, and W. Neuhauser, "Chorus Distributed Operating Systems," *Computer Systems 4*, 4 (Fall 1988), 305-370.

Saltzer, J. H., D. P. Reed, and D. D. Clark, "End-to-End Arguments in System Design," *ACM Transactions on Computer Systems 2*, 4 (November 1984), 277-288.

Sandberg, R., D. Goldberg, S. Kleiman, D. Walsh, and B. Lyon, "Design and Implementation of the Sun Network File System," *USENIX Proceedings*, June 1985, 119-130.

Satyanarayanan, M., "Scalable, Secure, and Highly Available Distributed File Access," *IEEE Computer 23*, 5 (May 1990), 9-21.

Satyanarayanan, M., J. H. Howard, D. A. Nichols, R. N. Sidebotham, A. Z. Spector, and M. J. West, "The ITC Distributed File System: Principles and Design," *Proceedings of the Tenth ACM Symposium on Operating Systems Principles*, December 1985, 35-50.

Saxena, A. R. and T. H. Bredt, "A Structured Specification of a Hierarchical Operating System," *Proceedings of the International Conference on Reliable Software*, April 1975, 310-318.

Scheifler, R. W., *X Window System Protocol, Version 11*, MIT Laboratory for Computer Science, Cambridge, MA, 1986.

Schroeder, M. D., A. D. Birrell, and R. M. Needham, "Experience with Grapevine: The Growth of a Distributed System," *ACM Transactions on Computer Systems 2*, 1 (February 1984), 3-23.

Schroeder, M. D. and M. Burrows, "Performance of Firefly RPC," *ACM Transactions on Computer Systems 8*, 1 (February 1990), 1-17.

Schroeder, M. D., D. D. Clark, and J. H. Saltzer, "The MULTICS Kernel Design Project," *Proceedings of the Sixth ACM Symposium on Operating Systems Principles*, November 1977, 43-56.

Schlichting, R. D., G. R. Andrews, N. R. Hutchinson, R. A. Olsson, and L. L. Peterson, "Observations on Building Distributed Languages and Systems," Department of Computer Science, University of Arizona, TR 87-25, Tucson, AZ, October 1987.

Schwartz, M. F., J. Zahorjan, and D. Notkin, "A Name Service for Evolving, Heterogeneous Systems," *Proceedings of the Eleventh ACM Symposium on Operating Systems Principles*, November 1987, 52-62.

Schwetman, H., *PPL Reference Manual (Version 1.1)*, MCC Technical Report, January 1987 .

Scott, M. L., T. J. LeBlanc, and B. D. Marsh, "Design Rationale for Psyche, a General-Purpose Multiprocessor Operating System," *Proceedings of the ICPP*, August 1988, 255-262.

Shaw, A. C., *The Logical Design of Operating Systems, First Edition*, Prentice Hall, Inc., Englewood Cliffs, NJ, 1974.

Shoch, J. F. and J. A. Hupp, "The Worm Programs - Early Experience with a Distributed Computation," *Communications of the ACM 25* (March 1982), 172-180.

Siewiorek, D. P., C. G. Bell, and A. Newell, eds., *Computer Structures: Principles and Examples (2nd Ed.)*, McGraw-Hill Book Co., New York, NY, 1981.

Silberschatz, A. and J. L. Peterson, *Operating System Concepts, Alternate Edition*, Addison-Wesley Publishing Co., Reading, MA, 1988.

Singhal, M., "Deadlock Detection in Distributed Systems," *IEEE Computer 22*, 11 (November 1989), 37-48.

Smith, A. J., "Disk Cache -- Miss Ratio Analysis and Design Considerations," *ACM Transactions on Computer Systems 3*, 3 (August 1985), 161-203.

Sollins, K. R., "The TFTP Protocol (revision 2)," RFC 783, MIT Laboratory for Computer Science, Cambridge, MA, June 1981.

Spector, A., "Performing Remote Operations Efficiently on a Local Computer Network," *Communications of the ACM 25*, 4 (April 1982), 246-260.

Solomon, M. H. and R. A. Finkel, "The Roscoe Distributed Operating System," *Proceedings of the Seventh ACM Symposium on Operating Systems Principles*, December 1981, 108-114.

Stein, M. and S. Ahnger, "Tutorial #M5: The Network File System," *Usenix Technical Conference and Exhibition*, June 1987.

Stoll, C., "Stalking the Wily Hacker," *Communications of the ACM 31*, 5 (May 1988), 484-497.

Stumm, M. and S. Zhou, "Algorithms Implementing Distributed Shared Memory," *IEEE Computer 23*, 5 (May 1990), 54-64.

Sturgis, H. W., "A Postmortem for a Time Sharing System," University of California, Berkeley, Ph.D. thesis, 1973.

Svobodova, L., "Performance Monitoring in Computer Systems: A Structured Approach," *Operating Systems Review 15*, 3 (July 1981), 39-50.

Svobodova, L., "File Servers for Network-Based Distributed Systems," *ACM Computing Surveys 16*, 4 (December 1984), 353-398.

Swinehart, D., G. McDaniel, and D. Boggs, "WFS: A Simple Shared File System for a Distributed Environment," *Proceedings of the Seventh Symposium on Operating Systems Principles*, December 1979, 9-17.

Tanenbaum, A. S., *Operating Systems: Design and Implementation*, Prentice Hall, Inc., Englewood Cliffs, NJ, 1987.

Tanenbaum, A. S., *Computer Networks, Second Edition*, Prentice Hall, Inc., Englewood Cliffs, NJ, 1988.

Tanenbaum, A. S. and R. van Renesse, "Distributed Operating Systems," *ACM Computing Surveys 17*, 4 (December 1985), 418-470.

Tanenbaum, A. S., R. van Renesse, H. van Staveren, G. J. Sharp, S. J. Mullender, J. Jansen, and G. van Rossum, "Experience with the Amoeba Distributed Operating System," *Communications of the ACM 33*, 12 (December 1990), 46-63.

Tay, B. H. and A. L. Ananda, "A Survey of Remote Procedure Calls," *ACM SIGOPS Operating Systems Review 24*, 3 (July 1990), 68-79.

Teitelman, W., "A Display Oriented Programmer's Assistant," Report No. CSL 77-3, Xerox PARC, March 1977.

Teorey, T. J. and T. B. Pinkerton, "A Comparative Analysis of Disk Scheduling Policies," *Communications of the ACM 15*, 3 (March 1972), 177-184.

Thacker, C. P., E. M. McCreight, B. W. Lampson, R. F. Sproull, and D. R. Boggs, "Alto: A Personal Computer," in *Computer Structures: Principles and Examples (2nd Ed.)*, D.P. Siewiorek, C.G. Bell, and A. Newell (ed.), McGraw-Hill Book Co., New York, NY, 1981.

Tsai, C.-R., V. D. Gligor, and C. S. Chandersekaran, "On the Identification of Covert Storage Channels in Secure Systems," *IEEE Transactions on Software Engineering 16*, 6 (June 1990), 569-580.

Tucker, L. W. and G. G. Robertson, "Architecture and Applications of the Connection Machine," *IEEE Computer 21*, 8 (August 1988), 26-38.

Ullman, J. D., *Principles of Database Systems, Second Edition*, Computer Science Press, Rockville. MD, 1982.

Vaucher, J. G. and P. Duval, "A Comparison of Simulation Event List Algorithms," *Communications of the ACM 18* (1975).

Walker, B., G. Popek, R. English, C. Kline, and G. Thiel, "The LOCUS Distributed Operating System," *Proceedings of the Ninth ACM Symposium on Operating Systems Principles*, July 1983, 49-70.

Wang, W. H. and J. L. Baer, "Efficient Trace-Driven Simulation Methods for Cache Performance Analysis," *ACM Sigmetrics Performance Evaluation Review 18*, 1 (May 1990), 27-36.

White, J., "A High-Level Framework for Network-Based Resource Sharing," *Proceedings of the National Computer Conference*, 1976, 561-570.

Wulf, W. A., E. Cohen, W. Corwin, A. Jones, R. Levin, C. Pierson, and F. Pollack, "Hydra: The Kernel of a Multiprocessing Operating System," *Communications of the ACM 17*, 6 (June 1974), 337-345.

Young, M., A. Tevanian, R. Rashid, D. Golub, J. Eppinger, J. Chew, W. Bolosky, D. Black, and R. Baron, "The Duality of Memory and Communication in the Implementation of a Multiprocessor Operating System," *Proceedings of the Eleventh ACM Symposium on Operating Systems Principles*, November 1987, 63-76.

Zimmerman, H., "The ISO Model for Open Systems Interconnection," *IEEE Transactions on Communications COM-28*, 4 (April 1980), 425-432.

INDEX

70284